Luminos is the Open Access monograph publishing program from UC Press. Luminos provides a framework for preserving and reinvigorating monograph publishing for the future and increases the reach and visibility of important scholarly work. Titles published in the UC Press Luminos model are published with the same high standards for selection, peer review, production, and marketing as those in our traditional program. www.luminosoa.org

ASIA PACIFIC MODERN

Series Editor: Takashi Fujitani

1. *Erotic Grotesque Nonsense: The Mass Culture of Japanese Modern Times,* by Miriam Silverberg
2. *Visuality and Identity: Sinophone Articulations across the Pacific,* by Shu-mei Shih
3. *The Politics of Gender in Colonial Korea: Education, Labor, and Health, 1910–1945,* by Theodore Jun Yoo
4. *Frontier Constitutions: Christianity and Colonial Empire in the Nineteenth-Century Philippines,* by John D. Blanco
5. *Tropics of Savagery: The Culture of Japanese Empire in Comparative Frame,* by Robert Thomas Tierney
6. *Colonial Project, National Game: A History of Baseball in Taiwan,* by Andrew D. Morris
7. *Race for Empire: Koreans as Japanese and Japanese as Americans during World War II,* by Takashi Fujitani
8. *The Gender of Memory: Rural Women and China's Collective Past,* by Gail Hershatter
9. *A Passion for Facts: Social Surveys and the Construction of the Chinese Nation-State, 1900–1949,* by Tong Lam
11. *Redacted: The Archives of Censorship in Transwar Japan,* by Jonathan E. Abel
12. *Assimilating Seoul: Japanese Rule and the Politics of Public Space in Colonial Korea, 1910–1945,* by Todd A. Henry
13. *Working Skin: Making Leather, Making a Multicultural Japan,* by Joseph D. Hankins
14. *Imperial Genus: The Formation and Limits of the Human in Modern Korea and Japan,* by Travis Workman
15. *Sanitized Sex: Regulating Prostitution, Venereal Disease, and Intimacy in Occupied Japan, 1945–1952,* by Robert Kramm
16. *Outcasts of Empire: Japan's Rule on Taiwan's "Savage Border," 1874–1945,* by Paul D. Barclay

Outcasts of Empire

The publisher and the University of California Press Foundation gratefully acknowledge the generous support of the Philip E. Lilienthal Imprint in Asian Studies, established by a major gift from Sally Lilienthal.

Outcasts of Empire

Japan's Rule on Taiwan's "Savage Border," 1874–1945

Paul D. Barclay

UNIVERSITY OF CALIFORNIA PRESS

University of California Press, one of the most distinguished university presses in the United States, enriches lives around the world by advancing scholarship in the humanities, social sciences, and natural sciences. Its activities are supported by the UC Press Foundation and by philanthropic contributions from individuals and institutions. For more information, visit www.ucpress.edu.

University of California Press
Oakland, California

© 2018 by Paul D. Barclay

Suggested citation: Barclay, Paul D. *Outcasts of Empire: Japan's Rule on Taiwan's "Savage Border," 1874–1945*. Oakland: University of California Press, 2018. doi: https://doi.org/10.1525/luminos.41

This work is licensed under a Creative Commons CC by NC ND license. To view a copy of the license, visit http://creativecommons.org/licenses.

Library of Congress Cataloging-in-Publication Data

Names: Barclay, Paul D., author.
Title: Outcasts of empire : Japan's rule on Taiwan's "savage border,"
    1874–1945 / Paul D. Barclay.
Other titles: Asia Pacific modern ; 16.
Description: Oakland, California : University of California Press, [2018] |
    Series: Asia Pacific Modern ; 16 | Includes bibliographical references and
    index.
Identifiers: LCCN 2017030926| ISBN 9780520296213 (pbk. : alk. paper) |
    ISBN 9780520968806 (ebook)
Subjects: LCSH: Taiwan aborigines—History—20th century. |
    Japan—Colonies—History. | Taiwan—History—1895–1945.
Classification: LCC DS799.42 .B37 2018 | DDC 951.249/04—dc23
LC record available at https://lccn.loc.gov/2017030926

27 26 25 24 23 22 21 20 19 18
10 9 8 7 6 5 4 3 2 1

For Naoko

CONTENTS

List of Illustrations and Tables   *ix*
Acknowledgments   *xiii*
Note on Transliteration and Translation   *xvii*

Introduction: Empires and Indigenous Peoples, Global Transformation
and the Limits of International Society   *1*

PART ONE. THE ANATOMY OF A REBELLION

1. From Wet Diplomacy to Scorched Earth: The Taiwan Expedition,
   the Guardline, and the Wushe Rebellion   *43*

2. The *Longue Durée* and the Short Circuit: Gender, Language, and
   Territory in the Making of Indigenous Taiwan   *114*

PART TWO. INDIGENOUS MODERNITY

3. Tangled Up in Red: Textiles, Trading Posts, and Ethnic Bifurcation
   in Taiwan   *161*

4. The Geobodies within a Geobody: The Visual Economy of Race
   Making and Indigeneity   *190*

Notes   *251*
Glossary   *293*
Index   *301*

LIST OF ILLUSTRATIONS AND TABLES

FIGURES

1. Japanese colonial-period ethnonyms for Taiwan Indigenous Peoples   *9*
2. Inō Kanori's ethnic map, 1898   *10*
3. Picture postcard map of Taiwan's ethnic bifurcation, ca. 1904   *34*
4. Two Atayal men engaged in "conjoined drinking," near Wulai, Taiwan, ca. 1900   *45*
5. Scorched earth guardline, ca. 1910   *47*
6. Surrendered Atayal at a stopover in Jiaobanshan, ca. 1910   *48*
7. Weapons captured from Atayal peoples, ca. 1910   *49*
8. Saigō Tsugumichi, Japanese soldiers, Paiwan headmen, and the interpreter Johnson, 1874   *72*
9. A certificate attesting submission to the Japanese Expeditionary Forces, 1874   *73*
10. Relics preserved from the 1874 expedition, ca. 1910   *74*
11. Bottle and can from the meeting at Dakekan, 1895   *84*
12. The Linyipu District Administrative Office, 1898   *92*
13. Gantaban men with severed heads, 1903   *97*
14. Guards warn of the approach of hostile forces, ca. 1910   *107*
15. Cutting trees to build the scorched-earth barricades, ca. 1910   *108*
16. The large Taiwanese labor force, during construction of the *aiyūsen*, ca. 1910   *108*
17. Porters hauling food and water for the guardline expeditionary troops, ca. 1910   *109*
18. Watan Yūra, ca. 1900   *123*

19. Watan Yūra, Kōan, Aki, and Pazzeh Watan, 1903   *124*
20. Kondō "the Barbarian" Katsusaburō, ca. 1910   *130*
21. Quchi-area residents posing with flag, ca. 1897   *132*
22. Kondō Gisaburō with Truku peoples, January 1915   *137*
23. Tata Rara with Japanese interpreter Nakamura Yūsuke, 1896   *143*
24. Tata Rara with her Puyuma militia, 1896   *144*
25. Pan Bunkiet, ca. 1900   *145*
26. The Wulai School for Indigenous Children, ca. 1910   *150*
27. Jiaobanshan model school for indigenous children, ca. 1930   *153*
28. Atayal textiles from Japanese ethnological survey, ca. 1915   *170*
29. A diorama from the 1913 Osaka Colonial Exhibition with Atayal red-striped capes   *171*
30. Trading post at Jiaobanshan, ca. 1913   *177*
31. Atayal women wearing imported clothing and weaving traditional clothing, 1936   *186*
32. Map of Taiwan, 1895   *193*
33. Japanese census map, 1905   *193*
34. Ethnic map of Taiwan, ca. 1912   *193*
35. An anthropology journal sketch of Watan Nawi, 1895   *200*
36. Jiaobanshan emissaries and Governor-General Kabayama as depicted in *Fūzoku gahō*, 1895   *201*
37. Photograph of the Jiaobanshan emissaries and Japanese officials in Taipei, 1895   *202*
38. Photograph of Habairon, Motonaiban, and Washiiga, 1895   *203*
39. Ethnographic drawing of Habairon, Motonaiban, and Washiiga, 1896   *204*
40. Photograph of Habairon, Motonaiban, Ira Watan, Marai, Pu Chin, and Washiiga, 1895   *206*
41. Textbook etching of Jiaobanshan emissaries, 1897   *207*
42. Jiaobanshan emissaries in fanciful setting, ca. 1900   *208*
43. Photo of Jiaobanshan emissaries in Western press, 1902   *209*
44. Etching of Sediq woman and Paalan headman in Ministry of Education textbook, 1904   *210*
45. Photograph of Sediq woman and Paalan headman, ca. 1897   *210*
46. Etching of Sediq woman and Paalan headman in commercial textbook, 1908   *210*
47. Photograph of Mori Ushinosuke, Japanese officers, and Truku headmen, 1910   *220*
48. Official commemorative postcard depicting indigenous customs, 1911   *224*
49. Men and women along the Quchi guardline, ca. 1904   *226*
50. Japan's Atayal allies along the Quchi guardline, ca. 1904   *227*
51. Dynamic and static maps of Taiwan's ethnic diversity, 1912   *231*

52. Jiaobanshan as staging area for Gaogan offensives, ca. 1910   *234*
53. Jiaobanshan woman with basket and pipe, ca. 1930   *237*
54. Postcard sleeve, "Jiaobanshan's hidden savage border," ca. 1930   *238*
55. Couple in Jiaobanshan, ca. 1930   *238*
56. Mountains of Jiaobanshan, ca. 1930   *239*
57. Contrasting photos of Jiaobanshan and Paalan, 1935   *240*
58. Second-order geobody of Atayal   *241*
59. Marai and Yūgai of Rimogan, ca. 1903   *242*
60. Wulai dwelling and granary, ca. 1903   *243*
61. Yūgai and Marai in textbook illustration, 1919   *243*

MAPS

1. The major indigenous ethnic groups of northern Taiwan   *7*
2. Overview of the major indigenous ethnic groups of Taiwan as portrayed in Japanese-period maps, ca. 1935   *8*
3. Taiwan, the Ryūkyū Islands, the Langqiao Peninsula, Mudan, and Satsuma, in East Asia   *51*
4. The Langqiao Peninsula, ca. 1874   *53*
5. Administrative centers, contact zones, and political boundaries in Taiwan, 1874–1945   *58*
6. Dakekan, Jiaobanshan, Quchi, Wulai, and Rimogan, ca. 1910   *80*

TABLES

1. Military encounters between the colonial government and Taiwan aborigines, 1896–1909   *100*
2. Sources of revenue for the colonial administration, 1897–1907   *101*

ACKNOWLEDGMENTS

The research for this book began in an undergraduate seminar room, decades ago. Since then, I have racked up a record of personal and scholarly debts disproportionate to the modest results achieved. These begin with my history professors at the University of Wisconsin, Alfred McCoy, Kathryn Green, Jean Boydston, John Sharpless, Kenneth Sacks, and Jürgen Herbst. Thanks, Al, for encouraging me to think big.

Several mentors who became friends at the University of Minnesota shaped this project and have earned my eternal gratitude. Advisors Byron K. Marshall and David W. Noble steered a comparative dissertation project to completion and spent countless hours counseling me on matters profound and trivial. Ann Waltner, Ted Farmer, Jeani O'Brien, Steven Ruggles, David Lipset, Russ Menard, Jennifer Downs, Chris Isett, and Wang Liping were all generous with their time, energy, and ideas. My fellow graduate students Sean Condon, Yonglin Jiang, Joe Dennis, Yuichirō Onishi, David Hacker, David Ryden, Matthew Mulcahy, Rachel Martin, Jennifer Spear, Jennifer Turnham, Martin Winchester, and Jon Davidann were the best classmates and extended family a graduate student could hope for. Jeff Sommers is a permanent friend and colleague from before and after graduate school; his outlook and insight have shaped this book profoundly.

Indulgent hosts, true friends, and brilliant associates have promoted my research in Japan. First and foremost, Vicky Muehleisen, Yamamoto Masashi, and Jerome Young put me up in Tokyo more times than I can recall. Fumu Susumu at Kyoto University and Sasaki Takashi at Doshisha University sponsored my early research and opened their doors and offices to a neophyte. Arisue Ken at Keio

University hosted me for a year of sabbatical research at Keio University and took the time to introduce me to everyone who was anyone in my area of research.

I emphatically thank Professor Kishi Toshihiko at the Center for Integrated Area Studies at Kyoto University for a residency, his friendship and guidance, myriad introductions, field trips, and workshops. Without Kishi-sensei's enthusiastic support, this book could not have been completed. Thanks to Professor Hara Shōichirō, director of the center, for making CIAS like a home away from home.

My research in Taiwan has been utterly dependent upon the friendship and assistance of several scholars and friends. University of Minnesota classmate Peter Kang (Kang Pei-te) has hosted me, shown me around, and provided the foundation for my investigations. Chen Wei-chi (Tan Uiti) and Chang Lung-chih have been superb teachers, comrades, and loyal supporters from the start. John Shufelt is a true friend, intellectual compatriot, host, and fellow explorer of Hengchun Peninsula. Douglas Fix is an indispensable mentor and model friend; Doug has forgotten more than I'll ever know about Taiwan. Caroline Hui-yu Ts'ai has written the most incisive and thoroughly researched institutional, legal, and cultural history of Japanese rule in Taiwan; more than that, she took great pains to host me at Academia Sinica's Institute for Taiwan History to finish research for this book. Paul Katz is a master of Taiwanese social history and religious studies and an endless supplier of shipped documents, connectivity, and *nomunication*. Professor Clare Huang (Huang Chih-huei) has taken me to field sites, introduced me to graduate students, patiently explained the nuances of the difficult postcolonial situation in Taiwan, and shared rare historical materials; she has changed the course of this research for the better. I also thank anthropologists of Taiwan Hu Chia-yu, Kuan Da-wei, Fred Chiu, Kerim Friedman, Scott Simon, Wang Peng-hui, Aho Batu, and Geoffrey Voorhees for camaraderie, mentorship, and vast repositories of knowledge. Wu Micha, Wang Ying-fen, Sandra Jiang, Lin Maleleve, and Yayut Chen have extended many courtesies and made this project fun. Chen Yi-fang of the Puli Municipal Library opened new doors and contributed wisdom, energy, and enthusiasm.

From the Shung Ye Japanese Research Group on Indigenous Peoples of Taiwan, anthropologist, historian of colonial ethnography, and über-*senpai* Kasahara Masaharu has inspired, mentored, and supported my work for two decades. Thank you so much, Kasahara-sensei! I also thank Nobayashi Atsushi for hosting me at the National Ethnological Museum in Osaka and trying to keep me in the loop. Professors Shimizu Jun, Miyaoka Maoko, Ōhama Ikuko, Yamamoto Yoshimi, and Tsuchida Shigeru have shared their networks, knowledge, and research in the true spirit of collegiality. Nagasako Minako at the Gakushūin Daigaku Archives provided access to collections and bibliographic support.

Thank you very much to Julia Adeney Thomas, Kirsten Ziomek, Janice Matsumura, Prasenjit Duara, Dennis Washburn, Chris Hanscom, Murray Rubinstein, Andrew Morris, Kenneth Ruoff, Hyung Il Pai, Rob Tierney, Alexis

Dudden, Barak Kushner, Ann Heylen, David Ambaras, Kate McDonald, John Shepherd, Robert Eskildsen, Joseph Allen, Tony Tavares, Emma Teng, Seiji Shirane, Matthew Fraleigh, Adam Clulow, Sabine Frühstück, and Austin Parks for the invitations, provocations, encouragement, panels, letters, edits, and shared documents.

My colleagues in the History Department at Lafayette College have been there for me in numerous ways over many years. Special thanks to Tammy Yeakel, Deborah Rosen, Josh Sanborn, Rebekah Pite, DC Jackson, Bob Weiner, Don Miller, Andrew Fix, Rachel Goshgarian, Jeremy Zallen, and Christopher Lee for intellectual community and a place to call home. I thank my Asian Studies Program compatriots: Seo-Hyun Park for brainstorms and crucial bibliography, and Li Yang, Robin Rinehart, Ingrid Furniss, Il Hyun Cho, and David Stifel for their intellectual companionship and ongoing commitment to my professional and personal development.

I am fortunate to have accomplished and unselfish colleagues in anthropology at Lafayette College. Thanks, Andrea Smith, Bill Bissell, Wendy Wilson-Fall, and Rob Blunt, for not allowing me to caricature your discipline. EXCEL Scholars Wu Haotian, Linda Yu, Li Guo, Sun Xiaofei, Sharon Chen, and Ning Jing have compiled tables, abstracted articles, and translated Chinese-language and French documents into English for me over the years.

Digital Scholarship Services colleagues Eric Luhrs, Paul Miller, Charlotte Nunes, James Griffin III, John Clark, and Michaela Kelly have built databases, constructed maps, captured images, hosted workshops, and provided more support than could be reasonably expected. John Clark created the six beautiful maps for this book. Neil McElroy, Diane Shaw, Elaine Stomber, Terese Heidenwolf, Lijuan Xu, Pam Murray, and Karen Haduck at Skillman Library unstintingly supported this project with access to funds, images, texts, databases, and interlibrary loan materials, not to mention accessioning and processing all manner of ephemera and curios. They have spoiled me rotten.

Matsuda Kyōko's pioneering research in the history of Japan's colonial anthropology in Taiwan has been an inspiration. I am also heavily indebted to Kitamura Kae, Kondō Masami, Kojima Rei'itsu, Matsuoka Tadasu, Yamaji Katsuhiko, and Matsuda Yoshirō for conceptualizing and documenting the history of indigenous-Japanese relations with admirable depth, nuance, and creativity. These scholars have set a high standard for this field. In addition, Chou Wan-yao, Wu Rwei-ren, Ka Chih-ming, Wang Tay-sheng, and Yao Jen-to have produced masterworks in the historical sociology of Taiwan; even where I've neglected to cite them, their ideas permeate this book.

Thanks to Donald and Michiko Rupnow for the picture postcard that adorns the cover of this book, and for supporting this research with other rare and wonderful images. Michael Lewis, Elizabeth and Anne Warner, Richard Mammana,

Lin Shuchin, and David Woodsworth have kindly donated, lent, or provided access to their private collections. Without their generosity and public-spiritedness, this book would not have been possible.

Sections of "'Gaining Trust and Friendship' in Aborigine Country: Diplomacy, Drinking, and Debauchery on Japan's Southern Frontier," *Social Science Japan Journal* 6, no. 1 (April 2003): 77–96, appear in chapter 1; "Cultural Brokerage and Interethnic Marriage in Colonial Taiwan: Japanese Subalterns and Their Aborigine Wives, 1895–1930," *Journal of Asian Studies* 64, no. 2 (May 2005): 323–60, in chapter 2; "Tangled Up in Red: Textiles, Trading Posts, and the Emergence of Indigenous Modernity in Japanese Taiwan," in Andrew Morris, ed., *Japanese Taiwan: Colonial Rule and Its Contested Legacy* (London and New York: Bloomsbury Press, 2015), 49–74, in chapter 3; and "Playing the Race Card in Japanese-Governed Taiwan, or: Anthropometric Photographs as 'Shape-Shifting Jokers,'" in Christopher Hanscom and Dennis Washburn, eds., *The Affect of Difference: Representations of Race in East Asian Empire* (Honolulu: University of Hawai'i Press, 2016), 38–80, in chapter 4. The editors and readers of these pieces offered valuable advice and suggestions.

Research for this book was funded by fellowships from the Japan Society for the Promotion of Science, the National Endowment for the Humanities, the Taiwan Ministry of Foreign Affairs, the Lafayette College Provost's Office, and the Andrew Mellon Foundation. The Friends of Skillman Library and the Lafayette College Academic Research Committee generously supported the publication of this book.

Thank you, Asia Pacific Modern series editor Tak Fujitani and Professor Jordan Sand of Georgetown University, for encouraging me to write a book. Tak offered counsel, advice, and support and deserves many thanks for reading this manuscript in its entirety, and parts of it repeatedly. Jordan has been an unselfish mentor and colleague. The book was improved thanks to their kind attention. Any errors of fact and interpretation that remain, despite all of this help, are wholly my own.

At University of California Press, senior editor Reed Malcolm and production coordinator Zuha Khan are amazing. Thanks for your timely responses to queries large and small! Jody Hanson designed the beautiful cover for this book, providing a much-needed lift as I came down the homestretch. Also, my heartfelt thanks to copy editor Erica Soon Olsen and production editor Francisco Reinking for their heroic labors in seeing this project through to completion.

Finally, my parents, David and Mary Barclay; Keiko Ikegami; and dearly departed Papa Ikegami cannot know the depth of my gratitude. Uncle Bill, Uncle Akita, brother John, and sister Barbara, thank you so much for a lifetime of inspiration and always being there.

I dedicate this book to my wife, Naoko. She and our daughter, Megumi, have lived this project without complaint and have supported it in more ways than can be expressed in writing.

NOTE ON TRANSLITERATION AND TRANSLATION

Japanese-language words in the text are transliterated in the modified Hepburn system, except for the place-names Tokyo and Osaka. The default system for Chinese-language words is Hanyu Pinyin. However, Taiwanese personal and place-names that are commonly transliterated in Wade-Giles or other non-Pinyin systems have been left as I have found them. There is no standard system for transliterating Austronesian personal names. Where possible, I have followed usage from Chou Wan-yao's *New Illustrated History of Taiwan*. Korean words are romanized in the reformed system. The McCune-Reischauer system is used for names of authors and publications that are cataloged under this system.

All translations from Japanese sources are by the author unless otherwise indicated. Chinese translations are the author's adaptations of translations by research assistants Wu Haotian, Linda Yu, Li Guo, Sun Xiaofei, and Ning Jing.

Introduction

Empires and Indigenous Peoples, Global Transformation and the Limits of International Society

PROLOGUE: THE WUSHE REBELLION AND
INDIGENOUS RENAISSANCE IN TAIWAN

On October 27, 1930, terror visited the small community of Japanese settler-expatriates in the picturesque resort town of Wushe, an administrative center nestled on a plateau in the central mountains of Taiwan.[1] On that day, some 300 indigenes led by Mona Ludao raided government arsenals, ambushed isolated police units, and turned a school assembly into a bloodbath. All told, Mona's men killed 134 Japanese nationals by day's end, many of them butchered with long daggers and beheaded. Alerted by a distressed phone call from an escapee, the Japanese police apparatus, with backing from military units stationed in Taiwan, responded with genocidal fury. Aerial bombardment, infantry sweeps, and local mercenaries killed roughly 1,000 men, women, and children in the ensuing months. A cornered Mona Ludao removed to the countryside and then killed his family and hanged himself to avoid capture. Subsequently, the Japanese government relocated the remaining residents of Mona's village, Mehebu, forever wiping it off the map.[2]

Over the course of Japanese rule (1895–1945), the Taiwan Government-General forcibly relocated hundreds of other hamlets like Mehebu. The invasive and exploitative policies that provoked Mona and his confederates also eroded precolonial forms of social organization, authority, and ritual life among Taiwan's indigenes. As it severed bonds between indigenes and their lands, in addition to prohibiting or reforming folkways it deemed injurious to its civilizing mission, the government-general nonetheless laid the groundwork for the emergence of Taiwan Indigenous Peoples as a conscious and agentive historical formation. By arresting the diffusion of Chinese language and customs into Taiwan's interior, restricting geographic mobility across the so-called "Savage Border," dividing the colony into normally and specially administered zones, and sanctioning a battery of projects in top-down ethnogenesis, the government-general inscribed a nearly indelible "Indigenous Territory" on the political map of Taiwan over the five decades of its existence.

This book will argue that successive, overlapping instantiations of state power's negative and positive modalities precipitated the formation of modern indigenous political identity in colonial Taiwan. This process paralleled other nationalist awakenings forged in the crucible of foreign occupation. As state functionaries smashed idols, compelled assimilation, and asserted the authority of a central government, their fellow nationals reified, commodified, and preserved the material, cultural, and territorial expressions of native distinction. These Janus-faced vectors of state building can be found wherever governments targeted citizenries, imperial subjects, or marginalized out-groups for inclusion into a new kind of national political space. Applying these axioms to the case of Taiwan Indigenous Peoples under Japanese colonial rule, *Outcasts of Empire* argues that the process Ronald Niezen dubs "indigenization" is a historical concomitant of competitive nation building in the age of high imperialism (1870s–1910s).

Rightly emphasizing the importance of transnational activist circuits, global NGOs, and the increased salience of international rights conventions, Niezen and others consider the decades following 1960 the incubation period for "international indigenism."[3] Laura R. Graham and H. Glenn Penny stress how indigeneity "emerged as a legal and juridical category during the Cold War era" in response to "growing concerns about environmental degradation during the twentieth century together with the emergence of human rights discourses...."[4] Writing about the Taiwan case study explored in this book, Wang Fu-chang asserts that indigenous political consciousness is a decidedly recent arrival, erupting in its current form in the 1980s.[5]

While recognizing the importance of the movements of the 1960s and beyond for indigenous cultural survival in the twenty-first century, this book argues that the early twentieth century is a better place to look for the systemic wellsprings of indigenism.[6] Rather than viewing indigenism as a postwar development enabled by a more or less functioning international system, *Outcasts of Empire* suggests that nationality, internationalism, and indigenism were mutually constituted formations, rather than sequentially occurring phenomena.

The pages that follow examine the politics, economics, and cultural movements that informed the Japanese colonial state's partitioning of Taiwan's indigenous homelands into a special zone of administration known as the Aborigine Territory. The administrative bifurcation of Taiwan began as an expedient measure in the 1890s, reflecting the dependence of the Taiwan Government-General on Qing precedents and straitened colonial budgets. By the 1920s and 1930s, however, the peoples today known as Taiwan Indigenous Peoples[7] were cast for good beyond the bounds of the colonial state's disciplinary apparatus. The so-called *Takasagozoku* (Formosan Aborigines) were accorded a special status as imperial subjects because they were believed to lack the economic competence to thrive in the colony's "regularly administered territories."[8] In a more positive sense, indigenes were invested with a cultural authenticity that marked them as avatars of prelapsarian Taiwan antedating Chinese immigration, based in part on high Japanese appraisals of Austronesian cultural production.[9] From the 1930s onward, the distinctiveness of indigenes as non-Han Taiwanese was elaborated and promoted by the state, the tourism industry, and intellectuals, laying the groundwork for the successor Nationalist Party government of Taiwan (*Guomindang* or GMD) to rule the island as an ethnically bifurcated political field.[10]

The deterritorializing and reterritorializing operations that underwrote the emergence of Taiwan Indigenous Peoples during the period of Japanese colonial rule had locally distinctive contours.[11] But these interrelated processes were embedded in a global political economy dominated by a capitalist business cycle and international competition. In East Asia, the Japanese state refracted these transnational forces throughout its formal and informal empires. A parallel and instructive set of events in neighboring Korea illustrates this point.

In 1919, the Japanese state brutally suppressed a Korean uprising known as the March 1 Movement. That year, across the peninsula, around one million Koreans loudly protested the draconian administrations of governors general Terauchi Masatake and Hasegawa Yoshimichi (1910–1919) on the occasion of former king Gojong's funeral. As was the case with the Wushe uprising of 1930 in Taiwan, the magnitude and vehemence of the protests were taken as a negative verdict on Japanese rule. The savagery of Japan's suppression of the uprising, which may have taken 7,500 Korean lives, became a source of national embarrassment. The sense that colonial rule should rest on more than naked force, and the awareness that the world was watching, impelled the Japanese state to embark on reforms that emphasized co-optation, the active support of Korean elites, and abolition of the most violent and hated forms of colonial police tactics, such as summary punishment by flogging.[12]

During the 1920s, the Korean Government-General launched a series of policies known as "cultural rule" in response to the March 1 debacle. As part of a larger program to legitimate itself, Japan's official stance toward Korean literature, architecture, music, and other cultural forms took a preservationist turn that tempered enthusiasm for the fruits of Korean ethnic genius with a wariness of insubordination and a long-standing belief that Koreans were developmentally laggard. The softening of the government's posture and policies entailed neither the implementation of a culturally relativist agenda nor the abandonment of the core principles of racial denigration. Nonetheless, Saitō Makoto's "cultural rule" policy represented a sea change, and it set into motion a series of reforms that laid bare the contradictory demands made upon the interwar colonial state.

On the one hand, state power was ultimately maintained through the threat of force and justified by a theory of Japanese racial superiority. On the other, the colonial state sought to attain hegemony through the politics of inclusion, which brought in its train practices that were conducive to the production of modern Korean subjects.¹³ Henry Em summarizes the paradoxical long-term effects of colonial rule in terms that mirror events in Taiwan:

> Thus, contrary to conventional [Korean] nationalist accounts that argue that Japanese colonial authorities pursued a consistent and systematic policy of eradicating Korean identity, we should see that the Japanese colonial state actually endeavored to produce Koreans as subjects—subjects in the sense of being under the authority of the Japanese emperor, and in the sense of having a *separate . . . subjectivity. . . .*
>
> *It was in this sense that Japanese colonialism was 'constructive' for both the colonizer and colonized. . . . Coercion, prohibition, and censorship, then were not the only (or even primary) forms through which colonial power was exercised. . . . there was a steady proliferation of discourses concerning Korean identity emanating from the Japanese colonial state itself—including studies of Korean history, geography, language, customs, religion, music, art—in almost immeasurable accumulated detail. . . . For the Japanese colonial state, the goal of exploiting Korea and using it for its strategic ends went hand in hand with the work of transforming peasants into Koreans, or 'Chōsenjin.'*¹⁴

Two parallels are in evidence here. First of all, well-coordinated attacks on Japanese state power (March 1 in Korea and Wushe in Taiwan), followed by clumsy and disproportionate responses (the open firing on civilians in Korea, the aerial bombardments in Taiwan), actuated regime change. In Taiwan, the heated debates surrounding the Wushe Rebellion pitted Japan's opposition Seiyūkai (Friends of the Constitution) against Governor-General Ishizuka Eizō, who was allied with the ruling Minseitō (Popular Government Party). The Seiyūkai capitalized on the Taiwan Government-General's incompetence to call for the resignation of Ishizuka, who actually stepped down along with his inner circle, a reshuffling reminiscent of Saitō Makoto's ascension to the governor-generalship of Korea in 1919.¹⁵

Again echoing events in Korea, the cowed successor administration in Taiwan called for a renovation of "Aborigine Administration" and a shift from rule by naked force and intimidation to government by co-optation and delegation. Importantly, for our purposes, Taiwanese highlanders were thereafter governed as members of ethnic groups, whose cultural, political, and economic distinction from the rest of Taiwan was selectively preserved, with certain elements even celebrated by colonial administrators, metropolitan voters, and consumers in Taiwan and Japan alike.¹⁶ As was the case for Japanese cultural rule in 1920s Korea, the new era of aborigine administration proved compatible with the emergence of a discourse on ethnic integrity, one that overrode localisms. The artifacts and structures that coalesced during this period would then resurface in the postcolonial era in the form of indigenous ethnonationalism.¹⁷

In contrast to Korea, public expressions of indigenous patriotism were suppressed in Taiwan for over four decades after the Japanese Empire crumbled in 1945.[18] The 1.5 million migrants to Taiwan in the Chinese Nationalist Party (GMD) exodus represented yet another wave of colonization for Taiwan's majority population.[19] During a long stretch of one-party rule under martial law (1949–87), GMD-sanctioned history excluded discussions of indigenes as autochthons because it regarded Taiwanese history as a regional variant of mainland China's.[20]

After martial law was lifted in 1987, politicians put distance between themselves and the GMD by supporting an indigenous cultural renaissance to signal the island's distinctiveness from the mainland.[21] On a parallel track, the founding of the Alliance of Taiwan Aborigines in 1984 ushered in a wave of organized indigenous activism.[22] Thereafter, coordinated action between Han Taiwanese nationalists and Indigenous activists produced a number of political and cultural reforms aimed at promoting a measure of autonomy and correcting the most egregious forms of public denigration. As a result, the notions that non-Han peoples are the island's original inhabitants and that Taiwan's multiracial composition should be celebrated rather than overcome are mainstream political positions[23]—much as they were in the 1930s, when Japan ruled the island.

Within this broader context of renaissance and revival, Puli-based freelance writer Deng Xiangyang's energetically researched oral and documentary histories articulate a local perspective on the Wushe uprising that posits indigenes as anticolonial heroes and avatars of an authentic, pre-Chinese Taiwanese past. Deng's books draw on biographical and family histories and photographs culled from his local network of Sediq acquaintances.[24] Along with graphic artist Qiu Ruolong, who also has extensive contacts and family relations in the Sediq community, Deng coproduced a television drama and children's book about the Wushe Rebellion. Qiu and Deng have popularized the heroic suffering of the Sediq people, the harsh labor conditions and sexual harassment that contributed to the revolt, and the brutality of the Japanese counterattacks. All of these themes were subsequently dramatized in the blockbuster John Woo production *Seediq Bale* (2011), a feature-length film that recounts the story of the rebellion in romantic hues that recall *Last of the Mohicans* and *Dances with Wolves*.[25]

As I watched and rewatched this film, I was struck by its fidelity to the Japanese inquest reports into the causes of the rebellion. The main characters, the key scenes, and the plot structure are immediately recognizable to anyone who has sifted through the documentation generated by the rebellion. Insofar as some Japanese characters are made out to be racist buffoons deserving of grisly deaths, this film can be considered anticolonial. At the same time, its deep engagement with a reservoir of colonial-era tropes, documents, and narrative structures highlights the entanglement of colonialism and postcolonial nationalism that marks the Korean experience, shown here in a new context: the making of an indigenous people.

While there were similarities, as noted above, the complex process by which residents of Mehebu and Paaran (see map 1) became Sediq was different from the trajectory that saw natives of Seoul, Gyeongju, and Pyongyang transformed into Chōsenjin (people of Joseon, or Koreans). In the case of Taiwan Indigenous Peoples, the translocal, subimperial, and putatively organic identities fostered under the government-general's variant of cultural rule were not *Taiwanese,* per se, but by turns Indigenous Formosan *(Takasagozoku)* or attached to particular ethnolinguistic groups (Amis, Bunun, Paiwan, Atayal, Tsou, Rukai, Saisiyat, and Yami) (see map 2).

For example, in 1930, Mona Ludao and his followers appeared in official documents, journalism, and commercial publications as "savages," "barbarians," or "Formosan Tribes" *(banjin, seibanjin, banzoku)*.[26] In many respects, they were governed as such: policy before 1930 emphasized their backwardness, mainly by excluding them from the tax base due to purported economic incompetence. The translocal identifier *banjin* ascribed little importance to matters of ethnic identity and was, in fact, symptomatic of a pre–Wushe Rebellion approach to governance that paid scant attention to subject formation.[27]

In the press, in government statistics, in police records, and in ethnological writing, indigenes were also identified as members of particular units called *sha* in Japanese (Mehebu and Paaran, for example). The *sha* were units of governance pegged to residential patterns, although they did not necessarily reflect local conceptions of territoriality and sovereignty. Rather, the category *sha* (in Chinese, *she*) was imposed by the Qing, long before the Japanese arrived, as a blanket term for any indigenous settlement or cluster of hamlets.[28] Like the *banjin* designator, affiliation with a *sha* did not confer ethnic or cultural status upon the governed.

Terminology anchored in derivatives of the terms *ban* and *sha* suggested continuity from Qing times and a relative disinterest in indigenous interiority. On the other hand, as early as 1898, Japanese ethnologists began to classify residents of Mona's hometown of Mehebu as Atayals. This neologism originated with Inō Kanori and signaled a different way of imagining Taiwan's non-Han population(s). The term *Atayal* first appeared in Japanese documents in 1896 to identify an ethnic group noted for facial tattooing, a common language that spanned several watersheds and valleys (and *sha*), and the production of brilliant red textiles.[29] The term *Atayal,* which connoted membership in a culture-bearing ethnos, rarely surfaced in policy-making circles during the first two decades of colonial rule. From early on, however, the term was inscribed in an academic counterdiscourse, as exemplified by a color-coded map. The map's novel subethnic components—territories for the Atayal, Bunun, Tsou, Amis, Paiwan, Puyuma, and Tsarisen peoples—overwrote Qing-period cartographic voids. This architectonic prefigured today's officially sanctioned view of Taiwanese multiculturalism (see figures 1 and 2).

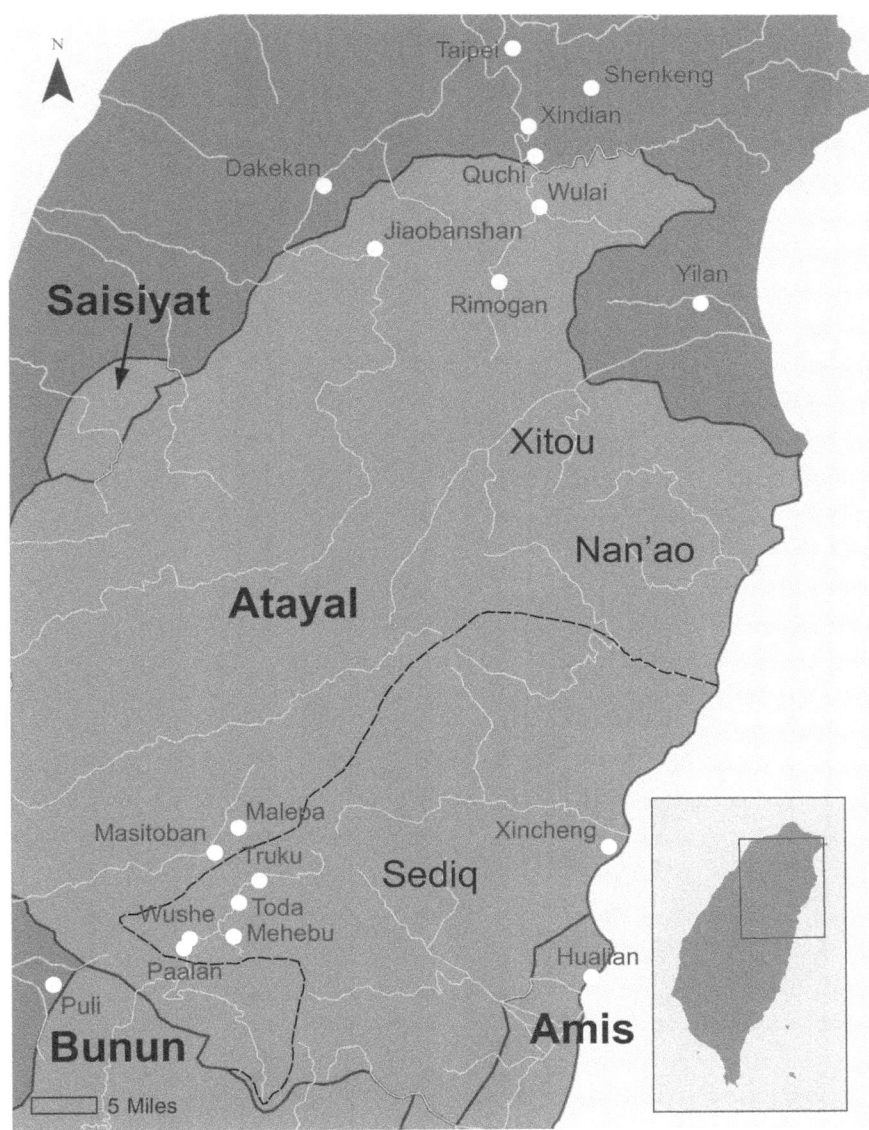

MAP 1. The major indigenous ethnic groups of northern Taiwan, with the Atayal and Sediq settlements most frequently mentioned in this book. The Sediq territory reflects the demarcations of Japanese official surveys in the second decade of the twentieth century. Today, much of the territory labeled Sediq by the Japanese is now considered Truku territory.

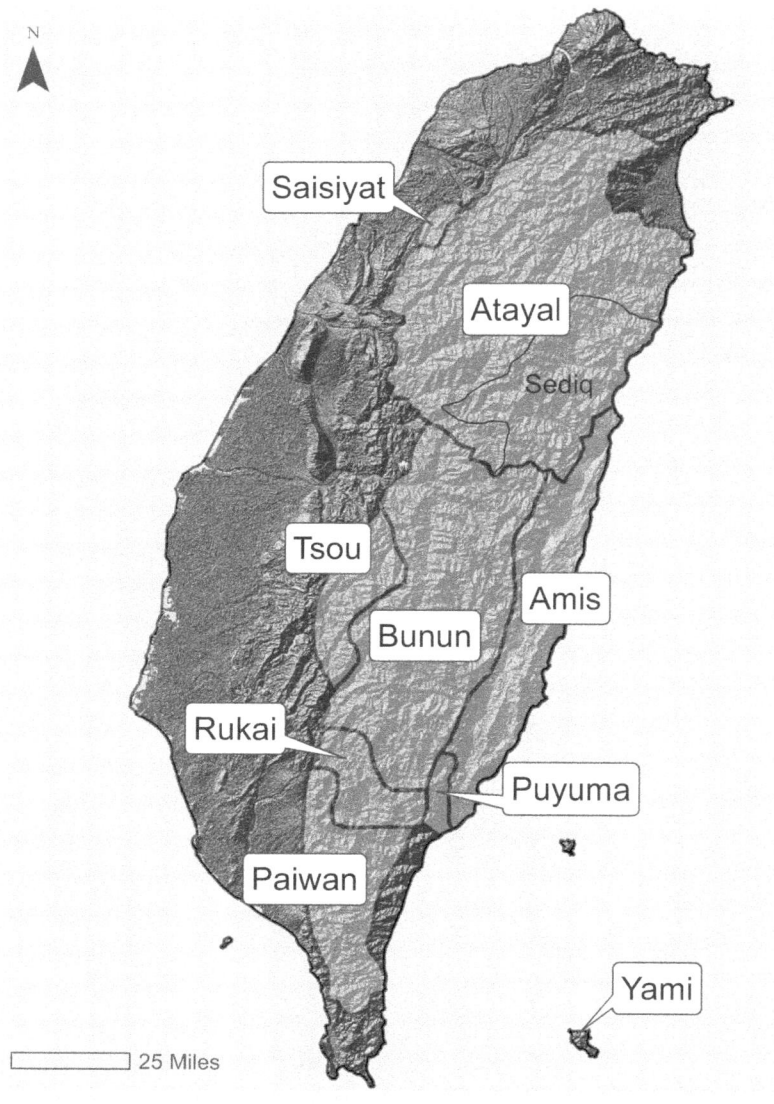

MAP 2. An overview of the major indigenous ethnic groups of Taiwan, as portrayed in Japanese-period maps, ca. 1935. As this book argues, the shapes of these territories, their names, and their numbers have been historically contingent.

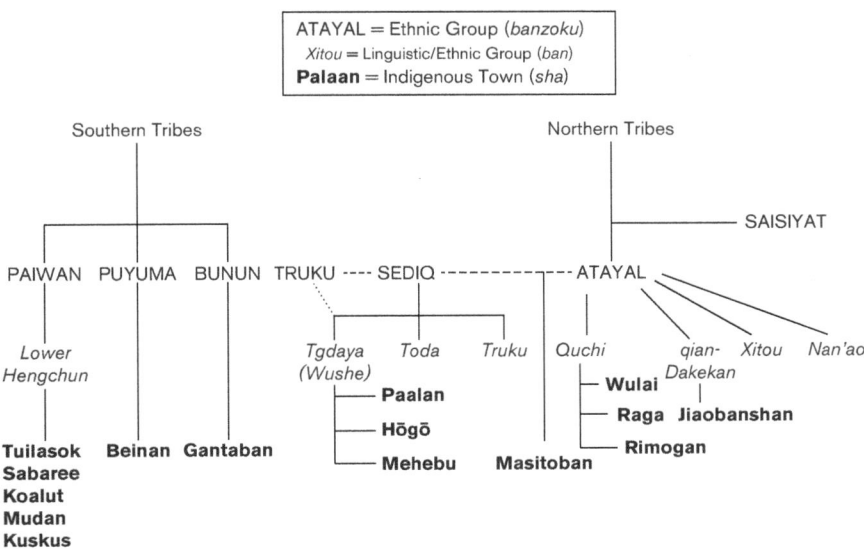

FIGURE 1. Japanese colonial-period ethnonyms for Taiwan Indigenous Peoples.

During the colonial period, the ethnic designator *Sediq* that marks Mona Ludao and his descendants was also slow to catch on, even after the Wushe uprising of 1930.[30] Nonetheless, the political and cultural salience of labels such as *Atayal*, under which the Sediq were subsumed at that time, increased in the 1930s. TGG-sponsored indigenous youth corps, a new locus of political power, were organized around these labels of identity and difference.[31] In addition, museum collections, censuses, and language dictionaries inscribed these categories for reactivation decades later.[32]

There are obvious differences in scale between modern Korean nationalism and Taiwan indigenous renaissance. The Korean Peninsula is populated by well over sixty-five million people, while the Sediq lands of contemporary Taiwan claim about ten thousand; Taiwan's sixteen recognized indigenous ethnic groups total roughly three hundred thousand souls. But for the purposes of this study, the more important issue is how these two former areas of the Japanese Empire have diverged, despite their common experiences as test cases for the efficacy of cultural rule, referred to above. Unlike Koreans who reside on the peninsula, Taiwan's indigenous peoples cannot claim a nation-state to express their shared heritage and territorial distinction in the hard currency of sovereignty. At the same time—and this separates them from ethnic minorities who cannot imagine themselves as indigenous—conditions are such for Taiwan Indigenous Peoples that territorial sovereignty in one form or another is a plausible, if not desirable, way forward.

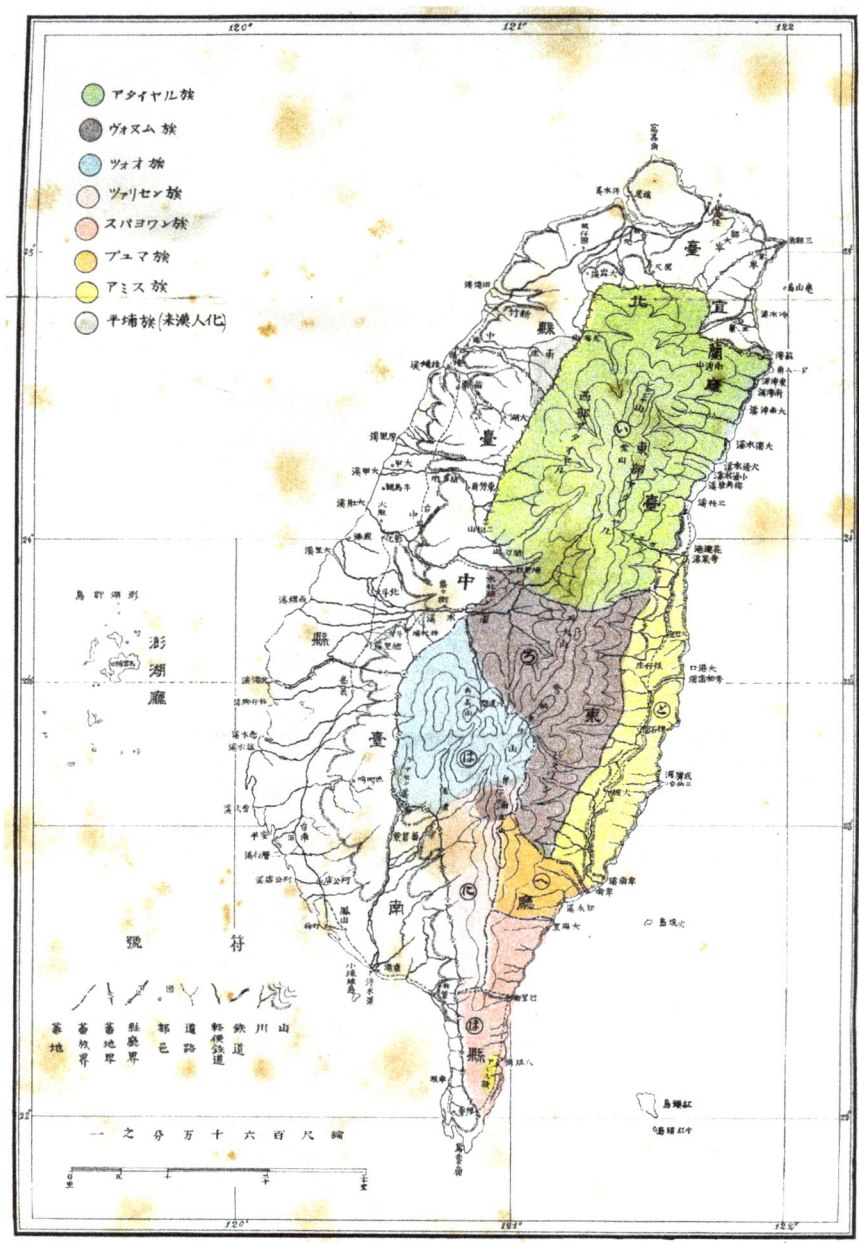

FIGURE 2. Inō Kanori's ethnic map of Taiwan's indigenous territory, 1898. The colored zones represent indigenous ethnic groups. The white areas represent nonindigenous (Han) Taiwan. A broken line indicates the borderline between the two. This map was published in 1900 as part of a government report: Inō Kanori and Awano Dennojō, *Taiwan banjin jijō* (Taipei: Taiwan sōtokufu minseibu bunshoka, 1900), n.p.

THE DECLINE OF NATIVES AND THE EMERGENCE OF INDIGENOUS PEOPLES IN WORLD HISTORY

American and Japanese successes in nation building during the 1870s and 1880s were not isolated events. After 1860, Germany and Italy also consolidated, and they, along with France, put into place new central governments. . . . A handful of nations put together the skills and aggressiveness to create concentrated industrial plants whose products and profits translated into military power. *The resulting new imperialism of the post-1860 years redrew the maps of Africa and Asia.*—Walter LaFeber[33]

As *there are no unoccupied territories*—that is, territories that do not belong to [a] state . . . *[T]he characteristic feature of the period under review is the final partitioning of the globe*—final, not in the sense that repartition is impossible; on the contrary, repartitions are possible and inevitable—but in the sense that *the colonial policy of the capitalist countries has completed the seizure of the unoccupied territories on our planet. For the first time the world is completely divided up, so that in the future only redivision is possible, i.e., territories can only pass from one "owner" to another, instead of passing as ownerless territory to an owner.*—V. I. Lenin[34]

In their recent intervention into the field of international relations, political scientists Barry Buzan and George Lawson make a strong case for the nineteenth-century origins of the "full international system."[35] They convincingly argue that a "global transformation" was occasioned by the confluence of shifts in the historically concatenated domains of production, state building, and ideology. Following historian Jürgen Osterhammel, Buzan and Lawson point out that today's international system is not a creature of Europe's landmark Treaties of Westphalia (1648) or Versailles (1919), but is rather a product of nation-state–sponsored industrial capitalism's global impact as an integrative and disintegrative force.[36] Osterhammel also views the nineteenth century as a world-historical pivot, while decentering the story of global modernity with a conscious move away from unreflexive Eurocentrism. Osterhammel and Buzan and Lawson take inspiration from C. A. Bayly in their regard for ideation and social formations as more than the epiphenomena of high politics and industrial progress.[37] But for all of their breadth, erudition, and nuance, none of these magisterial syntheses of nineteenth-century global political economy and history has accounted for a persistent phenomenon that was part and parcel of the transformations they so ably map. I refer here to the emergence of indigenous peoples, which is the other side of the coin of the birth of the modern nation-state system.

As Lenin asserted a century ago (see epigraph to this section), a handful of nation-states managed to write their sovereignty over the earth's surface during Osterhammel's, Buzan and Lawson's, and Bayly's period of global transformation. This feat was accomplished by harnessing the power of capitalism to a novel form of intra- and interstate sovereignty. In the emergent international system, state sovereignty was imagined as distributed evenly within clearly defined and limited national borders. Unlike their early-modern dynastic-state predecessors, with their relatively low state capacities and patchworks of graded, plural, and oscillating sovereignties, the new order was premised on the axiom that no space could belong simultaneously to multiple sovereigns. Perhaps even more radical was the axiom that no space on the globe could be excluded from the system.[38]

Colorful early twentieth-century globes and Mercator projection maps visually encapsulated the new system's logic. Formerly unknown white spaces and great deserts of the world were filled in with various imperial colors. One color ended where another began. The shapes given to these territories were serially reproduced and became instantly recognizable logos. Thongchai Winichakul called these entities "geo-bodies."[39] Today, we understand that these globes and maps expressed wishful thinking. Surely, the United States had not extended its authority over thousands of Philippine Islands and their millions of inhabitants with the stroke of a pen in Paris in 1898.[40] So too with the French in Vietnam in 1862[41] or the Japanese in Taiwan in 1895[42] at the conclusion of similar paper agreements. Superficially, such treaties, accords, and protocols transferred sovereignty from dynastic states to nation-states. But the notion of "transfer" obscured a thorny problem: dynastic states conceptualized sovereignty in significantly different terms, so the sovereignty that was inherited by nation-states was necessarily incomplete, partial, and unsatisfactory by the standards of "international society"[43] as it was being reconfigured in the nineteenth century.

In the years and even decades following annexation, each imperial nation-state aspired to reconcile the contradictions of an international system premised on universal reach but composed of legally plural empire-states riddled with semi-autonomous enclaves. Through negotiation, warfare, and experiments in applied colonial science, empire-states attempted to create a world of contiguous imperial geobodies in the face of deficits of intelligence, rebelling populations, challenging terrain, and fiscal constraints. As Jane Burbank and Frederick Cooper put it, " . . . when territories were taken over, colonized people did not simply fall into whatever role striving industrialists could imagine for them. Empires still came up against the limits of their power at the far end of lines of command, where they had to mobilize conquered communities and find reliable intermediaries—all *at a cost that did not exceed the benefits.*"[44]

Continuing in this vein, these historians point out that the far-flung European nineteenth-century empires, products and engines of a voracious industrial capitalism, were not sui generis entities. The great protagonists of high imperialism employed and built upon older imperial forms, albeit with more firepower and competitive edge. For them—and for Lauren Benton, another influential scholar of comparative imperialism—the ideal type of an international society exhausted by unitarily sovereign states was only that, an ideal. Giving it too much credence, as the telos of imperial history or as a dominant formation, belies an exclusive focus on the utterances of metropolitan visionaries and a disregard for how empires actually functioned.

This book shares the view of Burbank and Cooper and of Benton that empires are best understood as successors to other empires and that postcolonialism did not resolve itself into a world of sovereign nation-states based on former colonial boundaries. At the same time, it will argue that hallmarks of nineteenth-century imperialism—its symbiosis with industrial capitalism, a geostrategic setting of multipolar competition, and a susceptibility to liberal and anti-imperial inflections—produced a condition I will call indigenous modernity. Taking Burbank and Cooper's emphasis on the cost constraints of imperial integration to heart, *Outcasts of Empire* will describe a kind of fiscal exhaustion, one that occurred during the slice of world-time described above, as the ground for the emergence of indigenous peoples, autonomous regions, and other forms of quasi sovereignty that mottle the ideally solid surfaces of the international system's geobodies.[45]

A particular type of virtuous circle or positive feedback loop lay at the back of state efforts to call forth disciplined populations, the forerunners of today's national citizenries. In colonial Taiwan's "normally administered" districts, the government-general recovered its investments on a "big bang" of outlays for population censuses, land surveys, and a buyout of the old regime's elite because subsequent state revenues exceeded the costs of government. These monies were then plowed back into state building or reinvested in industry.[46] This virtuous circle of discipline begetting increased state budgets begetting governmentality was broken, however, in the militarily resistant, sparsely populated, topographically forbidding, and linguistically checkered highlands of Taiwan. In these "specially administered" territories, natives became indigenous peoples.

In our time, population recovery, courtroom victories, and cultural renaissance are integral to the story of indigenous peoples. The old tropes of dispossession, deracination, and endemic poverty remain relevant, but narratives of the "disappearing native" ring false in the twenty-first century. This book starts with the understanding that indigenous peoples did not become extinct. At its widest aperture, *Outcasts of Empire* asks how Bayly's, Osterhammel's, and Buzan and Lawson's models of global transformation might look different if the emergence of indigenism is viewed as an integral component of the international system.

To accomplish this task, this study chronicles the making of an indigenous people at a spatial and temporal junction of the aforementioned great transformation. The case study is the emergence of the Atayal, Bunun, Saisiyat, Tsou, Amis, Paiwan, Rukai, and Puyuma peoples in Taiwan under late Qing and Japanese rule from the 1870s through the 1940s. By shifting the optic away from interstate competition and the development of a global division of labor between the First and Third Worlds,[47] and focusing instead on the production of bifurcated sovereignty within nationalized *and* colonized spaces, this study attempts to explain disjunctions and discontinuities internal to emergent national political formations. The intensification and extensification of global capitalism,[48] it will argue, instantiated the political geography of bifurcated sovereignty in Taiwan.

The narrative begins in the 1860s, with a discussion of shipwrecks and ransoms on Taiwan's Langqiao Peninsula. On the southern extremity of the Qing Empire, Langqiao's political topography presented numerous hurdles to the extension of the international system.[49] Through an analysis of the diplomatic, military, and institutional solutions implemented to solve these problems, I show how a vision of world order became globally normative (although it remained aspirational at best). Subsequent chapters analyze how the Japanese colonial state attempted to implement the new models of sovereignty throughout Taiwan from the 1890s through the 1940s.

At a more granular level, *Outcasts of Empire* focuses on the lives, actions, and aspirations of men such as Kondō Katsusaburō (a Japanese colonist) and women such as Iwan Robao (daughter of a Sediq headman), individuals who left faint but discernible traces in the documentary record. Jun Uchida's term "brokers of empire"[50] describes them well, as does Daniel Richter's sobriquet "cultural brokers."[51] By either definition, these brokers thrived in the twilight era of the legally pluralistic dynastic empires—in our case, the Tokugawa, Qing, Joseon, and Shō dynasties in Japan, China, Korea, and the Ryūkyū Islands, respectively. *Outcasts of Empire* chronicles the shifting structural positions of the headmen, interpreters, trading-post operators, and trackers who dominated the political economy of the early-modern hinterlands as they were displaced or repurposed in the new international order.

As a narrative history that pays due attention to personalities who have yet to receive scholarly attention, the empirical heart of this study is pericentric.[52] The reconstruction of the particulars of long-obscured frontier history is necessary because it indicates that the nineteenth century's reterritorialization project was more costly and time-consuming than metrocentric histories would have it. At the same time, the macrohistorical frame cannot be ignored, because interstate competition propelled successive Japanese and Qing projects in state building on the edges of Taiwan's governed spaces. One cannot explain the lavish spending for these endeavors without putting them into a context of perceived national peril and the desire to create a world order that could accommodate much higher volumes and velocities of commerce, diplomatic communications, and migration.

I am not the first scholar to argue that indigeneity and the international system are related historical phenomena. However, the case that their co-creation dates back to the early twentieth century and that their entanglement commenced as part of the global movement to make the surface of the inhabited earth coextensive with national geobodies, has yet to be made. In making this claim, I argue that the historical process of indigenization was an integral component of the international system's emergence. The mechanisms uncovered by a study of their co-creation, I believe, provide an answer to one of modernity's big conundrums: why the dream (or nightmare) of a world exhausted by nationally governed territories is receding farther and farther toward the horizon, despite the exponential increase in state capacities and communication technologies.

Behind such seemingly innocuous statements as "Ankara spoke with Moscow, to Washington's chagrin" lies the conceit that there are people in Ankara, Moscow, and Washington who can speak for the populations containerized in Turkey, Russia, and the United States. These metonyms suggest that leaders have the power to restrain, encourage, and regulate their populations to the extent that agreements between them bind their populations, as well. Our ability to imagine that this system is operative, even as we are mindful of frictions and imperfections, presupposes a long history of state making that will be explored in the following pages. As we shall see, the project was animated by high ideals and mendacious ideologies, by altruism and greed. One can say that the UN charter presupposes such a world order, as did the Kellogg-Briand Pact of 1928 outlawing war. At the same time, the Berlin Conference of 1885, the Taft-Katsura accord of 1905, and the League of Nations Covenant of 1920 invoked the same ethos to justify collusion among powerful states to deny sovereignty to colonized peoples.[53]

This book contributes to the literature on global transformation by foregrounding the immense quantities of labor-power required to operationalize the ideal-typical political units that constituted the international system. For the women and men of Meiji Japan (1868–1912) who either went to Taiwan or participated in its colonization as citizens of the metropole, Taiwan's former Qing frontier was a vast, complex, unregulated, and challenging hinterland. Its conquest and pacification was chronicled in minute detail, because each negotiation, punitive expedition, or survey appeared as a necessary step to consolidate a Japanese empire that must either "eat or be eaten." And yet, for all of its intensity, momentum, and destructive fury, the project ran aground in the central mountains in the year 1915. The location and timing of the project's abandonment, I will argue, tells us much about the patchy sovereignty that still characterizes the earth's political geography.

STATES, SETTLERS, AND NATIVES

Historian C. A. Bayly has labeled native peoples "the losers" in the global transformation. Bayly's formulation helpfully avoids the anachronistic and circular term "primitive" and provides clues for identifying global patterns in the configuration of modern political space. Bayly writes, "What can be said is that small cultural groups which *were not centrally involved in intensive peasant commodity production* came under unprecedented political, cultural, and demographic pressure where previously they had been able to bargain with residents of the settled domains or early representatives of European and American power. The 'cultural terms of trade' moved decisively in favor . . . of all settled societies producing a permanent agricultural surplus or industrial artifacts."[54]

In our analysis, we will designate Bayly's "settled societies" as *settlers,* defined as social formations involved in "intensive peasant commodity production." Following Eric Wolf, we stipulate that *settler* populations are distinguished from "lineages, clans, tribes, and chiefdoms"[55] by their relationships to states. *Settlers* surrender surplus wealth to a state via some form of routinized taxation, whereas Bayly's *native peoples* (hereafter abbreviated *natives*) inhabited what James Scott terms the ungoverned peripheries of a world not yet exhausted by national borders or the direct control of dynastic states.[56] As Bayly intimates, demographically preponderant settlers overwhelmed smaller, relatively mobile populations of natives by squatting and organizing self-defense in the course of the nineteenth-century global transformation. More importantly, however, settlers yielded a portion of their surplus to states, which converted agricultural productivity into organized military force, at a remove from direct native-settler encounters.

Natives, in contrast, lived under political systems that fissured, subdivided, and recombined within the limits imposed by the politics of redistribution and reciprocity, which could never attain the surplus-extracting capabilities of states.[57] States, not settlers, turned geographically indeterminate margins, borderlands, and frontiers into demarcated and permanently defended political boundary lines. The dynamic of this tripartite state-settler-native relationship, then, is a central plotline in the delineation of the spaces of centralized state sovereignty in world history.

As a third party, the state could either mobilize agricultural surplus to restrain land-hungry settlers or deploy it to advance settler interests vis-à-vis natives, depending on a host of variables. One should not understand this process as an uninterrupted, unidirectional march, as depicted in Frederick Jackson Turner's frontier thesis, with the state an assumed ally of the tax- or tribute-paying settler. As Richard White has noted, based on the North American example, the state's intervention on behalf of settlers was often determined by the relative value central administrators placed on alliances with native peoples.[58] Moreover, when multiple empires were in competition, natives could leverage imperial backing against settlers. But as John Shepherd has shown regarding the Qing frontier in Taiwan, state support for settlers was also determined by a crude cost-benefit analysis. If the military expenses required for an aggressive settlement policy were justified by the projected increase in land revenues, the state would back the settlers.[59]

As White and other scholars have shown regarding the North American natives under British and U.S. colonial rule, it was when states abandoned native peoples in favor of taxpayers (actual or potential), in light of fiscal, geostrategic, or even electoral pressures, that nonstate spaces were likely to enter the realm of centrally administered territory. Broadly speaking, this dynamic of state expansion was reversible in the early modern period but became much less so with the advent of international relations undergirded by capitalist relations of production. As the increased volume and pace of global trade called forth greater regulation of ungoverned territory by centralized administrations, states sided with settlers to turn the tide against the natives.

An observer at century's turn might well have agreed with Lenin that states, by then, had carved up the earth's occupied territory. Bayly estimates that "only" four to eight million people constituted the world population of natives circa 1900, a number seemingly too small to stop the march of progress. But if the large portion of the earth's surface occupied by natives on the eve of World War I is taken into account, Lenin's statement appears premature. The remaining spaces of native autonomy constituted formidable obstacles to state-building visionaries and the settlers who acted as shock troops for national territorial expansion. To be sure, during the global transformation, vast tracts of the most productive native land were incorporated under the authority of nation-states and dynasties through dispossession, slaughter, or epidemiological catastrophe. Nonetheless, large areas remained administered by or in the name of native peoples beyond the spaces of national sovereignty.

LEGAL CENTRALISM AND LEGAL PLURALISM

The Japanese state in Taiwan aimed to effect "the transformation of differentiated and layered political order into an homogenous space"[60] from the early 1900s through about 1915, at the height of a historical epoch when "territory rather than status and allegiance increasingly defined the jurisdiction of the state."[61] Its predecessor state in Taiwan, the Qing, exemplified a contrasting regime of "weak" or multicentric "legal pluralism." Throughout the Qing Empire, heterogeneous communities and ranked status groups stood in differentiated legal relationships to the apical center of authority in Beijing. Implicit in the notion of multicentric legal pluralism is the possibility that sovereignty can be graded, and even diminished, at the margins of a polity. In contrast, nation-states ideally impose equal measures of sovereignty over the whole surface of their territories to facilitate defense, tax collection, conscription, economic development, and the mobility of labor, among other desiderata. At the least, expanding nineteenth-century empires attempted to shut down competing sources of authority and to bring plural systems under a hierarchical state-centered umbrella.

While the implementation of legal centralism was a costly affair, it was not a project abandoned lightly in the arena of competitive imperialism. At that time, border territories that appeared "ownerless," because they operated by nonstate logics, were subject to occupation by other states by the lights of Western international law. At the height of social Darwinism, Japanese leaders often felt compelled by geostrategic considerations to extend or consolidate territorial sovereignty in order to protect Japan's flanks, under time pressure and with finite resources. The end result of this conjuncture in Taiwan was its current bifurcated sovereignty.

Bifurcated sovereignty is a descendant of weak legal pluralism in roughly the same way that indigenous peoples are descendants of native peoples. In other words, the processes described by revisionist historian of American foreign relations Walter LaFeber and influential theorist of empire V. I. Lenin as the final push toward state ownership of the earth's inhabited space was halted where native peoples could not be brought within imperialism's centrally administered territories. Today these peoples are known as indigenous, and their territories are administered under different sets of rules from the rest of the nation's spaces. That bifurcated sovereignty is here to stay, despite the overwhelming pressure for administrative and legal integration brought to bear by industrial capitalism and international competition, requires historical explanation.

Thongchai Winichakul has described modern, Mercator-projection map-logos as geobodies. The geobody has a fixed shape—its borders are no longer expanding (or oscillating)—and its boundaries are clearly delineated. These two features distinguish it from most dynastic realms of the prenational era. Thongchai's case, Thailand's geobody, was formed in the context of international competition and technology transfer that characterized the long nineteenth century. To preempt encroachment by aggressive Western powers, who considered the ability to cartographically represent the precise limits of sovereignty to be an index of sovereignty, the Siamese court sent officials to its unmapped and unbounded peripheries to establish the geographic outer limit of Siam's sovereignty, defined as the exclusive right to govern the polities and populations within its national territory. The maps created under this modernizing regime, adopting the cartographic sciences and conventions of international society, established clear limits to the Thai state's spatial reach, while forestalling British attempts to extend the boundaries of Indo-Burma at Thailand's expense.

The inscriptions of national and imperial boundary lines over the erstwhile middle grounds that separated dynastic states were more than defensive projects to consolidate sovereignty within a container. The construction of geobodies can also be read as a multistate solution to a chronic problem facing maritime empires during the second industrial revolution.[62] The dynastic state's relatively laissez-faire approach to rule in distant borderlands was inimical to the orderly functioning of a world economy whose industrial plants and working masses were sustained by the timely shipment of oceangoing bulk commodities. This new epoch, wherein national populations became dependent upon long-distance trade for daily existence, I call the age of *high-velocity capitalism*.

High-velocity capitalism increased the number of disputes arising over shipwrecks in far-flung ports, while it swelled the vehemence with which states weighed in on such affairs. As the Qing and Tokugawa dynasts learned to their peril, foreign governments, representing the interests of the merchants and customers dependent upon oceanic trade, began to demand the right to negotiate with central authorities about incidents arising in the harbors and shores that shoguns and emperors had kept at arm's length since the mid-seventeenth century.

When authorities in Edo attempted to accommodate Washington's demands to facilitate the increased volume of oceanic economic activity in the 1850s, for example, they quickly ascertained that one central authority in Edo could not make the coastlines of Japan hospitable to foreign merchant marines by administrative fiat. The legacy of Edo's inability to command its borders from a central node of authority is well known: the Tokugawa government crumbled in a civil war that was ignited by confusion over how to deal with coastal traffic. Having learned how the fate of central government was now dependent upon the extension of sovereignty throughout the national geobody, the Meiji oligarchs made the eradication of legal pluralism and the instantiation of legal centralism key goals of the post-1868 Japanese state.

A mere five years later, the Meiji state joined the global war on legal pluralism by pressing the Qing court on its handling of the 1871 Okinawan shipwreck on Taiwan known as the Mudan village incident. In December 1871, Mudan villagers on the Langqiao Peninsula allegedly murdered fifty-four shipwrecked sailors from Miyakojima (Ryūkyū Islands). The fate of the castaways became a cause célèbre for ambitious Japanese politicians, who turned the islanders' misfortune into an opportunity for the young Meiji state to assert its territorial claims over the Ryūkyūs (later called Okinawa Prefecture). In April 1874, Japanese admiral Saigō Tsugumichi broke a string of diplomatic stalemates by descending on the Langqiao Peninsula at the rear of three attack groups to avenge the Ryūkyūans, recover their remains, and clear the coasts of wreckers.[63]

Within a month, Japanese troops laid waste to the southern Taiwanese villages it held responsible for the murders. Negotiations among Japanese, Qing, and British officials in Beijing prevented armed confrontation between East Asia's major powers. Nonetheless, over five hundred Japanese troops perished from disease and exposure awaiting Tokyo's orders. Ultimately, the Japanese recognized Qing suzerainty throughout Taiwan and secured a face-saving indemnity, while the Qing pledged to ensure the safety of distressed sailors on Taiwan's coasts.

Recast as a chapter in the clash between high-velocity capitalism and legal pluralism, the Mudan incident's family resemblance to the American shipwrecks off the coast of Japan in the 1840s and 1850s becomes apparent.[64] The Langqiaoans' plunder of shipwrecks was analogous to the hostility of shogunal officials who refused succor to stranded whalers or even imprisoned them.[65] From the standpoint of heavily capitalized maritime commercial powers, stronger central authorities with shared commitments to safeguarding commerce were a prerequisite to opening up East Asian markets.

In the myriad "Mudan village incidents" that litter nineteenth-century annals, one obstacle to resolution was the uncertain, broken, and long chain of command that connected border areas to dynastic capitals. When consular officials relayed the protests of distressed travelers or merchants to the shogun, emperor, or king about rough treatment on their peripheries, dynasts could hardly get to the root of the matter because their states functioned without the integrated, centralized, and ground-level bureaucracy that characterized nation-states.

Unlike the local hong merchants, interpreters, strongmen, and gentry who connected dynastic centers to their geographic peripheries, nation-state functionaries were dependent upon the center. Indeed, replacing intermediaries and brokers with centrally appointed officials was a venerable method of statecraft in East Asia long before the 1871 affair. During the Ming dynasty, the *tusi* system of inherited chieftainships was abolished in favor of staffing southwest China's frontier with appointed officials.[66] In the imperial Chinese case, the rule of avoidance, coupled with the centralized system of recruitment, appointment, and promotion, established an administrative grid united by common language, purpose, and chain of command. Institutionally speaking, the spatial extension of this grid represented the limits of the emperor's direct access to reliable information and the enforceability of his edicts.[67]

However, under the Ming and Qing, centralized bureaucracy only reached down to the district level. An unpaid subbureaucracy of gentry, yamen runners, and local notables took over from there to manage the day-to-day functions of government. The problem of central command and control was only exacerbated in Central Asia, where a completely different system of state-to-society mechanisms was instituted under the banner of the Bureau of Border Affairs. As Pars Cassel points out in his study of Qing legal pluralism, under the imperial system, nonofficials were not permitted the "luxury" of claiming to be subjects of the emperor in the sense that they might have any ritual, legal, or moral claims upon his attention, or he on theirs.[68]

From Beijing's perspective, then, the Mudan incident was "local" and "peripheral" because its Paiwanese perpetrators, and the Hakka Chinese who rescued the survivors, lived below and beyond the Qing's centralized administrative grid. One solution to the problem, attempted in the later 1870s and 1880s under the leadership of Shen Baozhen and Liu Mingchuan, was to put military pressure on Taiwanese border tribes in order to increase the size of the Qing tax base to pay for more expeditions to pacify and secure the interior.[69]

Such punitive expeditions required rudimentary military intelligence or the help of local allies, neither of which was beyond the reach of the Qing. As William T. Rowe put it, "when it chose to, the [Qing] state could certainly marshal the resources to despotically terrorize its subjects." In the new order, however, such power was insufficient. Rowe continues: "on a day-to-day basis [the Qing] left many of the functions we might think of as governmental to private individuals and groups."[70] It was these private individuals and groups who were considered threats to a system that sought to make the world safe for the circulation of higher volumes and velocities of commerce.

DISCIPLINE, GOVERNMENTALITY, AND BIOPOLITICS

In the 1874 negotiations with the Zongli Yamen over the resolution of the Mudan incident, Ōkubo Toshimichi claimed that the Qing were not sovereign in Langqiao because the court, the entity that answered to national leaderships in London, Tokyo, and Washington, lacked the capacity to regulate the daily affairs of Langqiaoans.[71] In Lenin's parlance, the Langqiao Peninsula was still among the ownerless territories of the world. For Ōkubo, who was being advised by French legal scholars and an American consul, establishing "ownership" or sovereignty over a governed territory meant educating and "improving" natives to prevent disruptive behavior, or punishing them for transgressions against merchants and outsiders in a timely manner. This type of sovereignty involved a level of territorial integration between borderland and capital unthinkable for the expansive, multiethnic, and legalistically plural Qing dynasty. As Meiji leaders themselves were to learn in the 1870s and 1880s, territorial integration on this scale, at this level of intensity, required new software and hardware for governance.

As Ōkubo was chastising Qing officialdom for its lassitude regarding southern Taiwan, the young Tokyo government that ruled in the name of Meiji was executing its own ideological offensives, administrative overhauls, and financial stratagems to avoid a repeat of the Tokugawa regime collapse (which was attributable to weak horizontal integration). This project entailed obvious centralizing measures such as replacing feudatory leaders with centrally appointed governors, raising a conscript army, funding and populating a public-school system, fielding a police force, and establishing a court system. These measures required tax increases, but getting citizens to pay such taxes, voluntarily and without recourse to revenue-squandering and economy-stultifying structures of oppression, presupposed the prior existence of these selfsame institutions.

To bootstrap itself out of this dilemma required nothing less than moving Japan from a society of *punishment* to one of *discipline*. This quantum leap entailed the instantiation of a *governmental* approach to statecraft. Here, I am borrowing from geographer Matthew Hannah's adaptation of Foucault's terminology to analyze the problem of state building in nineteenth-century North America. His model is apt because, as Yao Jen-to has observed, the government-general seems to have taken a page out of Hannah's playbook to govern Taiwan.

According to Foucault, the French dynastic state, for all its unchecked and terrifying power, was relatively weak. Beyond the palace precincts, he writes, a plethora of religious, clan-based, guild, and local leaders maintained the old regime's social order with recourse to bribery, corruption, and benign neglect. The problem with these "innumerable authorities," from the view of the insurgent bourgeoisie, was that they "cancelled each other out *and were incapable of covering the social body in its entirety.*"[72]

It was the Chinese and Japanese social body's uncovered areas and multiple sources of authority that vexed the Euro-Americans who asserted a "natural right" to protect commercial intercourse throughout the world in the mid-nineteenth century. For Foucault, as was the case for treaty-port powers vis-à-vis the Qing and the Tokugawa, the unpredictability of royal power from above was of a piece with its weaknesses when directed outward. Under multicentered legal pluralism, to borrow Benton's terminology, "each of the different social strata had its margin of tolerated illegality: the non-application of the rule, the non-observance of the innumerable edicts or ordinances, were a condition of the political and economic functioning of society."[73] Here Foucault speaks of poaching, smuggling, pilfering, unregulated use of the commons, and other petty offences that did not concern the crown directly. In Qing-era Taiwan, as we shall see, ransoming, or paying "aborigine rent" to borderland toll-states, or redeeming severed heads from sham battles for bounties, were functional equivalents of these tolerated illegalities.

The political economy of high-velocity capitalism, in Foucault's exposition, demanded a new approach to law and sovereignty. The late eighteenth century's increase in "commercial and industrial ownership [and] the development of ports," along with "the appearance of great warehouses . . . [and] the organization of huge workshops,"[74] found the sporadic and uneven consistency of royal authority insufficient for the protection of widely dispersed, ubiquitous, and moveable property. Privately held and deployed assets were now too numerous and valuable to be rendered secure, everywhere and always, by the king's punitive brand of justice. For the treaty-port powers, the same principle held: how could the emperor's or shogun's occasional displays of sovereign/punitive power, or the compromised and negotiable justice of magistrates, village headmen, and yamen runners, be entrusted with the volumes of commerce that would pass through multinational customs houses?

For Foucault, the bourgeoisie's solution was to instantiate "a *systematic*, armed intolerance of illegality," which he termed "public power."[75] Public power is the aggregate effect of *discipline*, or what may be termed panopticism. This modality regulates the conduct of millions across vast distances because it conditions individuals as objects and authors of a dispersed, circulating form of behavior-modifying power as teachers and students, doctors and patients, jailers and jailed, parents and children, and so on. According to Foucault, again recapitulating the demands of treaty-port consuls in East Asia, it

> . . . became necessary to get rid of the old economy of the power to punish, based on the principles of the confused and inadequate multiplicity of authorities, . . . punishments that were spectacular in their manifestations and haphazard in their application. *It became necessary to define a strategy and techniques of punishment in which an economy of continuity and permanence would replace that of expenditure and excess. In short, penal reform was born at the point of junction between the struggle against the super-power of the sovereign and that against the infra-power of acquired and tolerated illegalities.*[76]

Here, the "struggle . . . against the infra-power of acquired and tolerated illegalities" called forth a public power that would educate, diagnose, cure, and police populations to pay taxes, work hard, serve in the military, and respect private property *willingly* if not *energetically*. As Caroline Ts'ai puts it, "disciplinary power works through the construction of routine. This power is 'constitutive.' As such, the Foucauldian approach . . . locates power in the 'micro-physics' of social life."[77] Properly established, public power circulates continuously, everywhere and always. Its absence, as Ōkubo argued in his diatribes against the Zongli Yamen in 1874, signals a state's incompatibility with modern political economy made manifest in the international system. For Foucault, *discipline* (government through reeducation and behavior modification), rather than *punishment* (the use of terror, edict, and brute force to obtain compliance), was a sine qua non for nation-states with capitalist economies.

Following Foucault, Hannah demonstrates how societies cross the watershed from punishment to discipline through a burst of state-directed energy, in the form of censuses, land registration, and bureaucratic staffing. These projects lay foundations for rule by *governmentality*. Discipline and governmentality are overlapping concepts. As Hannah puts it, discipline constitutes individuals as objects and authors of knowledge and power, but it does so with a specific goal in mind—the creation of docile workers and obedient citizens. Takashi Fujitani's *Splendid Monarchy* provides a relevant example of discipline making in operation.

To unify a social body riven by horizontal and vertical cleavages, the Meiji oligarchs instantiated discipline by cultivating identification with the emperor, imperial history, and a new national culture. The enterprise aimed to flatten status distinctions and weld fissured territorial divisions.[78] First, the emperor was made visible across the realm by a series of lavish processions and tours, providing a common point of reference for a people only vaguely, if at all, acquainted with the image, person, or backstory of the state's new symbolic, unifying center. However, these costly processions were insufficient. Their evanescence, novelty, and circumscribed routes could not in and of themselves cover an entire social body to produce "a modern citizenry with an interiorized sense of themselves as objects of an unremitting surveillance."[79] But it was a start.

Statues of mythical and actual national heroes were installed across the landscape, while state-authored rituals and liturgies were publicized and enforced. Importantly, the imperial institution—including the imposing architecture of a national capital—was relocated to Tokyo as a node of panoptical power. Now the emperor would stay put, and the people would move. Meiji, instead of being the object of the public's gaze, was now the author of an omnipresent discipline-making gaze. Meiji's mass-produced portraits were made objects of daily rituals in public schools, allowing him to be seen looking down on his subjects, daily, to the far edges of Japanese sovereignty. The emperor's paramountcy was augmented by mass military spectacles that drew tens of thousands near the imperial palace, also presided over by the all-seeing emperor as the master of ceremonies.[80]

To simplify, the Meiji oligarchs used the imperial person and associated pageantry to both represent a body politic to itself and interiorize loyalty and obedience to a symbolic center. This massive project consumed not only the costs of mobile pageantry but also expenses associated with Tokyo's urban renewal and the building of a conscript army. In microcosm, Emperor Sunjong and his retinue traversed the Korean Peninsula in 1909 on a similar errand, to forge identification with a subordinate national monarch. However, Sunjong reigned at the pleasure of a Japanese resident-general named Itō Hirobumi. Consequently, Sunjong's procession was met by protests and ended up working against the rump Yi dynasty.[81] Its utter failure to replicate the effects of the earlier Meiji processions suggests that display and symbolism alone were insufficient in and of themselves to foment a sense of nation among a nascent citizenry. Moreover, Japan's 1909 exercise in imperial pageantry reveals that measures effective in the home country might not be exportable to the colonies.

While there would be no imperial processions in Taiwan,[82] other more portable methods of bootstrapping social formations into the era of discipline were imported from Japan. The Meiji land tax reform (LTR) was implemented from July 1873 until the end of 1876, at about the same time that the imperial processions were setting out from Kyoto and Tokyo. Like the grand imperial tours, the LTR involved meticulous planning by Japan's top officials. At a cost of about forty million yen,[83] the central government assessed "85.44 million parcels of rice paddies and all other types of land, and issu[ed] 109.33 million certificates of land ownership" to Japanese citizens.[84]

The purpose of the LTR was to simplify, standardize, and make more equitable (across prefectures) the patchwork system of Tokugawa land tenure and taxation. Under the old system, different domains were taxed at various rates, and taxes were paid in kind, based on a percentage of annual yield. For central planners *whose annual budgets required forecasts of income and expenses,* the unpredictability of the old system presented headaches. In addition, the differential tax rates caused discontent. Therefore, the two-and-half-year project sought to convince citizens that the new government was impartial. But more importantly for our purposes, the reformed system levied taxes based on assessed land value to make government receipts more predictable, to commoditize land (by issuing certificates), and to yoke peasants to market discipline by demanding cash payments.

In the short run, central-government receipts remained constant, and per capita tax rates declined in most years. Over the longer haul, Kōzō Yamamura argues, the reform strengthened the government while it enriched the populace, because efficiencies arising from a land market drove up aggregate productivity.[85] Less sanguine accounts do not deny the efficiency of the new system for administrators or its ability to generate national wealth. However, because tax rates were fixed and redeemable only in cash, bad harvests, isolation from market centers, or low prices often sent smallholders without reserves into tenancy.[86]

The LTR in Japan and the one implemented later in Taiwan exhibit a *governmental* approach to statecraft, rather than a *disciplinary* modality. Governmentality, rather than targeting individuals as objects of regulation, per se, targets the national political economy. As Hannah puts it, "Governmentality, like discipline, constructs (not merely "manipulates") its objects, but unlike discipline, it constructs them as objects that should not be unduly manipulated. . . . As such, governmentality, too, is fundamentally structured around cycles of social control linking observation, normalizing judgment and regulation. But unlike its genealogical predecessors, governmentality . . . helps the governing authorities decide whether there are limits to its ability to enforce or achieve the norm . . . In short, governmentality at a national scale involves more respect for the integrity and autonomous dynamics of the social body."[87]

Seen in this light, the 1873–76 LTR was the quintessential governmental project. A nationwide cadastral survey of farmholdings and the validation of holdings with land certificates were undertaken to lay the foundations for a national political economy that could be managed, in some sense, by accountants and actuaries in Tokyo. Government yields were increased not by the principle of "squeezing the peasant like a sesame seed to get additional oil" but rather by monetizing agriculture, establishing a fixed tax rate, and creating the conditions for a national land market, thereby letting "the invisible hand" (and the enforcement of eviction notices) raise overall yields.[88]

The Meiji state's LTR was repeated a quarter century later in Taiwan. Minister of Civil Affairs Gotō Shinpei (1898–1906) oversaw Taiwan's first national land survey and imperial Japan's first population census. As with the home island, the land registration, assessment, and deeding project was a gargantuan enterprise. The cadastral survey itself produced 37,869 maps of villages. The project cost over 5,225,000 yen. Like its 1873 Japanese predecessor, Gotō's LTR in Taiwan simplified and streamlined an early-modern system of land tenure and taxation. The old Qing system, with its multiple layers of usufruct and subsoil rights and various forms of payment, not only hid land from the tax collector but was difficult to administer from Taipei.[89]

The related population census, another measure implemented to regularize government receipts, took three years to prepare. Enumeration day was October 1, 1905. It required "842 supervisory staff, 1,339 assistants, and 5,224 census takers."[90] In terms of scale, level of detail, and cost, these two enterprises not only set Taiwan apart from less capital-intensive modern colonies—they also preceded the first national home-island census by fifteen years. From Yao Jen-to's perspective, the TGG's exorbitant spending and attention to detail distinguished the Taiwan Government-General from the British government in India, which staffed its census projects more lightly. Yao concludes that the Taiwan Government-General did not take its military dominance as an invitation to remain ignorant about subject populations.

Rather, Japan entered the imperial arena in the 1890s, after statistics had finally become a basis for statecraft in Europe. Therefore, the advantages of followership allowed Gotō to put the Taiwan Government-General on a scientific footing from its inception. In Yao's account, however, the censuses and LTR were punitive, and not *governmental* in the sense Hannah uses the term. Yao rightly points out that accurate statistical data render an alien population visible, knowable, and to some extent manageable for outsiders by representing it in "combinable, mobile and stable" units (borrowing from Bruno Latour).[91] On the other hand, Yao asserts that these expensive and scientific instruments were effective because they aided the government in hunting down rebels.[92] He also equates "capitalism" with organized theft by noting that land registration made Taiwan's real estate available for confiscation by Japanese corporations after the hidden acreage was exposed in the cadastres.[93] In these two instances, systematic and comprehensive knowledge was weaponized for naked exploitation.

In contrast, Ka Chih-ming has analyzed this same land reform program as a *governmental* undertaking. For Ka, the purpose of Gotō's land reform was only in part to increase the government's tax yield by registering more land. It also served to cement a TGG class alliance with Taiwan's smallholders against absentee landlords who collected "small rents" and then forwarded "big rents" to the capital (after skimming). According to Ka—and this echoes the circumspection with which U.S. and Japanese land surveys proceeded in noncolonized spaces— cultivators cooperated with the cadastres in exchange for fee-simple titles to their land. Moreover, the Taiwan Government-General could reallocate these titles thanks to a large buy-off from absentee landlords—paid for by funds raised on the bond market in Japan.

From a fiscal perspective, Gotō's gambit worked. From 1905 onward, Taiwan no longer required subsidies from Tokyo and became exceptional in the annals of Japanese colonialism by becoming a boon, rather than a drain, on Japan's national economy.[94] Ka writes, "With order restored and revenues ensured through deficit financing, the administration implemented a number of measures to increase production and expand the market: a thorough land cadastral not only revealed tax evasion but greatly facilitated the subsequent reform that created a modern private land ownership system. The land survey and reform guaranteed private property rights, facilitated the effective use of land, and provided incentives to increase production for the market."[95]

Anticipating Ka's analysis by many decades, the 1906 *Japan Yearbook* exclaimed that the "success of [Japanese] colonial policy in Formosa is conclusively demonstrated in the Revenue Column. . . . The item of 'Subsidies from Central Government' that was steadily diminishing finally disappeared . . ."[96] W. G. Beasley, also noting the parallel between Japan's 1870s and 1880s reforms and Gotō's early twentieth-century expenditures in Taiwan, concluded that the bundle of projects reviewed above had secured "financial stability which . . . made it possible to meet budget deficits by floating bonds, placed with a newly formed Bank of Taiwan."[97]

This quantitative yardstick for success—achieving black-ink balances on regularly scheduled budgets—represents the type of *governmental* rationality well articulated by Max Weber in his landmark study *The Protestant Ethic and the Spirit of Capitalism*. Weber's linked concepts of quantification and continuous renewal resonate strongly with contemporary governmental projects in colonial Taiwan. Weber writes:

> . . . capitalism is identical with the pursuit of profit, and forever *renewed* profit, by means of continuous, rational, capitalistic enterprise. For it must be so: in a wholly capitalistic order of society, an individual capitalistic enterprise which did not take advantage of its opportunities for profit-making would be doomed to extinction.
>
> . . . The important fact is always that a *calculation of capital in terms of money* is made, whether by modern book-keeping methods or in any other way. . . . *Everything is done in terms of balances*: at the beginning of the enterprise an initial balance, before every individual decision a calculation to ascertain its probable profitableness, and at the end of a final balance to ascertain how much profit has been made.[98]

This passage, on the one hand, reflects the "eat or be eaten" worldview of a number of Meiji intellectuals and statesmen in the 1890s. For example, influential author, public intellectual, and publisher Tokutomi Sōhō, who came to see Japanese imperialism as a means of national survival at century's turn,[99] would have assented to substituting "nation" for "enterprise" in Weber's quotation: nations that do not compete successfully *are doomed to extinction*.

Weber's formulation also encapsulates a core principle of governmentality in Taiwan under Japanese rule. Beginning with the LTR and the census, the Taiwan Government-General quantified human, environmental, and built assets in the colony, and more importantly, it set and recalibrated policy based on income and expenditure *projections*. As Hannah points out, a governmental state relies upon statistical record keeping and computation to manage its heterogeneous resources and budget for multiyear projects. In the competitive imperial setting, failure to balance the colonial budget portended scrutiny from the Diet, which held the purse strings of the military and supplementary budgets for the Taiwan Government-General. Therefore, Weber's foregrounding of capitalism's *continuously renewed* commitment to positive balances captures the spirit of capitalism as an ethos but also isolates a distinctive feature of statecraft in the postdynastic era. In this dispensation, national expressions of public power underwrote territorially aggrandizing war machines. National militaries, as income-starved institutional behemoths, not only competed against each other but also competed with domestic spending projects that sustained the public power presupposed by militarized states.

Weber's contemporary Takekoshi Yosaburō issued a book-length encomium to Gotō Shinpei and Japanese rule in Taiwan the same year that *The Protestant Ethic* first appeared. Takekoshi articulated the governmental ethos in his stout defense of the embattled government-general in Taiwan. In 1904 he wrote, "If the trade [between Taiwan and Japan] continues to grow as it has done during the last six of seven years, Japan will by about the year 1910 have received back an equivalent of all the subsidies [to the Taiwan Government-General], together with the interest upon them. From that time *Japan will have reached the goal of colonial enterprise,* and be able to look to her colony for substantial support."[100]

Based on his own projections, the economic historian Takekoshi inserted a table that projected TGG annual income, expenditures, public loans (principal plus interest), and a positive overall balance for the years 1903 through 1922. Unsurprisingly, each year cost more than the previous one.[101]

In another example of Weberian rationality at work in colonial Taiwan, TGG councilor Mochiji Rokusaburō issued his famous "opinion paper on the Aborigine problem" *(Bansei mondai ni kansuru ikensho)* in December 1902. With an eye to the bottom line, Mochiji declared that the "savage-territory problem" *(banjin banchi mondai)* was, strictly speaking, a land management problem. As peoples who did not submit to the Qing, the "savages" *(banjin/seibanjin/genjin)* were not covered in the articles of the Treaty of Shimonoseki that formally ceded Taiwan to Japan. Moreover, Taiwan's *seiban* (savage) population lacked recognizable organs of government and therefore stood outside the rules of civilized warfare and diplomacy. As Mochiji put it, "sociologically speaking, they are indeed human beings *(jinrui),* but looked at from the viewpoint of international law, they resemble animals" *(dōbutsu no gotoki mono).*

Mochiji reasoned that, insofar as "savage territory" could be made to pay for the expenses of punitive expeditions and policing, they would be launched. But if expeditions were sent simply for the purpose of revenge or a display of dominance, Mochiji argued that they should not be undertaken.[102] Accordingly, the military expeditions targeted the camphor-rich north and left the south mostly untouched. Mochiji here displayed a clear aversion to *punishment* (in Foucault's sense) and showed himself ever the rational bureaucrat.

Takekoshi added urgency to Mochiji's plan a year later with the plea that "time was running out" for a solution to the "problem of the savages." He wrote that the militarization of Japanese-Atayal relations "does not mean that we have no sympathy at all for the savages. It simply means that we have to think more about *our* 45,000,000 sons and daughters than about the 104,000 savages."[103] Takekoshi thereby embraced home-island Japanese as "sons and daughters" while banishing indigenes from the national family.

Thereafter, the Taiwan Government-General and the Tokyo government dribbled out funds to cobble together remnant Qing private armies and expand the police force in order to secure lucrative areas of camphor production. It took the political clout of fourth governor-general Sakuma Samata (1906–15), a hero of the 1874 invasion of Taiwan, to pry the lid off the imperial treasury. Drawing upon connections to Prime Minister Katsura Tarō and father of the conscript army Yamagata Aritomo, and with the Meiji emperor's blessing, Sakuma secured a whopping fifteen million yen, in 1909, for a five-year "big bang" spending program to solve the "aborigine question" once and for all.

While the scale, ambition, and cost of Sakuma's "five-year plan to control the aborigines" was commensurate with the 1873–76 LTR in Japan and the 1898–1905 Gotō spending package in Taiwan, its rationale was not quite the same. In the vein of these early programs, the idea was to create conditions for future wealth accumulation with a large initial investment. But in this case, the human beings in the targeted area were not considered sources of labor power or entrepreneurial skill but were seen instead as obstacles (unless they could be mobilized to subdue other indigenes). There was no attempt here to instantiate the virtuous circle of governmentality. Therefore, Sakuma's five-year plan, and the TGG policies regarding indigenes more generally, adopted a punitive and *biopolitically* inflected rationality of statecraft, to the exclusion of *disciplinary* concerns.

This was the crux of the matter: typically, in a nation-building context, discipline precedes or coincides with governmentality. However, in a colonial situation, wherein the "natives" (in Bayly's sense of the term) are not reckoned as a potential source of labor but rather as impediments to resource extraction, discipline is—by the yardstick of governmental calculations—wasteful. Foucault's notion of "biopolitics"[104] is operative here.

Sabine Frühstück's account of the "modern health regime" in Meiji Japan illustrates the positivities of biopower. Her study analyzes state initiatives to "force a population to be healthy." Several biopolitical projects, involving vital statistics, the regulation of sex, and government attention to nutrition, exercise, and inoculation, improved Japan's racial stock so it could stand up to the West and compete in the international arena.[105] This ensemble of state interventions, many coterminous with the LTR of 1873–76, was aimed at building a healthy conscript army and industrial labor force.

However, like the LTR, the regime of hygiene aimed to improve national power, not individual health and wealth. As many farmers were dispossessed by land reform, the health of state-regulated military prostitutes was sacrificed for the general health of the body politic. Turned outward or against internal Others, then, a biopolitical regime marks out subpopulations as expendable in the name of the greater good. Fujitani and Achille Mbembe follow Foucault by insisting that arrogating the power to sustain life entails the assertion of a right to extinguish it. This duality has been referred to as "necropolitics."[106]

Patrick Wolfe's analysis of the race politics in settler societies emphasizes this point. In North America, he writes, constituting the black race as a population and then nurturing its demographic resilience (partly through the legal fiction of the "one-drop rule") had a biopolitical logic: labor-pool management. On the other hand, the connected project of Indian removal (through both physical removal and the legal fiction that "mixed blood" Indians were, in fact, not indigenes) had a different economic logic: the land inhabited by indigenes was worth more, calculated in terms of cash value, if Indians could be removed.[107]

Importantly, in this model, racism creates races—not the other way around. Extenuating circumstances may even impel biopolitical regimes to reverse race-based policies in the name of self-preservation. In Takashi Fujitani's analysis of ethnic management during the Pacific War, the demands of mobilization pushed the Japanese and American regimes of the 1940s to transition from vulgarly to politely racist outlooks in the name of national security. As Japanese-Americans in the United States and Koreans in the Japanese Empire were identified as sources of labor and fighting power, each regime sought to inculcate that hallmark of discipline, the spirit of voluntarism, among formerly excluded populations. The shift to polite racism and the new emphasis on disciplinary measures such as compulsory assimilation programs aimed at the "conduct of conduct" announced a redefinition of marginalized communities in terms of cultural capacities or peculiarities, rather than as biologically defined Mendelian populations.[108]

Leo Ching has made a related argument regarding Taiwan's indigenes in the 1930s and 1940s. In Ching's analysis, a combination of alarm over the Wushe Rebellion and wartime mobilization requirements pushed the Taiwan Government-General to imagine the former "savages" *(seibanjin)* as the Formosan Aborigines *(Takasagozoku)*. This new politely racist rhetoric did not entail equal treatment or the end of exploitation, but it portended a shift in administrative rationality. Henceforth, the *Takasagozoku* would not be formally excluded with the vulgarly racist epithet *banjin*. They would instead be targets of disciplinary ministrations aimed at a particular kind of subject formation, one defined by a willingness to die for the emperor.[109] Huang Chih-huei's study of the *Takasagozoku* volunteers who claimed to have exhibited even more "Japanese spirit" than their home-island officers in the Philippines campaigns of 1943 and 1944 stands as a testament to the efficacy of "imperial subjectification" among some indigenes in Taiwan.[110]

This book argues that "imperial subjectification" among indigenes can also be understood as an indigenization movement. While Ching's chronology and analysis are persuasive as a two-stage model to chart the mechanisms and meanings of the shift from vulgar to polite racism in TGG policy, its emphasis on the ideational aspects of citizenship to the exclusion of its legal-economic bases leaves room for some debate.

The Taiwan Government-General's assimilation campaigns were preceded by the multistage trading-post and guardline projects. During the Kodama and Sakuma eras (1898–1915), northern tribes were the expendables in the government-general's biopolitical calculus. These punitive and often bloody campaigns encircled erstwhile borderland "natives" (in Bayly's sense) with administered territories, reconfiguring their homelands as an ethnic enclave.[111] While they were regarded as "savage," and governed largely through the negative techniques of sovereign power, as objects of *biopolitical* management they were sequestered, "censused, mapped, and museumed."[112]

As "specially administered" subjects, the Taiwan Government-General positioned indigenes as exterior to the more intensively disciplined and governmentalized territories governed by *baojia* (mutual-surveillance and tithing organizations) in "regularly administered" Taiwan.[113] From 1898 through 1902, the government-general revived the old Qing-period system of mutual responsibility and tithing as an efficient mechanism for registering, policing, and mobilizing a Han labor pool. By 1920, the surface of "normally administered Taiwan" was covered with *baojia* districts.[114] These had all been subject to land markets and taxation and were highly commoditized as integral parts of the imperial political economy. However, negatively defined indigenous territory, by 1920, was already "public land" and excluded from the *baojia* system. By the time the imperial subjectification campaigns of the 1930s were launched, access to the indigenous territory by outsiders had been suppressed by a permit system for three decades.

Against this backdrop, the imperial subjectification policies of the 1930s were implemented through a new generation of indigenous youth corps *(seinendan)*. These corps leaders had attained adulthood under Japanese rule in an ethnic enclave. As the government-general mobilized these corps through drill, parade, song, schools, panindigenous gatherings, and finally military recruitment, it solidified the standing of the indigenous territory as a separate entity, or what I have termed a "second-order geobody." Therefore, the "imperial subjectification" policies, even though they were conducted in the Japanese language, could only further isolate the indigenous territory from the social, political, and economic currents in Han Taiwan that were preparing the ground for postcolonial nationality.

During *kōminka* (imperial subjectification), indigenes became proficient in spoken Japanese. They hoisted Hinomaru (Japanese) flags and belted out imperial anthems with apparent gusto. Moreover, some abandoned "evil customs" such as in-home burials and face tattoos. Nonetheless, the notion that they were "becoming Japanese" overlooks an important aspect of modern citizenship: its material basis.

Unlike their neighbors, the specially administered peoples of Taiwan had never been citizens or subjects of agro-bureaucratic empires-cum-dynastic states. As "natives" practiced in the art of not being governed, most of Taiwan's Austronesians were not accustomed to the routines of unremitting, coordinated, and surplus-generating agricultural and manufacturing toil that characterized the lot of their lowlander neighbors under Tokugawa, Qing, and Joseon rule. Looking backward, it would seem that the success of disciplinary projects such as imperial panopticism, the Taiwan Government-General's graft of a Japanese police apparatus upon a Han Taiwanese *baojia* system, or the cultivation of national Korean and

Taiwanese bourgeoisies were all premised on *longue durée* processes begun before the great age of transformation.

Colonial rule in Han-dominated Taiwan took on a coloration of nation building in Japan, under a regime of governmentality/discipline,[115] whereas the indigenous territory of Taiwan was ruled under a hybrid regime of punishment and biopolitics, at least until the 1930s. However, these regimes did not operate independently but were built together, one upon the back of the other. Initially, Japanese officials thought that highlanders could be mobilized on Japan's side against lowlanders in the colonial state's war against armed Han resistance. Looking back at these early years, commentators considered 1895–98 to have been a "honeymoon period" of Japanese-Indigenous relations. During this interval, brokers like Kondō the Barbarian flourished as trading-post operators, land speculators, and contract employees of the state. But the debt incurred by the Taiwan Government-General to set off the "big bang" of governmentality in the plains put pressure on the inland sea of Taiwan's camphor forests.

As Japanese officials were well aware, frontier violence, which began to spike in 1898, could have been reduced by simply backing the rights of indigenes vis-à-vis Japanese lumber companies and their employees. Indeed, such a policy had much to recommend itself while Japan sought allies in its war against Han guerillas. In fact, the biggest camphor merchants in Xinzhu Prefecture in the late Qing- and early Meiji-period camphor industry were Saisiyat men, most notably Ri Aguai. Some indigenes were more than willing to sell camphor—the resource so ardently coveted by Japan's state builders and merchants—to outsiders for monetary gain.[116] But the state could not exercise regulatory functions to control the volume or quality of camphor under "middle ground" or "contact zone" conditions. State planners wanted to standardize quality, regulate output, and project estimated profits from its monopoly bureau for annual budgetary purposes.[117] However, unlike in the plains, where smallholders and some merchants, as well as scholars, could be co-opted to provide the means for igniting the motor of disciplinary rule, the Japanese found few property holders to make a parallel class alliance in the highlands. With this crucial element missing, the Japanese state pressed forward in its efforts to make the Aborigine Territory into a state space with a series of punitive expeditions and economic embargoes.

Sediq, Atayal, and Truku settlements surrendered their arms en masse and were at times relocated to valleys within reach of the police apparatus. After establishing this beachhead, the Japanese state embarked on a series of cartographic and infrastructural projects to make the indigenous territory legible to the state. But as Matsuoka Tadasu has demonstrated,[118] the post-1915 Japanese state balked, in a sense, by not following up its military victories with policies of reterritorialization that would have rendered the non-Han spaces of upland Taiwan indistinct from the rest of the island colony. Legible, yes, but subject to modern discipline—not quite.

To restate the main argument: national and indigenous political formations are homologous, historically linked, and symbiotic. Modern state building in the age of high-velocity capitalism entailed heavy governmental outlays to create commensuritized sociopolitical formations for sustaining the timely circulation of information, goods, and people, all under the pressure of international competition. In the emergent international system, at least ideally, one national geobody's sovereignty ended where another began. The indigenous geobody was distinctive. As an administered territory defined by its exteriority to the full array of citizen-making projects associated with governmental and disciplinary tactics, the indigenous geobody was a "second-order geobody." It was discrete and bounded, and it took on the formal properties of a geobody. Instead of achieving national sovereignty, however, it remains a subunit of a first-order geobody, the arena of discipline- and citizen-making projects in the age of global transformation.

In Taiwan under Japanese rule, the virtuous circle of governmentality that is presupposed by legal centralism reached its geographic limit at the boundary of the Aborigine Territory. Therefore, Taiwan's second-order geobody can be considered the ethnogeographic expression of the Japanese regime's aspirations to master a territory just beyond its grasp. A first-order geobody describes a spatially configured unit of administration within which a mixture of Foucauldian discipline and Gramscian hegemony produces more or less self-actuating populations who surrender revenues to central authorities over and above the cost of funding myriad projects in governmentality. Such policies, programs, and installations underwrite the accumulation of capital, and its diversion to state coffers, at rates sufficient to balance accounts as calculated in annual government reports. Second-order geobodies are found at the extremities of empire, where various combinations of local resistance, rugged terrain, sparse population, and other factors rule out the creation of revenue-neutral regimes of governmentality. Although not brought within the fold of governmentality, the second-order geobodies were nonetheless constituted as objects of accounting, surveillance, and biopolitical ministration because the modern international system—unlike the interdynastic order it displaced—did not allow for ungoverned territories to exist "beyond the pale."

INDIGENOUS MODERNITY

In its 1905 census, the Taiwan Government-General attributed Malayan and Mongolian racial characteristics to populations that also fell respectively under "special" (savage) and "regular" (civilized) administration[119] (see figure 3).

This innovation confirms Charles Hirschman's hypothesis that modern racial epistemology had a hand in hardening the once porous occupationally and confessionally defined sociopolitical boundaries that characterized the early-modern world. As was the case in colonial Malaysia, the racializing process in colonized Taiwan employed circular logic. In each colony, so-called Malays (indigenes) were

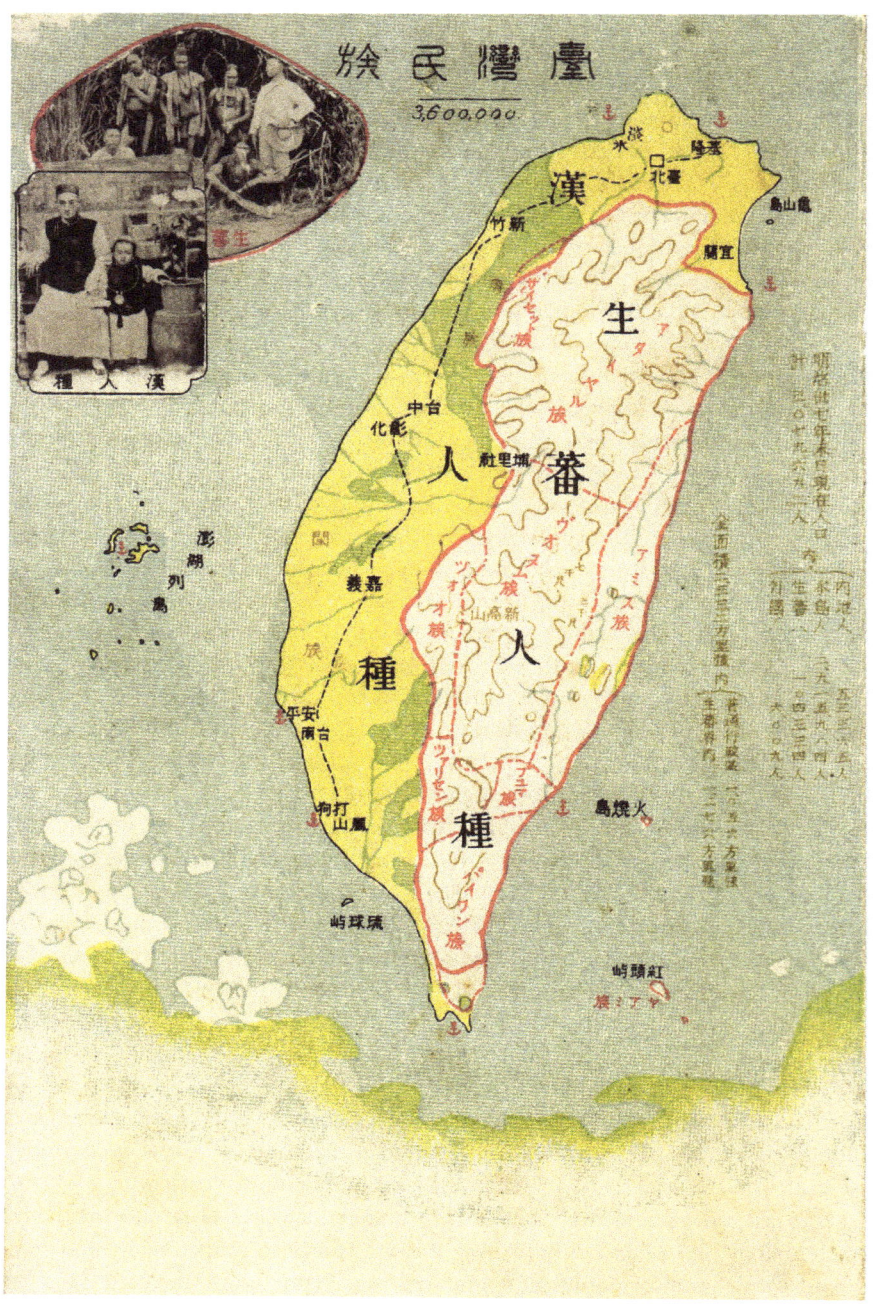

FIGURE 3. This ca. 1904 postcard divides Taiwan into two races, territorially defined as the "Han race" and the "savage race." Courtesy of the Rupnow Collection.

distinguished by their putative incapacity to participate in a modern, capitalist economic system, with all of its risks and benefits. Thus, Malays were placed under "special administration" and deprived of any chance to participate in a modern, capitalist economic system.[120] TGG officials asked: Did villagers have written deeds to their lands? Did they grow irrigated (surplus) rice? Could they honor contracts? If the answer was "no," then they were Malays.

On the one hand, Japanese men on the spot defined race by recourse to stereotypes and institutions disconnected from the craniometry and anthropometry that stood at the foundations of scientific racism. Nonetheless, at the back of the Malay label was a large corpus of Japanese race science. This bundle of scientistic ethnic maps, tables, photographs, and assessments of character mostly went ignored by policy makers in the early decades of Japanese rule. Yet it reemerged in the 1920s as the substrate for further elaboration, and it has been energetically revived in post–martial law Taiwan since the 1990s.

The classificatory work of three men in particular has drawn sustained attention from scholars of Japanese rule in Taiwan and of the history of anthropology in Japan's empire. They will play important roles in this study, as well. These three pioneering government ethnologists—Torii Ryūzō (1870–1953), Inō Kanori (1867–1925), and Mori Ushinosuke (1877–1926)—completed their most celebrated work during the first two decades of colonial rule, between 1895 and 1915. Methodologically, they arrayed various word lists, artifacts of material life, and elements of intangible culture into the tabular form that characterized fin-de-siècle anthropology's comparative method. Based on this data, they sorted Taiwan's diverse upland settlements into a nine-tribe schema. These tribes were represented as commensurate units juxtaposed like nation-states on a Mercator-projection map.

Reflecting their engagement with transnational currents in the young science of ethnology, these men were dissenters from the crudest forms of polygenetist racism that informed evolutionary anthropology. Rather, like Franz Boas and kindred spirits in England and Germany, these men advocated the worth and importance of nonliterate, small-scale societies as objects of study and subjects of history. To be sure, like Boas himself, they were self-assured in their superiority as members of industrial, urbanized societies. They neither aimed for nor achieved the Malinowskian ideal of empathy or access to the interior lives of members of the societies who were the objects of their taxonomic labors. As survey ethnologists, however, they were much more concerned about specificity, particularity, and the well-being of the peoples they studied than armchair ethnologists who did not concern themselves with face-to-face encounters. Reflecting their complicated relationship to the politics of conquest and ethnogenesis, their work was too fine-grained in some regards, and too abstract in others, to appear immediately useful to administrators in the early decades of colonial rule.[121]

However, on the heels of Governor-General Sakuma's campaign against the northern tribes, which ended in 1915, several trends conspired to put the latently pluralist conception of Taiwan devised by Torii, Inō, and Mori on a permanent footing, one that lasts to this day.[122] First, reflecting the post–World War I ethos of cultural appraisal (which was eclipsing racist denigration) that accompanied the Wilsonian moment, the new apostles of folklore and ethnic authenticity portrayed themselves as the stewards of territory inhabited by the non-Han Malayans.[123] This operation figuratively swept the landscape of Chinese claims to prior occupation. Moreover, an ethnic tourism trade emerged in Taiwan's highlands in the 1920s.[124] Its myriad graphic and material products were organized around the ethnic-pluralist model and institutionalized a view of indigenous Taiwan that rendered it a culture garden (see chapter 4).

To put these developments into global context, we recall that Bayly's narrative of displacement, depopulation, and dispossession ends in 1914 on a cautious note: he did not write off the small-scale societies that Eric Wolf once termed the "peoples without history." Bayly noted that indigenous resilience and creativity, the new human science of anthropology, a market for primitivist art in the metropole, and a growing revulsion to settler avarice in the mother countries had prevented the natives from becoming extinct. Turned on their heads, the forces Bayly regards as brakes on the extermination of natives can be reconceptualized as a seedbed for the creation of *indigenism.*

Anthropologist Ronald Niezen defines indigenism as the movement of First Nations and indigenous peoples to secure political rights, or even national self-determination, based on claims to primordial and prior ties to particular territories. Niezen has observed that indigenism has flourished with the *strengthening* of international society after World War II. He argues that the First Nations or indigenous peoples of the world, who number some "three hundred million people from four thousand distinct societies,"[125] are now a self-conscious, transnational force, whose current methods of rights articulation, preservation, and reclamation would have been scarcely imaginable in the prewar era. One of this book's tasks is to reconcile the corrosive effects of nation building and capitalism on the natives during the global transformation that left the world with "four to eight million" people existing on the margins of expanding states circa 1900 and the rise of indigenous peoples as an integral component of international society in the current dispensation.

In this case study of Taiwan under Japanese colonial rule, the period that separates Bayly's narrative of decline and Niezen's assertion of interstate system / First Nations symbiosis—1915 to 1945—brackets the years when central administrators in Taipei institutionalized and culturally invested the second-order geobodies that comprise Taiwan's indigenous territory. Prasenjit Duara writes that during the interwar period, Wilsonian notions of ethnic self-determination, combined with strains of historical pessimism in the West, blunted the impulse to conquer new colonies outright or to expand state borders at the expense of natives. Duara argues that a new, globally circulating "symbolic regime of authenticity" based political legitimacy on primordial ties to territory instead of on the rights of the conqueror to rule the conquered. Thus, "cultural rule" in Korea after 1919 and Japan's insistence that Manchukuo be ruled as a de jure nation-state rather than as a colony were consonant with the Wilsonian outlook. In both cases, Japanese ideologues anchored claims to legitimacy in the language of a brand of stewardship that was exercised in the name of the authentic nation/nationals of each dependency.[126]

In Taiwan, the discourse on sovereignty and authenticity dovetailed with an ethnic tourism trade that ennobled former "savage headhunters" as ethnic groups worthy of study, preservation, and even emulation. Indigenous artists, tourism industry workers, native informants, and politicians responded to those opportunities by producing the artifacts, icons, and performances that put flesh on the administrative-academic skeleton of territorially defined ethnic difference.[127] Under conditions of economic and physical isolation, coupled with cultural investment, the ungoverned peripheries of yore became the indigenous territories of today—now imagined as timeless, authentic, and buffered from the flow of world history.

Acknowledging that historical forces created indigenous peoples is not the same thing as claiming that indigenous claims for rights recovery in land, resources, or human rights rest on invented traditions and are thus hollow. As Arif Dirlik put it, "[a] critique of "cultural essentialism" that offers no articulated means to distinguish between the essentialism of indigenous ideology, and the essentialism of a Confucian revival or [political scientist Samuel] Huntington's vision of war among civilizations, may be methodologically justifiable; but it is, to say the least, morally irresponsible and politically obscene. Indigenous claims to identity are very much tied in with a desperate concern for survival; not in a "metaphorical" but in a very material sense."[128]

The example of the Saisiyat group in northern Taiwan provides a counterweight to breezy notions that indigenous peoples themselves, as self-defined collectivities, were *invented* by colonialist discourse or urban metropolitan longings. While the notion that their homeland is circumscribed by a fixed boundary line populated by bearers of a unique cultural ensemble is indeed a colonial invention, Qing-period records indicate that Saisiyat peoples identified themselves as Saisiyat before Japanese colonization. Moreover, they have retained and defended a sense of corporate identity without recourse to projected or reified cultural markers as core elements of identity. At the same time, colonial-period photographs, artifacts, and documents, as material objects, have—to use Hu Chia-yu's apt phrase—"enlivened" the past and served as touchstones for perseverance in the face of settler encroachment and institutionalized racism. Hu's invocation of Marshall Sahlins reinforces Dirlik's point and bears repeating: "The awareness of indigenous culture as a value to be lived and defended is not just a simple and nostalgic desire for the fetishized repositories of a pristine identity, but signifies the demand of them for their own space within the world cultural order, and recognizes their existence in the context of national or international threats."[129]

The goal of this book is to think through the processes and structures in world history that coproduced nation-states and indigenous peoples. It is less about the invention of tradition among indigenous peoples than it is about the incomplete consolidation of legal centralism characteristic of state building in the era of competitive imperialism and high-velocity capitalism. The world that was obliterated by the twin forces of capitalism and nationalism was not that of the natives but rather that of the in-between spaces of ambiguous sovereignty, the buffer zones at the margins or interstices of centrally administered, surplus-extracting dynastic and nation-states. In this niche, chiefs, interpreters, trading-post operators, trackers, headmen, and professional border crossers brokered the coexistence of political autonomy and economic interdependence during the *global transformation*.

As it turns out, the success or failure of projects to instantiate governmentality in Taiwan largely hinged upon whether or not a district or area had fallen under Qing administration. If this case study has broader applicability, the disciplined social fields considered normative in our models of international relations may, in fact, be products of *longue durée* processes that spanned successive empires. This finding suggests that today's international order is premised on sociological models that are relevant to a minority of the earth's population. Moreover, it suggests that bringing historically undisciplined populations within the ken of international society ("nation building") is probably beyond the means or will of any state that possesses the surplus wealth to pull it off. This is because such projects exhaust the patience of citizenries who must foot the bill, and because governments that ignore the centripetal pull of popular sentiment by definition lack the stability and resources to complete long-term projects for exporting discipline beyond their own borders.[130]

ORGANIZATION OF THIS BOOK

This introduction has argued that the process Ronald Niezen dubs "indigenization" and the phenomenon James Clifford terms "Indigènitude" are historical concomitants of nation building during the era of high imperialism (1870–1914). Anthropologists and sociologists consider the decades following 1960 to be the incubation period for the global indigenism movement. Indigenism, in their view, rests upon an infrastructure of interstate coordination anchored in UN human-rights conventions, transregional NGO activity, and democratically sanctioned political protest. By looking for the origins of indigenism in the late nineteenth century, I have argued that seemingly disparate formations—a supra-state, nation-states, and stateless peoples—emerged as contemporaneous formations. The case study of Taiwan under Japanese rule suggests that nationality, internationalism, and indigenism were mutually constituted, rather than sequentially occurring phenomena.

Chapter 1 of this study begins with the murders of fifty-four shipwrecked Okinawans on Taiwan's Hengchun Peninsula. This cause célèbre put the opposing logics of the dynastic and international systems on a collision course. Hengchun's mountain ranges were resistant to rule from a distance under the Qing, hindering the recovery of remains and the punishment of the alleged killers. The first part of chapter 1 explains how the lack of horizontal integration between the Hengchun Peninsula and the Qing Empire necessitated "wet diplomacy." This mode of interaction stressed particularistic, emotionally charged attachments requiring periodical renewal in the absence of administrators, courts, and policemen. To eradicate this obstacle to efficient resource management, which survived the transfer of sovereignty from the Qing to Japan in 1895, the colonial government built armed bunkers, relay stations, and guard posts along a scorched-earth trail known as the *aiyūsen* to enclose the Atayal settlements of northern Taiwan. From 1903 through 1915, government forces extended the barrier and then marched it inward. The Taiwan Indigenous Peoples, as a modern political-cultural formation, emerged from the ruins of these scorched-earth campaigns as a disarmed, geographically isolated, and dispossessed minority population.

Chapter 2 advances the argument that linguistic diversity occasioned institutional creativity and strategic frustration for colonialists in Taiwan. It examines state-led efforts to yoke an unruly Qing periphery to a centralized administration through its language and education policies. In Taiwan, administrators required methods to govern a patchwork of Chinese- and Austronesian-language-speaking populations. Commercial interdependency between the island's varied social formations spawned more organic solutions to the problem of cross-border communications, as well. Top-down, centrally installed measures, such as language training for colonizers or the colonized, were most amenable to administrative cohesion. However, formal language instruction was not scalable, due to cost constraints. Bottom-up arrangements, such as intersocietal adoption and marriage-centered alliance, were cost-effective but less answerable to central command. The Japanese state ultimately opted for intermarriages as a strategy—a holdover from Qing times. This policy came up short because it fostered identification with particular local power structures. It also allowed colonists to establish kin-ordered bases of authority independent of their bureaucratic chains of command. The political marriages, therefore, contradicted the more general colony-wide impulse to homogenize bureaucratic, legal, and economic space, and they led to intelligence failures and discontent among the ruled and even to the Wushe Rebellion of 1930.

The next chapter demonstrates how gifts performed multiple functions in the borderland economy of Qing-period and Japanese-ruled Taiwan. Travelers brought offerings to the mountainous hinterland to pay for services rendered or expectations of future assistance. In addition, the presentations of gifts were occasions for recording the emotional states of recipients and for gauging the dispositions of little-known peoples as either "greedy," "honest," or "uncorrupted." Gifts also fostered trade dependency among indigenes. As the Taiwan Government-General intensified resource extraction from camphor forests in the 1900s, it regulated gift giving as an arm of policy, to reform indigenous mores or to reward and punish highlanders. One class of these gifts, those involving dyed red thread or cloth, took on additional meaning, as these materials were disassembled and reassembled into "traditional" Atayal textiles. These were either consumed locally or reexported to trading posts, anthropologists, curators, and tourists. In this last guise, Atayal red-dyed textiles became exhibits in discourses on authenticity, progress, and primitivism. By tracking the uses of textiles across these many domains, chapter 3 illustrates the productive, though problematic, interdependence of indigenes, settlers, and metropolitans in the production of colonial modernity and global indigenism.

Chapter 4 examines a battery of twentieth-century Japanese official, academic, and commercial publications about Taiwan indigenes. These artifacts deployed texts, pictures, and maps to manufacture a "large reservoir of cultural imaginaries"[131] that have reemerged as reference points and resources for the indigenous renaissance in the twenty-first century. In what began as a quest to wrest resources, impose administrative order, and promote immigration to an erstwhile Qing borderland in the late 1890s and 1900s, Japan's colonial administration, tourism industry, and scholarly apparatus, by the 1930s, had completed numerous projects in ethnic typification, geobody construction, and racialization to institutionalize indigeneity in Taiwan. This concluding chapter analyzes these three interrelated processes to demonstrate how the increased intensity of resource extraction in colonial Taiwan intersected with historical trends in reprographic technology and new forms of state making to ethnically pluralize the island's non-Han populations as second-order geobodies.

PART ONE

The Anatomy of a Rebellion

1

From Wet Diplomacy to Scorched Earth

*The Taiwan Expedition, the Guardline,
and the Wushe Rebellion*

INTRODUCTION

On October 7, 1930, Japanese patrolman Yoshimura Katsumi passed through the hamlet of Mehebu (near Wushe) during a wedding celebration. There, a Sediq man, one Tadao Mona, beckoned him for a drink. Yoshimura brusquely refused, thereby slighting Tadao publicly. Tadao's hands were bloody from butchering meat for the festival repast. Nonetheless, he touched Yoshimura's freshly laundered uniform and left a red stain. Yoshimura angrily struck Tadao twice on the hand with a cane. Along with his younger brother Bassao Mona, Tadao wrestled Yoshimura to the ground and returned the blows. The next day, their father, headman Mona Ludao, went to the nearby Japanese police box with bottles of millet wine in hand to formally apologize. Much to Mona's chagrin, the branch chief, Sugiura Kōichi, refused the gift and apologies. Instead, Mona and his sons were reported to Sugiura's superiors. Mona was told to expect severe punishment; the possibilities ranged from detention to a punitive expedition against his entire village. Yoshimura's report and Sugiura's handling of the matter drove Mona into the arms of other rebellious Sediq men. Mona Ludao himself led the bloody Wushe Rebellion three weeks later. In the October 27, 1930, assaults, Tadao Mona's squad killed Yoshimura Katsumi in the first wave.[1]

These events of early October, known as the "Yoshimura beating incident" (*Yoshimura ōda jiken*) have been recounted (and sometimes embellished) in numerous government inquests, Japanese memoirs, document collections, and overviews of the Wushe uprising.[2] A popular 2001 comic book reconstructed the dispute for a general audience of post–martial law Taiwanese, while the blockbuster 2011 movie *Seediq Bale* dramatized it in a multilingual feature film.[3] There are conflicting facts in these accounts. We are left to wonder: What type of meat bloodied Tadao's hands? How many Japanese patrolmen visited the wedding? How many bottles of wine did Mona offer to Sugiura? Did Mona jump in and help assault Yoshimura, or did he break up the fight? But regarding the main sequence of events, all accounts agree: a wedding took place on October 7; a fight between Yoshimura and Tadao erupted; and Mona Ludao's attempt at informal mediation was rejected in favor of an administratively determined punishment.

From Mona's perspective, Sugiura's recourse to superiors constituted a rejection of Mona's chiefly authority to resolve disputes on the basis of his status as a revered Sediq headman. At the same time, the administrative hand-off subordinated Sugiura; it was an admission that he was not Mona's equivalent, a "local Japanese chief" with wide discretionary powers. This indeed was a momentous change, and it signaled the termination of rule by the outcasts of empire on both sides of the "savage border." The Yoshimura beating incident exemplified the regime's efforts to dispense with an intermediary layer of quasi officials at its geographic extremities.

In the new order, the authority of Japanese officials and indigenous leaders would be derived solely through competition and recruitment through the public-school system and the police bureaucracy. At least theoretically, this new hierarchy, on both sides of the ethnic divide, reached all the way up to the emperor in Tokyo, thereby unifying the island administratively—almost.

WET DIPLOMACY AND EARLY JAPANESE COLONIAL RULE

Six decades prior to Yoshimura's pointed refusal to drink with Tadao Mona, outsiders with business on the edges of Qing territory in Taiwan accepted alcoholic beverages from indigenes and stuck around to imbibe them at close quarters. We can think of such transactions as instances of "wet diplomacy." Throughout the island, alcohol was consumed as a liquid, but in northern Taiwan, the preferred method was called "conjoined drinking" *(gōin)*, which entailed contact with an interlocutor's saliva (see figure 4). The term "wet diplomacy" is therefore descriptive of a particular type of activity, but it also denotes an ideal-typical form of human interaction. The phrase is not used in this study to distill a particularly "Japanese" form of sociability but rather is adopted to account for the frequent and repetitive descriptions of diplomatic drinking in the source material, and for the insistence of historical actors themselves that the relationships thus consecrated were personal and not abstract or contractual. This ideal type contrasts with *durai* (dry) interaction, which is fungible. Wet bonds must be renewed with periodic expressions of fealty, while dry relationships are rule governed and attach to social roles or official ranks rather than individuals.[4]

In the late 1890s and early 1900s, the early years of formal Japanese rule in Taiwan, wet diplomacy was the coin of the realm along Taiwan's savage border. It

FIGURE 4. Two Atayal men engaged in "conjoined drinking," near Wulai, Taiwan, ca. 1900. The man on the right is Bato Watan of Rahao. Narita Takeshi, *Taiwan seiban shuzoku shashinchō* (Taipei: Narita shashin seihanjo, 1912), 39.

evinced continuity with the precedent-setting practices of the Taiwan Expedition in the 1870s. In both instances, Japanese officials, merchants, and scholars entered into personal relations with indigenes to secure forbearance, goods, labor, or guidance. In the course of these transactions, indigenous merchants, chiefs, and interpreters established bonds of trust with particular outsiders. These relationships frequently involved intermarriage (see chapter 2). In the wet diplomatic context, favoritism and loyalty were expected—in fact, they were the whole point.

Indigenous leaders sought access to Japanese goods and political patronage to gain advantage over local rivals or to shore up authority within their segmented polities. Therefore, from their perspective, the notion that all Taiwanese would be treated equally as children of the emperor was anathema. This Japanese policy was formally known as "nondiscrimination" *(isshi dōjin)*. Under it, all loyalty and obligation were directed toward a single apex, the emperor—thus making *isshi dōjin* structurally analogous to modern nationalism, which also channels loyalty upward as it postulates horizontal fraternities of juridically equal and interchangeable subject-citizens. Indigenous Taiwan's small-scale, nonstate polities were inimical to the instantiation of *isshi dōjin*, however, because they were held together by the politics of redistribution. Here, chiefly authority was augmented by public displays of favoritism vis-à-vis other indigenes and successful warfare against neighboring enemies.

Japanese *isshi dōjin* proclamations promised impartiality for all Taiwanese but were nonetheless premised on Japanese preeminence. That is to say, even the most fair-minded Japanese officials believed that indigenes were savages squatting on the emperor's land. However, as long as chiefs were receiving gifts, publicly engaging in joined-mouth drinking with Japanese colonists, or themselves apportioning banquet victuals, the vagaries of language allowed indigenous leaders to convert wet-diplomatic encounters into political capital vis-à-vis followers and rivals. But in the long run, the logics of centralized administration and bureaucratic rationality were incompatible with the protocols of wet diplomacy.

To overcome the paradoxes of wet diplomacy and establish a less particularistic and labor-intensive form of rule, the TGG stationed guard posts along a scorched-earth trail known as the *aiyūsen* (see figure 5) to enclose the Atayal, Sediq, and Truku settlements of northern Taiwan. This denuded landscape provided clear lines of fire, while it physically divided northern Taiwan into two distinct zones: one for imperial subjects and another for outcast rebels. From 1903 through 1915, government forces extended the scorched-earth barrier and then marched it inward.[5] The Indigenous Peoples of Taiwan, as a modern political-cultural formation, emerged from the ruins of these scorched-earth campaigns. The surrender ceremonies themselves, and the nakedly asymmetrical power relations they enforced, epitomized "dry" interpersonal relations—the lists of demands Japanese policemen read from their elevated platforms were couched not in the language of reciprocity and benevolence but as orders for compliance upon pain

FIGURE 5. Scorched earth guardline, ca. 1910. Narita Takeshi, *Taiwan seiban shuzoku shashinchō* (Taipei: Narita shashin seihanjo, 1912), 163.

of punishment (see figure 6). The trade-starved, bombed-out, and battered indigenous delegations were summoned to these spaces as supplicants. To resume trading relations and stop the shelling, they were forced to surrender their weapons and listen to lists of conditions enforced by carrot-and-stick methods, rather than renewed displays of friendship, as called for in wet diplomacy (see figure 7).

Yet after the highlands were largely disarmed, wet diplomacy did not dry up. The guardline campaigns had, in fact, exhausted the Taiwan Government-General. In the late 1910s through early 1930s, state-society relations were left in the hands of rural district police officers, their indigenous wives, and local chiefs such as Mona Ludao. These districts remained outside the tax base and were labeled "special," "savage," or "aborigine." I will refer to this phase of Japanese rule as the era of "native authority," following Mahmood Mamdani.[6]

Wet diplomacy solved several problems for the Japanese, as it did for the Qing in earlier times: with a meager budget, the government-general established itself in the highlands despite linguistic and cartographic ignorance. From the strategic choke points thus established, information could be collected and relationships forged. However, wet diplomacy hindered the efficient and reliable extraction

FIGURE 6. Surrendered Atayal at a stopover in Jiaobanshan, ca. 1910. Endō Hiroya, ed., *Banhi tōbatsu kinen shashinchō* (Taipei: Endō shashinkan, 1911), n.p.

of resources from the upland forests, and it blurred the boundaries of state sovereignty along the so-called "savage border." This chapter plots the history of indigenous-Japanese relations around the forced march from wet diplomacy to scorched earth, and then from scorched earth to native authority. It further posits an isomorphism between wet diplomacy and the low-velocity milieu of tributary interstate relations. By the same token, it will argue for a congruence between dry human relations and the horizontal integration of space that is presupposed by the regime of rule from a distance. This latter mode of governance, in turn, sought to facilitate the generation, accumulation, and funneling of surplus wealth to state coffers.

TREATY-PORT TAIWAN AND THE MUDAN VILLAGE INCIDENT

As with the 1930 Yoshimura beating incident, the 1871 shipwreck of the Ryūkyūans in Taiwan could have been resolved locally, on the spot. In each case, recourse to central authorities occurred in the context of increased volumes and velocities of resource extraction in these imperial peripheries. Such pressures catapulted

FROM WET DIPLOMACY TO SCORCHED EARTH   49

FIGURE 7. Weapons captured from Atayal peoples during Sakuma Samata's five-year plan, photographed at the Taiwan Government-General Museum in Taipei, ca. 1910. Endō Hiroya, ed., *Banhi tōbatsu kinen shashinchō* (Taipei: Endō shashinkan, 1911), n.p.

otherwise unexceptional events to historical turning points. The 1930 Wushe uprising was set off by the Japanese government's heightened demand for timber in central Taiwan. Yoshimura himself was brought to Wushe to supervise a Sediq labor force in felling and hauling gigantic cedars, at fixed wages, to complete a series of public works projects. Yoshimura was not locally embedded, as some of his superiors were, but was a specialist hired to accelerate the process of forest exploitation. When his tone-deaf rejection of Tadao's entreaty caused a ruckus, his supervisor Sugiura construed the wedding brawl as an assault on imperial authority and sent his report up the chain of command, escalating matters beyond the point of no return. Six decades earlier, a longer chain of events, with a larger cast of characters and an even higher body count, presaged a similar set of problems at the outer margins of state-administered territory in Taiwan.

The increase in Asia-bound commerce that followed the Opium Wars (1839–42) turned the Taiwan Strait into a major thoroughfare in the China trade. After two treaty ports were opened there in 1860, Taiwan's "poorly charted and still-unlighted coasts" and rocky shallow waters became a graveyard for boats and their crews. One tally estimates that about "150 foreign vessels . . . foundered in the vicinity of the Taiwan coast between 1850 and 1869 of which over thirty were plundered or burned."[7] Another calculates that at "least forty-six Western merchant ships" disappeared or were destroyed from 1861 through 1874.[8] Most infamously, in December 1871 near Bayao Bay, Taiwanese murdered 54 shipwrecked sailors from Miyakojima (Ryūkyū Islands/Okinawa), an act that occasioned the invasion of over 3,000 Japanese troops beginning in May 1874 (see map 3).

Most historical accounts of the 1871 shipwreck are based on the recollections of a Japanese official and two Miyakojima survivors. Oral testimonies of the protagonists, their rescuers, and local officials were jotted down in 1872 and subsequently combed over by generations of scholars in Taiwan, Japan, the Ryūkyū Islands, and beyond. Chou Wan-yao summarized this scholarship in a recent review article,[9] while Miyaguni Fumio has republished the primary-source materials.[10] Ōhama Ikuko has mined archives in Taiwan and Japan (including Okinawa) and reconstructed the events with great care.[11] In addition, local historian and native of Kuskus village Valjeluk Mavaliu has collated written evidence with his geographical and genealogical knowledge,[12] while Mudan resident and oral historian Gao Jiaxin (Lianes Punanang) has interviewed a dozen or so Paiwan elders (including Valjeluk Mavaliu),[13] to provide a local perspective.

The drama was set in motion by the November 30, 1871, departure of four tribute ships from the castle complex of Shuri (near Naha), on the island of Okinawa. The ships were returning to Miyakojima and the Yaeyama Islands in the Ryūkyū Kingdom. Within sight of Miyakojima, the ships were blown off course and succumbed to a typhoon on December 12, 1871. One of the ships from the Yaeyama Islands was lost forever, but another landed on Taiwan's western coast. The survivors of the latter wreck made it back to Naha through the good offices of Qing officials. Of the two Miyakojima ships, one made it safely back to its port of origin, but the other— the famous one—capsized off the east coast of southern Taiwan, near Bayao Bay.[14]

There were sixty-nine passengers on the ill-fated Miyakojima ship. Three of them perished trying to get ashore. The other sixty-six made landfall five days after the horrible storm. Soon after, they encountered two Chinese men who reportedly warned them away from traveling inland among dangerous Paiwan peoples. It is difficult to know what transpired at this juncture. The survivors' deposition indicates that the sixty-six Ryūkyūans were robbed by the Chinese and decided to part ways with their hosts. They spent the night in makeshift outdoor lodgings and set out the morning of December 18. As they wandered westward, they encountered men with large earrings and distended earlobes, presumably Paiwanese.

The Ryūkyūans followed the Paiwanese to a settlement of fifteen or sixteen thatched homes, Kuskus, where the lost mariners were given water and food and were put up for the evening. The provision of water by Kuskus residents, for them at least, symbolized an offer of protection and friendship, according to Valjeluk Mavaliu.[15] The deposition claims that during the night, they were robbed again by their Kuskus hosts. In the morning, a departing group of hunters ordered the

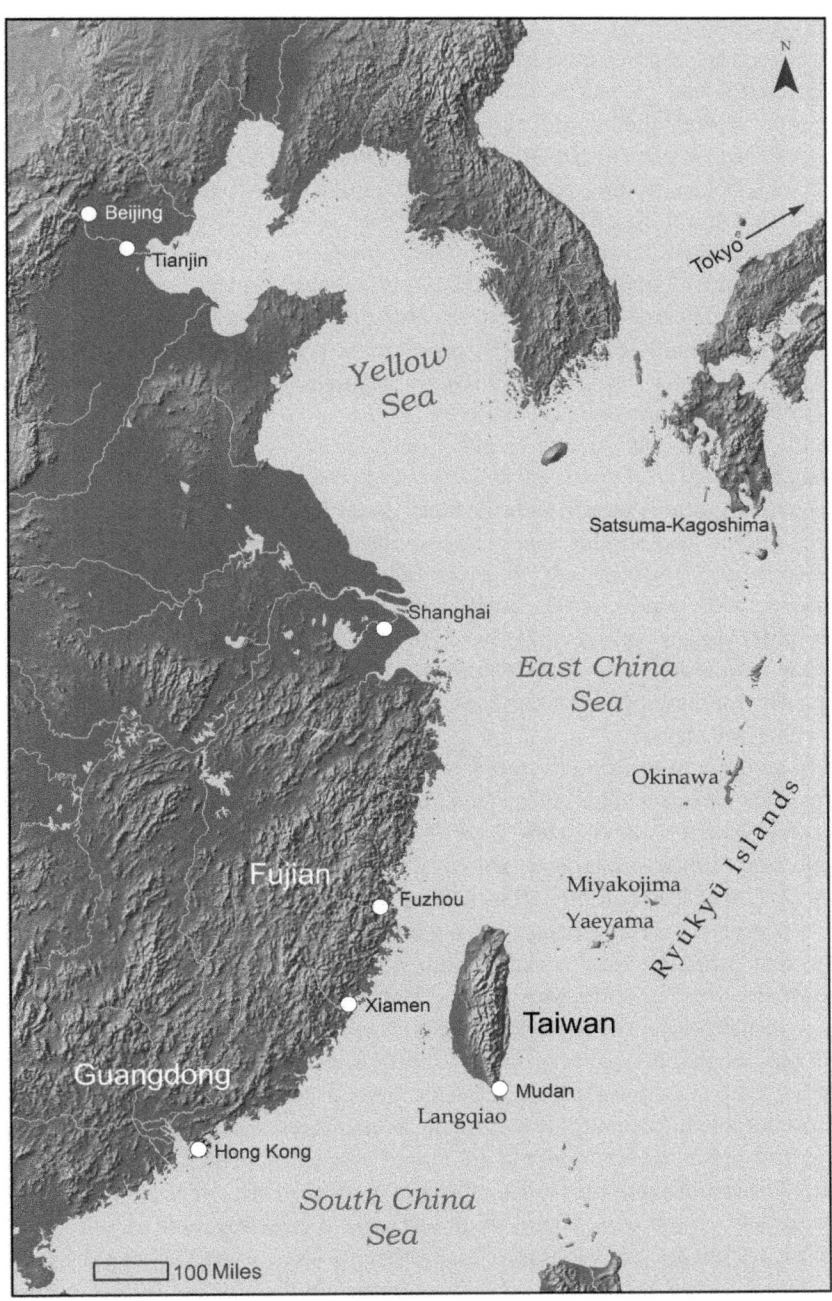

MAP 3. Taiwan, the Ryūkyū Islands, the Langqiao Peninsula, Mudan, and Satsuma, in East Asia.

Ryūkyūans to stay put and offered to return with enough game to provide a feast. However, the presence of so many armed men, coupled with the rumors of head hunting that had greeted them on shore two days earlier, impelled them to make a break for it while the hunting party was absent.

Dozens of the fleeing Ryūkyūans found shelter in the home of seventy-three-year-old Hakka trading-post operator Deng Tianbao (named "Old Weng" in the deposition[16]) and his thirty-year-old son in a nearby settlement of five or six houses. Most Taiwanese Hakka *(Kejia)* people immigrated from Guangdong Province. Throughout Taiwan, the Hakka established settlements in foothills and acted as commercial conduits between Austronesians in the mountains and Han people of Fujianese extraction (Hok-los) in the plains.[17] Valjeluk Mavaliu writes that Deng was married to a Paiwanese woman named Utjau,[18] a common practice for cross-border merchants in this area.

That same day, Paiwan men caught up with the Ryūkyūans. They forcibly entered Deng's compound. Dozens of Ryūkyūans were dragged out and slaughtered in a courtyard; others were caught in flight. Nine Ryūkyūans avoided detection in Deng's home, and another three escaped (and were captured by other Paiwanese subsequently). The other fifty-four were killed in the melee. The next day, the nine survivors were removed to the much larger Hakka settlement of Poliac (Baoli) and put under the care of the village head, Yang Youwang—Deng's son-in-law. Poliac was an ammunition depot, trade junction, and place of arms manufacture. Hakka merchants transshipped powder, shot, and guns to Paiwan buyers inland from this location (see map 4).

In addition to securing the safety of these nine, Yang also arranged for the ransom of the three separated men. Yang Youwang then sheltered these twelve survivors for about forty days, before sending them to the administrative seat of Taiwan Prefecture (Taiwan-fu, today's Tainan). The Ryūkyūans were returned to Naha in July 1872, over seven months after the four ships were hit by the typhoon.[19]

Although it became a truism among Japanese officials and subsequent chroniclers that Paiwanese Mudan villagers murdered the seafarers, residents of Kuskus, today known as Gaoshifo, were the assailants.[20] It has been proposed that the violence resulted from the Ryūkyūan visitors' ignorance of guest etiquette (they ate and ran), or that the captors could not find buyers to pay ransom and thus killed them.[21] Gao Jiaxin's oral histories provide another plausible explanation. Sixty-six adults, unable to communicate in the local languages, walked into Kuskus farmland and began taking food and trampling over hotly contested village boundaries. On top of these nuisances, efforts to feed and shelter dozens of strangers, who brought no provisions and could not make themselves understood, strained Kuskus resources and hospitality. Finally, the intruders were killed as punishment for their multiple misdeeds.[22] The best estimates put the population of Gaoshifo at 250 at the time.[23] Therefore, one can imagine that caring for sixty-six guests would have been a major, to say nothing of disruptive, undertaking in this sparsely populated area of rural Taiwan.

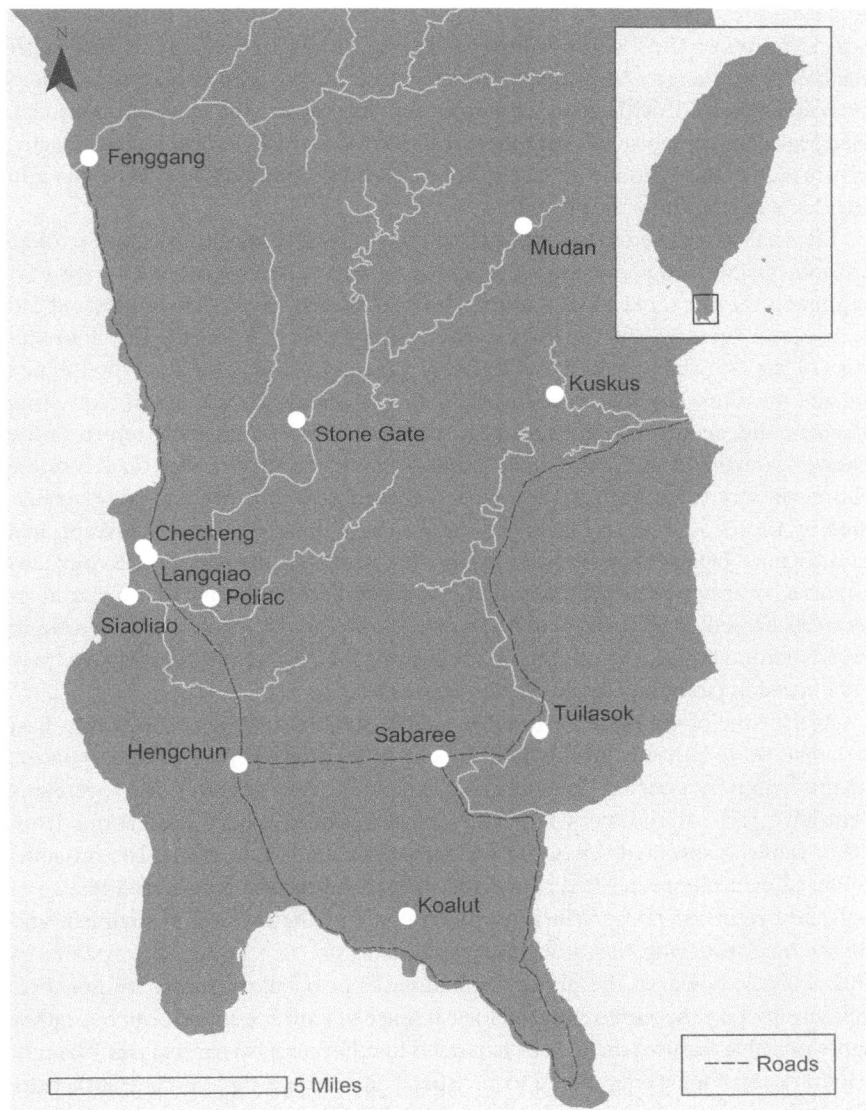

MAP 4. The Langqiao Peninsula, ca. 1874.

Whatever the motivations of the people who killed the Ryūkyūans, the slaughter did not immediately raise eyebrows in Japan. While a few officials who happened to be in Beijing or Naha in mid-1872 got wind of the massacre, it did not become a full-blown international incident until April 1874. The 1872 repatriation of the twelve survivors from Poliac to Fenggang to Taiwan-fu to Fuzhou appears to have been by the book. In fact, the Qing system for repatriating Ryūkyūan shipwreck victims on the shores of China (including Taiwan) settled 401 incidents over the course of the seventeenth to the nineteenth centuries. Qing policy throughout its realm was to provide food, clothing, and ship repairs for stranded mariners. Reciprocal agreements with neighboring powers returned Chinese shipwreck survivors to the Qing realm from Japan, Korea, Vietnam, and the Ryūkyūs in over 700 incidents during the same period.[24]

Edwin Pak-wah Leung has argued that this regional repatriation system worked without visible complaint until the arrival of the Western-centered treaty-port regime in the late nineteenth century. He notes that the Ryūkyūan court itself did not request Japanese officials to intercede on its behalf regarding the fifty-four victims of the 1871 shipwreck. It was Japanese officials visiting Okinawa who lobbied for the invasion. The Ryūkyū monarch Shō Tai (Shang-tai), instead of requesting Japanese aid, sent a reward to Chinese officials in Fuzhou after the return of the twelve survivors from Taiwan. In fact, Ryūkyūans had been stranded on Taiwanese shores on fifty-three recorded occasions between 1701 and 1876 and were repatriated by the Qing in each instance.[25] Because such incidents were unexceptional and because Japan's expedition to avenge the deaths of the fifty-four Ryūkyūans occurred over two years after the event, the question of the timing of the 1874 invasion has been of great interest to historians. Quite rightly, scholars have looked to Japan's national politics and diplomatic history for answers, decoupling the May 1874 invasion from the December 1871 shipwreck.

At the time of the Meiji Restoration (1868), state-to-state relations within East Asia had yet to become international and are more properly termed interdynastic, or the "tributary system." To assure that diplomacy demonstrated the sovereign's centrality and paramountcy, tributary courts received official delegations from other states at specified times and for periods of limited duration. The missions followed carefully prescribed routes, performed minutely orchestrated guest rituals, and returned home. Much has been made of the cultural chauvinism and hierarchical ordering that informed diplomatic practice under this system. In this analysis, however, the important hallmarks of tributary forms are not their validation of a generalized, transhistorical sense of Chinese superiority but rather more portable features that can be extended to other premodern regimes. Namely, tributary relations were tailored to the specificity of each diplomatic transaction. Guest rituals in this system were adjusted for differences between supplicant states or even for the size of missions. Tributary relations also eschewed the notion that interstate relations be put on a permanent, contractual, and routinized basis. In their emphases on the necessity for periodic renewal and forthrightly particularistic forms,[26] Qing, Tokugawa, and Joseon guest rituals bore a family resemblance to the "wet diplomacy" described above.[27]

According to Takeshi Hamashita, "modernity" did not overpower encrusted East Asian "tradition" with the coming of the Western treaty ports at the conclusion of the Opium Wars. Rather, the Atlantic powers overlaid a new set of institutions, practices, and personnel onto existing Chinese, Japanese, and Korean maritime trade circuits. Independent of the new trade, intra-Asian commerce experienced its own growth spurt in the nineteenth century. East Asian politicians and merchants themselves could be eager proponents of trade-volume expansion, tariff standardization, harbor improvements, and efficient customs agencies. In a word, Hamashita demonstrated that the routinization of cross-border commercial practices within Asia, rather than threatening dynasties, could, in fact, strengthen central authority.[28] The ideological divide in dynastic circles was not so much between moderns and traditionalists but about means to increase, regulate, or reject higher volumes of foreign trade in order to protect sovereignty.[29]

These debates about how to meet the challenges and opportunities presented by the arrival of industrial capitalism in East Asia raged in Japan during the interval between the December 1871 killing of the Ryūkyūans in Deng Tianbao's courtyard and the May 1874 Japanese invasion of Taiwan. Simultaneously, the Japanese government struggled to assert authority throughout its three major islands of Honshū, Kyūshū, and Shikoku. Rural rebellions against increased taxes, compulsory education, and military conscription, as well as the "chastise Korea debate" *(seikanron)* at the higher levels of government, formed the backdrop for the 1874 invasion. Saigō Tsugumichi's occupation of southern Taiwan, therefore, not only aimed to clear the Langqiao Peninsula of parasites who leeched wealth from the global system but also advanced the Meiji project to stamp out regionalism and resistance to central authority within Japan.[30] As Norihito Mizuno put it, the varied projects subsumed under the Taiwan Expedition—to colonize the Langqiao Peninsula, to siphon off samurai discontent with a foreign adventure, and to assert exclusive sovereignty over the Ryūkyūs—all conformed to a single logic: the young Meiji state's heightened threat perception vis-à-vis its industrialized competitors in the arena of nation-state imperialism.[31]

It will be recalled that the lack of succor for shipwrecked American whalers at the hands of Japanese local officials energized the U.S. government to pursue a "water and wood" treaty with the Tokugawa Shogunate (1603–1867) in 1853. The 1854 Treaty of Peace and Amity, signed between the United States and Japan on the heels of two U.S. naval missions led by Commodore Matthew Perry, was aimed at a Japanese government actively hostile to shipwreck victims, and by extension, to untrammeled access to the ocean's natural resources.[32] America's whalers were extending their range deeper into the Pacific, making the problem of shipwrecks on Japan's shores a persistent one if Americans were to keep increasing oil consumption. Under threat of naval bombardment, the Tokugawa Shogunate signed the 1854 treaty with the United States and a subsequent 1858 treaty to open trade and treaty ports.

The government in Edo managed to dodge the bullet of foreign invasion, but its actions met with dire consequences. After the shogunate signed these

56   THE ANATOMY OF A REBELLION

unpopular instruments, civil wars erupted throughout the realm, in addition to a wave of political assassinations. When rebellious Satsuma (a southwestern domain in Kyūshū) shore batteries fired on British ships in 1863, also to protest Japan's new policies of openness, British naval bombardment nearly decimated the castle town of Kagoshima.[33] Outgrowths of this civil strife, brought on by a central government's overreach to satisfy the demands of mercantile powers, fomented the collapse of the Tokugawa Shogunate in 1868.

As the Tokugawa regime was teetering on its last legs, U.S. consul to Amoy (Xiamen) Charles LeGendre reprised, on a smaller scale, the 1853–54 U.S. missions to Tokyo in Langqiao, Taiwan. In the fall of 1867, LeGendre concluded a verbal agreement with the Langqiao headman Toketok to protect shipwrecked sailors from assault, robbery, and ransoming on Taiwan's south coast.[34] The agreement, like the 1854 Japan-U.S. treaty, reflected the efforts of maritime powers to make the seas safer for greater volumes and velocities of commerce. The LeGendre-Toketok negotiations, like the U.S.-Japan talks of the late 1850s, averted armed confrontation in the short run, while they placed unbearable strains upon Toketok's ability to hold together a loose confederation of subordinate polities. Toketok's problems, in fact, mirrored those of the Tokugawa government vis-à-vis Western gunboats.

LEGENDRE EXTENDS THE TREATY-PORT SYSTEM TO LANGQIAO

In April 1867, LeGendre made his first journey to Taiwan to investigate an American shipwreck that became known as the *Rover* incident. The consul's visit ignited a seven-year fuse that exploded with the landing of four Japanese warships in Langqiao in May 1874. The barque *Rover* bottomed out on Taiwan's south cape in March 1867. After it capsized, the *Rover*'s captain, his wife, and his crew were murdered on shore by Koaluts (a Paiwan tribe) while trying to secure help. The one survivor of the attack, a Chinese man, reported the incident to authorities in Gaoxiong after making his escape. Thereafter, a British steamer left the same port to investigate but was turned back by the eruption of musket fire from the camouflaged and elevated positions of the Koaluts. LeGendre headed to the south cape for a ten-day tour.[35] He failed to find survivors or remains since he could not secure local guides.

While LeGendre plotted his next move in Xiamen, U.S. vice admiral H. H. Bell launched a frontal attack from the location of the *Rover*'s wreck. Ignoring the advice of LeGendre, Bell skipped a stop at the port town of Siaoliao. LeGendre had suggested that Bell activate the "mediating networks" of Hakka, Hok-lo, bicultural, and Paiwan villagers that connected the port of Siaoliao to the protected and isolationist Koalut polity.[36] Going it alone instead, Bell successfully landed, but soon after, one Lieutenant Captain Mackenzie was shot through the heart by a Koalut marksman during an uphill infantry charge against unseen defenders.

The American warship pulled anchor and shelled the Koaluts from a safe distance, apparently inflicting great damage. But without access to kin, trade, and alliance networks, Bell could not locate survivors or discover who specifically had killed the crew of the *Rover*.[37]

As a treaty-port consul in Xiamen, which subsumed Taiwan on the American diplomatic organizational chart, LeGendre took the Langqiao Peninsula's opacity as a professional and personal affront. A letter to LeGendre from the Taiwan circuit attendant regarding the *Rover* referred to Articles 11 and 13 of the 1858 Treaty of Tianjin to state "that whenever within the jurisdiction of the Emperor of China, anyone shall molest Americans, the military and civil authorities must, on hearing of the same, try to punish the authors." However, the note added—and this became the sticking point for years to come—"the Savage country does not come within the limits of our jurisdiction, and our military force is not able to operate in it."[38] Finding this response unsatisfactory, LeGendre took the matter all the way to the top (short of an imperial audience). In person, he proposed to the governor-general of Fujian and Zhejiang, Wu Tang, that the Langqiao Peninsula be occupied by Chinese inhabitants and garrisoned permanently by Qing forces.[39]

Langqiao's meager population—about fifteen thousand people, of whom three thousand were indigenous, seven thousand or so bicultural, and another four or five thousand Hakka and Hok-lo[40]—and its variety of unknown (to Chinese officials) languages and inaccessible terrain[41] did not commend the extension of civil and military administration to this remote corner of empire. Understandably, Wu did not formally consent to LeGendre's proposals, but neither could he ignore them. It is testament to the force of British and French arms and the demonstration effects of the 1860 sacking of Beijing[42] that LeGendre could obtain a meeting with Wu, who sat at the apex of an administrative unit that governed perhaps thirty million Qing subjects.[43] It was surely in this larger context that the American's numerous requests, if not honored, were generally entertained.

Wu Tang's successor, Ying Gui, therefore allowed LeGendre to accompany a military tour of Langqiao led by General Liu Mingdeng in September 1867.[44] LeGendre recounted travel to Langqiao from the prefectural capital, Taiwan-fu, as an arduous affair. Although ranking Qing officials extended LeGendre diplomatic courtesies, transportation was halting. LeGendre rode on a sedan chair in proximity to General Liu, but his journey was delayed by bad weather and slow communications. As one moved south, the last Chinese city on the coast, Fangliao, was literally the end of the road. To go beyond, Liu's troops (who numbered about five hundred), built a forty-mile path—supposedly at LeGendre's urging—before the expedition could proceed (see map 5).[45]

LeGendre's contemporary accounts of his progress through Taiwan, which he appears to have kept scrupulously accurate within the limits of his knowledge, do not suggest that Taiwan was divided into two separate zones, Chinese and indigenous (see figure 3). He would adopt this divisive view later, after his trips to the

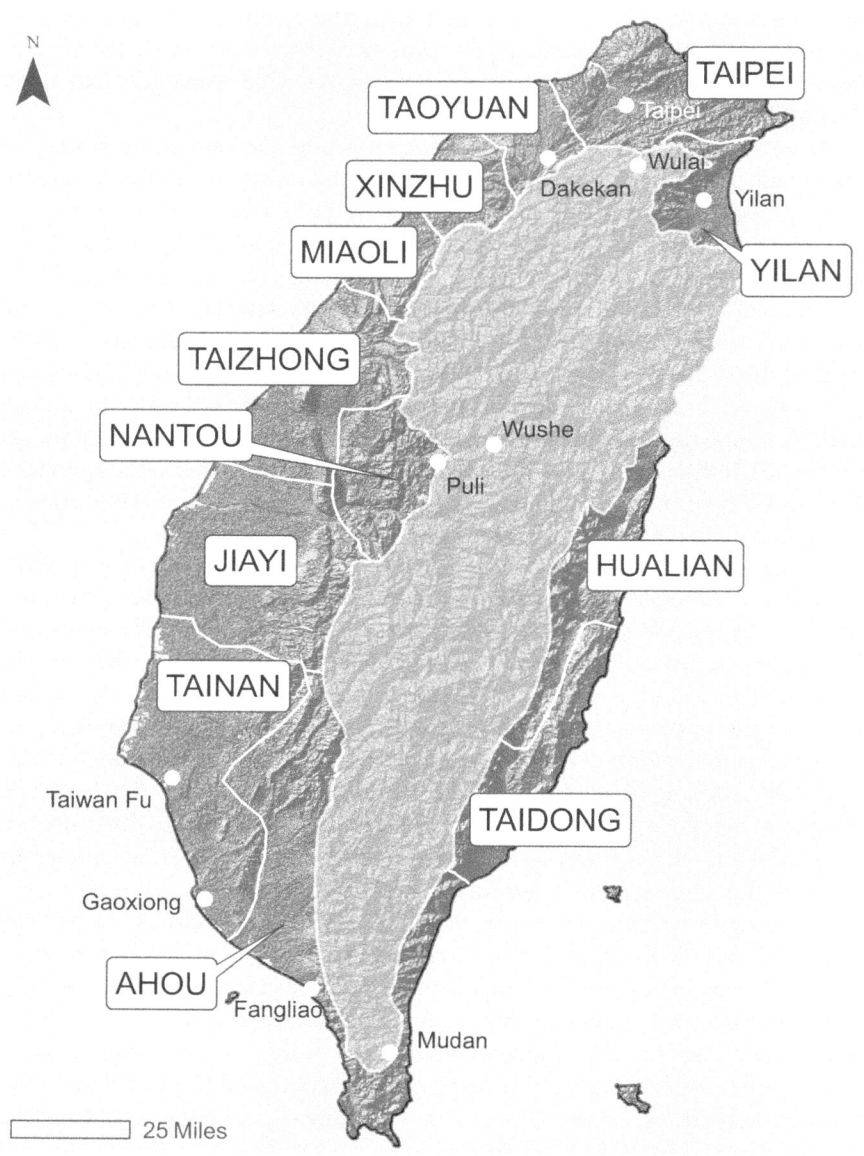

MAP 5. Principal administrative centers, contact zones, and political boundaries mentioned in this book. The Taiwan Government-General's 1909–20 prefectures are in all capitals. The lighter area of the map is TGG-demarcated Aborigine Territory (ca. 1905–45).

island ceased and his knowledge was, in a sense, weaponized for use in the diplomatic arena. As Bruce Greenfield wrote of the Lewis and Clark journals, expedition accounts subsume numerous genres of writing, each with its own source of authority. For LeGendre the amateur scientist and aspiring author, recording surfeits of local detail established his credibility and retained reader interest.[46] At the same time, LeGendre wrote in a combative, legalistic style to prosecute his official duties. In this register, later complicated by his advocacy of a Japanese invasion, his descriptions of Taiwan lost much of their veracity and took on a hortatory aspect.

During this 1867 procession and follow-up tours in 1869 and 1872, LeGendre entered a region of marked ethnic diversity and hybridity; its indigenes—predominantly Paiwan—presented outsiders with a confusing array of settlements, confederations, and diplomatic forms.[47] The principle Paiwan people that LeGendre dealt with are known as the Eighteen-Tribe Confederation. The eighteen tribes were considered to have been under Toketok's leadership in Western sources, though the bases of that leadership and what it entailed were murky to contemporaries and remain an object of research and speculation.

These eighteen tribes (including the Kuskus who killed the Miyakojimans and the Koalut who killed Mackenzie) were of Paiwan ethnicity. The primary political and residential unit was a village, with populations ranging from seventy-five to four hundred people; these villages were mostly located in the mountains beyond the western coastal plain. Paiwan villages were militarily predominant in Langqiao before 1875. They collected taxes and tribute from Han settlers. Among the Paiwan lived a smaller population of Amis people, migrated from Taidong, and people of plains indigene descent known as Makatao. Four lineages—of Puyuma or Beinan ancestry—produced the locally paramount "big stride chiefs" (*ōmata tōmoku*) such as Toketok and Isa. The four noble clans of lower Hengchun viewed themselves, and were treated by Paiwans, as distinctly "foreign." Later Japanese ethnologists referred to the lineages as Skaro peoples, or Paiwanized Puyuma. The four Skaro clans were revered as descendants of militarily powerful invaders; the southern clans that Toketok and Isa headed were also feared as efficacious and dangerous magicians.[48]

Villages, such as Kuskus, Sabaree, and Tuilasok, were located less than forty meters above sea level and sat astride well-traveled river corridors. Others, such as the feared Koaluts and Mudans, were more geographically isolated. Hakka peoples in Langqiao inhabited trade junctions between the plains and the mountains and frequently intermarried with Paiwan peoples. Today Hakka people are normally grouped with Han Chinese, but outsiders such as LeGendre and his interpreter, William Pickering, considered them a distinct people. Most remarked upon was the village of Baoli (Poliac), proximate to the two largest coastal Han settlements, Checheng and Siaoliao. This Hakka village also guarded the entrance to the valley that led to Kuskus (see map 4).

Less well-defined groups, variously called "plains savages" or "half-castes," are less easily described by ethnic labels. I will refer to them as bicultural, although many of them were tricultural. The man known to history as Miya belongs to this category. He was familiar with Paiwanic and southern Chinese languages and was related through kinship, commercial, and professional networks to a Paiwan confederation chief, a Qing general, and the headman of Siaoliao town. One of Langqiao's few ports, Siaoliao was a Han-dominated coastal village that LeGendre referred to as "half-caste." Miya would become LeGendre's factotum in Langqiao and then go on to help the Japanese establish military operations there in May 1874.

Han peoples known as Hok-los, mainly from Fujian, were the majority population of nonindigenous people in Taiwan. They also resided in Langqiao, and they were known to be in competition with Hakka settlements, if not engaged in actual armed conflict. As LeGendre and Pickering, his interpreter, were quick to point out, however, common cause, such as the arrival of Qing soldiers or defense against Paiwans, could bring these two groups together as temporary allies.[49]

The Paiwan peoples of the extreme south, who most concerned General Liu Mingdeng's Qing scouts in September 1867, maintained their military preponderance with supplies of shot, powder, and metal, purchased from Hakka traders in exchange for mountain products (furs, meat, medicinal ingredients, loot from shipwrecks). Further north near Fenggang, where Japanese troops would camp in mid-1874, Han settlements paid taxes or tribute to Paiwan villages.[50] So-called "aborigine rents" were relatively light; they did not fund infrastructure but were paid out as protection money. Villagers also paid taxes to Paiwans farther south, with the important exceptions of larger settlements such as Checheng and Siaoliao.

To summarize, for people who hoped to conduct business in Langqiao circa 1870, it was imperative to know how particular settlements were connected together and to secure the aid of people who could mediate the appropriate constellations of polities suited to a particular type of errand. Administrative ranks such as LeGendre's were of little help unless they were attached to armies on the move, generous caches of gifts, or personal connections to embedded locals.

Returning to LeGendre's mission: A little over two weeks after the U.S. consul's September 6, 1867, arrival, he and General Liu entered the town of Langqiao behind a color guard of fifty flag bearers. The townspeople prepared shrines and memorial tablets for the arriving mandarin and foreign dignitary. The locals prostrated themselves accordingly. Eight sedan bearers carried LeGendre. The consul was not bothered by the fact that he could neither read the ceremonial calligraphy produced for his benefit nor understand conversations between Liu and the reception committee. Separating himself from the seemingly unwholesome conditions of the Chinese town, LeGendre camped outside Langqiao with an interpreter and a few attendants. From there, he ran a shadow operation in parallel to the more expansive Qing effort, sending emissaries to find Toketok, the man whom General Liu had planned to negotiate with, as well.[51]

LeGendre believed that Liu's large armed retinue would impede negotiations, so he ended up meeting Toketok on neutral ground with five interpreters and a guide. The October 10, 1867, tête-à-tête lasted about forty-five minutes and ended abruptly. Toketok brought about two hundred men under arms; he had mustered some six hundred for a previous meeting in Poliac, even though his home village of Tuilasok had a population of less than one hundred.[52]

From LeGendre's perspective, Toketok was willing to negotiate because LeGendre himself and the war hero Lieutenant Captain Mackenzie (shot by a Koalut man) were brave men whom Toketok could respect. Time and again, LeGendre emphasized the personal nature of his relationship with Toketok and praised the frankness and simplicity of the Paiwan leader. He also claimed that Toketok would not deal with Han people or Qing emissaries because of their lack of courage.[53] During the 1874 expedition itself, Toketok's successor as paramount chief of the eighteen tribes reportedly expressed a reluctance to deal with anyone but LeGendre,[54] so important was the personal connection forged during the 1867, 1869, and 1872 visits to Langqiao.

It is impossible to weigh the extent to which personal ties such as the ones articulated by LeGendre mattered to the Langqiaoans. LeGendre's linguistic transactions occurred through interpreters, usually more than one. Moreover, he could not read or understand Chinese dialects. Thus the speech he imputed to Toketok, or that which LeGendre's successor, Commander Douglas Cassel, heard from Toketok's successor, Isa (see below), must be taken as approximations. While Toketok may have resented Qing officials and found common cause with the frustrated treaty-port official LeGendre, and while it was undoubtedly a bold stroke to meet Toketok with such a small escort, LeGendre's diplomatic offensive had at its back a massive Qing army and at its front a seasoned commercial interpreter who laid much of the groundwork for the meeting. Moreover, as shall be explored later in this book, Toketok was able to ritually incorporate LeGendre into a sphere of exchange and tribute by orchestrating the receptions of gifts and dispositions of banquets in accord with local forms (see chapter 3).

William Pickering recalled several visits to Toketok as an emissary from Langqiao residents and asserted that LeGendre's meeting was but an afterthought and a ceremonial ratification of negotiations largely completed by Pickering himself. More importantly, while LeGendre was discussing the finer points of shore safety with Toketok on October 10, over five hundred Qing troops, spies, and interpreters were fanning out across the peninsula threatening to exterminate the Paiwan and advertising the fact that many more Qing soldiers lay in reserve on the mainland.[55] LeGendre's introduction to the region, it should be recalled, was his grand entrance to Langqiao with General Liu at the back of a color guard and in the front of an army.

Despite this general atmosphere of intimidation, the actual terms of the "treaty" (which was never acknowledged by LeGendre's superiors in Beijing, despite his repeated efforts) suggest that Toketok was not overawed by the Qing troops. Some of the stipulations resemble the 1854 U.S. treaty with Japan: shipwrecked mariners were to be provided with basic provisions and shelter and would be brought ashore at only specified locations. However, there were major differences. For example, the 1854 treaty with Japan stipulates that U.S. sailors could not be confined at close quarters like the Dutch in their compound in Nagasaki but must be allowed to move about freely. It also leaves open the possibility of putting U.S. consuls at one or both "wood and water" stations (Shimoda and Hakodate). In contrast, Toketok's agreement restricted foreigners to coming ashore in a very specific location and did not allow them to "visit the hills and villages" of Paiwans. When Toketok revisited the 1867 discussions, he also asked for the right to kill visitors without red flags (unless they were victims of nautical accidents).[56]

It appears that some sailors were actually saved thanks to the agreement with Toketok. However, LeGendre's personalized brand of treaty making was insufficient to effect his stated aims. Upon returning to Langqiao in 1869 and 1872, LeGendre had to reactivate local networks anchored by Miya—who was not a salaried Qing official—just to locate Toketok. Then he was informed that the treaty would have more force if it could be renewed annually with personal meetings between the U.S. consul and the Paiwan headman. In addition, as the celebrated massacre of the Ryūkyūans revealed, Langqiaoans understood the agreement as valid only for sailors who could be linked to LeGendre himself (non-Asian mariners). And just as problematic, from a treaty-power viewpoint, was the fact that Toketok's promises did not carry much weight beyond Tuilasok, one of the smallest settlements of the eighteen tribes.[57]

After LeGendre left Taiwan in late 1867, Governor-General Ying Gui wrote a memorandum to the Qing central administration in Beijing with recommendations to keep foreigners out of Langqiao completely. Instead of backing LeGendre's proposal to integrate Langqiao more tightly into the treaty-port economy, he tried to prevent the area from becoming a flash point for diplomatic disputes with Westerners. Ying Gui also proposed stationing troops and officers and appointing a few local headmen (Hok-lo, Hakka, and bicultural) to rescue shipwreck victims after the fact. These representatives and troops would be stationed in coastal Fenggang and Fangliao, not in Paiwan territory as LeGendre had envisioned. The Qing plan was premised on an indirect form of supervision.[58] In short, these proposed Qing measures were consonant with the older, low-velocity tributary mechanisms described above for ameliorating, rather than preventing, incidents like the *Rover*.

The indefatigable LeGendre countered again. In an official letter to his Qing counterpart, he urged that better roads, a large garrison, and monthly displays of Qing naval force off the south coast—leavened with threats of trade embargoes on powder, shot, and other necessities—would bring the Paiwan to heel and reduce the menace they posed to commerce once and for all. Writing in 1869, LeGendre showed awareness that his propositions would dramatically increase Qing budget outlays. And indigenous villages would be forced to deal routinely with soldiers and settlers under his plan—a sure recipe for bloodshed.

According to the Qing records of the October 1867 proceedings, Taiwan officials agreed with General Liu that fort construction on the south cape would provoke the Paiwanese (whom they termed "savages").[59] Based on the events of 1875, we know that the Qing ministers had cause for concern. In the years immediately following the Taiwan expedition of 1874, Koalut, Saparek, and Mudan raids into lowland territory killed many, and one follow-up Qing expedition was massacred.[60] Even in 1867, without hindsight, it seemed to Qing officials that anything less than extermination or permanent occupation would add to the disorder that LeGendre sought to alleviate. As LeGendre himself pointed out, nonindigenous Langqiaoans who paid taxes to Paiwanese were getting off lightly. Were the Qing to extend its administration south of Fangliao, the financial burden would fall on them. Like his American counterparts who negotiated treaties with the Tokugawa Shogunate, then, LeGendre was urging the Qing to become more activist in ways that would surely create chaos, violence, and tax increases. The goal, in each case, was to expand the arena of global commerce in the name of a "general good" that, at least for the foreseeable future, did not include very many East Asians.[61]

It was not the case that all residents of Taiwan suffered at the hands of the activist American consul. For example, the residents of LeGendre's base of operations in Siaoliao, where Japanese troops would also set up shop in 1874, eagerly joined efforts to extend the treaty-port economy's reach. Wages for guide service, in addition to transshipment opportunities for the spoils of wreckage and profits from more legitimate forms of coastal trade, enriched Siaoliao residents in the 1860s and 1870s. Even before the arrival of LeGendre in 1867, the post–Opium War increase in intra-Asian junk traffic redounded to Siaoliao's economic benefit.[62]

When LeGendre received word in early 1872 that Toketok wished to see him again, it was through Miya (the son of a Siaoliao headman mentioned above) and his network that arrangements were made. Again the occasion was shipwreck trouble, this time the *London Castle*. To assist in this case, LeGendre took the initiative without an official invitation and started for Taiwan in his capacity as a "piracy-suppressing consular official." LeGendre briefly docked at the walled city of Taiwan-fu to apprise "civil and military authorities of the island" of his mission. Without personally visiting local officials in the prefectural capital, LeGendre steamed south and docked at Fangliao on March 1, 1872, with his picked men.

LeGendre expected to find a garrison at Fangliao, in addition to personnel entrusted with securing castaways from Paiwanese hosts or captors, per his negotiations with Qing officials in 1867 through 1870. LeGendre found instead that the Qing had attached a single "military messenger" to the local headman. LeGendre turned to unnamed civilians for aid, but they proposed a service fee that LeGendre declined to pay, perhaps on principle. The next morning, LeGendre's team disembarked farther south, near Siaoliao. When the party arrived on March 2, a U.S. consulate interpreter named James Johnson—himself a native of Xiamen, a veteran of the American Civil War, and a resident of New Jersey—sought out a Siaoliao man named Miya.[63] Miya had been LeGendre's guide to the area in 1867 and 1869, and for his efforts as a member of Liu Mingdeng's militia in 1867, he "was awarded the fifth military rank by the Taiwan" circuit intendant.[64]

Johnson finally located Miya. He and LeGendre then hatched a plan to visit Sabaree, a Paiwan settlement about an "hour's walk from" the coast. LeGendre and Miya hired another guide and "twenty seven Chinese coolies" to haul the required gifts for diplomacy with the Paiwans. LeGendre described Miya and his other Siaoliao guide as "half-castes," by which he meant people conversant in spoken Chinese (probably the Minnan variant) and a Paiwan dialect.[65]

A Paiwan man named Isa (also known as Esok or Yeesuk) presented himself to Miya and Johnson as the responsible leader in Sabaree, the via point for LeGendre's meeting with Toketok. Like Miya and Johnson, Isa had met LeGendre on a previous occasion. After spending one evening in Sabaree, the U.S. consul, Miya, the Siaoliao guide, James Johnson, and twenty-seven porters walked another two hours inland to Tuilasok. Today, Highway 200 in Pingdong County runs through this same corridor; it is about two and a quarter miles from Sabaree to Tuilasok. In 1872, Tuilasok was the abode of Toketok. In Tuilasok, LeGendre and his large entourage were made to wait because Toketok had been detained on matters in a different village. Upon Toketok's return, animals were slaughtered for a feast.

LeGendre inquired about the disposition of shipwrecked sailors in the area since the 1867 agreement. It turned out that Toketok had aided a few groups but had never heard from Qing authorities about their ultimate safety. LeGendre took this lack of communication or recompense as a sign of Qing bad faith. LeGendre's other reports emphasized that Paiwan settlements were jealous about the entry of outsiders and that Toketok was contemptuous of Qing officials. James Horn's reports, quoted approvingly by William Pickering, painted Toketok as a shrewd manipulator and ransom taker. It is not clear why LeGendre expected the relationship between Qing officials and a toll-state broker such as Toketok to have been more cordial, routinized, and intimate. In fact, despite having a Siaoliao network in place and having met Toketok on two previous occasions, it was no small matter for the U.S. consul himself to locate Toketok and conduct business.

It was during this visit to Siaoliao that LeGendre first heard about the plight of the fifty-four Ryūkyūans. Based on his interview with Toketok, LeGendre darkly hinted that the Chinese themselves were responsible for their deaths because the Qing government had refused to staff frontier outposts with agents who could expedite the ransom payments that would have saved the Ryūkyūans.[66]

The various eighteen tribes, as they were called, had populations of a couple hundred people—some more, some less. Their economies were of modest scale, compared to the nations that sent ships halfway around the world. Housing large groups of strangers who required shelter, food, water, and "supervision" strained local resources—to judge from the constant refrain that payment to the hosts was a sticking point for release. Sensibly, LeGendre urged that regular gift distribution and timely payments were key to securing the victims of shipwrecks. Oddly, LeGendre appears not to have considered the probability that large and routine payments to confederation leaders such as Toketok would have only increased their independence from the Qing, as well as the Hakka and bicultural settlements who provided LeGendre himself access to Paiwan representatives.

But if strong and independent chiefs posed threats to the smooth functioning of a treaty-port maritime economy, so did weak ones. As Toketok explained it himself at the 1872 meeting, his authority among the confederated eighteen tribes was contested and not wholly dependable. At the banquet, LeGendre maneuvered Isa of Sabaree and Toketok of Tuilasok into explaining their exact political relationship, which turned out to be one of rivalry. As the public face of diplomacy with outsiders, Toketok made plenty of local enemies by collaborating with outsiders. Accordingly, Qing officials did reward Toketok with gifts and payments to help him maintain that authority, noted LeGendre. (We will find Mona Ludao facing the same dilemma in 1930, when Taiwan was under Japanese rule.)[67]

Having said his farewells to Isa and the assembled Sabaree men at his second feast of the day, LeGendre headed back to Siaoliao on the coast, never to engage in palavers, gift exchanges, and toasts with Paiwan political leaders again. The date was March 5, 1872.[68]

THE MEIJI RESTORATION AND THE 1874 INVASION OF TAIWAN

Between 1867 and 1872, Charles LeGendre made a total of eight trips to Taiwan.[69] As LeGendre was shuttling back and forth from Xiamen to Taiwan-fu and making circuits of the island, the Tokugawa Shogunate in Japan was overthrown. The successor state was promulgated in 1868 with a sixteen-year-old emperor named Mutsuhito as the figurehead and symbolic apex/center. Mutsuhito is known to history as the emperor Meiji. A group of samurai, mostly from the old feudal domains of Satsuma and Chōshū, strove to build a state that could resist the impositions of industrialized Euro-American powers. Thus, the so-called Meiji oligarchs set out to collapse the status-group distinctions and regional inequalities sanctioned by the Tokugawa dynastic state. At the same time, they positioned the nascent national geobody within a complex regional system at the intersection of Western international society and the East Asian tributary system.

Almost from the start, Meiji diplomats tried to do away with tributary protocol because it diminished the dignity of the Japanese emperor by referring to him as a mere "king," a subordinate to the Middle Kingdom (Qing) emperor. Facing their neighbors, the Meiji oligarchs promoted the new form of state-to-state relations (see introduction). Japan's central authority, the Council of State, launched a number of ill-fated diplomatic initiatives to the Korean court in the 1870s to abolish older practices, finally imposing a trade treaty in 1876 through the use of force.[70]

Regarding Japan's more powerful neighbor, the Qing dynasty, negotiation was the only way forward. An early treaty was signed with the Qing in 1871. Many in Japan, however, found it objectionable for retaining the irksome extraterritoriality clauses of Western treaties with Japan and China. To revise the 1871 Qing treaty, diplomat Yanaihara Sakimitsu went to Beijing in 1872. There, he read about the murder of the fifty-four Ryūkyūans in Langqiao from the official gazette, *Jingbao*. Yanaihara sent the clipping to Minister of Foreign Affairs Soejima Taneomi in Tokyo in May 1872. This letter put the incident on the central government's radar even before the survivors returned to Naha. After the shipwreck victims were repatriated on July 12, a visiting Kagoshima man, Ichiji Sadaka, caught wind of their plights while in Naha and relayed the news to Kagoshima Prefecture governor Ōyama Tsunayoshi.

Since 1609, the Ryūkyūs had been tributary to both Satsuma domain (which subsumed Kagoshima castle town) in Japan and the Qing empire. On August 29, 1871, the domains in Japan were abolished, and the Ryūkyūs were, on paper at least, folded into the new entity of Kagoshima Prefecture.[71] However, there was still a court in Shuri castle of Naha, and the Ryūkyūans considered themselves tributary to the Qing. It was precisely during the Miyakojima sailors' ordeal in Taiwan (November 30, 1871, through July 12, 1872) that central administrators in Tokyo were devising institutional and pragmatic stratagems for integrating Ryūkyū into the Japanese state, destroying the legitimacy of the Shō dynasty, and separating Ryūkyū from China. Because of its timing, then, the shipwreck was a godsend for Japanese who sought a firmer international claim to exclusive sovereignty over the Ryūkyūs.

Kagoshima governor Ōyama's August 31, 1872, letter urged Meiji to punish the Taiwanese for harming his subjects (the ill-fated Miyakojima tribute mission) in order to "spread the imperial prestige abroad and succor the angry spirits of Your islanders below."[72] In October 1872, these bottom-up rumblings from Kagoshima gained traction in Tokyo with the aid of Charles De Long, the American minister to Japan. Seeking to drive a wedge between the Qing and Japan, De Long stirred the pot by drawing Minister of Foreign Affairs Soejima Taneomi's attention to the Taiwan shipwreck and suggesting that it be made the occasion of an armed expedition. To further his aims, De Long introduced Soejima to LeGendre, who was just six months past his last visit to the Langqiao headmen Isa and Toketok. The two statesmen discussed Taiwan with the aid of LeGendre's extensive map collection. By December 1872, Soejima convinced the Council of State to hire LeGendre as a high-ranking advisor to the Japanese court.[73]

The Meiji emperor himself received Soejima and LeGendre on March 9, 1873, and issued a rescript granting Soejima full authority to avenge the deaths of the Ryūkyūans.[74] They both set off for Beijing in mid-March 1873 to ratify a revised version of the Sino-Japanese Friendship Treaty of 1871.⁷⁵ But there was also an unannounced goal for this mission: Soejima and Yanaihara Sakimitsu would put the Ryūkyū shipwreck case before Qing officials to notify them of an invasion of the areas of Taiwan "beyond Qing government." LeGendre thought the Qing might actually cede a portion of the island and allow its permanent occupation by Japan without a fight. On June 21, back-channel negotiations conducted by Yanaihara, his interpreter, Zheng Yan'ning (Tei Entei), and three Qing officials named Mao Changxi, Dong Xun, and Sun Shida addressed the 1871 shipwreck.

The Japanese side, according to later testimony (the correspondence was not preserved), claimed to be the rightful defenders of the beheaded Ryūkyūans. They informed Qing negotiators that Japan would send a punitive expedition to Taiwan to find the murderers and punish them. The Japanese delegation argued that Taiwan was so starkly divided between its governed, Chinese territory and its ungoverned, indigenous territory that a foreign army could militarily occupy the latter without appreciably affecting the former.

Qing statesmen, led by Li Hongzhang himself, did not acknowledge these side talks as part of the formal diplomatic mission. The Qing view that emerged from the discussions nonetheless defined the Ryūkyū Kingdom as tributary to the Qing; the 1871 shipwreck was an internal matter. According to Beijing, the Qing magistrate's repatriation of twelve survivors to Naha demonstrated sovereignty. They considered the case closed. Qing officials stated that the savages *(banmin, seiban)* were but one of many border peoples whom the empire allowed to maintain separate customs and usages. Qing claims that the assailants were beyond the pale of civilization *(kegai)* and yet within the imperial realm were seized upon by Japanese negotiators, who made much of the term *kegai* in subsequent diplomatic squabbles regarding the righteousness of the 1874 invasion.⁷⁶

By failing to restrain wreckers on the south coast, the Japanese side reasoned, the Qing had forfeited its claims to jurisdiction in Langqiao. The Japanese delegates argued that it was their right and duty to "chastise" the "barbarians," either before a European power filled the vacuum by annexing Taiwan as a colony, or before enraged Japanese vigilantes stormed the island in defiance of all governments.⁷⁷ The diplomats returned to Japan with the Mudan village incident left unresolved.⁷⁸

Foreign Minister Soejima resigned in the aftermath of the October 1873 debates among Council of State oligarchs over invading Korea (the *seikanron* affair). Therefore, plans for the invasion of Taiwan remained dormant that winter. In the spring of 1874, however, they were revived to mollify Satsuma men such as Saigō Tsugumichi. In the wake of the *seikanron* hollowing out of Japan's central administration, the Taiwan invasion held together a fractured oligarchy by throwing a bone to expansionists who remained in Tokyo. On May 4, Ōkuma Shigenobu was put in charge of the "Taiwan Savage Territory Office" to occupy Langqiao. As the plans to invade Taiwan became public knowledge, Western diplomats declared their neutrality in deference to the Qing, though sub rosa support for Japan was also in evidence.[79] Recalibrating in light of foreign pressure, Ōkubo Toshimichi, a leading member of the council, cabled the expedition's commander, Saigō Tsugumichi, to delay the mission. In contravention of Ōkubo's order, on May 2, 1874, Saigō sent the first transport with 1,200 soldiers to Taiwan, with three more to follow.[80]

The Japanese expeditionary force deployed 3,658 men between May and December 1874. LeGendre himself did not participate, but his network was put to good use by General Akamatsu Noriyoshi and Douglas Cassel, a lieutenant commander in the U.S. Navy charged with operations planning. The first Japanese ship arrived in Langqiao Bay on May 7. It docked at Siaoliao, where LeGendre had disembarked for the 1872 mission recounted above.

The lengthy correspondence between Ōkuma Shigenobu and Charles LeGendre reveals that cooperation with local agents in Siaoliao was anticipated, as well as some sort of alliance with Toketok and the Tuilasok Paiwans. LeGendre recommended that Siaoliao headman Miya be sought out before troops disembarked. According to LeGendre's instructions, the Siaoliao and Tuilasok men were to be threatened with an invasion force of twenty-five thousand men and utter extermination. They had narrowly escaped suspicion for collusion in the deaths of the fifty-four Ryūkyūans, LeGendre warned through Cassel, because they had extended courtesies to LeGendre in 1872.[81]

Commander Cassel arrived in Langqiao with Fukushima Kunari, the Japanese consul at Xiamen, on May 6, 1874, aboard the vessel *Yūkōmaru*. Cassel had also taken a commission from the Japanese government to execute the punitive expedition to Taiwan. The Chinese-American interpreter James Johnson was sent ashore to locate Miya and his relatives. A payment of cash was offered to retain the services of the leading family of Siaoliao, while LeGendre's threats and promises were issued on shipboard. The following week, through Miya's orchestration, the Japanese hired around five hundred Chinese laborers, organized by headmen, at wages of thirty cents per day. The local economy received another boon from the sale of provisions and land rentals. Journalist Edward House remarked sardonically about the entrepreneurial spirit of local Langqiaoans, who leveraged their bargaining power without hesitation.[82]

On May 10, Cassel sent Johnson, Miya, and attached Siaoliao interpreters to arrange a meeting with Tuilasok leaders. Miya had reported Toketok's death earlier, so plans to work through his successor, Isa of Sabaree, were put into place. The first diplomatic encounter between Japanese officers and the Langqiao confederation was held on May 16. The encounter took place at the village of Wangsha, a small settlement called "semi-savage" in Japanese accounts and "half-caste" in English accounts—signifying its location in the foothills at the entrance to the areas of Paiwan domination.

Three Paiwan headmen agreed to meet with the Japanese on neutral ground. They refused to enter the Japanese camp near Siaoliao, and they resisted requests to enter their own villages beyond Wangsha in the mountains. The Sabaree chief Isa, who took charge of the Paiwan delegation, brought a large retinue of armed retainers. Cassel acted as General Akamatsu's translator, it appears, while he also issued his own declarations as LeGendre's surrogate. Johnson translated for Cassel (from English into southern Chinese), while Miya translated for Johnson (from southern Chinese into a Paiwan dialect). Journalist Edward House reported: "The interview was not very long, and although the colloquy was necessarily slow, requiring triple translation each way—from Japanese into English, thence into Chinese and again into the savage dialect, with the same process in reverse in replies—there was little occasion for extensive discussion. *The mere forms of meeting and recognition, and the interchange of a few reassuring words were about all that was really required."* Three Snider rifles were given to Isa and the other Paiwan headmen, and the meeting was concluded with drinks and a feast.[83]

Aspects of the scene described above were repeated late into the summer of 1874. In published writings, journalist Edward House and LeGendre emphasized the warm relations that permeated indigenous-outsider relations in Langqiao. Saigō Tsugumichi's 1902 obituary claimed that he wore the silver bracelet received from Paiwan headmen at one of these feasts into old age. This bracelet was immortalized in a postcard set issued on the twentieth anniversary of his death and in a photo attached to a 1936 tribute to his Taiwan days, financed by Saigō's family and admirers.

But Gatling guns, military parades, and intimations of larger troop deployments were subsequently brandished to intimidate the Paiwan emissaries who received Japanese gifts. And as Japanese troops began to use this firepower to destroy Paiwan bodies, villages, and landscapes, it became easier to arrange meetings. Thereafter, the conferences lost the character of diplomatic encounters and became occasions for the Japanese to enumerate demands and specify the parameters of acceptable conduct.

This paradigm shift is illustrated by the second major meeting between Japanese forces and Paiwan headmen, held on May 25, 1874. This meeting occurred three days after a battle that broadcast the Japanese Army's capacity for carnage loudly and clearly. The May 22, 1874, Stone Gate Battle broke out during the search for perpetrators of an earlier Paiwan ambush. According to Cassel, the Japanese troops blundered into Stone Gate for lack of discipline—merely to avenge the death of a single soldier. The two or three hundred Paiwanese defenders at Stone Gate were led by Alok and his son. Both were killed in the melee, along with another thirty or so Mudan warriors. Many more were wounded. On the Japanese side, between four and seven were killed and over a dozen wounded (accounts vary). News of Alok's death and the ferocity of Japanese troops—who severed a dozen Paiwan heads and brought them back to camp with other trophies of war—prompted Isa and other leaders to seek out Commander Saigō in order to avoid becoming the next victims.[84]

The May 25, 1874, conference was attended by Commander Saigō himself and was held at Miya's personal residence. The main forces of Paiwanese guards and

Japanese soldiers were kept away, since there was mutual suspicion. The five Paiwan delegates themselves arrived with a cow, ten chickens, hides, and millet wine. Saigō "ordered a very large package of very handsome presents to be brought,"[85] which "consisted of two superb Japanese swords, packages of silk, woolen and cotton cloths, and a variety of . . . 'fancy goods.'"[86]

The Japanese side, through the same three layers of translation that obtained during the first meeting on May 16, admonished Isa and the others that

> . . . there were two tribes of people with whom we [the Japanese forces] have a deadly quarrel, and that not one single man of these should escape the death which they deserved at our hands. These were the [Mudan], and the [Kuskus] who had helped them, and that, as sure as the sun rose in the East and set in the West every man of these wicked people should surely die by our hands. But that we had heard that some of the people from [Sabaree] and [Tuilasok], and the other Southern tribes had availed themselves of the mountain roads to go round and join our enemies, these treacherous and murderous [Mudan], and I wished to solemnly warn him that if this were really done, the most dreadful punishment would fall upon him and all his people.[87]

Isa, who led this delegation, did not require Miya's third layer of interpretation; like Toketok's brother and his adopted son, Bunkiet, Isa could understand spoken Chinese. He assented to the demands that Japanese troops have free access to the peninsula and that Mudan and Kuskus men not be harbored. Cassel then promised to distribute flags to sixteen of the eighteen tribes of Langqiao—Isa asked to receive them personally. The absence of the flags would then identify the Mudan and Kuskus foes as fair game for Japanese soldiers to fire upon at will. Imperial Japanese presumption of indigenous collective guilt, and the delineation of free-fire zones marked out for generalized punishment, would reemerge in the early twentieth century in the camphor wars against the Atayal, Saisiyat, Truku, and Sediq peoples of northern Taiwan.

Since the Japanese did not have actual flags on hand for villages to hoist for protection, numbered certificates with the names of the villages and headmen were issued and then distributed as promissory notes on the flags (see figure 9). It is hard to imagine how such placards might have shielded civilians from collateral damage or cases of mistaken identity. In any event, Japanese official histories reproduced facsimiles of them in their accounts of the occupation, as if to document the army's precision and discrimination, in the midst of a rough-and-ready display of brute force that sent a message not dissimilar to that of the French crown's execution of the regicide Damian, as famously reconstructed by Michel Foucault.[88] Against this backdrop of imminent threat, Cassel wrangled an agreement out of Isa for permission to build another fort in Langqiao, this time on the east coast. The sufficiently rattled Isa accepted. After these terse communications were relayed back and forth, Saigō's gifts were distributed while cups of "Chinese samshu" were passed around so the gathered parties could "drink Friendship" (Cassel's words) to conclude the proceedings.[89]

The expedition's only set-piece, scripted military operations—drawn up to punish the alleged killers of the Ryūkyūans—were raids on Mudan and Kuskus settlements from June 1 through June 3. These search-and-destroy missions were carried out by three detachments. They hacked through tough terrain and numerous improvised Paiwan defense works to cross the narrow peninsula. The sweltering heat, swollen rivers, Saigō's nocturnal bivouac, and army food shortages became part of the mission's lore. Although it was celebrated in press reportage and colorful wood-block prints as a glorious affair, the climax was less so: the burning of a few Paiwanese settlements in Mudan and neighboring Ernai. These villages were abandoned before the Japanese arrived, because they had been warned away by the skirmish at Stone Gate.[90]

To formalize the victory over Mudan, a triumphal procession was held at the Kameyama headquarters just south of Siaoliao on June 5. Three days later, delegates from numerous tribes came to meet Saigō. In American accounts, nine different certificates were redeemed for proper flags. In a Japanese account, based presumably on more detailed reports, sixteen flags were distributed that day.[91] At this meeting, the Japanese troops reinforced the lessons taught at Stone Gate and in the village-burning exercises of early June by displaying their Gatling guns and massed troops in formation. Resistance was futile. Again, gifts—though of a less generous nature—were distributed. Here, Isa consented to a Japanese fort at a specific location on the east coast, while refusing the offer of rent for the land.

The June 8 meeting can be interpreted as the culmination of a series of meetings with lower-Hengchun headmen that commenced in 1867 with LeGendre's first confab with Toketok. This sequence of complex encounters can be viewed as a progression of sorts. That is to say, over the course of seven years, wet diplomatic exchanges between Paiwan leaders and outsiders—effected by offers of gifts and pledges of mutual obligation—gave way to more scripted encounters wherein formalistic, rule-laden edicts were issued simultaneously with threats of violence. Initially, for LeGendre to meet Toketok on September 10, 1867, with a few interpreters, it required weeks of advance planning and mediation. Toketok made the U.S. consul wait and finally granted him a brief audience in his own compound. The first Japanese meeting with Isa, on May 16, 1874, was held on neutral ground, while the second one, on May 25, occurred in Miya's courtyard within shouting distance of Camp Kameyama. For the June 8, 1874, meeting, Saigō and his men didn't budge but instead waited for the Langqiao headmen to visit Saigō's headquarters (see figure 8). As Edward House reported, by then the Japanese had reckoned the total Paiwanese population of Langqiao at three thousand people—fewer than the number of Japanese forces brought to bear on the peninsula. The outcome of the military contest was longer in doubt by June 8. Therefore, the Paiwan emissaries were treated as supplicants.

FIGURE 8. Saigō Tsugumichi, Japanese soldiers, Paiwan headmen, and the interpreter James Johnson. [Saigō Tsugumichi and Mizuno Jun in Hengchun, 1874], lw0242, East Asia Image Collection, Lafayette College, Easton, PA, accessed May 13, 2016, http://digital.lafayette.edu/collections/eastasia/lewis-postcards/lw0242.

On July 1, a fourth meeting included the recently vanquished Mudan representatives. Sakuma Samata (who would become the fourth governor-general of Taiwan in 1906) acted as Saigō's delegate at this session, which was held in Poliac, the Hakka settlement that functioned as the gateway to the interior. Much had happened since the June 8 conference at Camp Kameyama. On June 22, the Qing plenipotentiary Shen Baozhen visited Langqiao and demanded that Saigō cease operations. Saigō was not empowered to negotiate with Shen, but the writing was on the wall. Japanese troops would be leaving in the near future and would not colonize Taiwan. Nonetheless, Sakuma read a battery of prohibitions and warnings to the assembled headmen and issued flags. By November, at least fifty-three flags had been doled out to Paiwan emissaries (see figures 9 and 10).[92]

But wet diplomacy was not yet dead in Hengchun, despite the complete reversal in power relations. In August, the Tuilasok headman invited Commander Saigō for a banquet with representatives from the interior of southern Taiwan. Saigō traveled by sedan chair across the peninsula. They stopped at Isa's compound in Sabaree and then arrived for a large banquet in Tuilasok. His translator Mizuno Jun's description documents indigenous-Japanese interpersonal relations at their dénouement. Mizuno recalled:

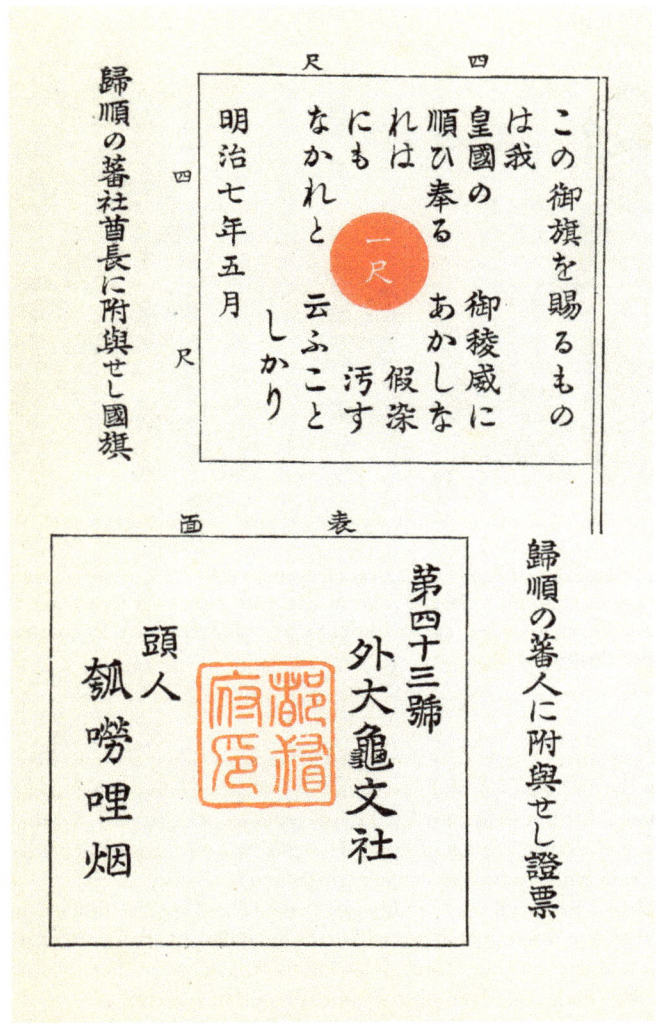

FIGURE 9. A certificate attesting submission to the Japanese Expeditionary Forces, 1874, and the schematic drawing of the surrender/alliance flag, from Inō Kanori's general history of Taiwan. Inō Kanori, *Taiwanshi* (Tokyo: Fuzanbō, 1902), facing p. 76.

A chief from a neighboring village with about ten men showed up, and a twilight feast ensued. A Chinese style wooden table was set up out of doors, and on top of it was pork gravy, deer, and pheasant with sweet potatoes, all cooked in a big pot and spread out on the table. The local sweet potato *shōchū* was ladled out of a big rice-cooking pot, and we were strongly urged to drink. While many of that day's

FIGURE 10. Photograph of families in Lower Hengchun, with relics preserved from the 1874 expedition, ca. 1910. Customs of Savage Tribe, ip2026, East Asia Image Collection, Lafayette College, Easton, PA, accessed July 24, 2017, http://digital.lafayette.edu/collections/eastasia/imperial-postcards/ip2026.

honored [Japanese] guests were renowned for their drinking abilities, they were no match for the amount of alcohol served at this banquet. This huge banquet appeared to consume a lifetime of wealth for the Indigenes to prepare, and this should have produced the best feelings of affection. However, the strong insistence that people continue to imbibe produced some uneasiness and perplexity . . .

Men then joined in a circle and began to dance and sing. Before leaving, Saigō attempted to do a little dancing himself, to the great delight of all present. The dancing was not unlike the obon dancing done in the Tokyo area. When the savages saw Saigō do their dance that evening, they were pleased beyond limit.[93]

Unlike the exchanges of toasts, drinks, and presents at the May 16 feast attended by Isa in Wangsha, Saigō's interactions with Tuilasok hosts in August were of no diplomatic import. By late July, all combatants had declared submission to Japan, and fighting had ceased. Monotony had set in among the soldiers.[94] Morale sank to new lows, and homesickness, boredom, and fatigue became widespread. Danny Orbach has unearthed a Japanese veteran's memoir stating that young recruits, egged on by their officers, were shouting from the treetops to Saigō himself, "Let's go home!," when the commander made his rounds.[95]

In addition to flagging morale, malaria visited Japanese military camps. From late August through November, the outbreak—abetted by insufficient shelter, heavy rains, lack of medicine, food scarcity, and poor sanitation—took over 550 Japanese lives. Of the army's 500-strong contingent of laborers, over 120 perished.[96] Reports in the Japanese press about illness at camps began to surface in late July; by October they had become routine. Journalistic reports were based on rumors and provided wildly fluctuating statistics. But all reports agreed that Taiwan's climate was "miasmic" and unhealthy for Japanese people, an image of the island that persisted into the twentieth century. As Chen Xuan has pointed out, however, many Paiwan people also died from diseases spread by Japanese troops and workers, while Fujisaki Seinosuke, a colonial official, himself blamed lack of resources, planning, and medical knowledge for the high death toll. In other words, the ravages of illness, which were fiftyfold more lethal than combat in Langqiao, cannot be attributed to "tropical conditions" but rather to imperial overreach.[97]

Up until the time of the troops' departure in December 1874, small groups of Japanese scouts made forays around the peninsula to learn about its social conditions and ethnic complexion. Numerous visits to headquarters near Siaoliao or the northern encampment in Fenggang for banquets or displays of military hardware were frequent. Importantly, no attempts were made to extract resources for commercial export from Langqiao or to police the day-to-day activities of the peninsula's inhabitants. There were reports of insubordinate troops committing sexual harassment and petty crimes,[98] but Langqiao did not become the site of the ethnic cleansing threatened by Cassel aboard the *Yūkōmaru* on May 7, 1874.

LANGQIAO AND THE SPECTER OF PUBLIC POWER

After the December 1871 killing of the fifty-four Ryūkyūans, Qing district and provincial officials treated survivors with utmost care; at the next rung below, local literati and traders in southern Taiwan paid ransoms to save some lives and took it upon themselves to properly inter the remains of the dead. The slain Ryūkyūans were enshrined in mass graves that were subsequently feted at biannual rites to calm their spirits. In short, the murders of Ryūkyūans may have occurred beyond the formal limits of Qing jurisdiction, but they did not occur beyond the pale of civilization, as diplomats contended. Edwin Pak-wah Leung's and Chou Wan-yao's contentions that the dynastic system for handling shipwrecks worked without complaint are important, for they speak eloquently to the Qing court's centripetal orientation, its narrow base of legitimacy, and its incompatibility with highvelocity capitalism.

As Chou and Leung indicate, the complaint against the Qing for the deaths of the Miyakojimans was launched by Kagoshima activists, not the Ryūkyūan court. The activists who remonstrated for revenge, it should be noted, were not interested in extending the parameters of the treaty-port system. Their project was nonetheless intimately connected to the horizontal integration of the Meiji state. As power was centralized in Tokyo, and the "general good" redefined as the bottom line on a *national balance sheet* instead of in terms of the exemplary moral conduct of officials,[99] the Satsuma activists—all samurai—advocated an attack on Taiwan to retain political relevance. While it is tempting to view them as members of an emergent national citizenry, aggrieved by the loss of newly imagined conationals from Miyakojima, the Satsuma men Kabayama, Saigō, and Ichiji were "domain nationalists," in all likelihood.[100] Nonetheless, the fact that low-ranking men in a geographically remote prefecture were able to exert political pressure on the Tokyo government is significant. The post-Tokugawa state could not ignore bottom-up expansionist impulses, for it had to shore up its multiregional coalition via appeals to patriotism. If the Meiji oligarchs were to build a state strong enough to remain sovereign in an unforgiving social-Darwinist world order, they would require more than tacit acceptance of the central government's primacy. Satsuma's active commitment to the Meiji modernization project was crucial, so Ōkubo and the central leadership launched the expedition even against foreign objections and those of fiscal hawk and pragmatist Kido Takayoshi.[101]

Qing support for limited forms of restorative justice and its tolerance of wrecking and unsanctioned violence on the periphery of its realm were relics of dynastic rule. The Qing did not rest its legitimacy on claims to embody, represent, nurture, and defend every one of its citizens, no matter where they were located. Its representatives even spoke of Paiwanese subjects as "beasts" and people of such low status that honorable governments would avoid any association with them. The Qing's inward orientation, as so many have noted, was not conducive to building national strength, as was made painfully clear when Li Hongzhang was left to fight Japan's imperial forces with his regional navy in 1894. Its anachronistic and low-velocity approach to diplomacy was best articulated in a formal response drafted by four members of the Zongli Yamen to pointed questions of Ōkubo Toshimichi at the September 14, 1874, negotiations for Japan's withdrawal from Taiwan. The Qing ministers wrote:

> In the aboriginal territory the Chinese Government let the indigenes keep their customs. Those who are able to pay tax pay it. Those who are talented enter nearby schools. We enforce generous and lenient policy to bring them up to a high level of edification. They are subject to the officials of the nearby districts. China stresses a gradual process of government, and has no intention to forcefully or too rapidly subjugate them. The natives of Hainan Island are treated the same. China has many regions of similar condition and every province has its own practices.[102]

In other words, the Qing realm included many areas deserving of special treatment, depending on local conditions and levels of economic development. In some areas, it was appropriate to govern very little, if at all. Consequently, at the margins of Qing rule in Langqiao, LeGendre and then Saigō were forced to rely upon a collection of headmen, brokers, and guides for hire to locate allies in their search for the remains of fellow countrymen or in pursuit of malefactors who had killed them.

Jürgen Osterhammel has argued that such "cross-border lobbies" of "pirates and partisans, semiprivate military operators and warlords" stitched the world of prenational empires together. It could not have been otherwise, given the limited state capacities of these far-flung multiethnic states, separated as they were by vast stretches of unadministered territory. As the international system consolidated itself around industrialized nation-states, however, these interstitial groups were displaced, ideally, with functionaries who answered to center-generated directives. Osterhammel terms this process "horizontal integration."[103]

Ōkubo rebutted the Zongli Yamen's position paper, quoted above, with point-by-point objections that called for the horizontal integration of Langqiao with the Qing empire. Ōkubo asserted that "a nation is responsible for the control of crimes, and when crimes are not punished, then there is no law, therefore no national jurisdiction." In addition, he stated that "tax is a contract agreed to between the ruler and the ruled, and must be applied uniformly upon every citizen and subject within the domain. Making any exception would reduce the payee into tributary status and as not owing allegiance to the ruler." To his list of criteria for demonstrating sovereignty, Ōkubo added compulsory education. He charged that "the education of only a very small minority of a tribe could not be regarded as 'civilizing' the whole aboriginal population."[104] Thus, Ōkubo advocated universal education for rural Taiwan at a time when the Japanese system itself only operated in fits and starts. Kido Takayoshi, Japan's minister of education in 1874, argued against Ōkubo's plan for outfitting an expedition to Taiwan for this very reason: Japan's own public-school system was woefully underfunded, and the nation could not afford foreign adventures until it put its own house in order.[105]

Ōkubo railed against Qing officials who "preside remotely and abandon the indigenes to their criminal undertakings." Such leniency, he urged, was "tantamount to not having any jurisdiction." Lastly, Ōkubo attacked Qing policies of attraction and voluntary submission, stating that "two hundred years of gradualism was a bit too slow."[106] Some thirty years later, Japanese parliamentarian Takekoshi Yosaburō would make an identical argument to his own central government: TGG policies of voluntary submission through benevolence were too gradual, leaving the empire vulnerable at its extremities, he argued.[107]

The endless rounds of wet diplomacy that characterized political transactions in Langqiao before 1874 were symptomatic of *"the infra-power of acquired and tolerated illegalities"* that provoked LeGendre and formed the basis of Ōkubo's case against the Qing. At the same time, as Carol Gluck, Takashi Fujitani, Robert Eskildsen, Marlene Mayo, Danny Orbach, and Hyman Kublin have demonstrated amply, the Japan of 1874 had barely made a beginning on stamping out tolerated illegalities, regionalism, dynastic myopia, and threats to central authority within its own borders. It is thus unsurprising that many of Ōkubo's charges against the Qing were based on international law as interpreted by Gustave Boissonade, who accompanied Ōkubo to Beijing on September 10, 1874, as his advisor.

The French legal scholar also coached Itō Hirobumi and Inoue Kaoru on the fine points of international law as they extended the treaty-port system to Korea by military force and diplomatic cunning in the mid-1870s. Therefore, when Ōkubo alluded to constructions of sovereignty in Beijing that resembled the instantiation of public power, he referenced the abstract writings of jurists such as Emer de Vattel, Friedrich Martens, and Johann Kaspar Bluntschli, and not conditions in Japan. Ōkubo was not suggesting that the Qing behave more like the Meiji government, but he was rearticulating his own fledgling government's centralizing aspirations in a different setting.[108] The Qing negotiators simply refused to play by these new rules (the Koreans would have less success rebuffing such arguments in 1876), and the Japanese ended up withdrawing from Taiwan that December.[109]

LeGendre himself did not envision the creation of a disciplinary society or the establishment of public power to end Langqiao's threats to shipping. While LeGendre was still getting his feet wet in treaty-port diplomacy in the late 1860s, his vision for southern Taiwan was indigenous autonomy under Qing suzerainty. Like Native Americans or New Zealand's Maori peoples, Taiwan's Paiwans could be left to manage their own affairs but would be denied the ability to enter into agreements with foreign powers. The Qing would be responsible for "restraining them" and indemnifying injured foreigners. If the Qing could not accomplish these tasks, it would forfeit the territory.[110] A few years later, in mid-1874, after LeGendre had been removed from Taiwan for a couple of years, his view hardened. His new plan B for treaty-port era reterritorialization was extermination. If they could not be pacified, foot draggers who impeded access to sea-lanes were expendable. As an alternative to extermination, LeGendre proposed making Langqiao into a Japanese penal colony, developing it along Australian lines.[111] In all of these scenarios, there was no provision for dispersing power throughout a population to make it self-actuating, as was the goal of the Meiji oligarchs vis-à-vis Japan's own citizens. At the same time, the Qing policy of gradualism, or letting border peoples maintain separate customs until they "came around," was also ruled out.[112]

This newly emerging liminal space between the old Qing posture of letting distant tribes in Hainan or Langqiao maintain their own customs until they came into the fold of "civilization" and the concurrent Meiji policy of horizontal integration at all costs for Honshū, Kyūshū, and Shikoku created the ground for the transformation of southern Taiwan's natives into indigenous peoples.

THE QING-JAPANESE INTERREGNUM AND UENO SEN'ICHI

In 1890, Foreign Minister Aoki Shūzō ordered Ueno Sen'ichi to Taiwan to investigate its commercial potential. In late December, Ueno set sail for Danshui (a port near Taipei).[113] In early 1891, Ueno departed Danshui "to meet a chief *(doshū)*" as part of his mission. Ueno described his destination as "the Tokoham region, which occupies a majority of the savage [territory] *(seiban chū mottomo daibubun o shimuru Tokohamu chihō ni shite).*[114] Ueno used the term "Tokoham" (Dakekan) loosely; the route he described brought him not there but rather to Atayal peoples then known as the eight villages of Marai (near today's Wulai). Ueno departed Taipei on a sedan chair, crossed a broad plain to Xindian, and from there traversed several creeks to the villages known as the Quchi tribes (Wulai, Raho, Raga, and Rimogan—see map 6).

By 1891 the Quchi area was a well-established trading junction for Atayal peoples to barter furs, bones, organs, and medicinal plants for cloth, iron, gunpowder, and ornaments with Chinese traders. It can be considered the functional equivalent of Poliac in Hengchun. Quchi analogously connected Xindian, and by extension Taipei/Danshui, to the mountain settlements and forests south along the Nanshi River (then known as the Xindian River). As early as 1871, European and American writers knew to travel there to pick up guides and information on their way to the interior. On the map Charles LeGendre published that year (which made its way into Japanese military archives along with Ueno's handwritten report), the river junction abutting "Koo-cheu" (Quchi) is tagged "Chiankoey the name of all the places where exchanges between the Chinese & Aborigines take place." According to Consul LeGendre, the Border Tower, just downriver, was a no-man's-land between a southward-moving Han frontier and the indigenous villages tucked in the mountains.[115] As was the case when LeGendre advanced south past Fangliao in Langqiao, traders moving south past Quchi were dependent upon such intermediaries as they could find and went past the "savage border" at their own peril.

In 1882 assistant Imperial Maritime Customs officer William Hancock also stopped in "Kochu" (Quchi) en route from Xindian. The year Hancock wrote, oolong tea exports from Taiwan were increasing annually, a trend that may have contributed to some of the frontier chaos and violence he witnessed. Hancock remarked on the presence of trading posts and Atayal-Chinese interpreters. According to Hancock, Chinese settlers in Quchi were still in danger of head-hunting raids, despite their inroads as settlers and tea cultivators. When he finally obtained passage to an Atayal village, he noted the presence of many severed Chinese heads. Since these borderland "illegalities," to use Foucault's terms, did not directly affect Westerners, Hancock did not remonstrate with the Qing to fix the problem, in contrast to the activist consul LeGendre just a decade earlier.

Hancock hired the services of a bicultural interpreter/tracker to continue inland. He stopped at a trading post to purchase samshu liquor for distribution. His guide, who quickly donned Atayal garb, weapons, and adornment before alighting, brought a small group from the interior, who were then duly plied with liquor. Convinced that Hancock was generous, they consented to a visit to an area that appears to have been close to Rimogan, upstream from Wulai. There, in a scene reminiscent of Saigō's big August 1874 feast in Tuilasok, Hancock danced in

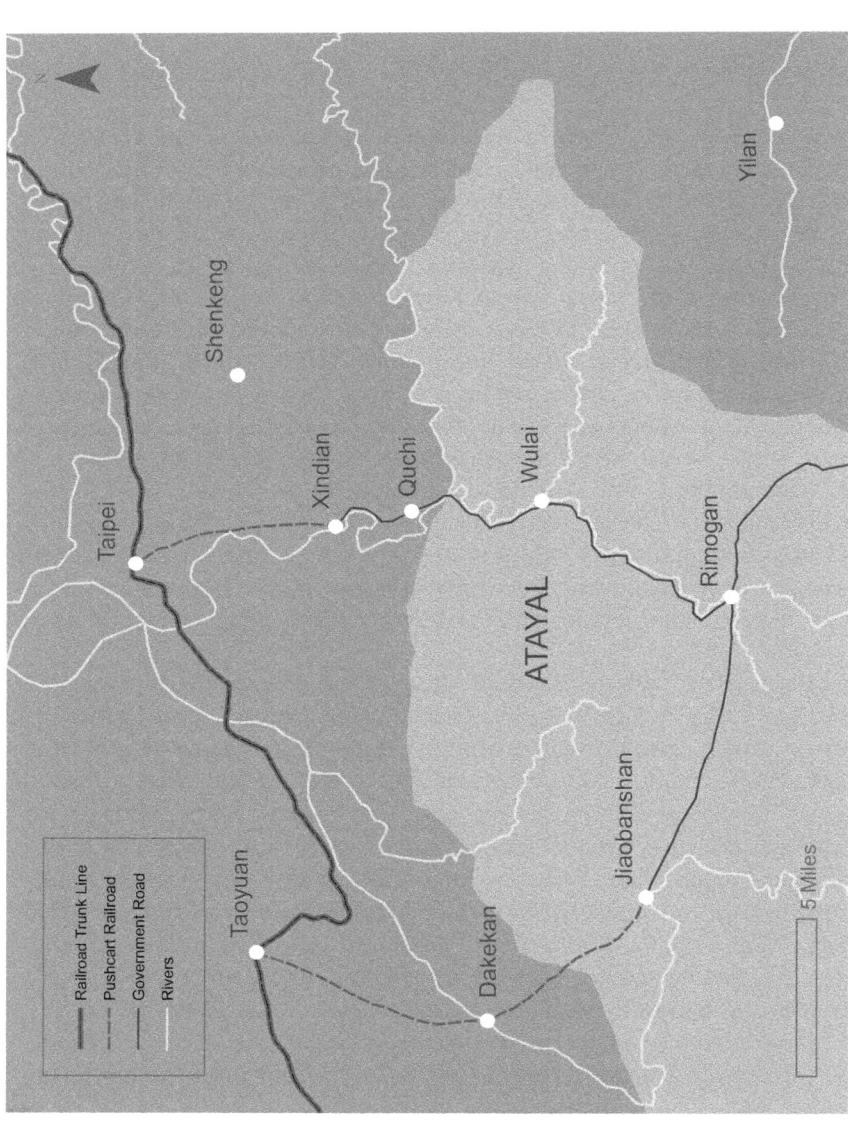

MAP 6. Dakekan, Jiaobanshan, Quchi, Wulai, and Rimogan, ca. 1910. The lighter area of the map represents the Aborigine Territory.

a circle with Atayal women, ate roast pork, and poured down cups of alcohol with his hosts. He was led back to Quchi by a different path than the one by which he had arrived, and he noted in his consular report that the village was well hidden from outsiders.[116]

Following in Hancock's tracks a decade later, Ueno finally found a guide "who could speak the Aborigine language a little."[117] Ueno ordered him to arrange a parley with the paramount chief *(shūchō no gotoki tōmoku)*. Taking his leave, Ueno's interpreter removed his "Chinese-style" clothing, pinned up his queue, donned a tunic, waist dagger, and Atayal-style cap, and set off to find the paramount chief.[118] After a long wait, the interpreter returned with six Atayal people. The guests were a "paramount chief" named Watan Yū, his wife and daughter, and three retainers. After Ueno distributed the expected presents, Watan Yū produced sweet potatoes and a bundle of rice stalks from a "head carrying bag." After this exchange of gifts, the chief, along with the other five, stood up at once and took turns striking Ueno in the chest with their right arms. Ueno asked the Chinese-language interpreter *(tsūben)* what this meant, and the interpreter replied that it was a sign of affection and happiness. It literally meant that the indigenes considered Ueno as kin, as a member of the "tribe/race" *(dōjinshu)*. Ueno then reciprocated by striking Watan Yū's chest with his right hand.

As the festivities continued, Ueno showed Watan a bottle of sweet potato *shōchū* purchased at a trading post along the way. As Ueno was about to open it, Watan asked if he could take the bottle back to his own village for later consumption. Ueno convinced him that both sides should consume it together, on the spot, in the spirit of fraternity. Quite joyfully, according to Ueno, the imported liquor was consumed. Ueno's attention to detail reveals his belief that every gesture and gift was freighted with meaning. Ueno noted that, as in a Japanese tea ceremony, after taking a drink, each person would wipe the rim of the bowl to show purity of intention before passing the bowl to the next person.[119]

Upon his return to Tokyo, Ueno published a detailed record of his observations, along with information gathered from Western missionaries and Qing sources he was privy to as a Japanese consul. These appeared in the February 1892 issue of the *Tokyo Geographical Society Journal*. Ueno also hit the lecture circuit to alert Japanese entrepreneurs about business opportunities in Taiwan and on the continent.[120] Ueno then addressed the Tokyo Geographical Society's March 22, 1895, meeting. Brandishing the earrings and cape he had received from Watan Yū and his wife, Ueno reported that the unconquered "savages" regarded the Chinese as enemies. Like Hancock before him, he portrayed Atayal people as innocents, who stood little chance against their cunning civilized neighbors, the Chinese.[121]

During his tenure as consul at Wonsan, Korea, Ueno recopied and edited his 1891 travel notes and submitted a handwritten draft to the Imperial Army's General Staff, signing the updated report October 25, 1894.[122] Three months later, the General Staff published Ueno's report under the title "A Gazetteer of Taiwan."[123]

All of these iterations institutionalized the notion that Taiwan's population was divided between victimized indigenes and Han aggressors and that the former constituted a population of natural allies who could be won over with gifts of cloth, jars of liquor, and a willingness to participate in wet diplomatic transactions.[124]

Because Saigō and Ueno were short-timers, their interactions with indigenes were perforce of a different order than those of Qing officials or Han settlers. Thus their codified and serially reproduced assurances that relations of hostility or intimacy were attributable to the respective characters of Chinese, Taiwan Indigenous Peoples, and Japanese were based on false premises. These Japanese visitors, backed by the armed might of an occupational force or the implicit threat of Qing armies, were not charged with extracting raw materials from Taiwan's interior, nor did they take responsibility for maintaining the peace between rival indigenous groups or between lowlanders and highlanders. Their faith in the efficacy of wet diplomacy would be severely tested when the Japanese government took over from the Qing and found itself torn between the notions of public power as expressed by Ōkubo Toshimichi in Beijing and the practical necessity of ruling within the constraints of finite resources. They would begin, as it turned out, by letting border peoples keep their own customs and by exercising leniency.

FEASTING, GIFTING, AND DRINKING: ATAYAL-JAPANESE DIPLOMACY IN THE COLONIAL ERA

On August 2, 1895, Admiral Kabayama Sukenori signed papers transferring the sovereignty of Taiwan to Japan aboard a ship in Jilong Harbor. Within a month, forty-six men under a garrison commander named Watanabe trekked southeast toward the mountains to initiate official relations with Atayal representatives. He chose the junction town of Dakekan, a gateway to the mountain trade. After marching for a couple of miles, Watanabe waited for a delegation of Atayals. Emissaries numbering seven, two of them women, showed up. The soldiers distributed gifts of liquor, tobacco, silver coins, and tinned mackerel to the seven red-caped representatives.

The expected drinking soon ensued. As two o'clock rolled around, the chief reminded Watanabe that a five-mile journey back into the mountains awaited. He promised to meet the Japanese later at the same spot.[125] On September 4, a mission headed by section chief of industrial development *(shokusan-buchō)* Hashiguchi Bunzō (future Taipei governor) set out from Taipei to follow up. After negotiating the actual spot and timing over days of weather delays and messages shuttled through an interpreter, the summit commenced on September 8.

The Japanese lined up the twenty-two Dakekan-area residents on a field. Then Taipei governor Tanaka Tsunatoku read a statement: "You have come from afar, down from the mountains, bringing even your women and children. We are overjoyed to meet with you here. We set out for Dakekan yesterday to meet with you because we wanted to establish good relations and to apprise you of matters of official import. To see you here in good health bearing a compliant *(onjun)* attitude makes all of us very happy."¹²⁶

These introductory remarks, made to "test the attitude of the indigenes," were followed by a toast, and the liquor was produced. Like Watanabe and Ueno before them, Hashiguchi and Tanaka found themselves at close quarters with their Atayal counterparts. In Hashiguchi's case, the intimacy produced mild discomfort tinged with amusement. Hashiguchi explained at a lecture before the Tokyo Geographical Society: "As everyone knows, when Germans make agreements, they face each other, put their hands like this, (Hashiguchi motions in imitation) and drink beer together. The indigenes are a little different. Touching their mouths together, they both drain the same cup. I don't mean to boast, but when I said 'how about some sake,' immediately one came at me with his mouth and I joined him . . . If one cannot bear to do such things, one cannot associate or communicate with the indigenes at all."¹²⁷

This was not the first time a high-ranking Japanese official joined mouths with an Atayal man. In September 1873, Mizuno Jun—then a government language scholar and interpreter—accompanied future governor-general of Taiwan Kabayama Sukenori to Suao Bay (near Yilan) on reconnaissance. Upon meeting a delegation in the Nan'ao area, Kabayama's group distributed spirits manufactured in Fujian in exchange for servings of the local alcoholic beverage, probably a fermented millet wine. Farther along, at a subsequent feast, *shōchū* was ladled out to the thirsty and tired Japanese travelers. The headman grabbed Kabayama's colleague Naritomi Seifū by the shoulder and forced their mouths together so they could down the liquor out of the same cup.¹²⁸

Returning to the September 1895 mission: after the initial toasts, Tanaka announced to the gathered men and women that the relationship between Japan and the Dakekan peoples would conform to the principles of nondiscrimination:

> Here we must communicate to you a matter of utmost importance. You should listen silently and with full attention. This island of Taiwan, the parts inhabited by you [Indigenes] and by the Chinese *(shinajin)*, has wholly become a possession of Great Japan, under the rule of our Great Emperor. Henceforth, the garrison troops and officials posted here will administer both Taipei and Dakekan, and govern everyone uniformly *(mina ichiritsu ni waga nihonkan kore o kanri suru)*. The previous Chinese administrators have fled and left, so from this day forward, you are all, just like us, the children of the Emperor, you are our brothers. Having listened well to our office's order, you will exert yourself to be loyal subjects of the Emperor and the Great Empire of Japan.¹²⁹

Tanaka's speech was communicated through Atayal interpreters and received in the context of joined-mouth drinking rituals and presentations of gifts. At the same time, it was filled with "dry" sobriquets written in lofty and abstract phrases

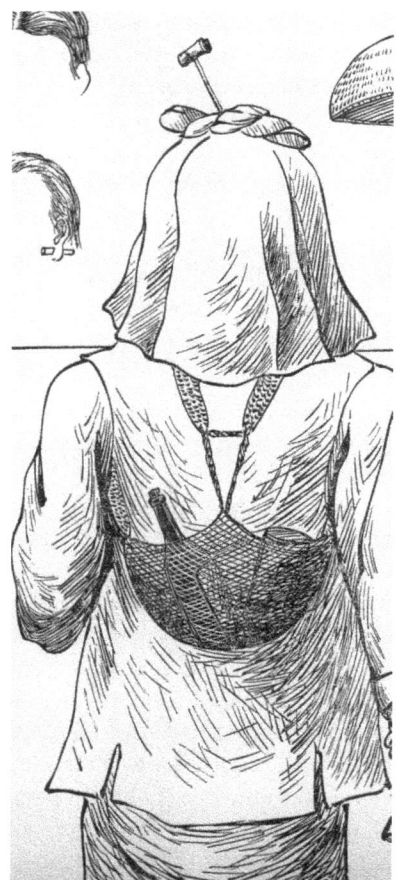

FIGURE 11. Drawing of Watan Nawi's wife, Lemoi Maton, present at the meeting during Watanabe's expedition to Dakekan. In the head-hunting bag, note the alcohol bottle and can, which were gifts brought back from the meeting with representatives of the colonial government near or in Dakekan (Daxi). *Tokyo jinruigakkai zasshi* 11, no. 115 (1895): back cover.

that disavowed special treatment or a budding personal relationship. Japanese officials would propagate these mixed messages throughout the interior in subsequent "first-contact" events.

Despite the layers of linguistic confusion, Hashiguchi's and Tanaka's adherence to Ueno's notes on hospitality and their willingness to participate in wet diplomacy achieved their short-term goal. Twelve of the original twenty-two Atayal were persuaded to visit the Dakekan garrison. Seven of these, including the Jiaobanshan headman Watan Nui (who had dealt with Watanabe on August 29), returned to Jiaobanshan soon thereafter (see figure 11). They were issued a beef cow and a written note signed by Hashiguchi and Tanaka as a receipt to commemorate Japan's expression of sincerity and its announcement that Taiwan was now "imperial territory." It is not clear from the documentation whether Watan Nui, like Toketok and his brother in 1867, requested this written record or if the Japanese team felt it served a purpose.

The remaining five Atayal emissaries were lured to Taipei with the promise of additional wool blankets. Accompanied by their Atayal interpreter, Pu Chin, they went to the capital for meetings with Governor-General Kabayama, presentations of gifts, and photo sessions. The Dakekan contingent of six (including Pu Chin) was welcomed by a brass band and feted at an elaborate banquet with Kabayama himself. They also visited a military police station, where they taunted a Han Taiwanese prisoner with threats to cut off his head and bring it home as a souvenir. These events generated sufficient excitement to be chronicled in several magazines and newspapers.[130] The Shanghai illustrated *Dianshizhai Pictorial* even published an engraving of the Japanese band serenading the tattooed Atayal men, women, and children as they dined in an ornate Chinese banquet hall.[131]

On September 12, the five emissaries were sent back to Dakekan on a boat, where they continued to drink, sing, and nap.[132] Thus the government-general established its initial method of rule in the uplands, whereby Japanese rural officials "governed" their indigenous subjects by personally distributing gifts to headmen and retainers at events that involved alcohol consumption and intimate physical contact, far removed from the habitations of the indigenes themselves.

As did Ueno Sen'ichi in 1891, Hashiguchi returned to Tokyo and publicized his observations and opinions regarding Taiwan's non-Han population. On October 13, 1895, he lectured at the Oriental Club (Tōhō Kyōkai). There, Hashiguchi reiterated Ueno's assertion that indigenes and Han were mortal enemies, thanks to the Chinese practice of breaking their promises. Hashiguchi characterized the "brigands" *(dohi)* fighting the Japanese government as Hakka from Guangdong Province. The *seiban* (raw barbarians), by contrast, were well disposed to the Japanese.[133] Hashiguchi showed up at the Tokyo Geographical Society on October 22, 1895, to repeat his performance.[134] Colorful speeches like Hashiguchi's, larded with asides, anecdotes, and speculation, remained popular in prewar Japan. At the same time, there was also an outpouring of attentive journalism and academic writing, including notes and observations about the indigenous alcoholic beverages mentioned in passing by LeGendre, Mizuno, Ueno, and Hashiguchi.

INDIGENOUS ALCOHOL PRODUCTION AND CONSUMPTION AS CULTURE

As a low-ranking official in the Bureau of Education, ethnologist Inō Kanori conducted Japan's first extensive ethnological survey of the island's non-Han population. Inō's influential descriptions confirm Hashiguchi Bunzō's report on the etiquette observed in the north and indicate that there were several types of liquor found beyond the pale of the former Qing administration. Here is Inō's description of Atayal spirit production:

> To make liquor, millet or rice is steamed in a wooden basket steamer. It is mixed in a pot with water and yeast purchased from the Chinese. This is covered with leaves

and brews for three or four days. Then the unfermented yeast is filtered out and the liquor is ready.

We should say a word about the related matter of the actual drinking. There is the special custom of two people touching the sides of their mouths together and drinking out of the same vessel. This should be called a drinking ritual *(inrei)* which expresses good will or courtesy.[135]

Based on more extensive fieldwork, fellow government ethnologist Mori Ushinosuke emphasized that Atayal people were not habitual drinkers; they manufactured and consumed spirits only on special occasions. Mori's account echoes Inō's but employs native terminology:

Rice or millet is placed in a steamer basket (called a *koro*) and then put on top of a kettle and steamed. It is transferred to a winnowing basket and cooled, and then the appropriate amount of powdered yeast is added and mixed in. It is put in a pot and a little water is mixed in, and the whole thing is covered with leaves. Then heat is applied to certain areas of the pot and it brews for three or four days. Now more water is added and the liquor is filtered in a device made from wisteria, and it is ready to drink.

In some villages, after brewing, the refined portion of the liquor is consumed first and then the rest is expressed. To distribute the liquid portion, a bamboo cup called a *zō* is dipped into the middle of the kettle.[136]

Inō's earlier account also provided recipes and commentary on manufacturing processes and consumption practices among Bunun, Tsou, and Paiwan peoples. Inō noted that Atayal and Bunun both engaged in joined-mouth drinking, while southern groups used double-chambered drinking vessels for the same purpose.

Inō Kanori's diary documents his own direct participation, revealing that even anthropologists were expected to get wet if they would ply their trade in northern Taiwan. On May 26, 1897, in Wulai (just south of Taipei), Inō was welcomed by a young *bantei* (brave) named Watosinai, whom Inō had previously met. Upon seeing his acquaintance, Watosinai struck Inō in the chest and then opened up some liquor. Subsequently, Inō and his men joined in a banquet with the village headman, Wataniurrak (Watan Yūra), and Watosinai, during which the younger man broke out into exuberant singing before the group turned in for the evening.[137] It is probable that this was the same Watan Yū who drank with Ueno in 1891.

Through firsthand observation and his study of Qing records, Inō also learned that in addition to welcoming strangers, indigenous Taiwanese engaged in communal drinking at fixed times on the ritual-agricultural calendar. On September 2, 1897, in Tōsha (near Sun Moon Lake), Inō's party was feasted on native liquor as part of a thirty-day harvest celebration. Inō and his party drank the festival liquor with young and old, finally joining in a ring, dancing and singing as participants in a scene reminiscent of Saigō Tsugumichi's 1874 adventure. Similar festivities were held when Inō's party arrived in Beinan on November 9, 1897.[138]

Okada Shinkō, prefect of Jiayi in 1905, recorded investigations of Tsou customs near Alishan. Okada emphasized that, though liquor was the staple beverage (excepting water) among the Tsou, it was not produced regularly and stored for everyday use but was only for special occasions.[139] This observation would be repeated in many later reports on various groups of indigenes in Taiwan. In sum, it is evident from contemporary firsthand observations that alcohol consumption, before 1905, was variable and often restricted to particular seasons, occasions, or festivals. For Japanese administrators in the early years, social drinking was an effective method of bringing indigenes down from the hills to government stations and trading posts in order to gather information.

ESTABLISHING CONNECTIONS THROUGH WET DIPLOMACY

Just as the five emissaries from Jiaobanshan were leaving Taipei in September 1895, Hashiguchi Bunzō ordered Captain Kawano Shuichirō to lead Japan's first official embassy to the Yilan Plain on September 14, 1895. Kawano reported that under the Qing, the border trade with the Nan'ao and Xitou Atayal was conducted privately by interpreters. In 1889, however, after a military campaign to establish a Qing presence in upland Yilan (at a cost of a thousand Chinese lives), a Pacification Office (*fukenju*) was built at the mountain pass Dingpobuwu to supervise trade with the Xitou tribes. Another *fukenju* outpost was built at Alishi to manage trade with the Nan'ao tribes. Thus, like Watanabe and Hashiguchi before him, Kawano headed for a well-established junction settlement to initiate diplomacy with Atayal peoples.

Kawano's expedition left Yilan on November 16, 1895, for Dingpobuwu and wound through narrow passes beset by bamboo thickets. The troop's ears were assaulted by howling dogs and shrieking waterfowl. The Japanese ferried across a large ravine and forded the same stream over twenty times. To avoid scaring the Atayal away, "fourteen or fifteen" men were ordered to take a rest under cover of a thicket. The government translator and two others were sent ahead. Kawano's men hiked along a valley from which they saw smoke rising from the many active camphor stoves. At a clearing, the Japanese presented themselves to ten emissaries from two Xitou villages, Xiyanlaowa and Mosu. Among them were eight men, including the Xiyanlaowa headman Yawa Ui, and two women—Kawano recorded all of their names and ages. Kawano's speech made no mention of nondiscrimination but emphasized Japan's military superiority, while it demanded compliance. Here is the text Kawano entered in his report:

> The Great Empire of Japan has recently defeated the Qing in battle. Now Taiwan and the Pescadores islands belong to us. Henceforth, you shall follow the directives issued by the Great Japanese Empire. Since the local villagers (*jinmin*) shall henceforth absolutely cease their violent acts, you shall in turn cease committing violent acts

against the residents of this district. Because they were enemies of Japan, we killed ten thousand Qing subjects in this region; we sent the other ten thousand back to China. You should not disobey the commands of the Japanese empire and bring disaster upon yourselves. [We shall pacify your hearts, everywhere cultivating virtue and encouraging industry. Eventually, we shall open a path of intercourse between yourselves and Japan.][140]

Echoing the June 8, 1874, meeting between Paiwan emissaries and Commander Saigō in Hengchun, Kawano and his men distributed a Japanese flag, gifts, drink, and food to the assembled Xitou men and women. The meeting featured trappings of a negotiation, with its attendant toasting, gifting, and oathing, but the visitors were backed with overwhelming military force just beyond the scene of the meeting. In this regard, parleys on Taiwan's "savage border" in the opening decade of Japanese colonial rule were not so different from treaty-port negotiations between Qing, Tokugawa, and Joseon officials and gunboat diplomatists.

In some cases, as with LeGendre's early meetings with Toketok or Akamatsu's first meeting with Isa, the threat was imperfectly understood or ignored. Such was the case with Kawano's mission. Despite the bluster, the Xitou men firmly refused Kawano's entreaties to visit the walled city of Yilan for further parleys, just as Watan Nui of Jiaobanshan refused a similar request from Hashiguchi to visit Taipei. They also rebuffed Japanese requests to travel farther inland. The Xitou emissaries did offer to distribute the remaining gifts to other tribes and act as intermediaries between the Japanese and the inland villages.[141] The mission succeeded in establishing rudimentary communication, but the new subjects of empire successfully parried Japanese attempts to visit their habitations.

The Watanabe, Hashiguchi, and Kawano missions all took place near the Taipei Basin or Yilan Plain, at active nodes of indigenous-Chinese-Qing communication, trade, and warfare. The junction city of Puli, farther south, shared these attributes but was farther inland and more remote from the coastal ports and cities. While the highest mountains in the Langqiao visited by Saigō in 1874 were about 200 meters above sea level, the Puli basin sat at about 500 meters, and Japan's first Sediq contact settlement of Paalan was at an altitude of about 1200 meters. At these higher altitudes, the Hiyama mission broke new ground among villages not found on treaty-port maps of Taiwan.

Puli prefect Hiyama Tetsusaburō made his first overtures to the Tgdaya (Sediq) tribes of Paalan in December 1895. Following precedent, Hiyama dispatched a "northern tribe" wife of a *jukuban* (cooked barbarian) to carry gifts and a message to the most powerful Tgdaya chief, the headman of Paalan.[142] After her second trip and much delay, four Sediq scouts came to test the waters in Puli. They were promptly treated to drinking, dancing, and photographs with a Captain Ishihara of the Puli garrison. On December 31, the Paalan headman brought five "subordinate" village headmen and a contingent of three hundred retainers, plus women and children, down to Puli. The Japanese put them up on the grounds of the old Qing Pacification Office post, sending them provisions of sake, rice, and salt. The next day Hiyama Tetsusaburō, a government interpreter *(tsūyakukan)*, and "two or three low-ranking officials" delivered an inaugural Japanese speech:

> We are overjoyed that you have come here from afar. From the beginning, we Japanese, as your brothers, have desired to meet and parley with you. Fortunately, the whole of the island has been restored as the emperor's territory. Now we have come to establish our administration on this part of the island. We are genuinely pleased to have this opportunity to meet with you.
>
> We have heard that you have always killed and injured Chinese people. This is a very evil practice. If you are really our brothers, as we have already mentioned, you absolutely must stop murdering. You may come visit our offices at any time. We, in turn, would like to go to your abodes. Today, since you have visited our offices, we have prepared a meager offering of drinks and side dishes. So let us drink with gladness to your arrival!

After hearing this initial Japanese declaration, the Tgdaya contingent replied with a counterspeech: "Murder and carnage do not come naturally to us. In the past, the Chinese have gathered strength in numbers and committed murder when catching one or two of us alone. Therefore, when we find a small group of Chinese, we murder them. But now that the Japanese are our brothers, we will certainly not act this way anymore."

With this exchange of solemn promises and admonishments, a stone-burying ceremony ensued. The anonymous correspondent who chronicled this exchange explained, "even should this stone and things thus buried disintegrate, our promises to each other shall not be altered."[143]

INSTITUTIONALIZING WET DIPLOMACY

In January 1896, district officials and Taipei authorities issued decrees and created organs of government for the purpose of routinizing and regulating contacts with indigenes. As a former Qing center of administration and hub of the border trade, Dakekan was the logical starting point. The old walled city of Dakekan housed the government-general's first dispatch station *(shutchōjo)*, the forerunner of the Pacification Offices.[144] Its chief, Miyanohara Tōhachi, applied to the government general for a modest 143 yen to fund "Barbarian Feasts" *(seiban kyōhi)* as a first step to addressing the area's endemic violence. Miyanohara acknowledged that a recent rash of murders and beheadings by Atayal people could be attributed to Japanese disarmament policies that left Chinese dwelling near the "savage border" defenseless. Nonetheless, Miyanohara trotted out a list of good reasons for Atayal to murder Han sight unseen: Qing policy was one-sided and relied exclusively on force; Han merchants cheated indigenes in trading; Han cultivators encroached on Atayal lands; and finally, Han were just as guilty of murdering uplanders as the mountaineers were of raiding the townspeople.

Miyanohara insisted that the Atayal were stubborn, obstinate, and unreasonable. However, they were very well disposed toward the Japanese and could be counted on to keep an agreement. Thus, to prevent further violence, Miyanohara invited over ten village headmen and admonished them to stop killing Han. To govern through suasion, Miyanohara argued, regular feasts for village leaders were the ticket.[145] The government organ that would forever be associated with feasting and drinking, the Pacification Office, was chartered to begin work on April 1, 1896, soon after Miyanohara made his recommendations.

The early years of Japanese "Aborigine administration" *(riban)*—the "Pacification Office period"—were later criticized for their leniency, along the same lines for which Ōkubo criticized lax Qing rule in Langqiao in 1874. As a policy that left border areas opaque and hindered Taiwan's economic integration, the gift policy became a lightning rod for invective. These criticisms perhaps overstated the government-general's largesse, however. The initial proposed budget of ¥1,293 for gifts, or about ¥215 per prefecture, was less than half the monthly cost of subsidizing a local Chinese militia to stand guard against the very same Atayal men and women targeted to receive these gifts. In short, the feasts and gift distributions held at the dispatch stations wrapped the savage-border militia's iron fist in a velvet glove. Just as LeGendre and Saigō professed the warm relations between non-Chinese foreigners and indigenes as a product of each side's sincerity, the actual meetings were held with overwhelming firepower in reserve on the side of the visitors.

As a veteran of the 1874 expedition, Satsuma man Kabayama Sukenori took a special interest in indigenous affairs. Yet his programs had to meet strict budget constraints, due to the cost of the war against Han insurgents and the fact that Taiwan was a drain on Tokyo's finances. Therefore, the twenty policemen originally requested by the governor-general for each of eleven proposed Pacification Offices, at a total cost of ¥111,181, were cut out of the budget. Instead, each station received one interpreter *(tsūyaku* of *hannin* rank), two assistants to the chief *(shujiho* of *hannin* rank), and two "operatives" *(gishu* of *hannin* rank); only eight out of the eleven stations would have a chief *(shuji* of *sōnin* rank), for a total of sixty-three officials, including chiefs.[146] In May 1896, Bureau of Industrial Development Chief Oshikawa Noriyoshi, under whose purview the Pacification Office fell, requested forty-two additional "staffers and special commissioners *(koin* and *jimu shokutaku)*" for the rural outposts.[147]

In our first concrete example of how Japan governed the indigenes "on the cheap," these 105 pacification officers were charged with intelligence gathering, diplomatic relations, commerce, and public works among a population commonly believed to cover 60 percent of Taiwan's territory and comprising at least eight major language groups (and many dialects). Although the indigenous population was estimated at around only 100,000 souls, they inhabited forbidding terrain and guarded their autonomy with widely available firearms.

Dispatch station chief Miyanohara Tōhachi was appointed first Dakekan Pacification Office head on May 25, 1896. The station itself commenced activities on June 30.[148] Within the month, local headmen accepted Miyanohara's invitations to Dakekan city for parleys. He was not sure exactly where these villages were located, however. Things got off to a rocky start when his Han *tsūji* (interpreter) refused to go inland for fear of a bandit leader known as Jian Ai. This so-called bandit was ensconced in the mountains beyond Dakekan in Shinajii, with his Atayal wife and a number of followers. Shinajii was home to many of the emissaries who had met with Hashiguchi the previous September.[149] Miyanohara heard that Jian Ai was turning the Atayal against the Japanese, so he wanted to apprehend him.

Miyanohara hired two local interpreters in Dakekan as well as two *banpu* (female Atayal) to accompany them to the interior. Their immediate target was the paramount headman Daima Weixian of Yiheng. The four interpreters reached him, and then Daima sent six scouts to Dakekan. They were duly feasted, toasted, and lodged on the evening of July 21, 1896. The Japanese sent them back to Yiheng with fancy cigars to entice Daima to broker a parley.

On July 28, a contingent of chiefs, men, women, and children representing six villages arrived at Dakekan. Miyanohara recorded, "When the indigenes arrived, the two *banpu* explained to us what sort of feast to prepare. They like nothing more than pork, salted fish, and native liquor." As it turned out, Jian Ai answered the call, while Daima did not. Miyanohara offered Jian Ai amnesty for his past crimes against Japan in return for a pledge to become an interpreter and informant on conditions near Shinajii, conditions to which Jian Ai apparently assented. Chief Daima's emissaries attributed his absence to an injured leg.[150]

Saitō Otosaku, the chief of the Linyipu Pacification Office (see figure 12), counted fifty-two villages under his charge. He reported that in August 1897, twenty of his twenty-seven men were in sick bay.[151] The turnover rate was high. In its second year, the total number of salaried officials in the Pacification Office increased to sixty-five (from fifty-seven the year before), but forty-one of these officials were new. In some posts, like Puli, the turnover rate was 100 percent for titled officials.[152] And here was a potentially fatal flaw: from the indigenous side, particularistic bonds were being forged via wet-diplomatic protocols, while from the Japanese side, duty on the savage border was a sort of exile to be endured and then left behind as quickly as possible.

The Pacification Office installations themselves were built over a period of two months, from June 2 to August 3, 1896. Oshikawa Noriyoshi, Hashiguchi Bunzō's successor in the Industrial Promotion Section, issued a thirteen-point circular defining the Pacification Office's mission. Oshikawa underscored the importance of explaining to chiefs and men of influence that the Japanese were impartial rulers. He wrote that the simple, savage indigenes could quickly be won over by

Präfecturgebäude in Linkipo, davor die Mitglieder meiner Expedition vor dem Aufbruch am 15. Dezember 1898

FIGURE 12. The Linyipu District Administrative Office, successor to the Pacification Office, on eve of expedition to the mountain tribes, December 15, 1898. Twenty indigenous porters are loaded down with gifts to bring to the interior. Karl Theodor Stöpel, *Eine Reise in das Innere der Insel Formosa und die erste Besteigung des Niitakayama (Mount Morrison)* (Buenos Aires: Compañía sud-americana de billetes de banco, 1905), 42.

gift giving, and he instructed officers to meet with headmen on appointed days, distribute presents, and explain Japan's imperial mission. Loyal villages would be rewarded with further gifts, while disobedient ones would be punished by withholding presents.[153] This last caveat presupposed that indigenous hunger for imported goods was strong enough to leverage cooperation in such operations as mapping, labor dragoons, and even turning over local peoples to Japanese police officers. For many areas of Taiwan, however, such conditions would not obtain until the 1920s or even later.

THE ORIGINS OF SPECIAL ADMINISTRATION

During the early years of Japanese rule, members of parliament and other public intellectuals advocated for the extension of the Japanese constitution to Taiwan. The debate was similar to ones raging in the United States about the Philippine Islands. At issue was the capacity of colonized populations to "play by the rules," or bear the rights and responsibilities of citizens. While the "extend the constitution" faction lost the early rounds of the debate, over the course of Japanese colonial rule in Taiwan, a great deal of legal integration between the mother country and the colony actually occurred. However, the geographic reach of this integration stopped at the areas beyond the old Qing savage border, in the areas placed under "special administration."

Early debates about the legal bifurcation of Taiwan, into normally and specially administered zones, occurred in the spring of 1897. Then, the Pacification Office heads met under the aegis of Oshikawa to chart a course for the future based on their first eight or nine months of field experience. One of the burning issues regarded punishments for head taking, robbery, and other violent crimes—the myriad "illegalities" that fester in ungoverned areas beyond the reach of "public power," to use Foucault's phraseology. Hiyama Tetsusaburō, the first Japanese prefect posted to Puli, argued that Japanese law could not be applied to the Sediq peoples under his charge. Echoing the Zongli Yamen members who contested Ōkubo two decades prior, Hiyama argued that, if penalized severely for murder, as called for in Japanese law, Sediq people would rebel en masse. Besides, Hiyama added, if Japan enacted a strict, consistent law code for the Sediq and Atayal peoples, it could only be applied to those who had shown themselves at the Pacification Offices. In the end, he recommended an ad hoc form of punishment, appropriate to the means at the disposal of the overstretched colonial state: "for those who take heads, cut off their gifts completely, stop distributing liquor, and stop giving them their needed salt."[154]

On the last day of the aforementioned conference, the Civil Affairs Bureau of the Taiwan Government General issued regulations to the prefects, subprefects, and gendarmes *(kenpeitai)* in regions with significant non-Han populations. The regulations are prefaced by a recognition that hunting was crucial to indigenous livelihoods, explaining that a complete ban on guns was inadvisable. Nonetheless, the following restrictions were put into effect to check what was perceived as rampant disorder:

1. Merchants must have a certificate/warrant *(shōmei)* from the Pacification Office head to supply indigenes with gunpowder—no exceptions *(kyokashō)* or special permits *(tokkyo shō)* are allowed.
2. Those who are not merchants must have a permit/permission *(kyoka)* from the Pacification Office to supply indigenes with gunpowder; for hunting rifles, the police and gendarmes may supply up to 3 *hyakume* (about 375 grams) of gunpowder or 500 percussion caps/fuses; to supply over this limit requires permission of the prefect.
3. The distribution of gunpowder to indigenes falls within the purview of the Pacification Office and therefore should be witnessed by officials.
4. The Pacification Office must issue a monthly report to the police and gendarmes stating the amount and kinds of gunpowder distributed to indigenes.[155]

Some Pacification Office heads judged the 1897 regulations on trade as too lenient. In the fall of 1897, Nagano Yoshitora, who replaced Hiyama Tetsusaburō as Puli

Pacification Office chief in July, argued that Atayal tribes were more bloodthirsty than the Bunun tribes who resided south of Puli. Nagano agreed that the new regulations on gunpowder and shot should be observed in the south, but that a complete ban should be put into effect for Atayal. In keeping with the early Japanese view that the indigenes were, at heart, good subjects, Nagano suggested that the northern "savages" be reformed by taking them on sightseeing tours of Taipei.[156] After sufficient transformation, the trade in gunpowder and shot, so vital to peoples who relied on hunting for protein, could be resumed.[157] In fact, Nagano's recommendation was taken to heart, and a delegation of indigenous representatives toured Japan that year; they were received by throngs of curious onlookers. In the short term, the tours did not have the intended effect of reducing violence related to camphor forests, however.

In response to a report that the Wuzhishan Pacification Office had punished a camphor worker's murder by levying a "traditional fine" of shell-money currency, Division of Interior head Sugimura Shun took exception. "Traditional" punishments, even if supplemented by embargoes of trade or the cessation of gifts, he argued, would embolden indigenes and cause them to despise the weak government. Outraged, Sugimura suggested that Pacification Office chiefs use gifts as weapons, and that trade embargoes, as means of collective punishment, could force the hands of indigenous leaders. Before resuming trade, the Pacification Office should

1. Order that the indigenous perpetrator be delivered.
2. After receiving the delivered perpetrator, deal with them by applying the law.
3. During the time that the perpetrator has not been delivered, the whole village should be held responsible: the distribution of gifts will be suspended; it goes without saying that the sale of arms and ammunition will be strictly banned.
4. During the period referred to in item 3, other villages will be ordered to cut off commerce/communication with the [offending] village.[158]

In July 1897, Kawakami Chikakata, Pacification Office head in southern Taiwan's Fanshuliao Prefecture, also railed against the patchy sovereignty that characterized Japan's government along the savage border. Kawakami noted that many camphor harvesters were forced to present gifts to indigenous headmen for access to the forests; some demanded rattan, others tea leaves. These audacious headmen even collected tribute outside the so-called Aborigine Territory. The indigenes were acting under the mistaken impression that they "owned the land" and could force outsiders to pay tribute, which in turn required the services of the hated "go-betweens," who were completely untrustworthy, according to Kawakami. In the end, commerce and "Aborigine education" were impeded because of blurred distinctions between public and private. Kawakami suggested that all lands abutting the Aborigine Territory be put under the jurisdiction of the Pacification Office.[159]

THE FUKAHORI MISSION AND THE END OF WET DIPLOMACY

While the Pacification Office was still operative, in February 1897, an expedition led by one Captain Fukahori Yasuichirō disappeared in the Neng'gao mountain peaks just northeast of Puli while searching for a potential railway route to Hualian Harbor. Captain Fukahori left Puli in late January 1897, and by March, all fourteen of his men were given up for dead. In April the local garrison chief initiated a prolonged, frustrating series of negotiations with area headmen to find the remains and the Fukahori expedition's murderers. Reminiscent of LeGendre's search for the remains of shipwreck victims in 1860s Langqiao, the usual methods of gift presentations backed by threats were used, but the area headmen stonewalled the investigation.[160] To pour salt in the wounds, a camphor worker was slain by Tgdaya locals at the same time. In retaliation for Fukahori's disappearance, the stymied investigation, and the fresh killing, the government imposed an embargo on salt, ammunition, and guns for eight whole years.[161]

As we have seen, the Pacification Office officials operated through concentric rings of intermediaries at this time. The whole structure was bound together by the distribution of material goods and the forging of personal bonds through drinking rituals. The first intermediaries were the "Aborigine interpreters," male and female, who were sent to mountain redoubts to bring headmen to the Pacification Office stations with promises of gifts, food, and drink. The next ring of intermediaries were the "conciliated/submitted" indigenes who carried invitations to other villages, bringing more headmen, interpreters, warriors, and children to the Pacification Office's banquets, gift distributions, and trading fairs. Although this system performed well enough for an understaffed, poorly informed, outnumbered set of rural outposts, it could not protect camphor harvesters from indigenes who felt cheated of customary tolls or were defending what they considered ancestral territory. Moreover, indigenes desperate for salt, guns, ammunition, or machine-made cloth traded through other indigenous groups to subvert the embargo.[162] Rightly sensing that the understaffed, lightly armed, and linguistically disadvantaged Pacification Office could not extend sovereignty by wet diplomacy alone, the government-general decided to abolish it altogether and place indigenous affairs within the purview of the Third Section of the lowest rung of the territorial administrative hierarchy, the District Administrative Office (*Benmusho*, hereafter DAO).

After the DAO replaced the Pacification Office in the summer of 1898, Japanese rural administrators repeatedly called for tougher measures against the indigenes who fought back against aggressive timber harvesting. Time and again, administrators called for trade blockades to be used as incentives for good behavior. In other words, now that the Japanese, like the Qing before them, were taking sides in an economic war for rights to harvest timber along the savage border, mentions of Japan's "special relationship" to indigenes disappeared.

In February 1900, Governor-General Kodama Gentarō lambasted the policies of his predecessors Kabayama, Mizuno, and Hashiguchi. With insurrection ebbing in the plains areas, Kodama declared, "we must shift our military forces to the savage territory. Those who live there are stubborn, and live like wild beasts; if we continue to feast them with liquor and food, staying with a policy of attraction, it will take many months and years for them to reach even a limited degree of evolutionary development."[163] And here was the crux of the matter: wet diplomacy would not make indigenes into loyal, governable, imperial subjects in a timely manner. For Kodama, the clock was indeed ticking, as Japan was a relatively poor country playing in the high-stakes international game of competitive colonialism. In late 1900, Japan was undergoing a massive armament expansion to prepare for war against Russia and could not afford to manage a colony in the red.

The years 1896 through 1900 paved the way for the aggressive measures that followed. During this interval, gift distribution centers became trading posts, with fixed exchange rates. Having established the posts as primary nodes of exchange, the government-general then began to impose selective embargoes against mischief-makers.[164] By this method, devised from expedience but also based on field reports about wet diplomacy from the 1870s and 1880s, Japanese officials in northern Taiwan's mountain districts had cultivated an effective network of collaborators, trading partners, informants, and mercenaries to go along with a rudimentary knowledge of local political conditions.

The effectiveness of wet diplomacy as a stepping-stone to the eradication of indigenous sovereignty is best illustrated by a notorious 1903 incident on the Sediq/Bunun border just south of Wushe. The grislier details and some of the specifics come down to us through memoirs many decades after the events, so there are factual discrepancies in these accounts. The cataclysm had its origins in the salt embargo placed on the Tgdaya tribes after the disappearance of the Fukahori mission in early 1898. On December 16, 1902, the Puli subprefect dispatched a "savage woman *[banpu]* named Iwan" to sound out Tgdaya tribes about an upcoming Japanese punitive expedition to the north. Iwan learned that they sought a truce with Japan in order to resume trade in salt. Besides, they were engaged in a cycle of revenge feuding with neighboring Toda and needed arms and ammunition.[165] Iwan was a common name in the Tgdaya region, so it is hard to say if Iwan Robao (see chapter 2) is the person mentioned in the above report. Nonetheless, Deng Xiangyang, Aui Heppa, and Pixo Walis have all attributed the planning of the "Bukai incident" that followed Iwan's reconnaissance to Kondō Katsusaburō and his Paalan wife, Iwan Robao.[166] This interpretation is consistent with other documented facts, but I have yet to find direct documentary evidence of Kondō's involvement.

On October 5, 1903, the continued economic blockade drove Tgdaya men into a bloody trap. Short of salt and firearms, men from Paalan consented to a meeting with Gantaban men of the Bunun group south of Puli, at Shimaigahara (Bukai).

FIGURE 13. Gantaban men at the Puli branch office with severed heads of Paalan and Hōgō men, October 1903. Jun'eki Taiwan Genjūmin kenkyūkai, ed., *Inō Kanori shozō Taiwan Genjūmin shashinshū* (Taipei: Jun'eki Taiwan Genjūmin hakubutsukan, 1999), 115. Photograph courtesy of the publisher: The Shung Ye Museum of Formosan Aborigines, Taipei.

The meeting's pretext was Gantaban's promise to funnel embargoed goods to Paalan behind the government's back. On the appointed day, the Gantaban trading delegation served the Paalan men large quantities of alcohol to initiate talks. Thereafter, concealed men rushed in, killing 95 of the 100 Paalan men and taking their heads.[167] The Japanese press reported 104 dead along with a yield of 57 rifles, 130 spears, and 127 daggers. The Bunun warriors brought 27 of the heads to the Puli subprefect, who appears to have expected this outcome (see figure 13).[168] The TGG file gives similar casualty figures while noting that Wushe's once reluctant posture toward the Japanese was much improved.[169]

THE CAMPHOR INDUSTRY AND THE GUARDLINE

The causes of armed conflict along the indigenous-Han border were multiple. Japanese officials reported a surge in revenge killings and ritually sanctioned head taking in the wake of Japanese arms confiscation sweeps that were part of the antibandit campaigns of 1896 through 1902. But most of the killings represented efforts by indigenes to defend hunting grounds, fallow fields, or forests previously subject to fees levied by headmen on camphor harvesters. These camphor-related killings dated from the treaty-port period (1860–1895), reached a fever pitch by 1900, and climaxed in a major battle between the Japanese state and Ri Aguai in late 1902.

The camphor tree (*Cinnamonium camphora,* or *Camphora officinarum,* or *kusunoki* in Japanese) "is a rather small-leafed evergreen, attaining . . . [a] height of from sixty to one hundred feet, with wide-spreading branches and a trunk two to four feet in diameter." By century's turn, the western plains had been denuded. Camphor was still abundant, however, in the "debatable land between the Savage territory" and the foothills.[170] The aggressive collection of the product in the latter half of the nineteenth century incited warfare between highlander and lowlander, creating a frontier that resembled a permeable membrane; commerce flowed through, but armies and lowlanders were kept at bay. During the last decade of Qing rule, government losses from these battles were horrendous, totaling hundreds of casualties per encounter.[171]

Camphor, traditionally used as an insect repellent and medicine, had been harvested in Taiwan since the seventeenth century, but developments in technology and politics increased the product's value sharply in the late nineteenth century. In 1858, Englishman Alexander Parkes invented a way to use camphor in the manufacture of celluloid, which meant that "combs, tobacco pouches . . . and indeed everything which had before been made of ivory, coral or tortoise-shell now came to be made of celluloid."[172] Camphor also became a crucial ingredient in the production of smokeless gunpowder during the latter half of the century.[173] In the same year that Parkes put camphor on the industrial map, the Treaty of Tianjin forced Taiwan's two major ports to open to international trade as part of the settlement of the so-called Arrow War. With demand for camphor up, increased numbers of foreign traders called on Taiwan's ports, and an influential comprador class emerged. By 1878, the export economy of camphor, tea, and sugar "absorbed about twenty percent of [Taiwan's] population."[174] The Lin family of Wufeng, who later supplied the Japanese colonial government with its first hired troops to guard the camphor districts, were part of this class.[175]

The old Lin guardline stretched from Taizhong city to Puli.[176] Iriye Takeshi, an infantryman who surveyed the area in 1896 for the army and wrote extensively for the trade press about Taiwan's indigenes, reported that these private guards *(aiyong)* could be bought off and had conspired to allow the murder of Japanese telegraph-wire stringers in February 1896.[177] By 1898 camphor manufacturers were hiring their own guards in addition to the ones employed by the Lins and subsidized by the Japanese government. One company paid out ¥1,200 per month for its own security.[178] That same year, the Taiwan Government-General began recruiting guards for its rural installations in the foothills. With the emergence of camphor as a pillar of state revenue collection, the government-general abdicated its role as referee between indigene and Han and jumped onto the playing field as a partisan of the lumber business. The total number of government and privately employed camphor guards totaled over 1,100 in 1898.

The majority were Taiwanese resident in the border areas, working under Japanese police officers. With these forces, sporadic Japanese-led military offensives were launched against villages accused of attacking government installations, experimental camphor plots, or Taiwanese plainsmen. These episodic "punitive expeditions" *(tōbatsu)* had mixed results—at times whole villages were burned, at other times companies of Japanese officers with their squads were routed and killed. Many battles were inconclusive.[179]

Recorded instances of armed conflict totaled 79 in 1897; they more than trebled to 271 in 1898. In each of the years between 1898 and 1901 (inclusive), over 500 deaths and 100 injuries were dealt out to government forces by indigenes near the guardlines. The great majority of the casualties were Han and *jukuban* Taiwanese (see table 1).

A look at the financial stakes for the central government in Japan explains why the Taiwan Government-General was willing to absorb so many losses. In 1896, expenses related to war and civil government in Taiwan cost the Japanese Treasury 11 percent of its annual budget. From 1895 to 1902, subsidies to Taiwan were about 7 percent of the Japanese national budget. By 1898 there were calls in Japan for the sale of the new colony back to China or to a European power.[180] In this atmosphere of crisis, Governor-General Kodama Gentarō and his civil minister Gotō Shinpei took charge of the colony in February 1898.[181] Gotō's short-term solution to the colony's financial problems was a government monopoly on opium, camphor, and salt. By instituting a government monopoly on camphor in June 1899, the government-general not only received the profits from a lucrative export product but also forced up the world price, since the only major competitor was Japanese camphor. As table 2 illustrates, with the exception of 1903, which showed uncharacteristically low yields for the monopoly, camphor consistently supplied 13 to 30 percent of the Taiwan-generated revenue for the colonial state during the critical 1900 through 1907 period of Japan's rule.

To finance projects in governmentality that would ultimately make the Han-dominated lowlands into a disciplinary society (see introduction), Gotō secured a Japanese government bond issue of ¥35 million in 1898. The proceeds were earmarked for railroads, land surveys, harbors, and other improvements. Between 1899 and 1905, the Taiwan Government-General received ¥31.2 million in installments from this bond issue, which gradually overtook and then replaced Tokyo's annual subsidies. (For this period, Taiwan's annual revenues, subsidies included, were a little over ¥10 million.) The home government released this money expecting the government-general to repay it out of the colonial budget.[182]

To increase the output of camphor and reduce injuries to the labor force, all privately employed guards were brought under the command and employ of the

TABLE 1. Military encounters between the colonial government and Taiwan aborigines, 1896–1909

Year	Cases	Killed		Wounded		Total		Total casualties	Casualties per case
		Jpn	Twn	Jpn	Twn	Killed	Wounded		
1896	41					63	16	79	1.93
1897	79					151	15	166	2.10
1898	271	21	536	8	126	557	134	691	2.55
1899	293	21	510	6	144	531	150	681	2.32
1900	314	95	430	34	81	525	115	640	2.04
1901	342	7	503	2	121	510	123	633	1.85
1902	273	8	303	23	98	311	121	432	1.58
1903	140	4	225	7	53	229	60	289	2.06
1904	185	27	254	13	100	281	113	394	2.13
1905	196	43	284	8	67	327	75	402	2.05
1906	169	71	173	15	103	244	118	362	2.14
1907	172	61	269	53	247	330	300	630	3.66
1908	89	24	68	14	38	92	52	144	1.62
1909	203	35	155	41	143	190	184	374	1.84
Total	2,767	417	3,710	224	1,321	4,341	1,576	5,917	2.14

SOURCES: Data from Formosa Bureau of Aboriginal Affairs, *Report on the Control of the Aborigines in Formosa* (Taihoku: Government of Formosa, 1911), adapted from table iv, 45; Mochiji Rokusaburō, *Taiwan shokumin seisaku* (Tokyo: Fuzanbō, 1912), 393; *Taiwan jijō* (Taihoku: Taiwan Government-General, 1923), 93; *Riban gaikyō* (Taihoku: Taiwan sōtokufu keimukyoku [Taiwan Government-General Bureau of Police Affairs], 1935), 70–71.

TABLE 2. Sources of revenue for the colonial administration, 1897–1907

Year	Tax revenue (¥ millions)	Net revenue from monopolies (¥ millions)	Revenue generated in Taiwan (¥ millions)[a]	Camphor profit (¥ millions)	Camphor as % of monopoly revenue	Camphor as % of local revenue[b]
1897	2.63	0.42	3.05	0.00		
1898	2.91	1.47	4.38	0.00		
1899	3.51	0.75	4.26	−0.24		
1900	3.27	2.63	5.90	1.75	66.5%	29.7%
1901	3.52	1.83	5.35	1.09	59.4%	20.4%
1902	3.81	2.64	6.45	1.10	41.8%	17.1%
1903	3.82	1.85	5.67	0.27	14.7%	4.8%
1904	5.67	3.00	8.67	1.29	42.9%	14.9%
1905	7.65	3.54	11.19	1.99	56.1%	17.8%
1906	8.34	5.16	13.50	1.77	34.3%	13.1%
1907	8.54	7.00	15.54	3.58	51.1%	23.0%

[a] For this calculation, I am only considering revenue generated in Taiwan (the total of tax revenue plus net revenue from monopolies); I am excluding subsidies from the Japanese treasury and bond sales.

[b] For this calculation, camphor profit is shown as a percentage of revenue generated in Taiwan.

SOURCE: Data from Ka Chih-ming, *Japanese Colonialism in Taiwan: Land Tenure, Development, and Dependency, 1895–1945* (Boulder, CO: Westview Press, 1995), 55–63.

Japanese government in 1902. Then, on January 27, 1903, all affairs pertaining to the indigenous territories were moved from various provincial and subprovincial offices to the jurisdiction of the central police headquarters in Taipei. In March 1903, Kodama and Gotō convened a conference of all high-ranking officials on the island to discuss a plan for ending "the Aborigine Problem." The committee was chaired by Mochiji Rokusaburō, a councillor in the Ministry of Civil Affairs.[183]

During his ten years in Taiwan, Mochiji worked in provincial administration, engineering, communications, and education.[184] In December 1902, he was sent on an inspection tour of the aborigine border. The resulting "Mochiji line" was approved and codified as a working document at the "Provisional Section for the Investigation of Affairs in the Aborigine Territory," convened in March 1903.[185]

As a proponent of the governmental modality discussed in the introduction, Mochiji urged calculated restraint after an initial "big bang" of brutal landscaping to create the playing field for modern economic growth. Instead of eradicating the indigenes, which would have been an expensive, drawn out, and ultimately pointless enterprise (from the standpoint of efficiency), Mochiji argued that Japanese offensives be limited to areas that would bring in enough revenue to justify the expenditures of life and treasure.[186] With these priorities in mind, Mochiji proposed a three-pronged approach to savage border policy: (1) to unify command under one head; (2) to divide the indigenous territory into the north and south—treating the northerners (Atayal, Saisiyat, Truku, and Sediq) as hostiles and the southerners (Bunun and presumably Paiwan) as allies; and (3) to revive the Chinese guardline system to surround the hostiles in the northern district.[187] Mochiji's academic credentials made him a true exemplar of "Meiji youth," a generation for whom social Darwinism formed the backbone of a modern, scientific worldview.[188]

According to Mochiji, in cases where inferior races came into contact with superior ones, "history" taught that the inferior race was either eradicated in the struggle for survival or assimilated to the superior race.[189] His analysis suggested that indigenous defense of local forests was an affront to imperial prestige: "Until we solve this problem with the indigenes, we will not have sufficient cause to boast to the outside world of our nation's will and ability to expand and be enterprising. The Aborigine territory occupies 56% of the island's surface, and is a storehouse of mineral, forest, and agricultural wealth. Unfortunately, the savage and cruel indigenes have thrown up a barrier to this storehouse of natural resources."[190]

Echoes of treaty-port rhetoric are audible in Mochiji's position paper. In the 1860s and 1870s, it was Paiwan treachery that endangered free trade and use of the sea-lanes, thus thwarting "progress." Now it was the "aborigine problem" on Taiwan's forested inland sea that frustrated imperial Japan's drive to become a first-rank nation-state.

From 1903 until 1909, the Taiwan Government-General extended guardlines around the perimeter of northern indigenous territories. The extension process involved building trails, stringing wire, and erecting guardhouses in cooperation with hired, allied, or coerced Taiwanese. The case study of the Quchi alliance in chapter 4 indicates that the networks, knowledge base, and control over trade established during the Pacification Office and DAO periods made it possible to close this perimeter before marching it inward. Large-scale coordinated military offensives were the exception during the 1903–09 extension period; more common were skirmishes that came from attacks on advance posts, camphor workers, and police installations. To build the first strongholds, Japanese forces put mortars and other forms of mountain artillery at commanding heights to provide cover for timbering, wire-hanging, and construction crews. All of these men were exposed to sniper fire, boulder cascades, and sabotage from above. The Bureau of Aboriginal Affairs recorded a total of 1,154 such confrontations for the 1903–09 period, for a total of 1,693 killed and 902 wounded on the government side. The great majority of the casualties were Taiwanese (see table 1). One estimate of the number of indigenous casualties put the figure at 30 percent of the number of Japanese casualties.[191]

The next phase brought overwhelming force to bear on mobile, motivated, and fugitive populations in the deeper mountain recesses of central northern Taiwan. The price tag for this endeavor and its timing support this book's contention that the attempted integration of former Qing peripheries into the Japanese polity was a continuation of the treaty-port project to accommodate higher volumes and velocities of global commerce by expanding the radius of public power. While Governor-General Sakuma lobbied to fund a military "surge" in Taiwan's northern and central mountain forests, the government-general also battled to secure funds to expand and deepen Jilong Harbor.

In sync with guardline construction to pipe flows of camphor from interior to port, Jilong Harbor had been subject to dredging and incremental improvements since 1898 to push bulk commodities, including camphor, onto the world market. Initially, the government in Tokyo dribbled out only small fractions of TGG funding requests, often reducing or suspending allocations. In 1906, the twenty-second Diet finally released a large sum—over ¥6 million—for a seven-year harbor improvement plan. But increased demand for Taiwanese rice and camphor exceeded the harbor's capacity to service sufficiently large cargo ships to clear the docks. Therefore, the Diet earmarked another ¥5 million in 1912, to be disbursed over a fourteen-year period.

By 1917, a total of ¥11,720,000 had been allocated, out of ¥15,700,000 million requested over an eighteen-year period, to build Jilong Harbor.[192] For the duration of colonial rule, Jilong dominated Taiwan's foreign trade in ship traffic and tonnage. Unlike the budget for Sakuma's punitive expeditions, however, the Jilong Harbor budgets were paid completely out of the Tokyo treasury.[193] Nonetheless, their roughly equal cost suggests the urgency and magnitude of the "Aborigine problem" for advocates of an aggressive policy circa 1909.

Sakuma's famous five-year plan (1910–14) was actually his second five-year plan. The first five-year offensive was launched in 1907. Sakuma sought mass surrenders and, apparently, glorious victories crowned with parades and triumphal arches. These failing, Sakuma's staff submitted a budget to the twenty-fifth Diet with ¥15,399,000 slotted for the construction, staffing, and movement of the guardlines, to be disbursed and spent over a five-year period.[194] This enormous sum was the lion's share of the estimated ¥18 million that Japan poured into the camphor wars from 1904 through 1916.[195] Even the abandoned first five-year plan was ambitious, financially. In 1907 and 1908, a total of ¥3.58 million was allocated for the extension and movement of the guardlines.[196]

The expense of this seemingly inconclusive war had its critics. At the February 1909 session of the twenty-fifth Diet, the firebrand representative Sasaki Yasugorō grilled Prime Minister Katsura, Communications Minister Gotō Shinpei, and Home Minister Harada Tōsuke for requesting large outlays of blood and treasure to subdue a "dying race." Sasaki was known as the "King of Mongolia" and as a "continental adventurer" *(tairiku rōnin)* for his exploits in Central Asia during the Russo-Japanese War.[197] While Mochiji invoked world history to espouse social Darwinism, Sasaki held up Zheng Chenggong and other imperial powers as models of competence in aborigine administration, compared to the Taiwan Government-General, which Sasaki considered inept.

Sasaki accused the cabinet members of refusing to answer questions, criticized them for their inattentiveness to the science of colonial statecraft, and even charged that measures to annihilate the indigenes were unconstitutional. At the heart of Sasaki's long harangue, which was interrupted by applause, was the charge that the cost of indigenous suppression had no end in sight and would increase ad infinitum until it broke the national budget. He doubted that suppression of the indigenes was an urgent national matter.[198]

Despite Sasaki's sharp questioning and the thirty signatures his inquiry garnered, the budget passed. Fujii Shizue attributes the approval to Sakuma's connections with Yamagata Aritomo. A hero of the Meiji Restoration, Yamagata was also the father of Japan's modern army, a prime minister, and a mentor to sitting prime minister Katsura Tarō. In addition, Fujii argues, the Meiji Emperor himself took a personal interest in the undertaking and lent his prestige to Sakuma's proposal.[199]

Out of an estimated 1909 aborigine population of 122,000, there were 28,242 Atayals, the principal targets of the guardline movements. These guardlines were manned and advanced by forces that varied between 6,000 and 7,000 inspectors, engineers, laborers, guards, and police officers (mostly Taiwanese guards).[200] A description of the guardline's physical aspect explains how these thousands were deployed:

> The guard-line has two components. The first is a road opened up in the mountain areas. . . . The other is the guard station. This is a kind of a dugout, a sentry box with

gun holes which is protected from bullets and shells by impenetrable sandbags, earth, stone, etc. Where necessary, electric wire fences have been hung and land mines have been buried. An electric current was passed through the wires, and many uplanders and their domesticated animals have died from electric shock. At this time, field and mountain artillery, as well as mortars were set up . . . As for the land mines, they were installed by the police inspectors and their assistants; the construction was left to police officers, who were all Japanese, and the assistant patrolmen, who were of Chinese descent, were not allowed to install them for the maintenance of secrecy. It appears that the electric wire fences began to be hung beginning in 1905. The electric switch was controlled by a Guardline Headquarters police inspector; since there were only one of these stations per guardline, even the guards were electrocuted from time to time.[201]

By 1912 the lines contained 756 guard stations, 427 branch stations, and 196 superintendent stations, extending to a total length of 226 miles.[202] The organization of these facilities was quite methodical, at least in its schematic form:

> The width of the guardline's path was 1.8 meters, and the foliage for 100 meters on either side of the path was cut down so for the sake of visibility. The Chinese guards protected the guard stations, and were equipped with rifles, which allowed them to be mobile. Two to four guards manned each guard post. A branch superintendent station was placed every four to five guard stations; officers and assistant policemen, as well as guards were stationed here. For every four to five branch stations a superintendent station built; besides the police and guards, inspectors and assistant inspectors were stationed here, as well as the intermittent medical personnel or reserve unit . . . amazingly, one of these posts was erected every 220 meters, which testifies to the strength of the resistance to Japanese rule.[203]

The guardline's organizational chart mirrored an ideal of centralized administration: priorities were set, and knowledge was concentrated, at the bureaucratic apex, while sacrifice was demanded from those at the bottom. At the pinnacle stood the police headquarters in Taipei, executing policy that was drafted with an eye to the "greater good" of imperial Japan, as defined by the imperatives to balance annual colonial budgets. At the nerve center of the guardline itself were the control stations. Here, Japanese inspectors were attended by physicians and heavily guarded. The inspectors were entrusted with the electrical switches, as well. Below them were Japanese nationals at branch stations and substations who were apprised of mine placement, and then at the bottom rung were the exposed Chinese and *jukuban* units. They absorbed the preponderance of casualties and, for fear of security breaches, were kept in the dark about operational secrets (the placement of mines or the ignition of the electrical fences), to their own physical peril.

Schematic maps from the extension and movement phases of these pacification campaigns represent the scorched-earth installations as circles and triangles arrayed on a "line." However, written accounts described a "hundred-meter-wide clear-cut" path, while photographs attest to three-dimensional, undulating ecological boot-prints. In a word, the term "guardline" *(aiyūsen)* soft-pedaled the physical magnitude of the scorched-earth installations. The photographs below document Japanese, Taiwanese, and indigenous guards, tree fellers, and porters who walked this tightrope during the period 1903–15 (see figures 14–17).

As guards, porters, and soldiers, Taiwanese recruits were exposed to enemy fire. In 1911, for example, 151 Taiwanese, compared to only 4 Japanese, were killed advancing the guardline.[204] Overall, over 2,000 government forces perished (including Japanese), with another 2,200 wounded, in the camphor wars of 1904 to 1915.[205] Taking a longer view, the death toll attributed to the war against indigenous people—including the spike in resistance from 1897 to 1901 and the dead from the Wushe uprising—amounted to 7,080 Taiwanese and Japanese, with another 4,116 wounded (1895–1935).[206] Caroline Hui-yu Ts'ai reports that some "55,600 [Taiwanese] men" were commandeered to serve in the subjugation campaigns as corvée labor.[207] At its peak, expeditionary forces proper numbered 12,000 men (including regular army and navy units).

Acknowledging the danger these exposed patrolmen, sentries, porters, and infantrymen faced, day and night, the Taiwan Government-General promulgated criteria to award special cash bonuses for meritorious service on the guardline in July 1905. The rationale stated that this type of duty was no different from fighting a war.[208] In April 1907, another TGG internal order announced that medals would be awarded to the bravest scouts and soldiers on the guardline; the governor-general himself would bestow top honors; battalion leaders would dole out lesser awards. The medals and prizes gave these punitive expeditions and related activities the trappings of a glorious undertaking.[209]

There were three tiers within which the pay levels for the one-time bonuses were set. Awards for inspectors and assistant inspectors ranged from the most meritorious award of ¥60 (grade A), down to the grade D award of ¥30. Policemen started at ¥35 and could earn as little as ¥12. Lastly, assistant policemen earned from ¥20 to ¥8 (descending from A- to D-class awards). In other words, the most meritorious assistant policemen would earn ¥10 less than the least meritorious inspector and ¥15 less than the most meritorious policeman.

A list of sixty-four awards submitted to Governor-General Sakuma by Nantou Prefect Koyanagi Shigemichi in May 1906 included commendations for twenty-eight assistant patrolmen, all with Taiwanese names. The remaining inspectors and policemen had Japanese names, meaning that Japanese guardline combatants outearned their Chinese compatriots handily, while casualties and the risk of death were much higher for Taiwanese participants.[210]

At the height of the five-year campaign, Ōtsu Rinpei, who directed operations as Sakuma's police chief, wrote the preface for a collection of *bidan* (glorious tales) about the brave men of the guardline. Some of the men lionized in this volume were killed in action; others were severely wounded. Ōtsu introduced these fifty-four sketches

FIGURE 14. Guards with bamboo and carved wood signaling devices to warn of the approach of hostile forces, ca. 1910. Narita Takeshi, *Taiwan seiban shuzoku shashinchō* (Taipei: Narita shashin seihanjo, 1912), 157.

FIGURE 15. Cutting trees to build the scorched-earth barricades, ca. 1910. "[T]here are many old trees with huge trunks, and it can require many days for a single tree...." Narita Takeshi, *Taiwan seiban shuzoku shashinchō* (Taipei: Narita shashin seihanjo, 1912), 161.

FIGURE 16. The large Taiwanese labor force, mostly sedan porters, at rest during construction of the *aiyūsen*, ca. 1910. At its peak strength, the Japanese guardline forces employed over fifty thousand Taiwanese laborers. *Tōbatsu junsatsu kinen shashinchō* (unpublished photograph album). Courtesy of the Chiyoda City Hibiya Library and Museum, Tokyo.

FIGURE 17. Indigenous Taiwanese hauling food and water for the guardline expeditionary troops, ca. 1910. "Savage of Hormosa [sic]," ip1219, East Asia Image Collection, Lafayette College, Easton, PA, accessed July 26, 2017, http://digital.lafayette.edu/collections/eastasia/imperial-postcards/ip1219.

by magnifying the importance of the war. He wrote that Taiwan presented three challenges to Japan: bandits, pestilence, and savages. The former two were eradicated with policing and medicine in the early years of Japanese rule, while the last obstacle was still being overcome. These tales describe the actions of men running into nests of headhunters to secure strongholds, fighting gamely against ambushes, or collecting intelligence in the face of grave danger. In total, the collection lauds the actions of twenty-six Taiwanese guards and twenty-eight Japanese policemen. In contrast to the cash bonus system's racially determined hierarchy of danger and compensation, the glorious tales were presented in chronological order with no preference for rank, age, or nationality.[211] The roughly equal representation and equalitarian format of Ōtsu's pamphlet stood in stark contrast to the patently discriminatory nature of day-to-day operations, be it measured in terms of risk or reward.

There were four major offensives in Sakuma's campaign, beginning with the attack on the Gaogan Atayal near Jiaobanshan in 1910. The picture that emerges is not so much that of a master plan coming to fruition as that of a centralized state with vastly superior technology and resources exhausting itself in a border region whose political economies, topographies, and traditions of armed resistance confirmed the wisdom of Mochiji's formula—some areas of Taiwan would not be worth the investment of blood and treasure to administer. In fact, the original

¥15.4 million budgeted for the campaign was insufficient. Supplementary requests drove the costs up to ¥16.24 million. Although official summary reports buried this figure, a contemporary economic analysis of the government-general's developmental policies discovered that over half of this burden—about ¥8.3 million—was paid out of the national treasury in Tokyo as supplemental funding.[212]

Although the five-year budget was drawn up with great precision, planners could not predict the course of the war. Early movements were repulsed, soldiers ran away, and the plan fell behind schedule. The 1914 *Japan Year Book,* which assiduously updated annual entries regarding the war's progress, reported ominously: "The [first] three campaigns cost about [¥9 million], but only about *one-tenth of the program was effected.*" In other words, well over half the budget had been spent, and four of the five budget years had passed, but only 10 percent of the plan had been completed.[213] Time and money ran out that summer. The vaunted plan abruptly ended with Sakuma's declaration of victory over the Truku peoples in August 1914.[214] Although southern and eastern Taiwan remained untouched, and the proposed network of roads and fences to secure the perimeter of the indigenous territory remained a dream, Sakuma and his officers erected triumphal arches in various parts of Taiwan and paraded to celebrate.[215] The Emperor Taishō granted Sakuma an audience on September 19, 1914. The seventy-one-year-old general reported to the throne, "the indigenous suppression undertaking has been concluded."[216]

Japan declared war on Germany on August 23, 1914, a week before the Truku campaign ended. The six-week siege of the German port at Qingdao cost 1,400 Japanese casualties (400 deaths), while the Japanese Navy steamed southward to occupy German holdings in the South Pacific.[217] The opening of the so-called Great War marked the end of imperial Japan's attempts to incorporate indigenous Taiwan into the empire. Sakuma's successor, Governor-General Andō Sadami, closed down organs and installations associated with the five-year plan between July and September 1915.[218] In 1917, the guard posts themselves were dismantled. Their personnel rotated into police administration as mobile units in more scattered but densely staffed police boxes.[219]

Tōgō Minoru and Satō Shirō, who finished their tome on Taiwanese colonial development in February 1916, wrote hopefully that the resources expended during the five-year campaign would be recovered as more indigenous territory in Taiwan was added to the tax base through incorporation into "normal administration."[220] The official digest of Taiwan's administration for 1915, however, was less optimistic. It issued a skeptical and prophetic warning: "The work of subjugation has thus been completed . . . , but this may not mean that the savages have been reduced to submission. Some of them *may still remain incorrigible at heart.*"[221]

The subsequent 1916 edition was more pointed. The "work of subjugation," it reported, "has thus been completed over all the aborigines' region, *at least for the present.* Strictly speaking, out of the total tribes of 672 with 129,715 inhabitants, 551 tribes representing 116,744 have vowed allegiance and the balance of the 121 tribes with 13,000 are *still to be dealt with*."²²² As testament to the TGG's lack of appetite for resuming Sakuma's aggressive policies after World War I, subsequent *Japan Year Books* repeated the 1916 summary verbatim, as boilerplate, for ten years running through 1927.

FROM MIDDLE GROUND TO NATIVE AUTHORITY

The historical contours of wet diplomacy in Taiwan's uplands recall the fate of North America's "middle ground." Historian Richard White's study of eighteenth-century frontier diplomacy argues that as long as Algonquians and Ojibwas had the leverage to force British and French agents onto the "middle ground" between state and nonstate spaces, gifts, feasts, and oaths were required to secure indigenes' provisional allegiance. By the early 1800s, writes White, the United States had neutralized the French and British threats to its sovereignty. Without rival powers to divide its energies, Washington trained its guns on Indians and enforced directives in Algonquian and Ojibwa territory with ultimatums and firearms instead of with banquets and gifts.²²³

Echoing this pattern, wet diplomacy in Taiwan prospered when indigenes occupied the middle position between contending powers: the Japanese state and Han guerilla fighters. The government-general's fear of a two-front war recommended a policy of negotiation, feasting, and gifting. Fiscal and political pressure to produce income from the camphor monopoly made wet diplomacy less tenable, however. After Gotō Shinpei's mass annihilation of Han rebels in 1902, Taiwan's middle ground became harder to maintain. Even so, while the Taiwan Government-General from 1903 onward trained its forces on indigenous peoples, *tōmoku* and *seiryokusha* (headmen and men of influence) remained important intermediaries, resembling the functional group "native authority" as described by Mahmood Mamdani.

The members of the native authority, who were recruited and coerced by the Taiwan Government-General in the 1910s and 1920s during the peak of the guard-line movements, had achieved local leadership status through prowess in mediation or battle, as leaders of ritual groups, or as members of chiefly lineages. The government-general supported the authority of these men with field trips to Tokyo and Taipei, stipends, badges, medals, and cash awards for meritorious service. This generation of mediators, despite these emoluments, were not utterly dependent upon the state for authority nor were they disciplined imperial subjects. Some remained *incorrigible at heart*.

By 1933, there were 186 Atayal, 92 Bunun, and 128 Paiwan officially recognized *tōmoku*. Of 431 headmen for all of Taiwan, only 22 could understand Japanese; a mere 20 had attended a Japanese educational facility (see chapter 2). Therefore, while members of the native authority might have been amenable to bribes, threats, or expedient alliances, they could not be counted on to prosecute Japan's interests for love of country, the emperor, or a belief that the new order would bring progress—the hallmarks of discipline (or interiority).[224] In short, Japan's version of native authority in Taiwan was a poor instrument for establishing public power in the interior, and it can be viewed as a stopgap measure for a government that could no longer expand its territory through the use of massed force.

Mona Ludao, who would lead the Wushe Rebellion in 1930, himself played the role of *tōmoku*. He traveled to Nantou City and Japan as a government-sponsored "tourist" in 1911, along with dozens of other *tōmoku* and *seiryokusha*. At the height of the guardline movements, four troops of headmen were brought to Japan to overawe them with views of Japan's economic, demographic, and military power. According to TGG police records, Mona himself was a revered warrior and a physically imposing man, recognized by other Tgdaya as a worthy successor to his father, Ludao Bai, a local chief *(domoku)*.[225]

Ludao Bai's adoption of Japanese son-in-law Kondō Gisaburō, in fact, had one foot in the world of wet diplomacy and another in the scorched-earth policy. To consecrate the marriage of Kondō and Ludao Bai's daughter Chiwas and activate the new Japan-Tgdaya alliance, the Taiwan Government-General contributed six oxen for slaughter and twenty oil cans of sake, most of it distributed at a wedding feast at Kasumigaseki (near Wushe) in 1909. Ludao Bai's son Mona Ludao mediated between Sediq men and their new Japanese in-laws during the drunken and tense proceedings. The debauch carried on for about a week. Afterward, about 650 of Ludao Bai's followers, thanks to this wedding feast and promises (unfulfilled) of enemy heads, supported guardline extensions at the expense of Truku and Toda settlements just north of Wushe (see chapter 2).[226]

A decade later, the government-general called upon Mona Ludao. Much has been written about the Salamao incident of 1920. Official sources consider Mona a conspirator against Japan during this affair, whose bad aims were thwarted by leaks. Oral histories and documentary evidence, on the other hand, suggest that Mona helped lead, or at least mobilize, about 560 Tgdaya troops to punish Salamao rebels. The incident began with an influenza epidemic attributed to the presence of outsiders. The most infamous in a series of Salamao raids and ambushes was an attack on a police station that took nineteen Japanese lives. As a condition of their earlier surrenders, and to avoid suspicion of conspiracy, warriors from Malepa, Xalut, and several Tgdaya villages signed on to fight with Japan. Fujisaki Seinosuke judged Japan's crushing victory a turning point, noting that the wrath of imperial forces frightened indigenes throughout northern Taiwan into submission.

Reminiscent of the Stone Gate Battle of 1874 and the Gantaban slaughter of 1903 (see figure 13), Salamao heads were displayed publicly to heighten the demonstration effect. Twenty-seven heads were photographed in front of the Wushe police station as trophies of the punitive expedition. Five heads were brought back to Malepa, where they were feted at a large head-taking festival—a long-banned practice that the police allowed on this one occasion, since the killings were government sanctioned.[227]

Mona Ludao's involvement in the 1920 maneuvers is sporadically documented; the contested nature of the records reflects his structural position as a member of native authority, which inclined him toward double-dealing. His clan expected material benefits for his family and followers by taking Japanese in-laws such as Gisaburō or contributing fighting men and laborers to Japanese expeditions. At the same time, chiefly cooperation was forced, on pain of the resumption of bombardment from mountain guns or of trade embargoes, leaving men like Mona with little choice. On the other hand, alliances with Japan, as the above campaigns showed, provided young Atayal, Sediq, Bunun, and Truku men opportunities to take heads and exhibit bravery in battle—rare occasions, since head taking had technically been outlawed.

But to favor Mona's men, thereby propping up his stature as a *tōmoku,* the Taiwan Government-General perforce eroded the prestige of Mona's Truku and Toda counterparts or the Salamao chiefs, just as the government-general had taken sides against Paalan (Tgdaya) in 1903, when they sanctioned the Gantaban head-taking binge. In other words, the favoritism entailed by wet diplomacy was anathema to the rationalization of state machinery, while it was the very antithesis of *isshi dōjin* (impartiality).

Mona himself, according to one memoir, was known to burst into anger at the mention of his role in Salamao. Official records describe him as a reluctant imperial soldier—the government-general marked him as a malcontent. Kondō himself complained that his Wushe in-laws had donated twenty thousand man-hours of labor to building the guardline in early 1909, while their fields lay unattended.[228] Kondō argued that long-term resentment at the government's ingratitude, which could have been allayed with a few kegs of sake and an official thank-you or a few more guns and bullets for Mona and his allies, ultimately led many locals to sympathize with and participate in the Wushe Rebellion of 1930.[229]

Therefore, Sugiura's rebuff of Mona's offer of mediation after the Yoshimura beating incident on October 8, 1930, should be seen as the last straw, one that added humiliation to long-standing torment. Of course, the relationship was also unsatisfactory from the TGG side. Accordingly, Japanese officials took steps to break their reliance on Mona's generation of headmen in the 1930s and to replace them with more dependent and reliable intermediaries, whose loyalty would not be purchased with canisters of alcohol, head-hunting licenses, or the promise of preferential treatment at government gun depots.

2

The *Longue Durée* and the Short Circuit

Gender, Language, and Territory in the Making of Indigenous Taiwan

Linguistic variation was the order of the day in nineteenth-century East Asia, as for most of the world. Before the advent of universal education and vernacular dictionaries, humanity's thousands of mother tongues were geographically circumscribed.[1] As we saw in chapter 1, communication by relay through chains of interpreters severely limited the scope and subtlety of linguistic transactions between Taiwan's natives and newcomers.[2] However, as long as states did not require routinized and rapid communication between capitals, and capitals between peripheries, the slow and halting process of cross-border translation did not become an overriding concern of central administrators.

Higher state capacities, longer imperial reaches, and administrative integration became imperative for dynastic states with the arrival of international society in East Asia on the helms of steam-powered gunships. This was the lesson future Meiji Restorationists learned from Perry's gunboats in 1854 and the Qing from the 1874 Taiwan Expedition that brought 3,658 Japanese occupiers to Langqiao. Now, a ship's crew running afoul of coastal wreckers on distant shores could be construed as injurious to national dignity or, perhaps worse, the steady flow of population-sustaining commerce. Left unresolved, such occurrences often spiraled into international incidents that brought indemnities and unwanted treaties in their wake.[3]

Accordingly, the Qing launched numerous attempts to extend its administrative reach deeper into Taiwan's interior after the shock of '74, with varying degrees of success. Nonetheless, when the Japanese regime replaced the Qing in the summer of 1895, the riddle of central command and control across Taiwan's complex linguistic landscape still awaited a solution.

When Japanese troops and officials arrived in northern Taiwan during May 1895, only a small minority of Taiwanese could speak the dialect of Chinese, Beijing "official speech," that Japanese interpreters could understand. The language barrier was made more insurmountable by the Meiji-period drift away from Chinese-language training in favor of Western languages. For example, of the forty students enrolled at the Army Staff College in 1885, "twenty-five studied French, fifteen German, and none Chinese." As for study abroad, the numbers reveal the same lack of institutional interest in China. Of the seven hundred ninety-two graduates of the Army Staff College in 1883–1914, eighty-one studied in Germany, thirty-three in France, twenty-nine in Russia, twenty-four in Britain, and thirteen in China.[4]

A few unconventional military men and commercial innovators kept their sights on China despite the "civilization and enlightenment" period's fascination with the West. Most famously, the "continental adventurers" *(tairiku rōnin)* advocated a China-first orientation for Japan's foreign relations. Foremost among them was Arao Kiyoshi, who transferred to the China section of the General Staff from the Kumamoto infantry in 1885. Aside from presumed cultural ties and a collective sense of grievance at Western gunboat diplomacy, *rōnin* of Arao's disposition believed that Japanese could not hope to compete successfully with Western merchants in Europe and the Americas. Therefore, Arao and like-minded *rōnin* saw Sino-Japanese trade as a potential engine for Japanese national wealth and large military budgets in the era of "survival of the fittest."

Arao was sent to Shanghai in 1886 to gather military intelligence. He conducted operations under cover of pharmaceutical giant Kishida Ginkō, founder of the Ginza-headquartered pharmaceutical company Rakuzendō. Kishida opened Rakuzendō branches in Shanghai, Fuzhou, and Hankou in the 1880s. Kishida was also Japan's first journalistic war correspondent, whose eyewitness coverage of the Taiwan Expedition of 1874 made him a national figure. On the mainland, Kishida provided lodging, food, and cover for Japanese students of Chinese language and for government spies. Under Kishida's and Arao's tutelage, Rakuzendō "employees," Japanese men wearing queues and dressed in tunics, fanned out across the continent to learn the languages, geography, commercial habits, and folkways of China.

After his return from China in 1889, Arao vigorously promoted plans for a large, government-assisted Japan-China Trading Company to coordinate strategy and resources for Japanese commercial expansion onto the continent. Arao also proposed an attached training institute for Chinese language, geography, and business practices. From cabinet members to public audiences of potential students, employers, and entrepreneurs, thousands of Japanese heard Arao's message. Promised public funding for the trading company and research institute, however, evaporated with the fall of the Kuroda cabinet and the seating of the fiscally conservative Constitution Diet in 1890.

Nonetheless, the *Nisshin bōeki kenkyūjo* (Sino-Japanese Commercial Research Institute) opened with a class of 150 students, selected by exam from a pool of 300 applicants that same year. Arao's *Nisshin bōeki kenkyūjo* established a rigorous four-year curriculum that taxed many students beyond endurance. The school was always on the brink of bankruptcy. Had it been a completely private concern, it surely would have collapsed. Arao's dense network of military connections in Tokyo made the difference. Vice-Chief of Staff Kawakami Sōroku, in charge of intelligence gathering in China, garnered emergency funding from the Diet and kept the research institute afloat. Though the institute cannot be called a government school, the Japanese Army lent it facilities for recruitment. In June 1893, its first graduating class of 89 finished just in time for the start of the Sino-Japanese War. Over 70 of these 89 graduates served as army interpreters or spies during the 1894–95 conflict.[5]

Arao's research institute could not, however, meet the demands of a protracted continental war. Apparently, the first call for interpreter applications met its yield target in September 1894. The theater of war quickly expanded, however, and by October the army began inducting less-qualified translators out of desperation. For example, forty students at the Kumamoto Kyūshū Gakuin were given accelerated training and pressed into service to make up for the shortage.[6] Mori Ushinosuke, who studied Chinese at a Nagasaki commercial school before the war's outbreak, recalled:

> At the time, anyone who could communicate in Chinese was recruited by the Army and sent to the Liaodong battle area; soon a shortage of manpower developed, and they began to use men who had barely a whiff of Chinese language training. If I think about it now, it is a kind of joke, because even those of us who could not understand Chinese were added to the ranks of these men. Since I did not continue with this work, I have long forgotten the words of Chinese that I did learn. But though I have no knowledge of Chinese at the present time, my associates and I, the ones unskilled in Chinese, were soon studying and being drilled, and we became very good Chinese translators.[7]

Those who answered the call to serve in the theater of war were classified as army auxiliaries and paid at the bottom of the officer's scale, between twenty-five and fifty yen per month. When the mainland phase of the war concluded in April 1895, many wartime interpreters went on to work for Japanese firms in mainland China, clustering around Shanghai and Hankou. Others went to Taiwan.[8]

Of the roughly 150,000 Japanese men activated for the Sino-Japanese War from June 1894 through the dissolution of imperial headquarters on March 31, 1896, over a third served in Taiwan at one time or another.[9] Eleven translators accompanied Colonel Fukushima Yasumasa's expedition to Danshui on August 9, 1895. Their mission was to establish a Japanese capital in Taipei. The interpreters came directly from Lüshun, Liaodong Peninsula, still wearing winter jackets. Highlighting the scarcity of interpreters, Fukushima refused an urgent request to spare a few to the Imperial Guard. Indeed, in the report he filed, interpreters accompanied every landing party and participated in missions great and small, dangerous and routine. For their contributions to the mission, completed on August 25, 1895, interpreters were awarded thirty-yen bonuses for meritorious service, on top of monthly salaries that ranged from thirty to sixty-five yen.[10]

Nonetheless, the bonuses did not provoke a flood of reenlistments. The *Daily Yomiuri* announced on September 12, 1895, that the military police *(kenpeitai)* in Taiwan "needed sixty translators." Of the three regiments sent from Hiroshima to Taiwan on September 2–3, one left with two translators; the rest embarked mute, waiting for help to catch up later, if it could be found. Men with abilities in spoken and written Chinese, who could "transmit orders, warnings, and information to the natives" were scarce indeed, pushing salaries to between thirty and seventy yen.[11]

The veterans and graduates of the commercial schools who could be persuaded to cross the strait did not speak Minnan dialects (in Japanese, called Taiwango or Forumosago, or Taiwanese) or indigenous languages. By the same token, most Taiwanese did not speak the Beijing dialect known to Japanese interpreters as Southern Administrative Chinese (to distinguish it from Manchu, or Northern Administrative Chinese). Therefore, additional talent had to be recruited in Taiwan itself. In the early years, the military hired Taiwanese fluent in Mandarin as "auxiliary translators" *(fukutsūyaku)* to work with the Japanese translators. Brush talking was heavily utilized, leading to frustration and miscommunication.[12] A Yomiuri correspondent provided a brief sketch of the early history of communication problems in Taiwan in this August 19, 1895, dispatch from Houlong, Miaoli:

> At first, when our military took Jilong and then occupied Taipei [May–August 1895], natives *[dojin]* who could speak Mandarin *[kango]* were rare. This caused difficulties for our official translators *[tsūyakukan]*, needless to say. It got to the point where certain lieutenants asserted they would not use official translators. Although the number of natives who spoke Mandarin was insufficient as far as the official translators were concerned, happily everyday communication could be conducted without too many tie-ups. Moreover, as the days passed, many of the official translators learned to understand Taiwanese *[dogo]*.
>
> As this division began its advance south, from Taipei to Xinzhu, and then from Xinzhu to Houlong, the language changed radically along with the topography. . . . The natives in the Houlong area do not speak Mandarin, so many discussions were conducted by brush talking *[hitsudan]*, which was bothersome. To be sure, Houlong's numerous so-called *jukuban* speak their own local version of Chinese, so some can speak a little Chinese. Nonetheless, unless some way can be found to translate this [local dialect] into Mandarin, the [Japanese] official translator cannot understand. This means that if another translator is brought in, three layers of interpretation have accumulated . . .
>
> Again, brush talking is no simple matter, there are many idiosyncratic characters and colloquial phrases [in use among the locals]; often standard Chinese writing is not understood.[13]

The small corps of Japanese and Taiwanese military police with smatterings of language training could not meet the demand for translators that came with the transition from regimes of punishment to regimes of discipline. By November 1896, the Civil Affairs Bureau and provincial administrations employed seventy-nine translators, all of them Japanese.[14] Since the colony was in acute fiscal crisis in its early years, augmenting this expensive corps was impossible. An economical compromise was proposed on July 25, 1897. Taiwan prefectural officials proposed ten-yen monthly pay supplements as incentives to keep policemen proficient in Taiwanese from escaping to the private sector and to encourage further efforts at language acquisition, but the proposal was rejected.

The administration of Kodama Gentarō and Gotō Shinpei (1898–1906) is often credited with bringing discipline to Taiwan. As part of a flurry of new measures, in April 1898, Imperial Order 68 was issued. It stipulated that *hannin* rank (fourth class) civil officials, police officers, and jail guards were eligible for stipends of up to seven yen per month as auxiliary translators. Qualified applicants would be paid bonuses to act as translators in addition to performing their prescribed duties.[15] Evaluations of the first round of applications for auxiliary-translator pay supplements *(kensho)* in May 1898 indicate that about 18 percent of Japanese policemen had at least some familiarity with "Taiwanese," while 6 percent of patrolmen and 9 percent of officers could "communicate effectively" or were considered "fluent."[16] Some 82 percent of Japanese policemen had no familiarity with a Taiwanese language in mid-1898. Even in the mother country, this state of affairs appeared alarming. In June 1899, the Taiwan Society, a group of powerful lobbyists that included ex-governors-general and some of Japan's top politicians,[17] lauded the *kensho* policy, explaining that the language barrier had fomented much "Taiwanese resentment and Japanese anger."[18] In October 1899, the government-general responded again. Taiwanese language institutes were attached to subprefectures *(benmusho)* and police stations to increase the number of qualified auxiliary translators. In September 1900, the Land Survey, Railway, and Camphor Monopoly Bureaus added language institutes to their local stations, as well.[19]

The Taiwan Government-General instituted the camphor monopoly in 1899 as one of several programs to address the fiscal crisis. After a rocky start, it established itself as a cash cow, thus impelling the state to abandon its role as peacemaker between indigenes and camphor workers. The government-general allowed existing private armies to guard camphor fields from the start. But with the camphor monopoly in place, it deployed its own policemen to protect the workers. It also devised legal machinery to dispossess indigenes of forest lands. These related projects touched off a rash of violent reprisals, which elevated the communication gap with rebelling Atayal, Sediq, and Truku speakers in Taiwan's north to a matter of national security.

The government-general thereafter launched programs in Austronesian-language education for Japanese policemen and Japanese-language training for Taiwanese. It also sanctioned and bankrolled intercultural marriages to overcome linguistic divides that were formerly bridged by unreliable, free-booting interpreters. In the short term, these policies appeared successful. By 1915, the government-general had achieved a military victory by disarming most "northern tribes," as we saw in chapter 1. But while the state more or less established a monopoly on the legitimate use of force along the savage border by 1923, it did not horizontally integrate the fractured political and linguistic terrain of the so-called Aborigine Territory, nor could it instantiate a disciplined society beyond the edge of the *baojia* units (regularly administered territory). The costs associated with training its own officials in myriad indigenous languages or building a school system that could shift the burden of translingualism to the indigenes proved too high for the always cash-strapped government-general.

Therefore, the government-general abandoned its mission to enforce the standard of sovereignty outlined in Ōkubo Toshimichi's 1874 admonitions regarding the Qing's uneven and dissipated sovereignty on its borderlands. What had been an expedient policy of benign neglect in the late 1890s hardened into a conscious policy of legally pluralistic, ethnically bifurcated administration in Taiwan.

During the 1920s, budgetary constraints and the appearance of calm reduced further the state's allocations for manpower and infrastructure in the highlands.[20] Yet the Taiwan Government-General stepped up its resource-extracting activities. Postmortems of the Wushe Rebellion blamed the overbearing demands of the state, in the disciplinary vacuum left by government on the cheap, for the conflagration. As we shall see, the stunted communications network encouraged by recourse to political marriages and reliance on *tōmoku* (headmen) created numerous blind spots for the state. As the 1874 invasion shocked the Qing, the 1930 Wushe uprising prompted the government-general to launch sweeping administrative reforms.

The first order of business was to reform the police service and rid aborigine administration of underachievers and shady characters.[21] The *tōmoku* who remained "incorrigible at heart" were the next targets. A concerted effort to reform aborigine customs utilized discipline-making techniques, with an emphasis on "imperial subjectification" (inculcating "Japanese spirit"). However, although these policies were superficially assimilationist, they did not portend the horizontal integration of the colony but rather reinforced the boundaries of an ethnic enclave.

To intensify imperial subjectification *(kōminka)*, the government-general demoted "chiefs" *(shūchō, tōmoku, shuryō, domoku)* or "village elites" *(seiryokusha)*[22] and promoted a generation of young "pioneers" *(senkusha)* and youth associations *(seinendan)*[23] to replace them as intermediaries. In the bargain, the daughters of the chiefs and village elites ceased to function as prominent political actors. Women such as Tata Rara, Iwan Robao, Yayutz Beriya, Yawai Taimu, Chiwas Ludao, and others, and the Japanese men who married into their families, were no longer needed to maintain imperial rule in the uplands. This shift appears to have smoothened the linguistic interface in the indigenous territories, preparing the ground for its horizontal integration into the rest of the colony.

At the same time, decades of legal discrimination, economic protectionism, and third-rate education had locked the majority of indigenes, no matter how proficient in Japanese, into the status of perennial subalterns. By 1930, aborigine administration had become its own interest group, with publications, associations, and an esprit de corps. Moreover, the ethnic tourism industry, academic anthropology, and Japanese literary production discursively constituted the indigenous territory as "the real Taiwan."

To be sure, indigene enrollments in night schools, police-station annexes (small installations dedicated to education), and elementary schools increased in the 1930s, as did the number of years of schooling for a minority of students. On the other hand, the variety of subjects taught, the quality of instructors, and opportunities for higher education remained limited by comparison with the lofty rhetoric of imperial subjectification. By the 1930s, although it went under the banner of assimilation and was dedicated to the diffusion of Japanese language and elements of home-country comportment, indigenous education came to mean "education to remain indigenous."[24] At the time of war's end in 1945, the second-order geobody of Taiwan's indigenous territory had achieved unprecedented levels of linguistic and infrastructural integration, via Japanese language-training programs, state-organized pan-indigenous institutions, and the Taiwan Government-General's road building program. In some respects, the indigenous territory bore many features of a community that could be imagined as a nation on the eve of Japan's departure with the empire's defeat. On the other hand, the indigenous territory's denizens lacked rights in property, were cut off from the economic life of the rest of Taiwan, and were relegated to the role of toiling, honest, and loyal children of the emperor. In a word, the 1930s imperialization policies finished the job of turning erstwhile Qing border peoples into modern ethnic minorities.

THE GENDER DIVISION OF LABOR IN CROSS-BORDER COMMUNICATIONS

Before the Qing government could even sign the Treaty of Tianjin of 1858, foreign adventurers in Taiwan were testing the waters for trade and missionizing possibilities. In 1857, future British consul Robert Swinhoe wrote: "I had the pleasure of seeing a few [Indigenous] women, who were married to Chinese at . . . [Langqiao] . . . a Chinaman named Bancheang, of large landed property, traded with the Kalees [Rukai] of the hills . . . He was constantly at variance with the Chinese authorities who had outlawed him, but could not touch him, as he was so well defended by his numerous Chinese dependants, and the large body of Aborigines at his beck. This man was wedded to a Kalee."[25]

As we learned in chapter 1, there was no shortage of "outlaws" like Bancheang in late nineteenth-century Langqiao. Swinhoe's vignette, however, is notable for exposing an element of Qing borderland society obscured by the outsized impact of the Mudan village incident on historiography. The preponderance of documented transactions between natives and newcomers in 1860s–1870s Langqiao ran through the Siaoliao-Sabaree-Tuilasok corridor, or the Checheng-Poliac-Kuskus route along the Sichong River corridor. Male mediators such as Siaoliao native Miya and Poliac subofficial Yang Youwang (see chapter 1) are prominent in these records, because of their pivotal roles in the dramatic events of the epoch. Douglas Fix's research into Langqiao social history suggests, however, that female mediators also operated in this milieu: "Another group, unnamed older women—nearly all labeled 'aborigine' wives of headmen—seem to appear just as frequently as the [Miyas] in my sources. Their existence and recorded activities indicated that cross-community mediators were 'born' at the intersection of kinship connections, munitions markets, and castaway exchanges. Furthermore, the regularity of their mediation suggests that a gendered analysis of the historical constitution and reproduction of frontier communities is long overdue."[26]

Xu Shirong's quantitative study of late Qing Hengchun social structure also notes the high incidence of intermarriage between Hakka residents of Langqiao and indigenous peoples. According to Xu, these intermarriages were woven into relations of mutual economic interdependence.[27] It may well be that male intermediaries such as Miya or Yang, who would qualify as "local gentry" under some definitions, typically dealt with conspicuously marked and well-armed official retinues of outsiders, while female interpreters such as those mentioned by Swinhoe, Fix, and Xu interfaced with smaller parties of traders, explorers, and missionaries.

For example, while traveling in a small party, William Pickering—whom we met earlier as LeGendre's interpreter—encountered a chief whom he referred to as a "T'ong-su" *(tongshi)*, the "headman of the tribe, responsible to the Chinese government." Pickering spoke to him through an "old woman, named Pu-li-sang, [who] was no novice to the ways of civilization, as she had, years ago, been married to a Chinese, and also had lived for some time with the [Tsou] Bangas . . . "[28] On the eve of the Japanese invasion in 1874, American naturalist Joseph Steere also noted the role of indigenous women as mediators, writing that the "Kale-whan [Rukai], in times of scarcity, frequently sell their daughters to the Chinese and Pepo-whans [plains indigenes], who take them as supplementary wives and make them useful as interpreters in thus bartering with the savages. While we were among the Kale-whan the chief offered to sell us three girls of the tribe at twenty dollars each."[29]

In world history, this was not an unusual arrangement; there are numerous examples from other times and places. In many cases, intercultural marriages were symbiotic, because outsiders provided access to far-flung trade networks or military alliances that could shore up a family's ascendancy in a fragmented milieu of stateless polities. In Taiwan, examples of such unions can be found in records going all the way back to the early seventeenth century. In fact, the term *tongshi,* employed by Pickering above, evokes a long history of semiofficial, bicultural intermediaries who functioned on the fringes of Qing territory beginning in the Dutch era (1622–61).[30]

Over the centuries of Qing rule (1683–1895) over Taiwan, *tongshi* were the primary conduits of trade and diplomacy during the era of tributary interstate relations in East Asia. The English word "interpreter" is a good approximation, but *tongshi* were more than linguistic adepts. They organized commerce, mediation, and taxation in the most sparsely populated areas of Taiwan. As would be the case during the period of Japanese colonial rule, *tongshi* often appeared as suspicious, disruptive, and not altogether trustworthy characters in Qing records.

Many of these intermediaries provided continuity between the successive Qing and Japanese imperial regimes in Taiwan. It is evident that ample room for cross-border maneuvering existed in Taiwan even after two centuries of Qing rule. On the eve of the handover to Japan in 1895, for example, Qing critics judged Shen Baozhen's and Liu Mingchuan's *kaishan fufan* policies to "open the mountains and pacify the indigenes" a failure. After twenty years and "several hundred million taels spent on road construction, military deployment, suppression and pacification of aborigines," Han settlement had not increased appreciably outside southernmost Taiwan, while outlays remained exorbitant.[31] Nonetheless, several individual campaigns and measures bore fruit, which supplied a small coterie of seasoned intermediaries who in turn formed the basis for the successor Japanese state's attempt to integrate the indigenous territories into its empire. In the south (to be discussed in more detail below), a walled city, Hengchun, was built in 1875 as a base for pacification campaigns into the mountains. There, veteran Paiwan and Puyuma participants in the treaty-port diplomacy of the 1860s and 1870s signed on as Qing subofficials; many would later work for the Japanese. In the north, administrative beachheads were established near Wulai, Yilan, and Dakekan, which also became early base areas for Japanese rule in the indigenous territory.

The latter three northern examples were gateways into Atayal-dominated mountain interiors. There, various types of Atayal-Chinese interpreters mediated mountain-plain or state-society relations. Males, whether as subofficials or commercial operators, were called *tongshi* (interpreter). This title could be attached to a chief who collected information and mobilized labor for the Qing or to an interpreter for hire who had acquired language proficiency and political connections through intermarriage. In 1885, Governor Liu Mingchuan dispatched his son Chaohu to Quchi (near Wulai) at the head of three thousand soldiers. The eight villages of the area were named for the paramount chieftain Marai, who submitted to Liu that year. Marai was then deputized to collect information, coordinate gift distribution, and report to Liu for six Qing liang (Japanese *ryō*) per month.

Marai passed away around 1888 without a successor. A Wulai chief named Watan Yūra, the man we met in chapter 1 as Ueno Sen'ichi's drinking partner and source of Atayal clothing and jewelry, filled the vacuum as the paramount headman of the Quchi tribes[32] (see figure 18). The interpreters known to us as Aki and

FIGURE 18. Watan Yūra, ca. 1900. Goto Shimpei, "Formosa Under Japanese Administration," *The Independent* 54, no. 2,796 (July 3, 1902): 1,582.

Kōan have been photographed with Watan Yūra (see figure 19). Aki and Kōan were Chinese by birth but became "Atayalized" over the decades. They moved into the mountains sometime in the 1870s.

Kōan was married to an Atayal woman and worked with the Japanese regiments stationed in Xindian in February 1896. Taiwan was still under military rule; the Xindian garrison was fighting Han rebels in Yilan. As the troops set out to survey a direct overland route from Taipei to Yilan, Kōan presented himself as an interpreter with local connections to the Quchi tribes. He arranged for Japanese forces to meet with the paramount chief of the eight villages, Watan Yūra, near Quchi on February 10. This led to a long series of parleys. The Japanese provided rice, liquor, gifts of various kinds, and assurances of protection from Chinese settlers in return for Quchi acquiescence in Japanese roadbuilding. These negotiations were carried out through an official Japanese translator, Kōan, and an Atayal man named Shiron, who had lived in Taipei and learned Chinese in the 1880s at Governor Liu Mingchuan's Academy for Aborigine Boys.

If Kōan's wife participated in these negotiations, her name was not mentioned. Female interpreters were referred to not as *tongshi* but as *banpu* (indigenous

FIGURE 19. Watan Yūra, Kōan, Aki, and Pazzeh Watan in 1903. Mori Ushinosuke, *Taiwan banzoku zufu*, vol. 1 (Taipei: Rinji Taiwan kyūkan chōsakai, 1915), plate 23.

females), though they often performed the same tasks as *tongshi*. The Atayal woman Awai and the Sediq woman Iwan Robao, for example, took the marriage route to becoming interpreters, as had Kōan. The most celebrated Atayal female interpreter, Yayutz Beriya, married a Japanese pharmacist named Nakano. Beyond taking the marriage route, Yayutz subjected herself to years of rigorous formal training in the Japanese school system to achieve prominence as a language teacher for Japanese policemen and as a famous interpreter.[33]

In addition to the *tongshi* and *banpu* who learned languages through immersion, another type of Qing-period interpreter is exemplified by Pu Chin, a Dakekan-area native who learned to speak and write Chinese in a Qing school for indigenous children. In response to the booming export economy in camphor (see chapter 1), Governor Liu Mingchuan established the *Fukenju* (Bureau of Pacification) in 1886 to regulate relations between indigenes and Taiwan's Han population.[34] Its charter specified that "barbarian women *(banba)* should . . . greet and feast the barbarians *(banjin)* who come down from the mountains." The Japanese gloss to this passage added, "these are taken mainly from *banpu* (indigenous women) married to Chinese men *(Shinajin)*.[35]

To mitigate the influence of the *banpu*, whose loyalties were necessarily divided, Governor Liu built a school to create a loyal corps of male interpreters. His academy opened in 1890 and accepted twenty students; it added ten more in 1891—all sons of chiefs or men of influence, aged sixteen or seventeen *sui*.³⁶ Graduate Pu Chin was twenty-three years old and working in industry when he was hired by the Dakekan garrison to interpret for the Japanese in August or September 1895.³⁷ As recounted in chapter 1, the talks orchestrated by Pu Chin were initiated by the Dakekan garrison commander, one Captain Watanabe. On August 29, Watanabe sent a *seiban tongshi* ("savage interpreter") to arrange for Jiaobanshan-area Atayal peoples to come down the mountain to speak with the Japanese. The next day, two women and five men showed up on neutral ground—down from the mountains, but beyond the rice fields abutting Dakekan walled city. Watanabe's retinue brought over forty people, including soldiers, porters, and military police. It is likely that the younger of two Atayal women was an interpreter as well. She was about eighteen, wore manufactured Chinese clothing, and "could pass for Japanese but for her braided hair." She appeared to be Atayal village's delegate in dealings with Chinese.³⁸

A week later, current Taipei governor Tanaka Tsunatoku and future Taipei governor Hashiguchi Bunzō, each with a couple of staffers, left Taipei by train to meet the Dakekan garrison. This time, the Japanese arrived with an official translator *(tsūyaku-kan)*, who translated Japanese into English and vice versa, and an unnamed Portuguese "temp" *(koin)* who translated between Taiwanese *(Taiwan dogo)* and English. In addition, they utilized two Atayal-Chinese interpreters, Pu Chin and Washiiga, to translate between Taiwanese and the Dakekan dialect of Atayal. At this parley, the relays were as cumbersome as those of Captain Cassel and Isa near Sabaree back in 1874 (see chapter 1).

The female Atayal interpreter named Washiiga was about nineteen years old. She had divorced a Chinese man at age sixteen, wore some "old Chinese clothing," and understood the "Formosan-language somewhat." Pu Chin, probably with Washiiga's assistance, provided Hashiguchi and Tanaka with the names, domiciles, family relations, titles, and ages of the Atayal contingent in his all-important register.³⁹ Tanaka's report, Hashiguchi's report, and the Tokyo *Asahi* newspaper account, all based on eyewitness testimony, provide different names for the Atayal people, suggesting the uncertainty of the linguistic environment. Tanaka and Hashiguchi did not even agree on the number of Atayal people present at the lineup at their initial meeting, so opaque was the language situation.

While Governor Tanaka assiduously recorded the script of the speeches he made to the assembled Dakekan men (see chapter 1), he noted in his manuscript report that only the "gist" was communicated. His spoken words, after all, were converted from Japanese to English, English to Taiwanese, and then Taiwanese to Dakekan Atayal, so anything other than a few cardinal points would have been impossible to communicate.

To convince those who had traveled to Dakekan from Jiaobanshan to continue on to Taipei, the troops offered to surrender the four blankets they had lent to the Atayal contingent, one blanket per person. Hashiguchi reported that the soldiers tried to explain to the Atayal people that the blankets were not the soldiers' private property but belonged to the platoon. The Atayal, for their part, believed that they already owned the blankets, even before the offer was made. Hashiguchi concluded that the Atayal people could not distinguish the concepts of *lend* and *give,* partly due to the small number of words in their language.

Rather, according to Hashiguchi, they conflated the concepts of *give* and *lend* into an Atayal concept somewhere in between that meant "to turn over, relinquish."[40] While Hashiguchi admitted that he was speculating, he had hit upon an important sticking point. The concepts of private property, ownership of goods, or keywords like *lend* and *borrow,* as we shall see in chapter 3, went beyond language difficulties and suggested fundamental differences in political economic cosmologies.[41]

After duly filing his reports and recommendations based on this encounter (see introduction and chapter 4 for details), Hashiguchi ordered subprefect Kawano Shuichirō to Yilan's Atayal territory. In September, "quite fortunately and by chance," they located four *tsūji* (interpreters) of former Qing employ and their *banpu* (indigenous women) wives. Kawano described the women as "pure indigenes with facial tattoos." The male interpreters themselves were described as *kabanjin* (transformed barbarians), a term applied to indigenes who had assimilated politically or culturally to Han folkways, though to a lesser extent than the *jukuban* (cooked barbarians). Kawano deputized the women as *tsūben* (go-betweens/interpreters) and ordered them to bring the chief of Xiyanlaowa village (Xitou) to the plains for a parley. The women then went inland and convinced a chief to meet Japanese officials on neutral ground.[42] Awai, one of the *tsūben* hired by Kawano, was thirty years old and had been married to the *jukuban* Chen Xilai for eight years. Although she wore some Chinese clothes, she retained distinctive tattoos and spoke the local Atayal dialect.[43] Kawano also recorded the text of his lengthy speech. This long-winded admonition was presumably communicated through the government interpreter and the *tsūben* to the gathered Atayal men and women.

As was the case with the Hashiguchi/Tanaka mission and feasts during the 1874 invasion, Kawano's scribes were careful to transcribe and translate into Japanese a song relayed to the gathered listeners in Atayalic.[44] It is impossible to know if Japanese officials were putting words into the mouths of the gathered singers. In any event, Kawano, like Hashiguchi, was denied access to the abodes of these emissaries; he returned to Taipei satisfied that he had soothed the feelings of the Atayal people and allayed their suspicions of the new regime.

THE TROUBLE WITH TONGSHI

While male *tongshi* such as Pu Chin and female *tsūben* such as Awai, located in and around the Qing Pacification Offices, were readily available to lead Japanese

Army contingents to particular villages to read proclamations and distribute gifts, it would take many hundreds of interpreters to satisfy the needs of Japanese camphor industrialists, people in the tea business, and officials who were laying the groundwork for an island-wide infrastructure. As indicated by an early report in the magazine *Taiyō*, which described the frustratingly complex process of mediation in Taiwan's interior, locating and securing a sufficiently large and adept corps of translators would be a daunting task:

> An interpreter is a Chinese who is good at indigenous languages and is conversant with conditions among indigenes. Each hamlet or group of hamlets has an interpreter (a hamlet is similar to our *buraku* [village]). The "local man" *(shatei)* works under the interpreter, procuring whatever is needed for each side to facilitate communication, diplomacy, and so on. Each hamlet without fail has a local man. These local men and interpreters are not always to be found in the hamlets, though. They have their own households with affairs to attend to, and they hire themselves out to people.
>
> Moreover, these interpreters can apply for government service. Officials screen them, and . . . they become responsible for relaying directives and taking care of all manner of things related to the indigenes . . . One imagines that their income is not small.
>
> . . . The interpreters and local men assume an arrogant and insulting manner toward the indigenes, who in turn treat the interpreters very humbly.[45]

Saitō Kenji, a camphor merchant and engineer, reinforced the unflattering portrait of interpreters in *Taiyō* from a commercial perspective, for an audience of Japanese who were in Taiwan or likely to travel there. He wrote that most interpreters were *jukuban*, whom he described as "evolved savages" *(shinka no seiban)*. According to Saitō, Chinese interpreters were rare. As liminal figures of uncertain affiliation, wrote Saitō, interpreters swindled and cheated Japanese merchants at every turn, holding them hostage with threats of head-hunting reprisals should they be dismissed by their employers. Saitō noted that interpreters could be hired for a fixed monthly salary but that it would be better to spend a couple of months learning "the indigenous language" oneself, instead.[46]

According to a Japanese infantryman named Iriye Takeshi, who recorded his observations just after the cession in 1895, the availability of Atayal interpreters in the north was directly related to increases in trade volume in the treaty-port era. Iriye described the codependence of commerce and intermarriage:

> In *[jukuban]* territory, indigenes give their daughters away and force them to marry. This is a recent occurrence; it did not happen in former times. . . . All of these types of marriages are related directly to [cross-border] trade . . . A meeting of the minds is reached between man and woman, and the marriage is arranged. Before any immorality is committed, the chief's permission is sought and the marriage carried through. When a *jukuban* takes a *seiban* concubine, the new bride is given Chinese clothing and so on. . . . For the return trip home, they are given a water buffalo, two jars of liquor, and black and red cloth.[47]

Anthropologist, interpreter, and police informant Mori Ushinosuke recorded that bride price—in the form of red skirts (up to one hundred in some cases), cattle, pigs, guns, daggers, farming implements, and even farmland—was customary at Atayal weddings.[48] Therefore, the above marriages chronicled by Iriye, while financially motivated, were not casual unions. In fact, they were publicly sanctioned. Indigenous parties to such unions took care to assure that marriage alliances did not result in *too much* familiarity between lowlanders and highlanders—permission to visit natal villages was often limited to outmarried daughters and not granted to their husbands. Since chiefs enriched themselves and accrued political power by interposing themselves between villages farther inland and delegates of foreign powers, thereby monopolizing outflows of mountain products and inflows of imported prestige goods, such strictures make sense. They suggest that outmarrying was part of a complex political strategy to maintain power in a milieu that required the distribution of gifts to maintain leadership status.[49]

To contextualize these practices, it should be noted that the selling, purchase, and exchange of daughters to further the goals of a village, family, or economic unit was common in rural northern Taiwan among the Han, as were arranged marriages in Japan for the same purpose. Han Taiwanese families in the Taipei Basin out-adopted birth daughters in exchange for adopted female daughters, to raise the latter as future daughters-in-law. This practice prevented expensive wedding costs and forestalled problems related to bringing outsiders into the family compound.[50] In Japan, *mukoyōshi* (son-in-law) adoption was a way to preserve lineage property in a system of inheritance based on primogeniture for families without male offspring. That is to say, the apparent ease with which Atayal chiefs outmarried daughters to secure future commercial intermediaries would not have appeared callous or outlandish to Han or Japanese people at the time.

From these and many other reports, a general pattern emerges. A minimum of two interpreters (usually three) brokered Japanese-indigenous communication in the early years of colonial rule. Japanese men known as "official translators" *(tsūyakukan* or *tsūyakusei)* interpreted for government officials to the Chinese or "evolved barbarian" interpreters *(tongshi)*. They interpreted between the "official Chinese" spoken in Beijing and Taiwanese Chinese (Minnan dialect), while the intermediaries known simply as "local men" *(shatei)* or "aborigine women" *(banpu)* interpreted from Taiwanese Chinese to an indigenous language. Despite their low official status, the local men and *banpu* were indispensable for sojourns in the indigenous territories. When Pacification Office chief Saitō Otosaku's Japanese official translator, Shōjiro Kunitei, was incapacitated with malaria during an early circuit of Alishan's environs, Saitō's mission continued to function. Saitō would not proceed, however, without his local man.[51] An official from the interpreter's bureau in Miaoli underscored the point: four different languages were spoken behind the mountains abutting Miaoli city. It was simply impossible to conduct business there without local men.[52]

THE NEW CLASS OF JAPANESE INTERPRETERS

As recounted in the previous chapter, Hiyama Tetsusaburō's first mission to Puli took on the same trappings as other "first embassies" to plains-mountain interfaces. In one way, however, the Hiyama mission was unique. From their base in the newly established Puli Pacification Office, Hiyama himself, his associate Kondō Katsusaburō, and at least two other Japanese men made alliances with Tgdaya tribes by becoming sons-in-law. According to Irie Takeshi, Puli prefect Hiyama Tetsusaburō's wedding, held around January 1, 1896, was a major event. Hiyama doled out the expected blankets and jars of liquor at his wedding to Chiwas, the daughter of the Paalan headman Pixo Sappo.[53] By April 5, 1896, Hiyama's marriage was publicized in the Japanese press as a human interest story.[54] Hiyama was a colorful politician from Tokyo who was lampooned in the Tokyo press for absconding to Taiwan to make an easy salary by exploiting his connections to Mizuno Jun.[55] His tenure in Puli did not last; he was expelled from office on May 25, 1897, for collusion in a burglary that ended in a murder.[56]

Hiyama's most notorious associate, Kondō Katsusaburō, would spend the rest of his life in Taiwan, achieving fluency in Taiwanese Chinese and at least one dialect of a northern indigenous language, probably Sediq. He was considered by some to be an expert on indigenous affairs on a par with Mori Ushinosuke himself.[57] Contemporary references to Kondō label him as a *tongshi* (interpreter), *shokutaku* (commissioner), or *buppin kōkanjin* (aborigine trader).[58] Kondō was also a decorated translator/explorer, who is credited for brokering complicated deals with Bunun, Atayal, Sediq, and Truku headmen and emissaries (see below). His long analysis of the causes of the Wushe Rebellion were picked up in various official, journalistic, and popular postmortems, thus spreading his name, for a time, widely (see figure 20).

Kondō Katsusaburō was born on December 10, 1873, the eldest son of Kondō Mankichi and Chiyo (née Kawahara) of Myōzai County, Urashō Town, Tokushima Prefecture. His family was in the indigo business. Kondō himself was a restless youth and purportedly blew 130 yen of his family's money in Ōsaka's warehouse and entertainment district instead of procuring indigo. The penniless Kondō made his way to Kobe, built up capital as a jobber and peddler, and finally opened a profitable store. His earnings were sufficient to repay his family. Kondō next joined the Ōkura Group to work in the commissariat during the Sino-Japanese War. Kondō sailed from Shimonoseki to Inchon and returned to Japan with the Nagoya army for the triumphal return. Kondō could not raise enough money for passage to America to learn the milling business, so he ended up in Hong Kong via Shanghai. His interest in Taiwan, piqued by stories of headhunters in the newly acquired land, sent him there on the next ship.[59]

A fragmentary memoir asserts that Kondō actually swam into Jilong Harbor shirtless, after having been thrown overboard from an American ship for scuffling

FIGURE 20. *Back row center,* Kondō "the Barbarian" Katsusaburō, ca. 1910. Courtesy of the Rupnow Collection.

with crew members.[60] Kondō's first known destination in Taiwan, Puli, was a crossroads of savage-border commerce and a melting pot. Conditions there rapidly deteriorated after the Japanese declared themselves masters of the island. Puli's walled fortifications, coupled with its location on a plateau high up in the mountains, made it an ideal rebel ("bandit") base.[61] Puli was captured by opposition forces on July 11, 1896, as the last in a series of towns and cities under the control of one Kien-I. It was retaken by the Japanese on July 22.[62] The Puli Pacification Office *(bukonsho)* officially opened on July 23, 1896, the day after Kien-I's defeat, with Hiyama Tetsusaburō as its first chief.[63]

Under Hiyama's patronage, Kondō was granted a permit to "trade in indigenous products" in Puli on May 19, 1896.[64] As a first step to becoming a celebrated "aborigine hand" *(bantsū),* Kondō wed Iwan Robao, the daughter of a Paalan village headman named Chitsukku,[65] sometime in 1896.[66] By all accounts, Kondō was a talented linguist; he quickly became a much sought-after interpreter. In January 1897 Kondō and Iwan joined the ill-fated Fukahori Yasuichirō expedition. Before the expedition entered the high mountains beyond Puli, however, Kondō fell ill with malaria. Iwan accompanied the mission as an auxiliary interpreter, working with Kondō's replacement, a plains indigene named Pan Laolong, also a merchant specializing in the "aborigine trade."[67] Pan and Iwan survived because they abandoned the mission before it came to grief, rightfully fearing danger as the troop traveled beyond areas previously secured through parleys with local chiefs. The frigid weather warned off other potential interpreters on the mission. Fukahori was able to hire about ten Sadō (near Truku village) men to lead him, but their assistance was useless in Xalut, where a different language was spoken. Because Fukahori's team was engaged in the visible project of mapmaking and had famously scolded and beat curious Tgdaya men for inquiring about these activities, the Xalut people feared that Fukahori was an advance team for a punitive expedition.

The wanderings of this troop were not unlike those of the Ryūkyū castaways in Langqiao in 1871. Without a common spoken language, miscommunication was the rule. The local peoples, rightly fearing large numbers of mobile outsiders, finally reacted with violence and slaughtered all fourteen of Fukahori's men. An indigenous-district policeman who reconstructed these events in 1936 opined that Fukahori's mission would have succeeded had the locally embedded and multilingual Kondō Katsusaburō not fallen ill.[68]

Ostensibly to locate Fukahori's killers, on August 20, 1897, Kondō left his wife, Iwan, and headed north to the Truku-Toda village complexes toward Neng'gao Mountain. He brought two of his trading-post employees, Nagakura Yoshitsugu and Itō Shūkichi, in addition to securing the services of Itō's wife, a Toda native named Tappas Kuras.[69] After a grueling, rain-soaked march, Kondō secured the patronage of a trade-minded Toda headman named Bassau Bōran. The headman was a former customer at Kondō's Puli establishment. As Bassau's houseguest and adopted son, Kondō literally "went native" in the course of his twenty-month stay, earning the sobriquet Seiban Kondō (Kondō the Barbarian).[70]

In the meantime, the Second Combined Squadron and a search party from the Puli Pacification Office conducted independent investigations in March 1897. The latter was ineffectual, for the same reasons that LeGendre's and Bell's investigations of Koalut in 1867 failed: they had no means for incentivizing cooperation. The more heavily armed and staffed squadron, however, determined that Fukahori's party had died in battle on a forlorn riverbed deep in the mountains. They recovered a few tattered articles of clothing and a pair of eyeglasses.[71] In March 1900, two years after Fukahori's disappearance, Kondō himself accompanied Puli subprefect Ōkuma Hirotake to recover five of the actual skulls and more artifacts in Sado, the place Kondō had ingratiated himself with Bassau.[72]

While Kondō and Itō bartered their way around Toda-Truku territory with the assistance of their new extended families, other noteworthy unions between Japanese men and indigenous women began to sprout up, including that of Jiku Shō Min and his Atayal wife, Bariya Nōkan. In 1895 or 1896, Japanese army interpreter Jiku (aka Watan Karaho) married into a Wulai family near Quchi. He claimed to be the heir apparent to his father-in-law's chieftaincy.[73] Inō Kanori's diary entry for May 23, 1897, referred to Jiku as the point man for directing Japanese officials on journeys from Xindian to Quchi (Ueno Sen'ichi's route in 1891).[74] Jiku signed several of his reports with the moniker Savage Righteous Army. His associations

FIGURE 21. Quchi-area residents posing with flag, ca. 1897. East Asia Image Collection, Lafayette College, Easton, PA.

with camphor merchant and hydroelectric power entrepreneur Dogura Ryūjirō suggest that he used his relations as a labor force and perhaps as a private army.[75] As Inō Kanori's and Mori Ushinosuke's guide to Wulai, Jiku was also a key player in the birth of Japan's ethnology of Taiwan.[76] As Inō was making his famous tour, Jiku dispatched a Rimogan resident named Taimu to survey the location of dozens of inland villages. Jiku submitted a color map, several dozen sketches of cultural artifacts, and a taxonomy of Atayal language groups in an official report.

Jiku included a description of a Raga (south of Wulai) couple with his attached photograph—perhaps the first photo in Taiwan to accompany an ethnological survey. He described the sitters as a male named Yūmin and a female named Akashi. Jiku referred to them as pioneers of "aborigine civilization" because they requested flags and Japanese clothing (see figure 21).[77]

Kondō Katsusaburō also translated for ethnologists Inō Kanori and Torii Ryūzō,[78] while Kondō's wife, Iwan Robao, was subject to Torii's interviews and anthropometric surveys.[79] Therefore, the bicultural marriages described above were indispensable for gathering practical as well as more abstract forms of intelligence regarding indigenous peoples in the early years of colonial rule.

Despite their benefits, in 1899 Sanjiaoyong (near Jiaobanshan) district officer Satomi Yoshimasa complained to Taipei governor Murakami Yoshio that Japanese-Atayal unions were causing friction with local men. Satomi suggested that Japanese civilians be forced to apply for permits before marrying indigenous women. Murakami then proposed a system of punishments for Japanese men who abandoned their local wives. In addition, Murakami recommended state support for divorcées, whose local marriage prospects had been ruined by public association with foreigners. Murakami's questionnaire, circulated to magistrates and police posted in aborigine territory, illuminates official concerns:

1. To what extent are there contracts or gifts of cash or merchandise on the occasion of a wedding *(kashu no sai)*?
2. [Provide] the name and occupation of the person who married a *banpu (banpu o metorishi mono)*.
3. Is it possible for one who has been a secondary wife/concubine of a Japanese to remarry an aborigine *(naichijin no shō/mekake to naritaru mono wa futatabi banjin ni kasuru)*?
4. In the case of abandonment, how is the *banpu* managing? How do the aborigines feel about the situation?
5. Was the union with a Japanese *(naichijin ni kasuru)* entered into as a lifelong commitment, or was it rushed into avariciously for the short term?[80]

Despite these problems, there appeared to be no other way to establish paths of communication with Austronesian language speakers. Even if official interpreters could learn indigenous languages, they were not stationed in places where they might have been useful. According to the personnel rosters for the first year of the Pacification Office's operation (1896), there were eight translators posted among its eleven stations.[81] The following year, the translator positions were all gone, although four of the 1896 translators remained as administrative assistants *(shujiho)*, now performing "routine duties and tasks to be determined by the station chief, including interpreting."[82] In the late summer of 1897, one Pacification Office head reported in the *Daily Yomiuri* that even when translators were employed, communication was still difficult because they did not understand the local dialects very well.[83] The Pacification Office was dissolved the next year, and aborigine administration was moved to Section 3 of the new District Administrative Offices *(Benmusho)*. As a rule, the *Benmusho* stations lacked translators altogether.

But without Japanese staffers trained in indigenous languages, wrote one pacification officer in 1898, Japan was doomed to rely upon the shady local men who cheated indigenes by plying them with booze. The local men also frustrated Japanese policy by trafficking contraband rifles.[84] One obvious measure to dispense with Japan's reliance on interpreters, without relying on the fractious intercultural marriages, was formal language training for pacification officers and policemen. In March 1897, as a first step, the head of the Industrial Section in Taipei ordered Pacification Office heads to compile word lists and phrase books based on trading-post conversations, official meet and greets, and negotiations of camphor contracts with indigenes. The memorandum's author wrote that indigenous languages had no historical affinities to Chinese or Japanese and that mastering them was difficult. The circular proposed systematic word collection and phonetic analysis with the cooperation of the Pacification Office. Materials started trickling in by October 1897.[85]

However, as anthropologist Mio Yūko's careful analysis of the manuscript copies of the responses reveals, the stacks of word lists and conversational phrases were made by linguistic amateurs, written down in katakana (a Japanese syllabary), and they ended up collecting dust in government offices. The ambitious project did not produce training manuals or textbooks, leaving the Japanese to learn indigenous languages through immersion.[86]

To incentivize immersion learning, the so-called *kensho* (stipend) system was implemented. In this program, police officers and assistant policemen were given monthly pay supplements if they could pass language exams in Hok-lo, Hakka, or an Austronesian language.[87] The pay incentives for Han Taiwanese assistant patrolmen to learn Japanese succeeded. The Taiwan Government-General thus cultivated a cohort of Japanese-speaking Han Taiwanese to handle interpreting chores in the plains and ports. However, the stipend system was premised on the assumption that a comprehensive and fair exam could be administered in the target language. It is clear from the foregoing, however, that Japanese officials were not in possession of instructional materials or a language pedagogy that could produce examinations, examiners, and a curriculum for Austronesian languages.

Therefore, an exception was made. The indigenous-language tests would consist of abbreviated interviews with Japanese district officials, who determined if a candidate understood an indigenous language sufficiently to "communicate and understand complex matters" and "relay orders without doing damage." Examinees would be sorted into three categories of proficiency.[88] A set of 1907 regulations stated that exams for indigenous languages be limited to oral interviews. That same year, *bango* (indigenous language) was officially defined as nine separate tongues: Atayal, Saisiyat, Bunun, Tsou, Tsarisen, Amis, Puyuma, Paiwan, and Yami.[89]

The practical application of government ethnologist Inō Kanori's taxonomy (see figure 2) had important long-term consequences. There are many more Austronesian languages in Taiwan than the nine listed above. As Inō's colleague and rival ethnologist Mori Ushinosuke observed at the time, Inō's taxonomy lumped dissimilar languages together, while it split similar languages into separate categories. Mori himself advocated a sixfold classification that fused Saisiyat with Atayal and grouped Puyuma, Tsarisen (Rukai), and Paiwan together, based on his own research as the Meiji era's most dogged survey ethnologist of Taiwan. Despite Mori's reservations, however, these nine groups became census categories, museum labels, and place-names on ethnic maps. As inscribed ethnonyms, they were carried forward with considerable institutional momentum into the late twentieth century (with the exception of Tsarisen, which essentially became Rukai). Until indigenous activists themselves met with some success in revising the taxonomy in the twenty-first century, these nine language groups constituted the building blocks of indigenous Taiwan's second-order geobody.[90]

On July 27, 1909, police headquarters circulated another memorandum urging colonial police stationed in the northern districts to learn Taiwanese and indigenous languages. The Yilan district station employed three instructors in the office and another at a garrison. At other locations, however, no qualified instructors could be found, so the men were reduced to studying word lists on their own. One district head noted that lack of contact with Atayal people for actual practice hindered progress. The Xinzhu station chief claimed that most of his men could say a few words in an indigenous language but could not conduct everyday conversations. The best he could do was provide nonsystematic practice for the policemen under his command with indigenous mercenaries or the indigenous wives of Japanese policemen.[91]

It is not surprising that conversation partners for uniformed Japanese and Taiwanese officials were scarce in 1909. We saw in chapter 1 how Kondō Katsusaburō and Iwan Robao (or possibly other informants to the Japanese government) orchestrated a trap for Hōgō- and Paalan-village Tgdaya (Wushe) men, who lost most of their weapons and warriors on a single day, on October 5, 1903. After their defeat, emissaries from Wushe notified a local police office that the severity of the trade embargo had inflicted suffering, and they offered to supply troops and porters to help build a guardline. The Taiwan Government-General kept Hōgō waiting. They finally sent negotiators in late 1905. Kondō Katsusaburō then acted as the go-between to orchestrate Wushe's surrender in 1906. In order to resume trade, the Paalan and Hōgō headmen allowed the government-general to build a guardline path to the summit of Shoucheng Dashan, just below its 2,420-meter peak. This commanding height overlooked dozens of settlements of strategic interest in and around Wushe.[92] To avoid being shot on sight, the Wushe-area men were told to bring Japanese flags to the Kasumigaseki station and check in before hunting in the area.[93] From this new section of guardline, which cut the Tgdaya villages off from the trade hub of Puli, the government-general was able to encircle the Atayal, Truku, and Sediq tribes north of Wushe in subsequent campaigns.[94] For brokering the surrender ceremony at the Kasumigaseki station, Kondō was awarded seventy yen for meritorious service. This was an extraordinary bonus. At this time, the top cash award for ranking inspectors was only sixty yen.[95]

Perhaps hoping to reproduce the 1906 breakthrough attributed to Kondō Katsusaburō, who was married to Iwan Robao of Paalan, Police Bureau head Ōtsu Rinpei urged the government to actively encourage, instead of merely tolerate, mixed marriages between low-ranking Japanese officers and indigenous women from chiefly lineages.

THE POLITICAL MARRIAGES UNDER SAKUMA SAMATA'S ADMINISTRATION

Following the Russo-Japanese War (1904–05), Governor-General Sakuma Samata's administration (1906–15) accelerated the policy of military conquest over the Atayal villages that had refused to surrender their rifles and sovereignty during the previous decade of colonial rule. Although Wushe had formally submitted in 1906, many of the tribes farther upland and inland still remained defiant. Sakuma pledged to break the resistance of the northern tribes once and for all by extending the heavily armed guardline to the heart of Atayal country to encompass Xalut (which subsumed Masitoban), Truku, and Toda (see map 1).[96]

Sakuma's right-hand man on indigenous policy, Police Bureau chief Ōtsu Rinpei, inspected the forward posts of the guardline in spring 1907. His report proposed to remedy the alarming interpreter situation with a "political-marriage" policy:

> I have sensed an extreme paucity of indigenous-language translators at every installation on my tour. This being the case, it is not difficult to imagine that many, many more translators will be necessary as we bring the indigenes within the fold of government. I need not mention that success in managing the indigenes hinges upon the ability of our translators . . . . The quickest route to cultivating translators would be to give occasional financial assistance to the appropriate men and have them officially marry *banpu* .
>
> [We] recognize that such marriages can cause trouble because indigenes . . . will say that such marriages are unfair and benefit only the villages or lineages of the *banpu*'s new husband. By the same token, if the Japanese husband is rotated to another post and abandons his wife, it will offend indigenous sentiment. Nonetheless, our present lack of translators is troubling. Because marriage to an indigenous woman will raise living expenses, occasional moneys should be provided for the low-ranking men who cannot afford it.[97]

In August 1908 Ōtsu commissioned Kondō to secure Wushe allies in order to add another spur to the system of guardlines already in place. Kondō himself initially demurred but then reconsidered when Ōtsu offered him a land grant of thirty hectares near the Kasumigaseki police station outside Puli. In October Kondō

FIGURE 22. *Left, in Japanese clothing,* Kondō Gisaburō, with defeated Truku peoples, January 1915. The photographer, Mori Ushinosuke, attested to Kondō's linguistic prowess in Truku and credited him with helping to defeat the Truku pictured here. Note the oilcan in the foreground: a bamboo indigenous drinking vessel is resting on top. Mori Ushinosuke, ed., *Taiwan banzoku zufu,* vol. 1 (Taipei: Rinji Taiwan kyūkan chōsakai, 1915), plate 31.

found allies in the settlements of Hōgō (headman Aui Nukan) and Mehebu (headman Ludao Bai), two Tgdaya groups who considered Truku and Toda enemies.[98] According to Kondō, Ludao Bai and Aui Nukan demanded that he and his younger brother Gisaburō (see figure 22) take wives in Wushe to seal the bargain. Accordingly, Kondō paid the price of one pig to Paalan's chief to ratify his "divorce" from Iwan Robao to pave the way for his second marriage.[99]

In January 1909 the brothers Kondō were married to Obin Nukan and Chiwas Ludao. In late February, soon after the formalization of the alliance by marriage, Kondō Katsusaburō led some 654 Wushe warriors in the general attack on Toda and Truku, which was successfully concluded by March 1909.[100] The official report states that Wushe drew the Taiwan Government-General into a local feud by blaming Toda for recent attacks on the Japanese guardline. The report's authors were skeptical of the charges against Toda but went along because they thought it expedient to use Wushe's manpower to gain a strategic foothold in difficult terrain. In addition to Kondō's 654 Wushe (Tgdaya) allies, who apparently acted as laborers, the government fielded 580 fighting men for the climactic attack on Toda.[101] These maneuvers secured more commanding heights for Japanese cannon and mortars as well as strategic passes for communication, which allowed the government-general to effectively hem in the Sediq territory from all sides.[102]

As an eldest son and a future *koshu* (household head), Kondō Katsusaburō expected to secure his Japanese family's future by obtaining a large, government-registered farm near Puli for the care of his aged father, per Ōtsu Rinpei's promise in August 1908. Indeed, Kondō's father, who had immigrated to Taiwan by this time, passed away in March 1909, leaving Kondō legally responsible for the care of his mother, younger brothers and sisters, and a number of nieces. Kondō spent the years 1909 through 1916 pressing claims for the promised acreage while continuing to accept government commissions as a guide and interpreter.

As the years wore on, his patron Ōtsu Rinpei returned to Japan; other officials familiar with Kondō's case left Nantou Prefecture. Finally, Wushe district police inspector Kondō Shōsaburō (no relation) deeded the land to his own relative, pre-empting Katsusaburō's claim. This perceived slight angered Katsusaburō's younger brother Gisaburō to the boiling point, according to Katsusaburō's testimony. In 1916 Gisaburō tendered his resignation in Taipei but was instead transferred out of Wushe to a new post in Hualian District at Pushige.[103]

Sixteen-year-old Kondō Gisaburō had come to Taiwan in 1901. Gisaburō worked his way up through the ranks to become a sergeant in the indigenous-territory police by the time of his infamous transfer, thanks to his facility with the Sediq dialects spoken near Wushe. Igarashi Ishimatsu, a Japanese official of long experience in Wushe, recalled Gisaburō as a companionate husband to Chiwas Ludao and a figure of local respect. Igarashi claimed that Chiwas's devotion to Gisaburō allowed the Japanese to squelch an uprising by Xalut and Salamao in 1913. Overhearing the plan from her brother Mona Ludao, Chiwas alerted Gisaburō, who in turn sounded the alarm and averted disaster for the Japanese.[104] Such timely intelligence is all that Ōtsu Rinpei could have hoped for when he called for political marriages back in 1907. However, this success story would be short-lived.

After Gisaburō's 1916 transfer to Pushige, he never returned, leaving Chiwas bereft. She eventually remarried a local man but was never compensated with death benefits, nor was she given a sinecure, as was done with other abandoned wives.[105] Kondō Katsusaburō recalled that Chiwas had not been entered into Gisaburō's *koseki* (household registry), making it impossible for the elder Kondō to file a claim on Chiwas's behalf.[106]

THE TAISHŌ-PERIOD POLITICAL MARRIAGES

From 1909 to 1914, Sakuma Samata's "five-year plan to control the aborigines" (*gokanen keikaku riban jigyō*) brought most of Atayal country under direct colonial rule. When the temporary organ established to administer Sakuma's five-year plan (the Bureau of Aboriginal Affairs) was disbanded in July 1915, the Taiwan Government-General declared victory in the north.[107] Thereafter, the indigenous territory was governed by Japanese police officers who "possessed the power of life and death" over their colonial subjects. The indigenous-district police were charged with peacekeeping, educational, and medical functions. They became the eyes, ears, hands, and feet of the Taiwan Government-General in the lands under "special administration." Unlike their predecessors, who lived near trading posts or in border towns, Japan's new "aborigine hands" would reside among the tribes and villages that they governed. As salaried officials (in contrast to *tongshi*), they would take direct orders from their superiors and transmit these orders to the "submitted tribes."

Two particularly well-known Japanese-indigene marriages, both initiated to advance the guardline in Atayal country, survived into an era that saw increased surveillance and conscripted labor. One of these marriages ended in 1925 with the sacking of Shimoyama Jihei after a drunken altercation with his superior officer, the other in 1930 with the killing of Sazuka Aisuke in the Wushe uprising.

Shizuoka native Shimoyama Jihei arrived in Taiwan in 1907 as a young army veteran, two years before Sazuka's arrival in 1909. During Sakuma's five-year campaign, the Malepa dispatch station was overrun and its staff wiped out. To reestablish control, the Nantou District head of indigenous affairs sent Shimoyama to run things, after ordering him to marry Pixo Doleh, the daughter of Malepa's headman. According to Pixo's niece, Malepa assented to the marriage out of economic desperation to obtain needed patronage and rifles.[108] According to their son Hajime, Pixo became proficient at Japanese conversation. Shimoyama, on the other hand, could not speak Atayal. Pixo bore him two sons and two daughters. Shimoyama's other betrothed, Shizuoka native Katsumata Nakako, arrived in Puli after he and Pixo had started their Malepa family. Nakako also began to bear Shimoyama's children. For a time, Shimoyama shuttled between Puli and Malepa. No longer able to afford two households, he finally moved his Japanese family to Malepa. Pixo Doleh, the daughter and sister of local headmen in a fiercely monogamous society, was humiliated.[109]

Shimoyama's open display of contempt for Atayal sensibilities came to the attention of Neng'gao district commander *(gunshu)* Akinaga Nagakichi in 1925. One oral history claims that Akinaga was tipped off by a disgruntled Atayal youth. In any event, Akinaga broached the delicate issue of bigamy in front of assembled Malepa men. Shimoyama retorted that Pixo's relatives had consented to this arrangement. Besides, an angered Shimoyama replied, he had been assured that he could break off the political marriage to Pixo after three years' time, even if there were children. For his part, Akinaga took umbrage at being contradicted publicly by a subaltern. Tempers flared. Shimoyama challenged Akinaga by grabbing his lapels. Akinaga then threw Shimoyama down on a table. Shimoyama was dismissed for insubordination the next day, a fact that demonstrated clearly that the government-general believed it could handle affairs in Malepa without him. Although his abrupt departure left Pixo bitter, Shimoyama secured a job for her at a Wushe infirmary at a salary of forty yen per month before he left. Nonetheless, Shimoyama's son Hajime recalled that his mother was never entered into Shimoyama's family register *(koseki)* as a legally recognized wife. Nonetheless, due to Pixo's high status in local society and official concerns about the ramifications of mistreating a headman's daughter, Shimoyama was not able to treat her as a disposable concubine.[110]

Nagano Prefecture native Sazuka Aisuke (1886–1930), unable to abide impoverished country life in Japan's "snow country," fled to Taiwan via Tokyo one January morning in 1909 with money stolen from his father.[111] Five years later, as combined police, army, and navy forces bombarded resistant villages near Hualian Harbor in the last spasms of Sakuma's "campaign to end all campaigns," Sazuka married Yawai Taimu, the daughter of an Atayal headman in Masitoban, just north of Wushe.

Sazuka's wife, Yawai, was remembered as one who spoke proper Japanese and worked harder than other Atayal women to assimilate to Japanese customs.[112] As one postmortem account of the Wushe Rebellion put it, Yawai married outside her local society only to be mistrusted by her fellow Atayal. She was also looked down upon by Japanese colonists for being a "savage."[113] In a word, Sazuka and Yawai were representative outcasts of empire. One left the bleak prospects of Nagano behind to seek fortune in a colonial periphery, while the other was cast out by her father to shore up his position as a local headman.

For his willingness to persevere in aborigine country, Sazuka was finally made chief of the Wushe branch station on March 31, 1930.[114] Wushe was an administrative center and showpiece for Japanese policies vis-à-vis the northern Taiwan Indigenous Peoples, a real step up from isolated Masitoban. There were eleven settlements under his new watch, and Wushe boasted a post office, schools, hot-springs inns, trading posts, and dormitories for students and government workers. Although it was a promotion, the reassignment to Wushe turned out to be Sazuka's death sentence. Because of their roots in Masitoban, Yawai and Sazuka were viewed suspiciously in Wushe. Residents in Wushe's villages were Sediq Tgdaya, who spoke a different language than Masitoban Atayals. Shimoyama Hajime recalled that Sediq visitors to Atayalic Malepa spoke Japanese with their hosts, since Sediq and Atayal were mutually unintelligible.[115] In the Xalut settlements of Malepa and Masitoban, Sazuka relied upon his wife's Masitoban networks for local knowledge and, to some extent, for his legitimacy as a leader for some two decades. His linguistic facility and political experience in these former posts, however, provided Sazuka with little useful intelligence in the new setting. On the contrary, Sazuka's affiliation with a non-Sediq Atayal—his wife, Yawai Taimu—and her father inclined Tgdaya residents within his jurisdiction to accuse Sazuka of favoritism toward Xalut peoples. They expected Sazuka and Yawai to exact vengeance against Tgdaya peoples in relation to recent intra-indigenous (though state-aided) violence.[116] And although Ōtsu Rinpei thought low-ranking rural policemen such as Sazuka could maintain bicultural households on their modestly supplemented salaries, Sazuka was an infamous embezzler, who was known to withhold pay and salt it away for his personal use. After his death in the rebellion, it was discovered that he had amassed ¥2,000 in a savings account and ¥20,000 in cash.[117]

Shimoyama Jihei's ignominious firing and Sazuka Aisuke's violent demise can be considered the final blows to a system of rule predicated on a gender division of labor for cross-cultural communication that dated back to early Qing times. In this system, locally embedded women, as the daughters of headmen or local indigenous notables, were either adopted or married into outsider families to act as buffers between politically separated but economically linked social formations. The men in this equation—be they Han merchants, settlers, or officials, or Japanese policemen or trading-post operators—capitalized on their wives' bilingualism and local kin networks to make a go of it on the so-called savage border. In hindsight, it is clear that this ad hoc arrangement was perhaps adequate for maintaining a certain volume of cross-border trade or for gathering military intelligence for short-term expeditions. But intercultural marriages fell far short of providing a mechanism to consolidate a stable system of outsider rule among the Sediq, Atayal, and Truku peoples of northern Taiwan.

According to statistics compiled by Kitamura Kae, twenty-nine Japanese policemen stationed in the special administrative district were proficient in an Atayalic language circa 1930, to rule over hundreds of settlements—many of them still hostile. According to Shimoyama Hajime, the son of Pixo and Jihei, the language barrier forced Japanese policemen to use blows instead of admonishments. Hajime extrapolated from his father's beatings to hypothesize that generalized physical abuse was a long-term cause of the Wushe uprising. In an interview years after the fact, Hajime even wondered if better language skills among the Japanese police could have averted the slaughter that took place on October 27, 1930.[118]

TEACHING JAPANESE TO INDIGENOUS PEOPLES

As Atayalic language competence among Japanese policemen declined in the 1920s, the Japanese language skill of indigenes was on the rise. The formal instruction of indigenous peoples in Japanese language was consonant with the generalized imperial impulse to diffuse national culture outward. It also aimed to cultivate a corps of interpreters whose loyalty was directed toward the state rather than their Taiwanese in-laws or private trading houses. While this project did not bear fruit in time to prevent the Wushe uprising, it represented the centerpiece of Japan's assimilation policies toward indigenes.

In 1896, soon after establishing itself in Taipei, the Taiwan Government-General established fourteen Japanese-language training institutes *(kokugo denshūjo)* throughout the island. Older students took crash courses in language and basic arithmetic to clerk and translate for the government. Younger students, as objects of the regime's "attraction policy," studied "written Chinese, geography, history, singing and gymnastics."[119] The Hengchun walled city institute in southern Taiwan served a mixed population of "acculturated indigenes" *(jukuban)* and Han students. Nearby, an annex school *(bunkyōba)* was built in Tuilasok; it was the first government school for indigenes.

The Paiwan settlement of Tuilasok was the home of Toketok, the man with whom LeGendre had struck agreements in 1867 and 1869. Toketok died in 1873, thus leaving his nephew Tsului to represent Tuilasok in meetings with Saigō Tsugumichi and other foreigners. By Tsului's side sat Jagarushi Guri Bunkiet—the son of a Tuilasok woman and a Guangdong immigrant surnamed Lin. Bunkiet was born in Checheng or Poliac in 1854 and was purchased by the sonless Toketok, who groomed the bilingual Bunkiet to be a headman.[120] Bunkiet came to the notice of Qing officials when Hengchun walled city was built in 1875 as a base for Shen Baozhen's "open the mountains, pacify the indigenes" campaigns.

For his success as a labor recruiter, the Qing awarded Bunkiet the surname Pan. He thereafter worked, presumably as an interpreter, in the 1890s campaigns to pacify the Hengchun tribes, earning a Qing meritorious rank of the fifth order *(wu-pin)*.[121]

In November 1895, Bunkiet, bearing a flag his family had received from Saigō twenty-one years earlier, attended Hengchun dispatch-station chief Sagara Nagatsuna's first official audience.[122] That same month, a Japanese garrison stationed in Sabaree mistakenly killed several men and burned down even more dwellings. According to one version of the story, the garrison heard shots fired from the direction of a Koalut village. In another version, they mistook an armed contingent of Paiwan men for hostiles. In any event, skittish Japanese troops responded by tying eight villagers to trees. While Koaluts were fleeing, the Japanese proceeded to torch twelve houses. They also shot and killed six residents in the confusion. News of the depredations had spread to neighboring settlements when Bunkiet stepped in. With Bunkiet's intercession, the Japanese government assuaged local anger by disbursing twenty yen each to the families of the dead and five yen each to the victims of the massacre. For this service, Bunkiet was appointed commissioner attached to the Hengchun dispatch station.[123]

As the government-general's new point man for the lower Hengchun, Bunkiet, in concert with other local leaders, brokered the formal submission of forty-four tribes in Taidong that same February.[124] Bunkiet and another bicultural mediator, a Puyuma woman known to us as Tata Rara, most famously assisted the government-general on May 18, 1896. Instead of merely brokering an agreement, Tata mobilized Paiwan and Puyuma troops to militarily defeat a remnant Qing officer named Liu Deshao (Liu Tek-chok) and his followers.

The Qing formally surrendered Taiwan on April 17, 1895, but (because of numerous rebellions) it took until April 1, 1896, for Japan to officially declare an end to

FIGURE 23. The Puyuma "Joan of Arc" Tata Rara with Japanese interpreter Nakamura Yūsuke, 1896. Adolf Fischer, *Streifzüge durch Formosa* (Berlin: B. Behr Verlag, 1900), 323.

the state of war and institute a civil government. Liu Deshao remained in southern Taiwan, operating as a local potentate beyond the reach of the government-general past the cessation of military rule on the island.[125] In accord with Shen Baozhen's "open the mountains, pacify the indigenes" program, the Qing had begun to station officials and soldiers in Taidong (near Beinan) in 1875. Around two thousand men were posted throughout the Hengchun Peninsula. They were not especially brutal, wrote the Japanese commentator Hara Segai, but they did make inspections, conscript labor, and take millet and rice without paying. The Qing government accordingly became loathsome to the people, inciting head-hunting attacks on plainsmen and provoking armed standoffs. According to Hara's report, when the Japanese took Taiwan in 1895, the Qing abandoned these forces without alerting them of the cession. The remnants resorted to looting and stealing to feed themselves, and the area descended into chaos.

During his first diplomatic mission to Taidong in February 1896, Sagara Nagatsuna consulted with Zhang Yichun, a prominent merchant and husband of the multilingual interpreter Tata Rara. Zhang's wife, Tata, then lobbied Sagara's translator, Nakamura Yūsuke, to intervene against Liu's remnant troops (see figure 23).[126]

Tata Rara was the daughter of Chen Ansheng, a chief who dealt with LeGendre during his perambulations in the 1870s. One source even referred to her as "Chen Tata."[127] Tata Rara spoke Southern Min Chinese, as well as the Puyuma, Paiwanese,

Tatta mit Pilamleuten.

FIGURE 24. Tata Rara with her Puyuma militia, 1896. Adolf Fischer, *Streifzüge durch Formosa* (Berlin: B. Behr Verlag, 1900), 324.

and Amis languages. Like Bunkiet, she earned a salary of six yuan per month as a Qing subofficial,[128] presumably for services rendered during the *kaishan fufan* campaigns.

In May 1896, Tata and Bunkiet organized a militia of three hundred indigenes to expel the Qing remnants. Tata Rara herself personally led the men through a hail of musket fire to secure the surrender of a thousand Qing troops. She appears to have been a formidable commander. One German publication referred to her as the "Puyuma Joan of Arc," while a Japanese report referred to her as a "heroine" (see figure 24).

Bunkiet and Tata, as liaisons and military leaders, earned cash rewards and plaudits for the defeat of Liu Deshao. Bunkiet received a commendation called Order of the Sacred Treasure, Sixth Rank, on December 15, 1897 (see figure 25).[129] Tata Rara belatedly received her reward of forty yen on February 9, 1900.[130]

After the suppression of Liu Deshao, Bunkiet and Sagara Nagatsuna applied to have the colony's first Japanese-language institute built for indigenous students. On September 2, 1896, a plan to build this modest school was approved. Bunkiet then mobilized his followers to supply land, building materials, and labor in time for a September 10 opening ceremony. One encomium to Bunkiet reports that he registered his own nephew to lead by example and that over thirty youths in Tuilasok followed suit.[131] A less celebratory account by a Japanese teacher reported

FIGURE 25. Tuilasok interpreter, headman, and Qing/Japanese official Pan Bunkiet, ca. 1900. The medal on his suit is a sixth-grade Order of the Sacred Treasure, conferred in 1897 by the Japanese government. Jun'eki Taiwan Genjūmin kenkyūkai, ed., *Inō Kanori shozō Taiwan Genjūmin shashinshū* (Taipei: Jun'eki Taiwan Genjūmin hakubutsukan, 1999), 177. Photograph courtesy of the publisher: The Shung Ye Museum of Formosan Aborigines, Taipei.

that the first group of twenty-seven students did not know why they had matriculated, except that the headman Bunkiet had sent them.

Three neighboring Hengchun Paiwan settlements, Koro, Tekiri, and Kauwan, responded to Sagara's announcement of the "urgent matter" of Japanese-language education with much less enthusiasm. They temporized by convening councils to deliberate the matter. Tekiri and Kauwan did not apply for schools, and by 1900, only two institutes had been built in all of Hengchun. Koro village finally applied on the condition that the school be combined with a gun and ammunition depot. As Kitamura points out, the language institutes were not gifts from the government but were built with locally provided materials and labor. "Buy-in" could not be assumed. Several Paiwan schools were shut down temporarily or closed because of armed attacks from neighboring settlements.[132] Reminiscent of the Meiji state's early efforts to spread compulsory schooling throughout Japan, central ambitions outstripped budgets, parents could not always spare the foregone labor of the children in the fields, and resentment by locals who paid for these unfunded mandates led to hundreds of cases of vandalism.[133]

Despite these hiccups, the lower Hengchun villages were far ahead of indigenous settlements in the north in terms of formal education.[134] We recall here that Ōkubo Toshimichi's parting shots to Qing officials in Beijing at the conclusion of his negotiations in 1874 included criticism of the lack of schools in the Paiwan settlements in Langqiao. While the Qing did not exactly dot the landscape with schoolhouses, it did make a beginning. After Japanese forces left in 1874, Hengchun city drew population by decree but also through attraction, as the Qing filled in an administrative grid with *baojia* (mutual responsibility) units and *zhuang* (administrative villages). Educational institutions to transform indigenous peoples into Sinophone Qing subjects were also piloted. This flurry of activity directed at horizontal integration tipped the balance of power in favor of the Han, vis-à-vis the formerly dominant Paiwan, during the twenty-year interval between the Taiwan Expedition and the assumption of Japanese rule.[135]

When Inō Kanori arrived in Hengchun at the behest of the TGG education bureau, the Tuilasok annex school was already in operation. In late October 1898, Inō stopped in the walled city, visited the local Pacification Office, and finally reached Tuilasok. During his tour, Bunkiet invited Inō into a ceramic-roofed home, well appointed with Chinese furniture. Bunkiet put on an elaborate feast for his Japanese guests and showed Inō a treasured copy of the admonition that Saigō Tsugumichi had issued in 1874, warning the Paiwan to be obedient to the Qing.[136]

In his synthetic report on conditions throughout Taiwan's interior, Inō wrote that the lower Hengchun towns such as Tuilasok were the most "advanced" of all indigenous peoples, due to frequent intermarriage with Chinese in their proximity. Inō singled out Tuilasok and Sabaree especially as places where tiled-roof homes and the use of Chinese language were common—these villages were, in fact, hardly distinguishable from Han settlements, according to Inō. The "lower

Hengchun tribes," south of the line stretching from Mudan to Fenggang (see map 5), were therefore geographically advantaged compared to the more isolated and less "advanced" upper Hengchun villages, according to Inō's evolutionary taxonomy.[137] After the Qing began to fund reclamation and Han migration, the southernmost Paiwan tribes, such as Sabaree, Tuilasok, and Koalut, were forced to adopt the Qing hairstyle, the queue. In the northern part of the peninsula, however, around Mudan and Kuskus, Paiwan men retained their Paiwan hairstyles.[138]

In 1902 the Japanese Hengchun district officer applied to abolish the status of Mudan, Kuskus, Sabaree, and Tuilasok as "savage villages" (Japanese *sha*, Chinese *she*) and promote them to "townships" (Japanese *shō*, Chinese *zhuang*). The application, like Inō's survey ethnography, noted in-migration of Han and Paiwanese acculturation and intermarriage with Han as factors in favor of township status. Another reason the lower Hengchun tribes qualified for "normal administration" was their cultural competence regarding private property and the conduct of commerce. Most notably, unlike indigenous peoples more generally, the lower Hengchun Sinicized indigenes understood how to calculate the worth of trade-goods in abstract monetary units—rather than in terms of customary equivalences in bartered goods (see chapter 3). In a similar vein, the application noted that lower Hengchun Paiwanese adjudicated disputes through mediation. They did not follow formal court proceedings, but at least disputes were not solved by feuds, vendettas, or divination.

As a surplus-producing, stockbreeding, and agricultural area, lower Hengchun, it was argued, should contribute to the cost of government by paying taxes—which meant extending all rights and obligations of colonial subjects *(hontōjin)* to Koalut, Sabaree, Tuilasok, and selected other villages. Thus, on April 28, 1904, the former abodes of Isa, Toketok, and the wreckers of the *Rover* were, administratively speaking, no longer "savage" in the eyes of the Japanese government.[139] Bunkiet himself is said to have led a group of Paiwan residents out of the mixed-residence Tuilasok to resettle in Mudan Bay in 1901.[140]

The evidence offered above suggests that Japan's "savage border," reckoned as a cultural boundary that separated economic moderns from indigenous peoples, reflected the extent of the Qing government's reach by 1895: wherever Paiwanese had been forced to wear the queue, normal administration followed. In fact, the lower Hengchun settlements of Mudan and Kuskus (the villages whose men reportedly did not wear the Qing queue), located just north of Sabaree, Tuilasok, and Koalut, remained classified as *sha* (savage settlements) well into the 1930s. As map 4 and figure 51 indicate, Japan's ethnic classification excluded Tuilasok, Koalut, and Sabaree from the Paiwan zone by 1912, while most of lower Hengchun remained firmly within it. The colorful maps attached to 1930s statistical compendia followed suit. On the Paiwan side, as late as 1934, Mudan and Kuskus were still sending children to the "aborigine schools,"[141] despite the region's status as a relatively wealthy and economically developed location. Thanks to its suitable riverbanks, Mudan became an early site for the cultivation of paddy rice in 1909. Within a couple of decades, Mudan was a model rice-production center,[142] though it still remained within the indigenous zone.

This seemingly arbitrary line—which divided fellow Paiwanese in a surplus-producing and fertile area of Taiwan into normally and specially administered peoples—had one important consequence. Like the qualifications for indigenous-district policemen (see chapter 1), which were lower than those for policemen stationed in Han districts, the indigenous school curriculum was adapted to special conditions—it was watered down. From the beginning, indigenous students were not expected to perform as well as their Han counterparts in Hengchun city or the other common schools and language institutes. Even under auspicious conditions—with an eager and powerful collaborator in Bunkiet and a surplus-producing Paiwan population versed in the Southern Min dialect of Chinese—Sagara Nagatsuna and the higher-ups in Taipei designed the Tuilasok annex school to keep Hengchun residents of Paiwan ancestry "down on the farm." Although it has been celebrated as the first indigenous education facility in the history of Japanese colonial rule, the Tuilasok annex was, in fact, a precursor to the third-tier educational system that would define Japanese rule in the highlands.[143]

By March 1898 the Taiwan Government-General had built sixteen Japanese-language training institutes and an additional thirty-six annex schools; four of the latter were for indigenous children (all in Taidong or Hengchun, in the south). That same year, the institutes were discontinued and replaced by a more ambitious common-school *(kōgakkō)* system. Its six-year curriculum "consisted of ethics, Japanese language, classical Chinese (composition, reading, calligraphy), arithmetic, music and gymnastics."[144] However, in two locations, Hengchun and Taidong, the vocationally oriented institutes were left in place until 1905. As one official report put it, the "reason is not far to seek. The existence of so many aborigines in these districts accounts for this exception."[145] In 1904, thirteen language institutes and annexes served indigenous children, with an enrollment of 803 (759 males and 44 females).[146]

Even after the remnant language institutes for indigenous children were discontinued in 1905, indigenous schools remained separate and inferior, but under the new name aborigine common schools *(banjin kōgakkō)*.[147] The government-general's own English-language propaganda was forthright: "According to the new [1905] arrangement, the school course covers only four years instead of six . . . while the number of subjects was made less than those of the [common schools]. The aborigine pupils have in the regular course only three subjects: Morals, Japanese, and Arithmetic. They have no need of Chinese classics, Science, and Commerce. Only Agriculture, Manual Training, and Singing (one or all three) may be added to the regular course of study according to the intellectual development of the tribe."[148]

Because the residents of Tuilasok, Sabaree, and Koalut bore the burden of taxation after their incorporation into the regularly administered territory, their children were theoretically eligible to attend six-year common schools with a full curriculum.¹⁴⁹ Aborigine common schools were built among Amis and Paiwan peoples who lived under normal administration and remained concentrated in the "advanced" south and the eastern rift valley into the 1930s. By 1935, there were exceptions: five aborigine common schools had been built in the specially administered territories. Of these five, only one was located in the north among the Atayal, Sediq, and Truku populations.¹⁵⁰

Eika Tai has noted that the common schools for Han children were aimed at creating "citizens" *(kokumin)*, whereas that term was absent in planning documents and curriculum for the indigenous common schools. This nomenclature reflected the government-general's pre-1930s approach to indigenous education: it would create not fellow nationals but rather docile and useful subjects.¹⁵¹

THE EXPANSION OF INDIGENOUS EDUCATION TO THE NORTH

Due to the violence surrounding the camphor wars, which surely fed into Japanese officialdom's low estimation of Atayal cultural capacity, the first "northern tribes" school was established in Quchi in 1908. The Quchi school was called an aborigine youth school *(bandō kyōikujo)*, a new institution that complemented the aborigine common schools. The youth schools were creatures of the guardline movements discussed in chapter 1. In contrast to schools for Han, making "citizens" was not part of their writ.¹⁵²

At the Quchi school and others like it, indigenous children were taught comportment (bowing, sitting respectfully, interacting with superiors), lifestyle "improvement" (wearing geta [clog-sandals], using chopsticks, wearing pants), ethics (loyalty), farming (intensive, fixed plot), and handicraft production (see figure 26). The youth schools were staffed by policemen and district-office staffers. The guidelines were drawn up in 1908, in the midst of the war against northern indigenes. They were built in part to win over the indigenous peoples and also to train interpreters.¹⁵³ The pioneering Quchi school was moved upriver to Wulai in 1911. The bulk of instruction was in field cultivation, tree felling, and other "regular employments. Japanese-language training was the second most important pursuit."¹⁵⁴

In 1915, the same year that Japan's major military offensives against indigenous peoples were terminated with the retirement of Sakuma Samata, the Taiwan Government-General issued first-year and second-year readers for indigenous children titled *Banjin dokuhon* (A reader for indigenes).¹⁵⁵ A user's manual for *Banjin dokuhon* (published in 1916) forecasted an ethnically bifurcated administration and the birth of indigeneity in modern Taiwan. Taiwan's educational administrators in effect hardened the line that LeGendre drew between indigenes and Han for political purposes in 1872 (see chapter 1), that census-bureau desk

FIGURE 26. The Wulai School for Indigenous Children, which opened ca. 1910. The standing adults wear the trademark embroidered upper garments with decorative buttons, as immortalized by Mori Ushinosuke's Quchi portraits. The male children sport Japanese-style haircuts and imported clothing, while the girls wear Atayal leggings with Chinese-style upper garments. THE SCHOOL OF URAI SAVAGE TRIBE, lw0410, East Asia Image Collection, Lafayette College, Easton, PA, accessed July 26, 2017, http://digital.lafayette.edu/collections/eastasia/lewis-postcards/lw0410.

jockeys inscribed between "Mongolians" and "Malays" in 1905, and that guardline architects scorched into the earth in the 1910s. The manual explained:

> In April 1914 . . . aborigine common school regulations were promulgated, beginning a new chapter in indigenous education. [Initially . . .], the aborigine common schools used the Ministry of Education elementary-school reader designed for *naichijin* (Japanese), or the Taiwan Government-General common-school reader for *hontōjin* (Han Taiwanese). . . . However, it goes without saying that these two readers were inappropriate for aborigines, who are of a different race, who differ in language, whose environment and climate is not the same, and whose lifestyles and cultures are varied. Therefore, the government-general ordered the formation of an editorial board for a new set of *Aborigine Readers*. . . .[156]

While this manifesto suggests that indigenes had varied cultures and lifestyles, it was premised on the notion that they were all subunits of a Malay race that was also inscribed in the 1905 census categories. Education bureaucrats thus based the different levels of education, for Han and indigenous Taiwanese, on perduring attributes such as environment, race, and culture. The phrasing of the guidelines amplifies Matsuoka Tadasu's view that 1915 was the turning point when Japanese colonists began to accept the specially administered territory as a permanent, rather than expedient, division.

In 1902, by contrast, the district officer of Hengchun applied to move Tuilasok, Sabaree, and Koalut under normal administration ostensibly because these communities had been Sinicized. However, *Sinicized* referred to those who spoke Minnan Chinese (a Fujianese tongue) and wore a Central Asian hairstyle (the Qing queue). Therefore, the term *Han* in this case did not have an ethnic referent but served as a proxy for the ability to produce surplus wealth and participate in a commodified economy. We can read this circa 1904 usage of *Han* as equivalent to *liangmin* (good subject), an old Qing term that separated most imperial subjects from pariahs, bannermen, nobles, and outlanders.

But under the 1916 educational guidelines for indigenes, reflecting wider currents in the post–World War I Wilsonian dispensation, indigenous status was being moved out of the plastic category of "uncivilized" and into the static category of "possessing unique attributes" as a racial/cultural marker, while the term *Han* moved in the same direction as it also became particularized as an ethnonym. As Sakano Tōru has argued, the first decades of Japanese colonial rule saw a conflation of "civilization" with "Sinicization" in the discourse on "aborigine improvement." However, by the 1930s, "imperialization/Japanification" had become firmly entrenched as the telos of progress in official discourse.[157]

The pointed suppression of Chinese-character (Japanese *kanji*, Chinese *hanzi*) use in the 1915 readers furthered the ethnic bifurcation of Taiwan into Han and indigenous moieties. While common schools for Han students[158] and late Qing indigene schools in Taiwan focused on Chinese reading and writing,[159] Japanese authorities in post-Sakuma Taiwan regarded Chinese characters as optional for indigenes, almost a luxury. The first two years of indigenous instruction, according to reformed rules, were conducted in katakana (a syllabary). Teachers stressed oral communication and diction; hiragana (another syllabary) was added in the third year, with some very elementary Chinese characters. In the fourth year, indigenes learned a few dozen *kanji* related to their customs, surroundings, and vocations but not nearly enough to read a Japanese newspaper or a Chinese poem.[160]

Of course, Japanese itself, like Chinese, was hardly a monolith, and what constituted Japanese in 1915 required spelling out. Because many indigenous-district policemen hailed from northeastern Japan and Kyūshū, the 1916 teacher's guide, echoing those for "national-language" teachers in the home islands, mandated the use of Tokyo-standard pronunciations. It inveighed against the rural Japanese policemen's "ragged Japanese" and "vulgar colloquialisms" and "mispronunciations," and it urged proper diction.[161] Shimoyama Jihei's son recalled that the Kyūshūans and Okinawans who staffed the aborigine police passed their rough Japanese on to their students; female Atayal women commonly used locutions like *ore* and *o mae* (very casual forms of male speech).[162]

Again promoting ethnic bifurcation, Japanese educators also pushed the notion that, as members of the Malay race, the indigenes were ethnic affines of the Japanese. Teachers could use the fourth-year reader's account of the emperor Jimmu's eastward conquests, it was suggested, to incline Taiwan's "Malays" (indigenes) to disidentify with the Han race and imagine themselves as long-lost cousins of the Yamato (Japanese) ethnos.[163]

So while the emphasis of indigenous education was practical and focused on everyday conversation, it also held within it the seeds of more complex forms of indoctrination. The fourth-grade reader taught students that a typical *ban-sha* (aborigine settlement) contained about 30 families and 150 residents. Indigenous residents generally farmed their plots but occasionally hunted in the mountains. Within each *ban-sha*, two buildings were most prominent: the schoolhouse and the police station. According to the reader, before the police station arrived, farming was difficult because indigenous peoples were in a perpetual state of war. Now they could farm peacefully. And, if they studied hard enough in school, they might be sent to the capital to study Japanese. One sample lesson reproduced postcards from a fictitious older brother in Taipei. The postcards reproduced pictures of the governor-general's residence and a large, ornate school building, as well. In addition to the large buildings of the capital, the reader also illustrated the countless thousands of Japanese troops that paraded in Tokyo and stood ready to put down rebellious imperial subjects.[164] In short, the reader reproduced in miniature the cardinal lessons of the indigenous sightseeing tours to Taipei and Tokyo, wherein headmen were made to understand imperial might and wealth and, hopefully, were dissuaded from further rebellious activity.

On the one hand, after 1928, some institutes adopted more challenging curricula. Thereafter, making *kokumin* (citizens) was a stated goal of indigenous schooling. Chinese characters were now part of the curriculum, as well.[165] However, proposals to send professional teachers to the indigenous territory, either to sharpen and reinforce the education outlined above or to improve the lives of indigenes, were continually thwarted. Indigenous schools were staffed by policemen for the duration of colonial rule. Throughout the 1920s, enrollments in aborigine youth schools actually increased. Nonetheless, allocations for instructional materials and physical plant were routinely diverted to fund shortfalls elsewhere in the colonial budget. In the end, writes Kitamura Kae, most Japanese-language schools for indigenous peoples, with the exception of the demonstration school at Jiaobanshan (see figure 27), became thinly disguised work camps.

Crops were raised by students to pay for their upkeep and the costs of infrastructure. Language lessons were dispensed in rickety buildings with chronic shortages of desks, chairs, and school supplies.[166] While common schools for Han students faced financial constraints because they were paid for with local taxes levied on colonized Taiwanese, the indigenous schools faced even tougher constraints because they were funded by a central government that was perpetually cash-starved.

FIGURE 27. Jiaobanshan model school for indigenous children, ca. 1930. [The Kappanzan School and Classroom], ip1532. East Asia Image Collection, Lafayette College, Easton, PA, accessed July 26, 2017, http://digital.lafayette.edu/collections/eastasia/imperial-postcards/ip1532.

With the arrival of Taiwan's first civilian governor-general, Den Kenjirō, in 1921, a few highly qualified and ambitious Han and indigenous students were permitted to enter elementary schools with Japanese children. In 1921, eight indigenous students throughout Taiwan met the tough standards. The denigrating word "savage" was dropped from the name of the aborigine common schools in 1922, but the course of study remained restricted to four years of practical education. The exceptions who proved the rule were children of Japanese policemen and indigenous women who entered the elementary school in Wushe alongside Japanese schoolchildren. Most indigene school attendees—themselves a slight percentage of the total population—went to the Wushe aborigine common school. This was the only common school for indigenous children for all of northern and central Taiwan; all other Truku, Sediq, and Atayal children, if they attended at all, were taught at Japanese police stations.

Two Wushe common-school graduates, Hōgō natives Hanaoka Ichirō (Dakis Nobing) and Hanaoka Jirō (Dakis Nawi), entered the Puli elementary school as teenagers in 1921. Puli was a walled city and gateway to the mountain settlements in central Taiwan. The two subsequently took jobs as a school instructor and a police assistant, respectively, near Wushe, and became famous for the suicide note they left on the morning of the October 27, 1930, Wushe Rebellion.[167] While they were not directly implicated in the attacks, they blamed "excessive forced labor" for the rebellion and reported that they had "been detained against [their] will by the barbarians." The passionately scrawled note criticized both sides, reflecting the painfully torn identity of men who had ascended the meritocratic ladder but also identified with the people they had left behind.

The Hanaokas (not related) had married local Hōgō women at a Japanese-style wedding ceremony near a government office in the 1920s. Their wives, Kawano Hanako (Obing Nawi) and Takayama Hatsuko (Obing Tado) were the daughter and niece of a leading Sediq political figure, the Hōgō paramount chieftain *(sōtōmoku)* Tadao Nōkan. Hanako and Hatsuko were frequently photographed in Japanese clothing and attended the Puli elementary school, like their husbands. According to Deng Xiangyang, these marriages were arranged by the government to provide examples of successful assimilation by indigenous peoples.[168]

The rumors of the two Hanaokas' complicity in the October 27, 1930, slaughter of Japanese civilians and police in the model indigenous administrative hub of Wushe suggested that too much education for indigenous peoples would only produce malcontents. Matsuda Yoshirō has written that after the 1930 uprising, indigenous peoples were no longer permitted to enroll in advanced educational institutes.[169] Kitamura Kae's statistics show that in the 1920s, fewer than ten students from the indigenous territory per year were selected to attend the elementary schools; by 1930 there were only twenty-eight total indigenous graduates of elementary, middle, normal, nursing, medical, and women's schools combined.[170] But the more important trend was the content, context, and purpose of indigenous education in the post-Wushe years, which shaded into the full-blown mobilization period after 1936. If the Taishō period can be characterized by the vocational bent of indigenous education, the Shōwa years featured an emphasis on spiritual transformation and imperial subjectification.

Inspector Yokoo Hirosuke took a leading role in framing post-Wushe policies for the indigenous areas. Yokoo obliquely referred to the "Hanaoka" syndrome with a reference to French colonial education in Africa. Yokoo believed that the French were moving too quickly on their assimilation policies. Therefore, the African educated elite returned to home villages resenting their own countries. Some suffered the anomie that bedeviled proletarian intellectuals in other colonies. Yokoo was not against education per se. He insisted that its quality and extent be improved and that Japanese-language training be more thorough. Yokoo stated his belief that indigenes should internalize and themselves propagate loyalty to the emperor and a sense of imperial mission. Somewhat paradoxically, Yokoo emphasized respect for the indigenous character (although he called for the reform, if not eradication, of many indigenous practices). While he was an advocate for imperial subjectification, Yokoo also believed that indigenous education should not exceed the cultural capacities of its targets.[171]

TGG policies indeed reflected the twin priorities of imperialization and respect for indigenous particularity in the 1930s. The period saw decreasing expenditures per indigenous student for education[172] but also saw renewed efforts to propagate Japanese language through other forms of schooling, including ubiquitous night schools attached to police boxes. One official estimate in 1937 put the overall "can understand basic Japanese for everyday tasks" rate for indigenes at 34 percent for males and 24 percent for females. Among Atayal peoples (Atayal, Truku, Sediq), these numbers were 40 percent and 32 percent, respectively. By 1942, roughly 50 percent of all indigenous peoples were proficient in conversational Japanese, with 58 percent of Atayal men reaching that level of proficiency.[173]

As indigenous proficiency in Japanese increased during the 1920s through the 1940s, the Taiwan Government-General hollowed out the incentive structure for Japanese policemen to learn indigenous languages. Before 1922 all policemen who passed a language test received stipends, but after 1931 that number decreased to 90 percent for a minority of "fluent" policemen and to only 20–30 percent of the majority "proficient" Austronesian language speakers. Diminishing incentives were reflected in low proficiency rates: in the 1930s, only 2.5 percent of indigenous district policemen were *fluent* in a local language, while 26 percent were merely *proficient*. That meant that about one in twelve dispatch stations had an officer fluent in a local language. But since the percentage of lower-ranking Japanese patrolmen in the indigenous area also decreased, while the number of indigenous policemen increased to about 50 percent of the police force,[174] the number of bilingual indigenous policemen actually increased; they just weren't Japanese.

During the period that I have characterized as falling under "native authority," circa 1910 to 1930, cross-cultural communication was anchored by female indigenous relatives of influential headmen who married Japanese policemen. The problems encountered by Kondō Gisaburō, Sazuka Aisuke, and Shimoyama Jihei revealed that system's limitations and contradictions. The reliance on chiefs not only circumscribed the influence and knowledge of policemen attached to them, but as we saw in chapter 1, the older generation of headmen themselves were unreliable vectors of public power. Therefore, after Wushe, they were replaced by new leadership: the indigenous youth corps *(Takasagozoku seinendan)*.[175]

These new youth leaders were called "pioneers" *(senkusha)*. They replaced the *tōmoku* and *seiryokusha* (headmen and men of influence) as the intermediaries between Japanese officialdom and the Taiwan Indigenous Peoples. With the advent of a new indigenous leadership recruited from aborigine youth schools, a less locally embedded intermediary cohort emerged. This new leadership was groomed to lead a society of farmers, stockbreeders, and fishermen who were destined, if Japanese colonial rulers had any say in the matter, to live their lives out in the indigenous territory. There was no question of integrating the highland economy with the rest of Taiwan. After the Wushe Rebellion, it was determined at the highest levels of government in Taiwan that Taiwan Indigenous Peoples could only thrive under the paternalistic care of a functionally specialized aborigine administration.[176]

As Japanese became the language of governance within the indigenous territory, Japanese policemen were rotated more freely over the surface of the territory. But their new ethos and sense of professional identity tied them to the second-order geobody of indigenous Taiwan. The new role of indigenous women in the post-Wushe era is perhaps best symbolized by the famous Atayal heroine Sayon. In September 1938, Sayon and ten other Atayal women were helping a local Japanese policeman named Takita cross a river to get to his military post and join the war in China. Weighed down with three of his suitcases, Sayon herself fell in and drowned, becoming a martyr and the subject of song, film, a memorial bell, and more.[177] The seventeen-year-old Sayon was neither an interpreter cohabiting with Takita nor a leader in war on the order of Iwan Robao or Tata Rara.

Instead, she was carrying luggage to help a mobile, uniformed, male agent of Japanese empire exit her village peacefully. While many treatments of Sayon emphasize the hoopla generated by her supposed spirit of sacrifice, she was essentially a porter. In fact, as the indigenous territories became sites of ethnic tourism in the 1930s, the luggage-carrying indigenous woman became a common sight.[178]

To be sure, the "normal administration" that indigenes were being excluded from meant heavy taxes, floggings by policemen without a trial (until 1921), and discrimination in public schools, administrative jobs, and the police force. Moreover, public education in the normally administered territories was far from universal or equal to the quality of education for children of Japanese colonists. Only 2.19 percent of school-age Taiwanese children attended schools in 1900. The rate reached 4.66 percent in 1905 and 5.67 percent in 1910.[179] By 1930, however, the rate was 30 percent, and by 1940, 60 percent.[180]

Even after Gotō's administration put an end to large-scale armed Han resistance in 1902, rebellions continued through 1915. In 1907 rebels led by Cai Qingrin killed twenty-four TGG policemen and frontier sentries in the "Beipu incident." The next day, insurgents killed all Japanese residents of Beipu town, for a total of fifty-seven fatalities in two days. The government-general killed about ninety rebels in its suppression sweeps. Over one hundred suspected rebels were arrested; nine were sentenced to death, and ninety-seven were either confined or put on corvée labor. Other planned rebellions were discovered before they came to fruition in 1912 and 1914. The hundreds of conspirators apprehended, however, suggests that Han-dominated lowland Taiwan could not be classified as a disciplinary society before World War I, insofar as brute force was required to maintain order.[181]

The Ta-pa-ni or Xilai'an incident of 1915 marked the last spasm of Han armed resistance.[182] Former colonial policeman Yu Qingfang (1879–1915) and associates led this millenarian uprising. According to Paul Katz, author of a definitive social history,[183] "the number of Taiwanese and Japanese killed during the fighting

[was] estimated to have exceeded 1,000 people. A further 1,957 Taiwanese were arrested... of whom 1,482 were put on trial and 915 sentenced to death. A total of 135 Taiwanese were executed before the Taishō Emperor issued a decree of clemency, while scores more died in prison."[184]

Han armed resistance never again reached the scale and intensity of the Beipu and Ta-pa-ni revolts. According to Caroline Hui-yu Ts'ai, by "1920, when the colonial administration of Taiwan delegated part of its power to local governments... structural integration by and large had been completed." In other words, over a two-decade period of experimentation, the Taiwan Government-General had effectively co-opted the *baojia* system for taxation and vital statistics while mobilizing it to make even Taiwan's rural population visible and amenable to policing and labor mobilization. Despite the coextension of territorially defined Japanese policing units *(gun)* with local self-responsibility units *(baojia)* throughout Taiwan, Ts'ai concludes that structural "integration... did not necessarily result in social integration. It took the two decades of the interwar period... for the colonial administration to appropriate Taiwanese society for its use."[185]

Nonetheless, in comparison to the indigenous territories, lowland Taiwan can be said to have become a disciplinary society in many respects. After the Ta-pa-ni rebellion was put down, normal administration began to diverge more sharply from special administration. By 1915, the year the reader for indigenes was published, a middle school had been established for Han Taiwanese. A few vocational schools were added after 1919 and a university (with only rare seats for Taiwanese) in 1928. Despite its restrictive and discriminatory nature, the Japanese education system for Han Taiwanese was robust enough to foment "major changes in the structure of Taiwanese elites. In the 1910s, the landlords and gentry... had begun to give way to the rising groups of professionals trained in colonial institutions."[186] Over the next two decades, the court system, especially for commercial law, became more equitable; corporal punishment was abolished; and a great number of rights guaranteed by the Meiji constitution for citizens on the main four islands were extended to Taiwanese under regular administration.[187]

Although social mobility through education for Taiwanese was restricted to medicine and education, it was structurally homologous to Japan's home-island system. Most students would obtain basic, functional literacy and morals education, and a small percentage of the population would be trained to lead the rest of society. Under colonial rule, these leaders were supposed to be models for collaboration and assimilation, but many led movements that challenged TGG prerogatives. The formation of a Taiwanese political class capable of mobilizing a petition movement for home rule and equal treatment in Japan had developed by 1914. This large-scale civil-society activism attests to the power of precolonial educational traditions and the strength of island-wide networks among Han Taiwanese. But the nonviolent political resistance movements of the 1920s and 1930s, as

Ming-cheng M. Lo has demonstrated, evolved in the colonial school system. In contrast, residents in the specially administered districts did not mount petition movements, establish opposition newspapers, or lobby the government in Tokyo. Instead, they attacked, burned, and looted exposed police boxes or Japanese settlements on occasion, most infamously on October 27, 1930.

PART TWO

Indigenous Modernity

3

Tangled Up in Red

Textiles, Trading Posts, and Ethnic Bifurcation in Taiwan

For a major exhibition titled *Rainbow and Dragonfly,* held from September 2014 through March 2015 at the National Taiwan Museum in Taipei, a large billboard greeted visitors and passersby with four distinct examples of Taiwanese indigenous textile manufacture, of varied pattern and age, all dominated by the color red. Inside, displays of Atayal cloth occupied fully one-half of the palatial museum's first floor. It was a complex installation: one-hundred-year-old, disembodied fabrics were juxtaposed with updated designs on sleek black mannequins; colonial-era ethnological surveys shared space with large color photos of contemporary weavers consulting them; and numerous imperial-era postcards illustrated the diversity, antiquity, and daily uses of the displayed fabrics.

The Taiwan Government-General established the National Taiwan Museum in 1908, at the height of Japan's camphor wars against the Atayal, Sediq, and Truku peoples who produced much of the cloth in this exhibition. The museum's current structure was completed in 1915, the year Sakuma Samata left office and declared victory in the war against the northern tribes. As the scorched earth, free-fire zones, and land-dispossession policies of that era displayed the negative effects of sovereign power, the coterminous planning, construction, and stocking of the museum exemplified the positivities generated under TGG auspices in the colonial period.

The *Rainbow and Dragonfly* exhibition, housed in a neoclassical, neocolonial edifice, was in good measure a dusting off, repackaging, and repurposing of the artifacts collected among indigenes during the Japanese occupation. Therefore, it revealed how colonial ethnography, museum practices, and photography were (and remain) active partners in the sustenance and revival of Atayal culture, which was also packaged in this exhibition as an element of Taiwan's national heritage. The silhouette outline maps of Taiwan's geobody that decorated the exhibition mark out Atayal and Paiwan homelands as the familiar second-order geobodies found on Inō's 1900 map (see figure 2). *Rainbow and Dragonfly* illustrated the difficulty of imagining modern Taiwan without its indigenous complement or indigenous Taiwan without its modern complement.

This chapter recounts a 150-year history of indigenous-outsider transactions centered on red-dyed cloth. It explains how the oldest artifacts in the *Rainbow and Dragonfly* exhibition conjoined global trade circuits, cross-cultural technological adaptations, colonial collecting, and Atayal social reproduction. In a word, this thread of colonial and postcolonial history illustrates how indigeneity and modernity coproduced each other.

GLOBAL ENTANGLEMENT AND LOCAL RESPONSES

U.S. consul to Taiwan James W. Davidson dated the "beginning of the commercial career of [Taiwan] . . . from 1858, when the two Hong Kong firms, Jardine Matheson & Co. and Dent & Co. first engaged the Formosan trade." Between that year and 1865, British, Russian, French, and American diplomats signed treaties with the Qing to open Danshui, Tainan, Jilong, and Gaoxiong to foreign commerce.[1] The next decade saw a lucrative tea, camphor, and sugar export boom. Taiwanese merchants and laborers organized and directed most of the trade, while a few scattered Western missionaries, exporters, and a lone British consul constituted the meager foreign presence.[2] However, the frequent disappearance of mariners on and off the coast (see chapter 1) prompted a few foreign agents to leave the security of ports to ransom survivors or locate their remains. Others traversed the island out of curiosity, to find commercial opportunities, or to win souls for Christ.

The guarantees of safety to foreigners spelled out in the Treaty of Tianjin of 1858, however, were moot in interior destinations beyond the limits of Qing administrative control. For such journeys, local trading-post operators and subofficials known as *tongshi* (interpreters) outfitted visitors with provisions, advice, and guides. Among the most noted items of purchase were gifts for indigenous hosts. U.S. consul to Xiamen Charles LeGendre's 1869 meeting with the Tuilasok chief Toketok (nudged to fruition with a baggage train of gifts) and Captain Douglas Cassel's 1874 meeting with Sabaree chief Isa (also concluded with lavish displays of generosity) are two prominent examples of the importance of gifts for borderland diplomacy (see chapter 1). So too with the aforementioned treks by Ueno Sen'ichi, Hashiguchi Bunzō, Kawano Shuichirō, and other Japanese emissaries to the "savage territory" in the 1890s. Gifts performed multiple functions in these settings. They were initially a means of paying for services rendered or expectations of future assistance, to be sure. But they were much more.

Presentations of gifts were also occasions for recording the emotional states of recipients and gauging the dispositions of little-known peoples as either "greedy," "honest," or "uncorrupted." Gifts also fostered trade dependency among indigenes. The regulation of gift giving was also implemented to reform mores, punish misdeeds, and incentivize compliance. Finally, gifts were recycled and repurposed. Manufactured containers were brought back to villages for reuse, while red-dyed textiles were disassembled and reassembled into traditional cloth and clothing, to be reexported to anthropologists, curators, and tourists as cultural items. As commodities in the Japanese curio, art, and souvenir markets, or as objects of aesthetic or scholarly contemplation, the reexported cloth and clothing became touchstones for metropolitan discourses on progress, primitivism, and cultural relativism. As such, these objects took their place next to the Gwanghwamun Gate in Seoul, Korean celadon wares, or bamboo and wickerwork from Taiwan.[3]

In a famous consular report that recounted his 1869 encounter with Toketok, Charles LeGendre wrote:

> I gave the chief one hundred and eighty yards of red camlet, a small pistol, a single-barrel shot gun (unserviceable), and a spear . . . an ivory spy-glass and case . . . some beads, and a quantity of rings, bracelets, and a case of gin . . . *Toketok had not expected this attention, and he was evidently much touched by it.* "If you have brought all this to buy me," said he, "you have taken a useless care, for you had my word; but if you hand me these presents as a token of friendship, I receive them with pleasure."[4]

Toketok's reported speech, to the effect that the 180 yards of red camlet and other gifts were mere "tokens of friendship" and that LeGendre had "taken a useless care," is significant for reprising assertions that indigenes were disinterested in material gain or profit. Toketok's soliloquy, recorded after the fact and at the end of a translation relay from Paiwan to Minnan Chinese to English, does not jibe with less florid descriptions of similar transactions. Other travelers to Taiwan recorded Toketok's businesslike collection of cash fees for the upkeep of stranded sailors.[5] LeGendre himself remarked in unpublished writings that Toketok's leadership of the eighteen tribes was financially draining and that the leader was known to drive hard bargains for ransoms of foreigners.[6] Douglas Fix has argued that when LeGendre arrived in Langqiao in 1867, Toketok's influence was at an apogee. By 1869, his hold on power had become precarious, in part for lack of funds.[7] But if LeGendre's imputation of native simplicity to a master negotiator rings false, it was not exceptional.

Edward House, a journalist who accompanied the Japanese invasion in 1874 and championed all of LeGendre's political positions, made similar observations. House had occasion to witness coastal Han Taiwanese bargain with troops for land, provisions, and wages as the army built its first camp, while House also reported on Japanese conferences with the Tuilasok and Sabaree leaders to negotiate alliances, passage, and land for an east coast garrison. At a June 8 meeting,

House wrote of Paiwan emissaries that "hints of the presents that were awaiting them at head-quarters did not affect their resolution, and it seemed impossible to move them, when suddenly Isa, stirred by what impulse I cannot imagine, unless it may have been the recollection of having made a promise at the time of his last visit, announced that he would go."[8]

For House, as for LeGendre, indigenes were indifferent to gifts but anxious to honor commitments. When Isa and a group of his confederate Paiwan headmen ceded a plot of land on the east coast for Japanese occupation, House wrote that offers "of payment were made, but the chiefs declined compensation, with the carelessness to gain which I have spoken of as characteristic of them."[9] House drove home his larger point with a comparison: "The savages [House's term for the Paiwanese] have nothing whatever of the Chinaman in their exterior aspect, and their ways of life are totally separate. The divergence of their disposition is most strikingly shown in the contrast between the insatiate greed of the West Coast [Han] and the indifference to gain of the mountaineers."[10]

LeGendre himself had several occasions to express vitriolic attitudes toward assorted Chinese officials and interpreters for their bad faith and greed, presaging Japanese scorn for Han Taiwanese who purportedly cheated indigenes in the so-called "border trade." In detailed reports of individual encounters, however, we find that the stark line House and others drew between the "Chinaman" and the "mountaineer" did not hold, calling into question their judgments that Han and indigenous attitudes toward profit or material gain were antithetical. For example, Toketok—the quintessential noble savage in the passage quoted above—himself slept in a Chinese bed, while one of his brothers could read and write Chinese. Isa, his successor as the dominant political figure in lower Hengchun, understood spoken Chinese. The "half-caste" allies and hirelings whom LeGendre and House distanced from China for having lived beyond the reach of Qing territory were referred to as "Chinese" by Douglas Cassel in unpublished correspondence—a contradiction that the American consul adjusted with a heavy editorial hand.[11]

In the long run, as this chapter shall argue, the triad of reinforcing stereotypes—impartial Japanese, avaricious Chinese, and innocent indigenes—became a self-fulfilling prophecy, as Japanese policies grounded in this discourse would eventually isolate Atayal, Sediq, Truku, Bunun, and Paiwanese from the market economy.[12] To be sure, the economies of upland rural Taiwan were not nearly as monetized or commoditized as the Han-dominated lowlands when Japanese colonists arrived in 1895. Therefore, a different sensibility and approach to commerce, gain, and valuation plausibly obtained in and beyond the savage border of Taiwan. At the same time, since this stereotype was resistant to empirical disconfirmation and durable in the face of historical change, it also functioned as a racial attribute, fixing certain populations with particular immutable characteristics in the discourses and legal apparatus of the colonizing power.

Like other travelers during the treaty-port period, LeGendre had an ax to grind with the local Qing officials, who seemed to thwart his every initiative, and Hakka intermediaries who profited from their monopoly on access to interior settlements. The everyday forms of resistance LeGendre faced are unsurprising, since his ability to travel to the interior of Taiwan was a direct result of the success of British arms in mainland China. Traders and diplomats in post-1842 Chinese treaty ports, LeGendre prominent among them, discovered that the stroke of a pen in Tianjin or Beijing did not magically transform Taiwan into a welcoming site for foreign residence or an arena of untrammeled access.

There is probably more than a kernel of truth to the perception that indigenes were more open to negotiation with foreigners than Han Taiwanese, since they sought allies in struggles against settlers or Qing officials over resources and territory. That is to say, the "greedy Chinese, innocent indigene" trope may have fairly reflected the experiences of individual diarists. There is also the possibility that Toketok's attitude toward gifts was context specific, dynamic, and grounded in a cosmology more intricate and meaningful than the sort of crass considerations that suggest themselves in LeGendre's and House's accounts. Anthropologist Kamimura Tōru has suggested as much by reconstructing a network of Parijarijao ("Paiwanized" Puyuma) chiefs and big men that was connected by patterned exchanges resembling a kula ring.

In Kamimura's view, the Langqiao Peninsula's indigenous Skaro lineages, with Tuilasok's Toketok first among them as the big stride chief *(ōmata tōmoku)*, ritually subordinated common Paiwan village chiefs (such as the Mudan headman, for example) through gifting relations. These transactions resembled tributary relations in some regards—as they featured hierarchical yet reciprocal ritual exchange—while they partook in some aspects of a kula ring, insofar as hierarchies were ratified only when equilibrium was restored at the termination of a cycle of gifting and countergifting. In Kamimura's reconstruction, Toketok, as the big stride chief, and Isa and the secondary great chief *(futamata tōmoku)* traveled widely to seasonal festivals to present finished goods such cloth, ritual daggers, alcohol, and millet cakes "downward." In return, subordinate chiefs, themselves members of aristocratic Paiwan lineages, countergifted "upward" with domesticated and hunted meat and presentations of large quantities of alcohol at banquets. When LeGendre and his men showed up with a large cargo of finished goods, which he lavished upon Toketok in exchange for alcoholic beverages and roast meat, Toketok situated LeGendre, quite publicly, in the position of one to whom fealty is rendered in return for protection, thereby inverting the *ōmata tōmoku*'s place in the gifting cycle—he became a receiver of finished goods instead of a supplier. If such were the case, then Toketok's hesitation to receive gifts can be interpreted as appropriate behavior for an *ōmata tōmoku* in a ritual gifting context. Kamimura regards the instances of Toketok's more avaricious bargaining as "enclave" transactions conducted outside the sphere of ritual relations and networks.[13]

Paiwan and Puyuma chiefly genealogies, foundation myths, and the specifics of prestations at festivals were not recorded until after the Japanese arrived as a colonizing power in 1895. Therefore, this more nuanced view of indigenous dispositions to gifts was not available to LeGendre, House, Mizuno, Kabayama, and the other men who became Toketok's and Isa's unwitting amanuenses. In the absence of countervailing explanatory frameworks, their treaty-port era jottings were elevated from commercial intelligence reports to sociological verities. For one, the musings of LeGendre and House, a U.S. consul and a journalist for the *New York Post*, respectively, were widely disseminated and archived for posterity in libraries and repositories. In addition, and more importantly, hundreds of LeGendre's reports, missives, and memoranda were translated into Japanese and read by Japanese officials. Ueno Sen'ichi, an assiduous consumer and translator of treaty-port documents, elaborated upon LeGendre's discourse in his seminal official writings in the 1890s, while Mizuno Jun himself echoed similar sentiments. Mizuno's early pronouncements as Taiwan's highest ranking civil official in 1895 cemented the "greedy Chinese, innocent indigene" binary in TGG circulars and archived reports.

As a permutation of the above-mentioned treaty-port era discourse, the trope of the "innocent" indigene took on new valences in colonial Taiwan. The Qing dynasty and its corrupt mandarinate were no longer relevant. The new foils were the untrustworthy bicultural border denizens discussed in chapter 2, the "interpreters" *(tongshi)*. This substitution of *tongshi* for mandarins mirrored the configuration of northern Taiwan's camphor forests as another "closed country" to be opened as an arena for high-velocity capitalism. Partly because they contained forests that sustained populations of animals, sources of clean water, fish, vegetables, and other resources, indigenes defended these lands with alacrity.

Nonetheless, the contest here was not between proto-environmental subsistence producers and rapacious capitalist invaders. Rather, the savage territory was an active zone of ongoing economic exploitation, like Chinese ports before the arrival of Western gunboat diplomacy. As Takeshi Hamashita has written of this maritime economy, the new entrants—this time the Japanese—did not displace an isolated traditional economy with profit-driven, translocal commercial activity. Instead, they overlaid a new system of rules and procedures and connected an existing system to wider currents of global trade. In this milieu, aptly described by Antonio Tavares as a late-imperial exchange economy, indigenes, Han Taiwanese, and operators who straddled both groups exploited these forests for commodities, not just birds, deer, firewood, and mushrooms.

As the Taiwan Government-General turned its attention to camphor as a fiscal boon for its ailing balance sheet, Japanese attributions of greed and faithlessness to *tongshi* (interpreters) reflected frustration with "toll states" that earned money by taxing and monopolizing access to camphor producers. For actuarially minded administrators in Taipei and Tokyo, this intermediary layer of brokers presented an obstacle to the efficient extraction of high volumes of product.[14] The trope of Chinese greed and indigenous honesty also justified colonial rule. As Japanese displaced interpreters, private militias, and Qing armies as agents of dispossession, the insistence upon indigenous innocence and victimhood validated Japanese policies to annex land, engage in forced relocation, and restrict Han immigration. Because indigenes did not understand the concept of private property, ran the argument, they could not make legal claims to title deeds for land. Consequently, their legalistic transformation into economic wards of the state allowed the government-general to sell off "excess land" to logging companies, in a repeat of the gambit used in Hokkaidō vis-à-vis Ainu peoples in 1899.[15]

Like any other colonial project, however, Japanese rule contained its own internal tensions, while it underwent historical vicissitudes. A competing discourse generated by these same cross-border exchanges identified Atayal red-striped capes as an element of a distinctive cultural ensemble. From the viewpoint of colonial ethnology, any cloth, implement, word list, or social convention that attached to "Atayalness" possessed a measure of intrinsic worth. As Scott Simon has noted, the ethnonym Atayal is a Japanese-era creation. Today, this imposed category has become an object of heated political contestation in the postcolonial period.[16] On the other hand, its origins were far from nefarious. The Japanese man who put the word *Atayal* into play recorded it as an autonym, a term provided to him in collaboration with agentive Atayal peoples.

In fact, the term *Atayal* had its origins in a dissenting discourse. Yamaji Katsuhiko's study of the centrality of Atayal textiles and Paiwan woodcarving to Japanese-indigenous relations over the past century is important in this regard. Echoing the findings of Hu Chia-yu, Yamaji notes that early Japanese descriptions of Atayal cloth juxtaposed them with other elements of ethnic identity—face tattoos, housing architecture, origin myths, and so on—to construct Atayal people as an ethnos. Hu's translation from Inō's famous 1900 survey is instructive: "The less abstract the costume design becomes, the higher its intellectual level tends to be. The more concrete [a] costume decoration becomes, the higher its intellectual level.... Thus, the weaving patterns of the Atayal costumes consist of straight lines and angles and elements arranged without clear order ..., which reflect a lower intellectual level. The embroidery designs on the Paiwan costumes consist of pictorial animal figures ... which demonstrates a higher intellectual level."[17]

By the 1920s, however, such antiseptic (and at times derogatory) descriptions gave way to aesthetic engagement and emotional investment. As was the case with Paiwan wood carvings, Bunun song, and Amis dance, Atayal weaving provided Japanese academics, tourists, and impresarios with a means to rejuvenate a Japanese self ravaged by the atomism and dislocations of urbanized modernity.[18]

Haruyama Meitetsu has argued that the colonial history of Taiwan cannot be written in isolation from political developments in Tokyo. For Haruyama, the twists and turns in the history of Taiwan's administration were intimately linked to regime turnover in Japan's central government. Haruyama rightly insists that Japan's ruling elites were a dynamic and internally divided group and that one must specify "who, what, and where" when imputing motives and causality to "the metropole" in the study of colonial Taiwan.[19] The same can be said for Japanese consumer, artistic, and literary tastes. They too were various and protean, and they constituted a dynamic aspect of Taiwan's history, as well.

In his 1991 book *Entangled Objects,* Nicholas Thomas devised a useful framework for elucidating the long-term imbrication of indigenous renaissance with colonialism and its legacies, and for bringing translocal networks and economies to bear on the siloed studies of nationalist history or community-based ethnography. In his study of asymmetrical historical interactions between British imperial agents and Fiji and Samoan Islanders, Thomas proposes the "entanglement" metaphor as an alternative to "incorporation" (a triumphalist or extinction narrative of global capitalism's rise to dominance) or "comparison" (the critique or lionization of capitalism through comparison with putatively alternative economic logics). The "entangled objects" model, which I employ in this analysis, steers a course between ascertaining the rate and extent of the periphery's transformation by the core ("incorporation") and the meticulous reconstruction of internally coherent ideal-typical systems of meaning ("comparison").[20] The former method is that criticized by Haruyama as too deterministic and reliant on Marxist stage theories, while the latter approach comes from the efforts to write "internal" histories of indigenous peoples that filter out "external" influences.

To illustrate, from an "incorporation" perspective, LeGendre's presentation of the red cloth to Toketok is salient because it facilitated an agreement between a U.S. emissary and a powerful chieftain. The arrangement was but one in a series of ad hoc accords whose breakdown fomented the Japanese invasion of Taiwan in May 1874. As a result of this invasion, the Qing initiated more aggressive policies against indigenes from 1875 through 1895, further eroding their autonomy. Shortly thereafter, mechanized Japanese military might brought indigenous populations to heel beginning in 1903. By 1915 or so, Japan delivered the coup de grâce to indigenous sovereignty, ushering in an era of subordinate existence in the global division of labor and the colonial racial pecking order. In this rendering, 180 yards of red camlet is fungible—any gift might have served the same function. This conclusion is at odds with the inordinate attention paid to the specific contours of materiality by contemporary observers. Moreover, as an extinction narrative, the "incorporation model" does little to help us understand current developments in indigenous peoples' rights recovery and renaissance or the continued attractions of primitivist consumerism.[21]

Using the comparative method would lead us in a different direction, and it also raises problems. Based on the voluminous travel reports and diplomatic correspondence available for southern Taiwan and anthropological fieldwork studies of Paiwanese kinship, political structure, and ideology, one could ascertain the role of red camlet in the redistributive political economy of the Eighteen-Tribe Confederation. Using models constructed by political anthropologists of Polynesia, one could then hypothesize to what extent Toketok was a chief or a big man, or try to figure out how his brushes with the global economy transformed his leadership style from one type to the other.

Having established the internal logic of Langqiao's political economy and the meaning of gifts within it, one could then contrast it with the logic of monopoly capitalism and national sovereignty to identify what is distinctive, autochthonous, and original about Paiwanese social organization.[22] Like incorporation analyses, comparativist studies yield important insights. But as Thomas notes, the methodological insistence upon "difference" in comparative work has a tendency to consign actors in these systems to parallel, containerized temporalities, an analytical fiction that is belied by the phenomenon of meaningful cross-cultural exchange.

An "entangled objects" analysis instead lingers a bit longer on the materiality of LeGendre's gift to take notice of the fact that indigenes refashioned imported red cloth to create what has come to be known as Atayal traditional clothing (see figure 28). Illustrations and Japanese ethnological displays (see figure 29) helped stabilize this marker of Atayal tradition.

These garments in turn took on a variety of local meanings, values, and usages that had little relevance to the story of international relations but were, nonetheless, crucial for social reproduction in indigenous societies.[23] Following LeGendre's red camlet through another iteration, we observe that the articles that have come to be known as traditional Atayal cloth were in turn reappropriated by Japanese of various stripes for a multitude of purposes during the colonial period (and beyond). As museum pieces, objects of study, and popular items at souvenir stands, Atayal textiles came to symbolize either a particular ethnic group or the artistic genius of an ancient, vanished race of Austronesians (see below).

Fast-forward to contemporary times: Taiwan Indigenous Peoples have refashioned elements of Japan's colonial-period repository of material culture. The revival of Atayal weaving practices, partly based on consultation of textiles collected during colonial times and preserved in Japan, now illustrates claims of Atayal distinctiveness and autochthony.[24] The same can be said for Paiwan, Rukai, and Saisiyat cultural revivals in the post-1980s milieu.[25]

As we have seen in the introduction and the first two chapters of this book, indigenes received, in the form of gifts (with strings attached), tons of red cloth—as remnants, garments, bolts, or even flags. We have also seen how the Taiwan Government-General clamped down on gifting by 1900. In the post-Pacification Office dispensation, what LeGendre called "tokens of friendship" were deployed as the candy backed by the whip of trade embargoes and punitive expeditions. During the period of Japan's "primitive accumulation" of an indigenous storehouse of cultural artifacts, anthropologists entered into these transactions. They wrote about,

FIGURE 28. Illustration of Atayal textiles from Japanese ethnological survey, ca. 1915. Kojima Yoshimichi and Kōno Kiroku, eds., *Banzoku kanshū chōsa hōkokusho* (Taipei: Rinji Taiwan Kyūkan Chōsakai, dai 1-bu, 1915), n.p.

sketched, photographed, and collected these items, then supplied museums and expositions with evidence of indigenous ethnic integrity, local genius, and archaic vibrancy. Concurrently, trading-post operators accepted Atayal cloth as specie and retailed it to tourists and collectors, diffusing weavings widely to Japanese and international collectors.

FIGURE 29. A diorama from the 1913 Osaka Colonial Exhibition with Atayal red-striped capes prominently displayed as "The household of the Taiwanese natives and its customs and manners." "Grand Colonial Exhibition at Tennoji Park," ip1472, East Asia Image Collection, Lafayette College, Easton, PA, accessed July 26, 2017, http://digital.lafayette.edu/collections/eastasia/imperial-postcards/ip1472.

Much of the indigenous cultural material that was photographed or preserved for posterity was collected during the "lost decade" of Japanese rule (1895–1905), which is usually considered a period of passivity, at worst, or simplistically as one dominated by a policy of "nurture." However, during this decade, the peoples beyond the savage border who had kept the Qing state at arm's length dazzled Japanese officials in search of allies and informants with their song, dance, festivals, folktales, and handicrafts. Indigenous emissaries to feasts and parleys posed for photographs and paintings; indigenous artifacts were collected by rural officials in exchange for tobacco and red thread that was subsequently distributed to shore up headmen's claims to authority; and indigenous textiles purchased in cross-border trade were boxed up and shipped to Japanese museums and industrial expositions to line the pockets and enhance the profiles of Japanese anthropologists (see figure 29). These myriad transactions had the cumulative effect of institutionalizing a view of indigenes as racially and culturally distinct from each other and from Han Taiwanese.

The contemporary world is politically and economically dominated by settler states and their majority populations.[26] Therefore, indigenous peoples, for both commercial and political reasons, often find themselves forced to perform identities that meet the expectations of outsiders, whether in court or in the marketplace. Cultural reification was certainly a prominent legacy of Japanese colonial rule in Taiwan. The objects discussed in this chapter, then, remain in play as articles of ethnic pride and as exhibits in the high-stakes game of indigenous renaissance and recovery.[27]

TOKENS OF FRIENDSHIP AND THE INNOCENT ABORIGINE

The themes of victimization, trade dependence, and exploitation punctuate descriptions of indigenous-outsider relations from the very first written records about Taiwan. Chen Di's 1603 *Account of the Eastern Barbarians (Dongfan Ji)* explains that Fujianese traders brought "agates, porcelain, cloth, salt, and brass" to Taiwan to trade for deer horns, hides, and meat. Chen laments that indigenes had "developed some desires" leading "rascals [to] cheat them with junk."[28] Two decades later, Commander Cornelis Reyersen observed indigenes exporting diverse animal products for "coarse porcelain and some unbleached linen." These exports were brokered by the "Chinese living there, who . . . married local women."[29] A February 1624 Dutch East India Company record suggests that trade dependency gave Chinese immigrants near the future Taiwan-fu leverage disproportionate to their numbers: "In almost every house . . . one, two, three, nay sometimes even five or six Chinese are lodged, whom [indigenes] keep very much under control. . . . Likewise they themselves are bullied by the Chinese for not giving them food or not working hard enough. *The Chinese immediately threaten to deprive them of salt, which means they are dependent on them.*"[30]

As we saw in chapter 2, the history of interpreters throughout the Qing period reveals a long record of economic ties that exceeded the boundaries of imperial administration. Jumping ahead to the treaty-port period, we return to the disappearance of fifty-four shipwrecked Ryūkyūans on Taiwan's southern peninsula in 1871. The calamity brought Meiji Japan's first official visitors to Taiwan. In particular, the observations of Mizuno Jun merit scrutiny. Mizuno would return to Taiwan as the top civilian official in the Taiwan Government-General at its inception in 1895.

In 1873, Ambassador Soejima Taneomi dispatched a twenty-two-year-old Mizuno, who was studying Chinese on the continent, from Hong Kong to Danshui to investigate conditions surrounding the deaths of the Ryūkyūans.[31] Upon arriving at Dakekan, Mizuno's party trekked eastward on a steep woodcutter's path toward the so-called savage border. Mizuno was told that areas of Chinese habitation were marked by the russet color of denuded forests, while the indigenous areas were lushly green. Mizuno's informants told him that this divide ran the length of Taiwan. It was patrolled by armed Han and indigenous guards on either side.

In a clearing used to initiate cross-border parleys, on May 23, 1873, Mizuno hailed a group of passing Atayal people. The men fled to the hills at the sight of Mizuno's armed Chinese guides. Two Atayal women, however, stayed behind. They explained that their village had been the victim of a ruse. Chinese traders had promised the delivery of Western goods to lure unsuspecting Atayal people into the clearing. The Chinese subsequently kidnapped the Atayal men and ransomed them later in exchange for titles to land. To overcome their reticence, Mizuno offered to distribute large quantities of red cloth, à la LeGendre, if the two women could bring an Atayal headman down from the mountains. Mizuno noted that indigenes coveted red cloth most of all. The next morning, he presented the two women with gifts of red cloth, matches, small daggers, and pearls. That afternoon, the chief sent a different women's contingent down the mountain. Mizuno supplied each with a "foot or two" of red cloth. Finally, Mizuno presented the chief with a live pig and two large jars of *shōchū* liquor. With this presentation of "tokens of friendship," Mizuno had accomplished the "principal goal of his mission, to look into savage strengths and weaknesses, degrees of intelligence and ignorance, and manners and customs."[32]

Although Mizuno did not record population figures, estimates of military strength, or routes to interior villages (as later travelers would), the intelligence he collected on his mission to Dakekan was put to use a quarter century later. Every transaction in Mizuno's account was premised on the Dakekan peoples' desire to obtain imported goods—twenty-two years before the onset of Japanese colonial rule. At the same time, as first governor-general Kabayama Sukenori's civil administrator, Mizuno issued proclamations and oversaw policies based on his estimation that the *seiban* (raw savages, i.e., unassimilated) were generally victims of the cunning and duplicitous Han Taiwanese.

George Taylor, an imperial maritime customs agent for the British crown, attested to the popularity of red woolens in southern Taiwan during the same era. Taylor observed that the red color alone made the cloth desirable, since the brightness achieved by Western dyeing techniques could not be achieved by local methods. These "serges," as they were called, were quickly pulled apart and combined with sturdier local ramie, hemp, and china-grass fiber to make durable clothing. Taylor complained that for everyday use, Taiwanese weaves were still dominating the market, much to the embarrassment of the British official, who had hoped that his machine-made cloth would flood the market.[33]

Ueno Sen'ichi's 1891 report (see chapter 1) stated that purchasing presents for the indigenes was most necessary for entering the savage territory. Accordingly, Ueno brought along "liquor, tobacco, glass beads, Western red-dyed thread, brass buttons, white ceramic buttons, and so on." Like so many Japanese officials who followed him, Ueno insisted that presents to indigenes be distributed equally, from the youngest child to the paramount chief. If one indigene were treated too kindly and another too carelessly, hard feelings would result, wrote Ueno. In return for these "tokens of friendship," chief Watan Yūra produced sweet potatoes and a bundle of rice stalks from a "head-carrying bag" and presented them to Ueno. After this exchange of gifts, Ueno's mission ended. He concluded that Atayal people were simple and trusting, but they were also quick to anger and never forgot a slight.[34]

Like Ueno, Captain Watanabe, during the previously discussed August 29, 1895, mission to Dakekan, distributed gifts equally among Atayal emissaries to a diplomatic meeting. According to Watanabe's report, Atayal valued manufactured goods highly, as they swaddled the empty liquor vessels, great and small, into bundles to carry back to their villages (see figure 11). Yet the chief showed no interest in the silver coins he was given.[35] Hashiguchi Bunzō's follow-up mission also commenced with the distribution of red cloth, tinned meat, handkerchiefs, ornamental hairpins, short daggers, tobacco, and alcohol.[36] Hashiguchi wrote that the Jiaobanshan embassy men were adorned with trademark Atayal red-striped capes. Hashiguchi emphasized the importance of red serge (a rough woolen), which he distributed in equal shares. To produce the distinctive red garments, Hashiguchi reported, the women took the serge apart and wove the dyed thread together with locally produced ramie fiber.[37]

Based on his experience with the Jiaobanshan emissaries, Hashiguchi, as director of the Office of Industrial Promotion *(Shokusan-bu),* proposed that each Japanese garrison near the savage border stock gifts for distribution to neighboring tribes. The Civil Affairs Bureau accordingly sent memoranda to the subprefects of Tainan, Miaoli, Yunlin, Yilan, Hengchun, and Puli explaining their importance. It specified that scarlet cotton fabric, red beads, flower hairpins, cigars, daggers, red blankets, red serge, and hand towels were all to be stocked. Every item on the proposed inventory matched one that was distributed by Hashiguchi to the Dakekan emissaries three days earlier, on September 8, 1895.[38]

As recounted in chapter 1, after the Pacification Office was opened in mid-1896, station chiefs were ordered to meet with headmen on appointed days and distribute presents. The belief that indigenes treasured their gifts and would do just about anything to receive them informed the office's optimistic charge. With bolts of red cloth, bags of salt, and bottles of sake as inducements, these hundred men would survey the political, demographic, mineral, vegetative, and military strength of some seven-hundred-odd settlements in uncharted territory.[39]

In addition to having power as political and diplomatic implements, red-dyed textiles were also known as inducements to commence trade relationships. On September 30, 1895, an anonymous Civil Affairs Bureau translator *(tsūyakukan)* told a Japanese metropolitan readership that adroit gifting could open Taiwan's interior to Japanese camphor merchants. The cost of gifts to chiefs was about one yen per camphor tree in Miaoli, he reported. These gifts included red, black, brown, or purple cloth scraps for women and guns, swords, sake, and tobacco for men. To obtain the camphor trees, he wrote, local Chinese also traded Nanjing coins or rings and bracelets made of pearl and lead. The selling price of a camphor tree was sixty or seventy yen—a more than sixtyfold return on investment. This particular correspondent surmised that indigenes did not understand the value of currency or the difference between silver and gold. He wrote that they accepted one or the other based on color preferences for yellow or white and that one could even use shards of glass or chunks of metal for currency in some areas.[40]

In October 1895 Ueno Sen'ichi's 1891 report resurfaced in a commercial guide published by the Japanese Ministry of Agriculture and Commerce in Tokyo. The guide reiterated Ueno's advocacy of red cloth as a rain-making gift and as the price of entry to the "savage territory." Moreover, it duly reproduced Ueno's capsule history of Han aggression, which partly attributed land dispossession to the supposed indigenous character traits of simplicity, illiteracy, and lack of foresight. The Chinese, according to this iteration of Ueno's now recycled report (itself a distillation of translated, paraphrased, and plagiarized passages from Western travelers), were greedy, cunning, and unscrupulous.[41]

A November 1896 report issued by the Industrial Promotion Section began its discussion of camphor with a predictable admonition that travelers stock "liquor-meat-cloth," especially Western imported red-dyed cloth. It then excoriated the residents of Beipu as dishonest indigenes to justify stationing armed guards in the area to protect camphor workers. In addition, countering the economic innocence argument, the report announced that indigenous headmen in Qing times required frequent cash payments, in addition to feasts and gifts, to keep the peace.[42]

A series of internal memoranda from the Luodong (Yilan) section chief for aborigine affairs also engaged in the rhetoric of indigenous victimization in commerce. He urged honest, fair-dealing Japanese immigrants to insert themselves into the "aborigine trade." If they didn't, he warned, the profits would remain in the hands of unscrupulous Chinese who set off violent cycles of revenge feuds by cheating Xitou and Nan'ao peoples.[43] The Luodong office claimed to have brokered marriages between the commercially minded *jukuban* (acculturated savages) of Alishi village and daughters of the Atayal Nan'ao villages to strengthen government ties with the mountain peoples. The district office held a large wedding banquet at which over a hundred Nan'ao Atayal guests were feted in May 1899. The Japanese official also encouraged the adoption of indigenous males into *jukuban* households in order to recruit these bicultural couples to act as interpreters. Qualifying the stereotype of Atayal disinterest in material gain, this scheme was premised on the lure of trade goods and wealth to inspire the Nan'ao villagers to place their daughters and sons among the trading villages at the foot of the mountains.[44]

As we have seen, Japanese accounts of diplomatic gifting repeatedly insisted that indigenes were acutely sensitive to "equal distribution," whether it was equal measures of cloth or portions of boiled meat. It is hard to discount such reports as projections or stereotypes, since they exist in so many forms. But did such behavior mean that indigenes were egalitarian, unselfish, and innocent of the profit motive?

At distribution events, a Japanese official could proclaim that his emperor would not play favorites. In kind, indigenous emissaries equally distributed goods among their own followers, at least in the presence of Japanese officials. But these happy structural isomorphisms had their limits. According to infantryman Irie Takeshi, Puli prefect Hiyama Tetsusaburō doled out the expected blankets and jars of liquor at his wedding to the daughter of the Paalan chief near Wushe. Complications arose, however, when Hiyama, unable to distinguish Toda and Truku men from the Paalan men, distributed gifts to everyone. Angered by the fact that their rivals from Toda and Truku received gifts, the Wushe men ambushed them after the banquet and took their gifts at gunpoint. Irie reported that the Wushe men asserted their right to receive the gifts first and then to redistribute them to other locals as they saw fit. After all, their chief had conducted a marriage alliance with Hiyama.[45] Hiyama's successor in Puli, Nagano Yoshitora, triggered the same response by distributing presents to Toda emissaries after a feast in 1898. On their way back home, the Toda men were ambushed by Wushe men. In the ensuing battle, Toda and Wushe suffered fifteen and two casualties, respectively.[46]

Moreover, detailed lists of gift items in the manuscript records of traveling district officials reveal that more expensive gifts were earmarked for headmen. These unequal distributions were, in fact, routine.[47] In summary, some individuals and groups of indigenes did not view material goods as fungible commodities that could be reduced to a value expressed in monetary terms. Nonetheless, these goods were still highly valued, were sites of contestation and competition, and were deployed by indigenes as either commodities or political currency.

TRADING POSTS, BEHAVIOR MODIFICATION, AND PUNITIVE EMBARGOES

Saitō Otosaku, Pacification Office chief in Linyipu, articulated the growing chorus of criticisms directed at Hashiguchi's gifting policy in an 1898 white paper. In his preface, Saitō wrote: "One must take care in distributing gifts to the indigenes; if it is done carelessly, it can lead to feelings of injustice and foment anger, or it can cause lethargy and shiftlessness . . . We must not distribute gifts without a reason; we must certainly not distribute luxury goods; we must not give in to demands for goods; when gifts are requested, we should give no more than is absolutely necessary."[48]

In language that reflects a newfound confidence in the Japanese government's ability to command rather than placate, Saitō composed a well-calibrated scale of gift categories. He reserved the Hashiguchi-style "tokens of friendship" for first-time visitors to government offices. Return "guests" would have to earn their gifts. For example, to receive goods classified in Saitō's top-shelf categories, indigenes would have to perform "labor on roadwork, afforestation projects, or stock-raising/farming enterprises . . . or service as savage auxiliaries *(banhei).*" Such efforts would be rewarded with "thick cotton shirts; black cloth, light cloth, table salt,

FIGURE 30. Trading post at Jiaobanshan. *Riban Gaiyō* (Taipei: Taiwan sōtokufu minseibu banmu honsho, 1913), n.p.

matches, and so on"; "buttons, all colors of wool thread, combs, tobacco, Nanjing pearls, and so on"; and, for especially meritorious service, guns and ammunition.

Saitō recommended that farm tools, seeds, and stock be freely given because they would wean the indigenes from their hunting economy. He argued that firearms and ammunition, though necessary for the time being, should be phased out, because hunting in and of itself was a vestige of savagery. Saitō also envisioned the government-managed trade as a source of profit. Lesser categories in Saitō's typology, which ranged from hoes and hatchets to hairpins and fans painted with *nishiki-e* scenes, were to be stocked as trade items.

A plan that may have been influenced by Saitō's report was implemented in Yilan in mid-1901. It restricted trade to government-licensed agents who would operate with set exchange rates. For example, one deer pelt was listed as equivalent to two feet of red woolen cloth or nine catties of table salt; one bear bladder equaled two iron pots or one suckling pig; three catties of wood ears equaled five catties of salt or a skein of thread; and so on. The government would profit from this trade and use the proceeds for "indigenous betterment," which meant building schools and transporting and lodging chiefs' families who came down the mountain to enroll in the pilot education programs.[49] The conversion of gift-distribution centers into trading posts was central to the trade-for-education program attempted in Yilan in 1901 (see figure 30). While these projects can be understood as attempts to give indigenes a "fair shake" vis-à-vis their wealthier Han neighbors, these trading posts quickly turned into instruments of punishment, conquest, and income generation for the Japanese state.

In 1899 Gotō Shinpei launched the Taiwan Government-General's camphor monopoly, along with other measures, to increase revenue to support his vision of an efficiently run surplus-extracting colony. As Antonio Tavares has shown, the official Japanese plan for camphor—to export large quantities of uniform quality with profits accruing to Japanese capitalists—posed a direct threat to the Atayal, Saisiyat, and other northern indigenes, whose leaders were accustomed to leasing forest land, collecting tolls, or organizing production themselves. Accordingly, cases of Atayal and Saisiyat violence against Japanese officials accelerated.[50] In response, the Pacification Offices were abolished in June 1898, and rural installations for aborigine management began to emphasize the importance of embargoes, smuggling, illicit trade, and contraband. As northern tribes put up stout armed resistance to logging-company encroachments, government officials began to worry less about the injury done to indigenes by crafty Chinese and to express outrage that Han traders would subvert Japanese bans on weapons, ammunition, or even salt to blacklisted tribes.

Taipei prefectural governor Murakami Yoshio urged that the tribes responsible for a June 1900 armed uprising near Dakekan, which cost over a thousand Chinese and Japanese lives and destroyed much property, be completely cut off from trade and from receiving gifts. Friendly villages would have only a partial ban on trade, in Murakami's plan. Murakami sent out strict regulations requiring merchants to be registered and calling for a complete ban on commerce in guns and salt to troubled areas. Murakami believed that villages could be crushed and brought to heel after a few months of deprivation of life's necessities.[51] In September of the same year, the Balisha district chief in Yilan sent out a similar memorandum, calling for selective trade embargoes against villages who defied the government's authority. He stipulated that feasting and trade would be permitted for tribes who had made amends for their crimes or who were above suspicion.

Such a policy might have seemed wildly optimistic in the era when Ueno and Hashiguchi were being led by their guides into terra incognita to purchase interviews with "demanding" headmen and chiefs. Yet, by 1900, by following the Pacification Office's directive to regularly supply gifts to headmen as an incentive to "heed invitations to arrive and be transformed," the Yilan district offices rerouted enough traffic or created enough new demand to be in a position to open and close the spigot.[52]

In 1902 two major developments conspired to minimize the centrality of the diplomatic and pedagogical functions of "entangled objects" and accentuate the punitive power of their regulation. First, the Ri Aguai Rebellion, which pitted an indigenous–Hakka–Han coalition of camphor producers against the government-general, taught the Japanese that force would be required to make northern

Taiwan's interior safe for capitalism. Under Ri Aguai's domination, camphor production was too decentralized, too beholden to toll-state politics that ran on bribes, and too unproductive to meet the camphor monopoly's requirements for black ink on the annual balance sheet of colonial management.[53] Second, Gotō Shinpei, through a combination of adroit manipulation and cold-blooded assassination, brought the Japanese campaign against armed Han resistance to completion that same year. In late 1902 an Indigenous Affairs Section was placed under the Police Bureau.[54]

In July 1905 Government Order 56 strictly regulated all "aborigine trade" merchants. Although private traders were still allowed to operate, they required government permits. All trade items were to be registered and declared, along with the names of all employees and coworkers.[55] The long list of surrender ceremonies that punctuate the annals of aborigine administration after 1906 shows that resumption of borderland trade was important to indigenous leaders. In January 1906 the four villages of Fanshuliao (Ahou Prefecture) promised not to seek contraband trade goods from camphor workers on the savage border as a condition of resuming trade. In May 1906 the Wushe (Tgdaya) tribes agreed to leave their weapons at home to conduct business at trading posts and to stay at specially designated lodgings during sojourns for commerce.[56]

In the summer of 1909, the government-general put strict embargoes and rations at the center of its much publicized "Five-Year Plan to Subdue the Indigenes." On October 9, 1909, after applying for terms of surrender, certain Dakekan tribes were permitted "one rice-bowl of salt per month per person" as "gifts," though not as "trade items." The tribes agreed to cease taking heads, to surrender their guns, and to submit to biannual inspections for weapons. Toda's terms of surrender on October 17, 1909, also stipulated that indigenes could not negotiate the price of goods at the reopened trading posts. Moreover, matches, salt, and daggers would be excluded from the list of trade items and supplied as gifts to Toda residents in amounts determined by the government-general. The following day, the Malepa tribes submitted to similar terms, accepting a ban on trade in salt, matches, and daggers in exchange for subsistence-level handouts. On November 11, 1909, the Xalut tribes also surrendered, again foreswearing the right to trade in salt, matches, and daggers.[57]

On April 1, 1910, the government-general began to operate its own trading posts, instead of merely supervising trade. The management of this trade was entrusted to the Taiwan branch of the Patriotic Women's League *(Aikoku Fujinkai)*,[58] while the former system of privately run licensed trading posts remained as a parallel system operated by Han Taiwanese. Echoing Saitō Otosaku's memorandum of 1897, this system announced its intention to reform indigenous character by suppressing the instinct to hunt.[59] Special commissioner Marui Keijirō inspected these trading posts in 1913 and urged that the Women's League be stripped of the contracts (and that private trading posts be abolished, as well). In a painstakingly detailed accounting of exchange rates for adzuki beans and salt rations, among other commodities, Marui pointed out that the Women's League was fleecing the indigenes. He believed, consistent with earlier reports about Han avarice, that such unfair dealing would provoke anger in the long run. Marui argued against the participation of Chinese merchants on the grounds that their bad moral character was corrupting by its very nature. He even linked the presence of venereal disease among indigenes to Chinese traders. As a substitute, he recommended the Saitō plan as the only way forward: use indigenous consumer appetites and trade dependency as a lever to reform indigenous character through the promotion of weaving, planting, and stock breeding.

A heavy hand was required, Marui argued, because indigenes were still mentally deficient in terms of their capacity to function as economic moderns. For example, Marui suggested that they be paid only in tools or other durable goods instead of cash for labor on roads and other public works. Why? They might foolishly spend their wages. Marui expressed frustration that indigenes hiked kilometers of mountain trails to save six thousandths of a yen on a catty of salt. He attributed this stubbornness to the well-known desire of indigenes to be treated fairly—if salt cost 5 sen per catty in Wushe, he wrote, then Toda men would not pay 5.6 sen for it at the nearest trading post but would instead walk all the way to Wushe to get the "fair price."[60]

Soon after Marui's report was released in October 1914, Government Order 85 called for the establishment of official trading posts to replace the Women's League institutions. These posts would be operated by police captains *(keibu)* and assistant captains *(keibu-ho)*, who would report to district heads. All posts would work with fixed barter schedules, to be set at the prefectural level. Following Marui's plan nearly to the letter, the circular that accompanied the new trading-post regulations stated:

> The goal of trade in the indigenous territory is completely for education. To have success, we will pay high prices for cereals, legumes, ramie, rattan, and wicker goods; we will sell farming implements and pig and cattle stock at low prices. We want to instill an agricultural ethos among them. We will pay low prices for deer antlers, deer penis, animal pelts, and bones, to discourage hunting.
>
> Moreover, villages that are not submissive will have their rations of salt severely limited. If we interrupt the flow of salt, that will give them some time to reflect upon their situation. This is a way to exercise coercion without resorting to brute force. It is a "soft policy." We are willing to sacrifice profit for the government to attain our goal of making the indigenes into farmers.[61]

In the short term, the new policy failed to deter hunting. In the February 1917 issue of the government organ *Taiwan Gazette,* ethnologist Mori Ushinosuke explained that 70 percent of the value of indigenous "exports" exchanged at trading posts consisted of animal products obtained in the hunt. Mori wrote that indigenes could not afford metal pots, salt, or fabrics without hunting. In addition, hunting put meat on the table. Mori highlighted the economic irrationality of indigenous agriculture when prices for crops were so low: at the time of his writing, a deer penis still brought five yen, bear bladders ten yen, and a good set of deer antlers thirty to forty yen in some markets.[62] In short, a couple of well-aimed shots or smartly set traps was equivalent to months of toil in the fields or on road crews.

As we have seen in the foregoing, indigenes were, at least in some contexts, demonstrably motivated by the prospect of cash earnings, material benefit, and personal advantage, according to the records of the Taiwan Government-General itself. But these anecdotal examples, no matter how legion, did little to disrupt the view that indigenes were ipso facto irrational, childlike creatures who lived on the "fruits of the chase" and required tutelage. A 1935 article in a Japanese policemen's magazine titled "The Economic Sensibilities of Savages and [Savage] Customs" provides but one of many examples of this resilient trope.

It maintained that indigenes did not customarily buy or sell goods based on considerations of market price but instead valued them in accord with traditional value. This estimation was the same one that ruled out the upper Hengchun Paiwanese from being included in the regularly administered territories with the lower Hengchun Paiwanese in 1904 (see chapter 1). With so much home-brewed liquor to be had for free, the article continued, there was little incentive for drink-loving indigenes to worry about having cash on hand. Therefore, they spent their ready cash until they were flat broke. These sweeping generalizations were illustrated with a large photograph of several Tsou men downing bamboo cups of wine with gusto. The author conceded that some indigenes maximized profit and adopted a market mentality, thanks to colonial policies of tutelage. He congratulated the police and hopefully noted that the indigenes were losing their backward habits and becoming more like Japanese.[63]

But if indeed some Atayal and Saisiyat farmers were making profits in business, it is hard to see how Japanese policies were to thank for this result. Imposed trade dependency, embargoes on necessities, fixed prices at the trading posts, and an onerous licensing system were not aimed at producing profit-seeking, utility-maximizing individuals but rather hard-working, surplus-producing, and pacified imperial subjects.

TEXTILES IN EXPOSITIONS, MUSEUMS, AND PHOTOGRAPHS

Colonial-period writers, especially officials, considered the early years of the occupation to have been ones of passivity regarding aborigine policy. Outposts were lightly staffed and underfunded, to be sure. Moreover, most of the government's resources were poured into the war against the so-called "bandits" *(dohi)* from 1896 through 1903—who were mostly nonindigenous, as far as the Japanese could tell. Therefore, there is some truth to the view that the era of "red-cloth diplomacy" was a historical cul-de-sac. But for the ethnologists whose taxonomic work, photography, collecting, and display efforts are still bearing fruit in Atayal ethnic revival movements, the years 1895–1903 were remembered as a golden age.

To bring our story full circle, then, we return to the National Taiwan Museum, site of the *Rainbow and Dragonfly* exhibition. The revered aborigine expert Mori Ushinosuke was the first curator of the indigenous materials at the museum, and he left a long shadow. Mori was an interpreter for Tokyo University anthropologist Torii Ryūzō, who made four anthropological surveys of Taiwan between 1896 and 1900. Mori was also a junior contemporary and sometime rival of the famous historian, folklorist, ethnologist, and taxonomist Inō Kanori (1867–1925), a formidable collector in his own right. To this day, Mori Ushinosuke's ethnographic photographs are prominently displayed in the National Taiwan Museum's permanent exhibition and in other Taiwanese museums. Along with Inō's and Torii's collected materials, photographs, and biographical information, these collectors and the artifacts that contributed to ethnology are often celebrated and, to the best of my knowledge, the collectors are rarely considered as plunderers or exploiters of indigenous heritage.[64]

During the first decade of colonial rule, at the pacification outposts, government halls, and army garrisons, these Meiji-period anthropologists photographed, measured, interviewed, and collected artifacts from the indigenous representatives who showed up to receive gifts or have a social drink. Inō Kanori's field notes, Torii Ryūzō's published travelogues, and Mori's serialized memoirs all describe the period as a time when demobilized Japanese soldiers, Han-indigenous interpreters, ethnologists, government officials, and indigenous headmen assembled to conduct business, exchange information, and size each other up.

In the era before participant observation, anthropologists like Inō worked quickly and gathered evidence opportunistically. Discussions about gift items, as we saw with Hashiguchi's confused conversations about the loan/gift of blankets to the Jiaobanshan emissaries, acted as prompts to initiate discussions between parties that had very little to discuss, given the language problems that plagued these encounters. The precious materials also functioned as the currency of access.

Inō wrote that in the "course of distributing various items colored red, which they generally like, such as scraps of red cloth, red yarn, red Japanese flags, and ornate hairpins," he had divined key aspects of the Atayal guests' mental life *(shisō)*. There are echoes of Ueno Sen'ichi's 1891 report in Inō's 1896 update, but there are important differences. Like Ueno, Inō observed a reverence for the gifts, polite manners in receiving them, and a lack of selfishness among the recipients: they insisted that everyone receive the same gifts.

But Inō's report did not compare the Atayal people (as he would later call them) favorably to the Han Taiwanese, nor did he dwell on their simplicity or innocence.[65] Instead, Inō learned the local names for the numerous types of clothing and adornment that were fashioned from these gifts and illustrated his account with several carefully labeled sketches. Having established that the female visitors from the Wulai area were similar in appearance to the women brought from Dakekan by Hashiguchi in 1895 (see above), Inō classified them as coethnics. To the question, "By what name do you refer to yourselves?," Inō heard the reply, "Taiyal," from members of each contingent. Inō recorded this term in Roman script, announcing a new scientific outsider's perspective on non-Han peoples in Taiwan. As he noted, the Qing terms *shengfan* and *shufan* (literally "raw savages" and "cooked savages") were externally imposed political categories. *Atayal*, in contrast, was a self-designated ethnonym, according to Inō.[66]

In 1898, Inō launched a bulletin to publish research on Taiwan Indigenous Peoples. For the inaugural issue, he published a photomontage with representatives of eight tribes. The Atayal man in the montage was from the Wulai area, probably a member of the troop that visited Taipei in 1896. Due to technological constraints and the infrequent access Inō had to sitters, Inō's montage was cobbled together out of black-and-white studio portraits and field photographs of uneven quality. This illustration could not capture the brilliant reds that were distributed to Atayal woman at Japanese outposts as the raw materials for the textiles that would in turn mesmerize Japanese souvenir hunters, ethnographers, and art fanciers. To remedy this problem, Inō commissioned a color painting as a substitute for display at the 1900 Paris Universal Exposition. While the photomontage displayed the Atayal man and woman in a simple vest and Chinese blouse, respectively, the painting took considerable artistic license to adorn them in ornate, bright-red traditional Atayal clothing.[67]

It appears that Inō rarely left ethnological-survey encounters empty-handed. Inō Kanori's large collection of cloths, carvings, and other implements formed the basis for the Taiwan National University Museum of Anthropology collection. The lion's share of Inō's over 430 specimens were obtained from his family in Iwate Prefecture by Utsurikawa Nenozo in the late 1920s, and they were the material foundation for the academic study of indigenous material culture in Taiwan at the PhD level.[68]

Mori Ushinosuke returned to Inō's site in late 1902 and early 1903 to photograph Watan Yūra and his family. Mori took multiple portraits of individuals and groups from Wulai and Rimogan (just upriver), with a focus on garments and cloth production especially. Five of these portraits were exhibited in nearly life-size reproductions for the five million visitors who attended the 1903 Osaka Industrial Exhibition. The Osaka posters were transported to the 1904 St. Louis World's Fair and then picked up by American news services for further reproduction (see chapter 4). Besides the large impact the Osaka Expo had on the propagation of Inō's map and taxonomy and Mori's photographs, it also had a direct link to contemporary Taiwan. According to the National Taiwan Museum's hundredth-anniversary guide, Mori first came into contact with the exhibit of aboriginal culture at the [Osaka Industrial Exhibition] in 1903. Five years later, the Japanese government established the Affiliated Memorial Museum of the Business Property Bureau to commemorate the completion of Taiwan's railroad network. Ranging from collecting objects for display, assortment of exhibit facilities, to the allotment of proper space, Mori had a hand in every aspect of exhibits. In 1915, the Taiwan Viceroy's Office Museum . . . was finally completed and the specimens . . . were transferred to the new location. Mori transferred to the new museum and worked there until his retirement in 1924.[69]

To the extent that the TGG museum was the first stop for visitors and a school of colonialism for Japanese officials, Mori's foundational work as the supplier, curator, and analyst of large collection of Atayal fabric in Taipei perhaps did more to associate "Atayals" with culture bearers than any of his myriad activities. On the photographic front, at the height of their popularity, Mori's textile-rich Wulai photographs were reproduced in Japanese geography textbooks, commercial publications, and government reports, while Inō's ethnic map found its way into the Japanese school curriculum.[70]

By 1915, the year Sakuma's scorched-earth campaign terminated, any primary or high-school teacher in Japan had at hand the materials to demonstrate that Taiwan was inhabited by a number of ethnic groups, each in possession of its own customs, languages, and territories. With the installation of Mori's collection at the Taipei museum, the same could be said of any important guest or ambitious official in Taiwan. This was a true accomplishment for the ethnologists. At this time, the overwhelming image of Taiwan Indigenous Peoples, even in textbooks but especially in newspapers, photo albums, and postcards, was of armed savage enemies of the state who would either soon go extinct or assimilate to Japanese culture.

ETHNIC TOURISM AND INDIGENOUS ART FORMS

As the frontier wars over camphor wound down in the 1910s, Atayal villages near Jiaobanshan and Wulai became regular stops for Japanese tourists and visiting dignitaries. The Atayal textiles that incorporated the red threads introduced in the treaty-port period could now be obtained at tourist-friendly trading posts as authentic indigenous cloth. During Japanese colonial rule, these garments made the transition from items of local consumption and everyday use to exported, high-quality handicrafts and art objects. In 1920, the protagonist of Satō Haruo's novella *Wushe* reported that the trading posts were stocking inferior knockoffs of the "genuine indigenous textiles" he sought,[71] while visiting Crown Prince Hirohito himself viewed an Atayal weaving demonstration in a Taiwan exhibition hall in 1923. The prince reportedly expressed admiration for their purity, color, and boldness of expression.[72] The indigenous trading posts and weaving demonstrations were also on the itineraries of Prince Chichibu in 1925 and Prince Asaka in 1927. A photo of the sword-bearing Asaka and his police escorts towering over three female Atayal weavers was splashed on the cover of the December 1927 issue of the *Taiwan Gazette*.[73]

In 1933 the eminent scholar and critic Ozaki Hotsuma urged colonial officials to enforce Japan's Important Arts Preservation Law in Taiwan so that traditional Atayal textiles, along with Paiwan woodcarvings, could be preserved as "national treasures." Ozaki rued the extent to which indigenous culture had been degraded in Taiwan since its golden age. He believed that Atayalic artistic abilities had peaked in the distant past, when the world's most archaic form of linear patterned cloth had emerged in the mountains of Taiwan. He argued that these artifacts, if preserved in a repository for scholarly and artistic appreciation, would reflect well on the empire itself. For Ozaki, the "normally administered areas" of Han residence possessed nothing of interest, except for derivative pieces imported from the continent.[74]

Like the Japanese aesthetes who praised the genius of Goryeo-era pottery while Japanese merchants undercut its production by flooding Korea with cheaper manufactured wares,[75] Ozaki did not connect the current "degraded state" of Atayal weaving to Japanese imports or other policies that eroded traditional forms of production. As early as 1900, the Government-General began to facilitate the construction of textile factories in Xindian. The local indigenous affairs field office recorded with satisfaction that Atayal women were being trained in Xindian and in Wulai to run the machines.[76] By 1938 journalist Harrison Forman, who shot numerous photographs at the same indigenous village visited by Princes Hirohito, Chichibu, and Asaka in the 1920s, observed that Atayal textiles had become luxury goods for local people. Traditional clothing required two weeks of labor to produce a single garment, wrote Forman, while secondhand Japanese clothing sold for about the price of two day's labor on a road gang.[77] In a letter to the editor of *Natural History,* Forman lamented that "the women too are dressed by the Japanese in cotton kimonos, which are symbolic of a movement that will rob another one of the few remaining native groups of the world of their own traditions and culture."[78] Forman's photograph, like a similar one by journalist Adachi Gen'ichirō taken in 1936, depicts Atayal women in Japanese clothing at work producing traditional garments for export, all while consciously posing for ethnic-tourism photographs (see figure 31)

LEGACIES AND DILEMMAS

Since the late 1980s, NGOs, the central government, and county offices have dispersed funding for indigenous language school curricula, the revival of dormant public rituals, and the manufacture of indigenous textiles, sculptures, and other items of material culture. As a result, the post-1990 affirmations of face-tattooing and head-taking, and the rediscovery of Atayal textiles and traditional music and

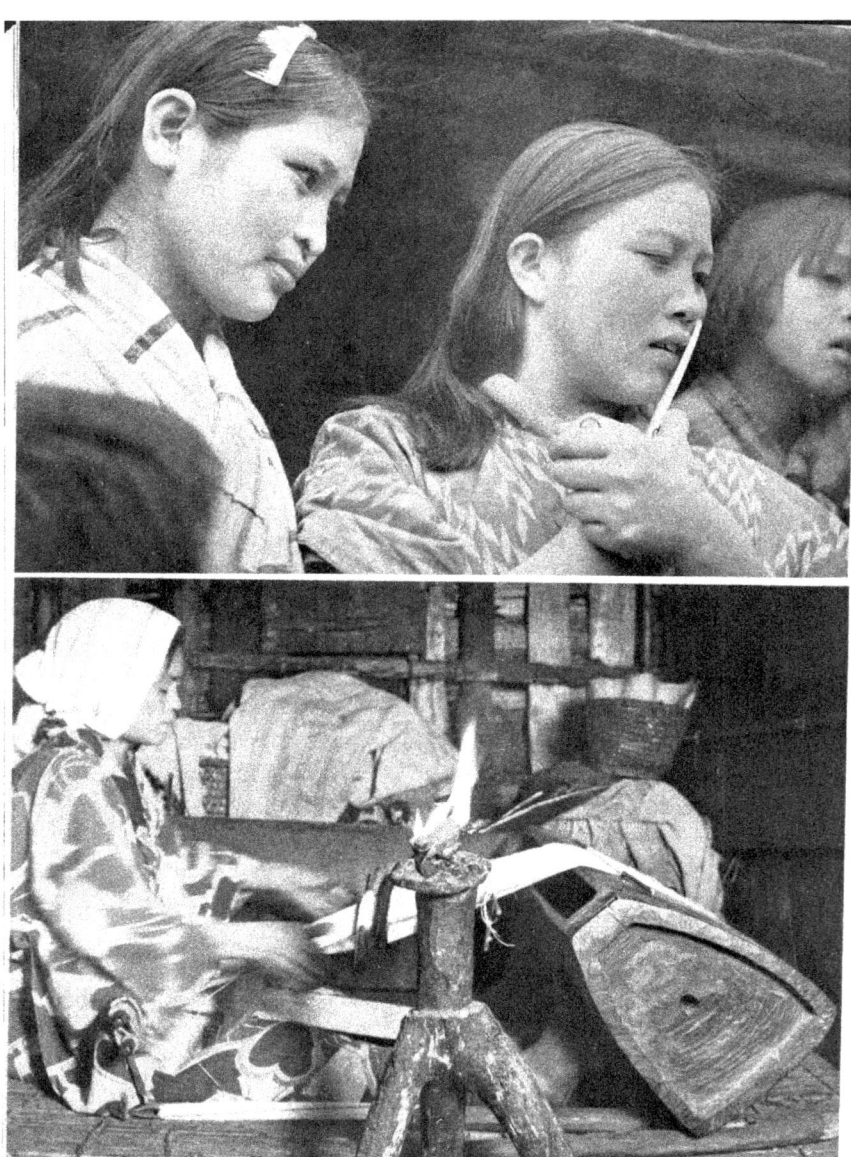

FIGURE 31. Atayal women wearing imported clothing and weaving traditional clothing, 1936. Tanaka Kaoru and Adachi Gen'ichirō, *Taiwan no yama to banjin* (Tokyo: Kokon Shoin, 1937), facing p. 92.

dance, have erased much of the public and private stigma formerly attached to Atayal culture by Japanese and Han neighbors over the past century.[79]

The consultation of colonial-era ethnological writings, illustrations, and photographs has been a crucial component in many, if not all, of these revivalist projects.[80] The Japanese-period documentary record has been important for the authentication of native traditions in Taiwan. This recourse to materials preserved and stored by outsiders is testament to the transformative effects of the government-general's relocation and assimilation policies, followed by decades of cultural oppression under the GMD. In a word, both the Japanese and the Taiwanese states have had a hand in deracinating Taiwan's Austronesian populations. Perhaps more significantly, under GMD rule, 80–90 percent of Taiwan's indigenes converted to Christianity, while roughly 50 percent migrated to urban environments antithetical to the maintenance of early twentieth-century markers of ethnic distinction.[81]

Recent ethnographic research suggests that top-down cultural politics are integral to the twenty-first-century indigenous renaissance in Taiwan. Anthropologist Michael Rudolph has noted that, as Christians, many indigenes did not initially identify with the revitalized symbolism, languages, and ceremonies that were being promoted by "elite traditionalists." A period of time was required for adaptation and reappropriation. Scott Simon has written extensively about the emergence of an indigenous elite in the 1950s in response to GMD changes in property law and rural administration. These political operators often use identity politics to fulfill their own political ambitions and are sometimes viewed with derision by their rank-and-file constituents. Mitsuda Yayoi corroborates the general pattern: educated elites formulated and promoted particular versions of indigenous ethnic identity and subsequently mobilized followers to achieve state recognition for a given interpretation of tradition.[82] Hu Chia-yu has identified the same dynamic but tempers this view with the judgment that after a period of elite domination, the revitalization movement found a home in everyday life and rural indigenous villages. In the twenty-first century, she argues, "the enhancement of local cultures and indigenous identities are intertwined with the promotion of Taiwanese consciousness and identity . . . "[83]

Can indigenous renaissance in Taiwan, therefore, be likened to top-down cultural revitalization projects in other postcolonial situations? Critical scholarship of the Indian case has suggested that unifying symbols of Indian, Hindu, or Maharashtra continuity, cohesion, and distinctiveness have been invoked by cultural elites to quash internal dissent in the name of national survival.[84] In Taiwan, on a much smaller scale, energized groups of activists have won official recognition for their ethnic groups to become eligible for office holding, public funding, and political patronage that accrue with the state's imprimatur. Since 2001 the number of recognized indigenous groups in Taiwan has climbed from nine to sixteen.[85] While the motives of such leaders and their followers are mixed and complicated, these battles have occurred in an institutional framework that incentivizes the homogenization of particular ethnic identities and the accentuation of differences among them.⁸⁶ And it was precisely these two processes that Inō Kanori and Mori Ushinosuke sought to consolidate as collectors, exhibitors, editors, and writers in the early twentieth century.

Some would consider it irresponsible to put the Taiwan indigenous renaissance on a par with postcolonial Indian nationalism. The move to historicize putatively timeless entities such as the Atayal can undermine indigenous claims to an autonomous political identity, according to this line of thought.⁸⁷ James Clifford's classic study of the courtroom travails of the Mashpee Indians, whose legal claims to rights and resources hinged on their ability to document the autochthony and continuity of their community by recourse to visible markers of culture, is a case in point.⁸⁸ To suggest that any indigenous identity has been staged, as I have done in this chapter, can be considered an attack upon the claims to collective redress that are part and parcel of indigenous rights recovery movements.

However, not all proponents of preservationism are indigenes laboring against staggering odds to regain stolen rights or establish a modicum of dignity. In post–martial law Taiwan, Han intellectuals who have invoked indigenous "otherness" as a tool for revitalizing Taiwanese national culture or for pulling Taiwan out of China's cultural orbit are primarily interested in Taiwan Indigenous Peoples as symbols. The symbolism of authentic, timeless, and non-Han indigenous peoples secures Taiwan's Austronesian heritage in this discourse.⁸⁹ The problem here is that the preservationist ethos encoded in essentialist definitions of ethnic belonging can backfire by creating unreasonable expectations that have grave real-world consequences. The notion that indigenous peoples are inauthentic or not truly indigenous if they do not wear traditional clothing or bear other markers of ethnic difference easily recognized by outsiders is, in fact, a common one. This fixation on authenticity shades into the political view that visibly assimilated indigenous peoples should ipso facto lose rights or privileges (such as access to waterways and hunting grounds or preferential treatment on university-entrance or civil-service exams).⁹⁰ The specter of the inauthentic (and undeserving) indigenous person is never far from the surface.

As was the case in the period of Japanese colonial rule, there are scholars today who find certain elements of indigenous cultures intrinsically valuable and of high aesthetic worth. Han anthropologists have worked in recent years to reinstate reconstructed forms of indigenous dance and song into the fabric of everyday life by promoting public performance as education. One critic of this movement has asked:

> Shall those young [indigenes] who have been in contact with Han society for a long time identify with an image . . . that has stagnated for several decades or centuries? Or shall they identify with a culture that has—as a result of inevitable historical development—interacted with other ethnic groups? And what kind of "Aborigines" shall non-Aborigines identify with? Is it possible that [Han preservationists]—in

order to redress the Han's former hegemony or for reasons of political correctness—unconsciously bring all possibility for the Aborigines' pluralist cultural development to an end?[91]

In this view, the interests of curators, ethnologists, neoprimitivists, and progressive Han activists are pitted against the majority of indigenes who have lived among the Han for many decades and who do not wish to turn back the clock. This proposition assumes that visible markers of identity, which perhaps define indigenes to outsiders, somehow exhaust self-conceptions of belonging from an emic perspective. Hu Chia-yu's study of Saisiyat memory, identity, and ritual life controverts such a view. She indicates that indigenous ethnic identities in Taiwan are also maintained through oral transmissions that interact in complex ways with material artifacts. Hu writes:

> . . . non-verbal expressions are heavily emphasized [in] Saisiyat ritual practices. However, the persuasiveness of ritual materials is combined with elaborated multisensory operations. The process of practicing rituals, touching sacred objects, tasting ancestral foods and drinks, listening to ritual speeches or songs, and making body movements are all perceived as major sources of sensory multiplicity. The senses as embodied powers are mediated through the material properties of sacred objects, ritual foods, or stylized bodily actions. Thus . . . the ancestral past is continuously sensed, recognized and articulated in the present to build and secure permanence in the Saisiyat community.[92]

In other words, the meanings of these objects for those who treasure them as mnemonic sites cannot be divined by mere visual inspection or abstract contemplation. They derive their identity-making efficacy through use in specific contexts that are largely unavailable to outsiders.

The three Meiji-era collectors who did so much to preserve, categorize, and enliven these objects for outsiders, Inō Kanori, Mori Ushinosuke, and Torii Ryūzō, could scarcely have imagined, I think, that Saisiyat, Atayal, Bunun, and other indigenous groups would still be around in the twenty-first century to utilize their collections. If their taxonomic labors and collecting proclivities have furthered indigenous renewal and persistence, as it seems they have to some extent, this long-term consequence was unintended, although not contrary to the spirit of their work in its own context.

4

The Geobodies within a Geobody

The Visual Economy of Race Making and Indigeneity

In the early twentieth century, Japanese official, academic, and commercial publications deployed texts, pictures, and maps to manufacture the "large reservoir of cultural imaginaries"[1] that have reemerged as reference points and resources for Taiwan's indigenous renaissance in the twenty-first century. In what began as a quest to wrest resources, impose administrative order, and promote immigration to an erstwhile Qing borderland in the late 1890s and 1900s, Japan's colonial administration, tourism industry, and scholarly apparatus, by the 1930s, had completed numerous projects in ethnic typification, geobody construction, and racialization to institutionalize indigeneity in Taiwan. This concluding chapter analyzes these three interrelated processes to demonstrate how the increased intensity of resource extraction in colonial Taiwan intersected with historical trends in reprographic technology and new forms of state making to ethnically pluralize the island's populations under the umbrella of an Aborigine Territory.

THE GLOBAL TRANSFORMATION AS THE AGE OF ANTHROPOLOGICAL TYPIFICATION

... [I]n premodern European discourses, non-Western peoples tend to be characterized not in any anthropologically specific terms, but as a lack or poorer form of the values of the centre.... My analytical fiction ... [postulates] ... a shift from an absence of "the Other" (as a being accorded any singular character) to a worldview that imagines a plurality of different races or peoples. The distinctively *modern* and *anthropological* [discourse] projects natural differences among people that may be rendered at one time as different "nations," at another as distinct "races" or "cultures." The underlying epistemic operation—of partitioning the human species—makes possible a variety of political and ethnographic projects: particular populations may be visible as objects of government; they may serve as ethnological illustrations or subversive counter-examples in comparative social argument; and these reified characters may be available for appropriation in anti-colonialist, nationalist narratives.[2]

In his definition of pluralism, or anthropological typification, Nicholas Thomas argues that modern colonial epistemology "partitions" subject populations into internally cohesive, distinctive, ontologically stable groups whose unique traits are embodied in representative figures, or anthropological types. To put these modern anthropological paradigms into relief, Thomas defines premodern ethnology as its foil, in terms strikingly similar to the assessment of Qing ethnology by Japanese ethnographer Inō Kanori. For Thomas, anthropology's interest in the languages, technologies, and belief systems of remote and small populations reflects, in part, modern cultural pluralism's axiom that all peoples are inherently worthy as members of the human race. Pluralism represents an epistemic rupture from Christian and Enlightenment paradigms of incorporation/assimilation, argues Thomas. This is so because difference configured plurally has something to offer multiple constituencies, as it gains traction as the object of scientific inquiry, exotic interest, ethnic pride, or racialist pessimism. In the new dispensation, pluralism is invested with an emotional intensity that forestalls the withering away of diverse cultural formations under the impact of the homogenizing forces consolidated during the long nineteenth century's global transformation (see introduction).

For Meiji ethnologists, who defined themselves as pluralists in Thomas's sense of the word, the first Chinese travelers to Taiwan were the very picture of premodern traveler/anthropologists. They postulated an intellectual chasm between themselves and their Qing predecessors in terms not unlike the ones Thomas uses to separate premodern and modern anthropological imaginaries. For example, in 1905, a decade into Japanese colonial rule in Taiwan, Inō wrote:

> When the Chinese first learned of Taiwan's location, they acknowledged the existence of the island's own people, or "the natives." . . . But at the time, they only recognized the natives as a different people, with different language and customs, but did not give them a particular name. . . . In Ming times, the name "Eastern Barbarians" *(dongfan)* was used . . . .After the Qing occupied Taiwan, there were two major divisions, based on the presence or absence of political compliance, the *seiban* and the *jukuban* . . . They did not, [however,] make observations about race.[3]

As the Qing period wore on, Inō wrote, Chinese observers began to add details to their reports and make distinctions among the various non-Han peoples of Taiwan. They even propounded theories for the origins of the Taiwanese natives. But in the final analysis, the "Chinese observations about the Taiwanese natives' essential nature, in relation to race, were extremely crude. There are no theories propounded here worthy of reference in scholarly discourse. The reason for this can be attributed to one cause: they based their theories on a general view that recognized the natives as beyond the pale of civilization, almost as a different species, one largely excluded from humanity."[4]

It is clear from this passage that by "race," Inō meant something more than a bundle of genetic traits that defined a Mendelian population, biologically or somatically. While Inō's project, as we shall see, essentialized and homogenized each subgroup of indigenous people through the process of typification, it also vindicated their humanity.

Thomas rightly insists that modern colonizers were far from unified in their conceptions of populations that underwent "anthropological typification." For Thomas, typification could shade into a version of relativism. Preservationist ethnologists or missionaries, in some cases, attempted to militate against the necropolitical Darwinian outlook of their fellow colonialists. In our case, Gotō Shinpei's point man on aborigine policy, Mochiji Rokusaburō, wears the black hat. In the face of their exculpatory discourse, Mochiji excoriated anthropologists for their relatively positive assessments of indigenes. In Mochiji's view, there were only two kinds of "savages": compliant and rebellious. The rebels existed beyond the bounds of sovereignty. Mochiji had little patience with pluralists and implicitly blamed them for Japan's lack of industrial progress in the uplands.

MEIJI NATIONALISM AND GEOBODY CONSTRUCTION IN COLONIAL TAIWAN

For Thomas, "colonialism's culture" locates positivities ("cultures") among the "ungoverned," "undergoverned," or "savage" peoples who are the objects of commercial, missionary, or military forces in the expanding international system. In contrast, early modern ecclesiastical/dynastic agents in such areas posited a negativity, or an absence of attributes thought to be constitutive of the imperial center, in their accounts of "barbarians/savages."[5] In this analysis, Taiwan's solidly colored secondary geobodies became placeholders for the positivities, or cultures, that displaced the blank, absent spaces of "savagery" in the Qing imaginary. The maps in figures 32–34 illustrate a sequence of contrasting logics.

The map in figure 32 is taken from an 1895 Japanese commercial publication; it is based on Western maps of Taiwan from the treaty-port era. In it, Taiwan is bifurcated into an eastern "savage" half and a western "Chinese" zone. The line separating the two zones is two-dimensional, stark and clear. This cartographic convention, which does not demarcate administrative boundaries or conform to natural land forms or emic senses of place but is rather a purely ideological construction, replicates the discourse on "separate Taiwans" advocated by Charles LeGendre after 1872 (see chapter 1).[6] In LeGendre's view, over half of Taiwan lacked government and civility. These maps, in fact, made the argument that over half of Taiwan was terra nullius, and up for grabs in terms of international law.

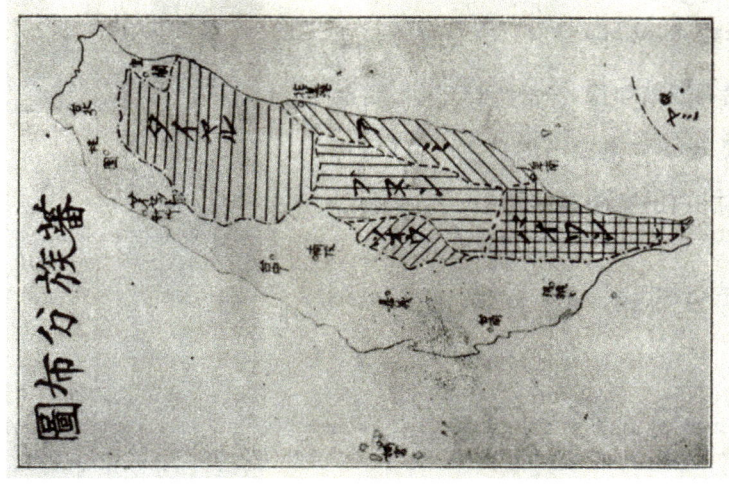

FIGURE 34. Ethnic map of Taiwan, ca. 1912. Takeuchi Sadayoshi, *Taiwan* (Taipei: Taiwan nichinichi shinpō, 1914), 620.

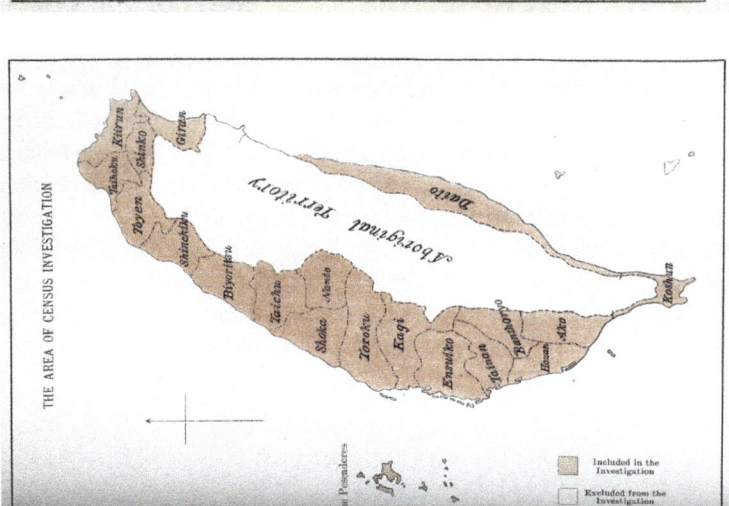

FIGURE 33. Japanese census map, 1905. *The Special Population Census of Formosa 1905: Report of the Committee of the Formosan Special Census Investigation* (Tokyo: Imperial Printing Bureau, 1909), n.p.

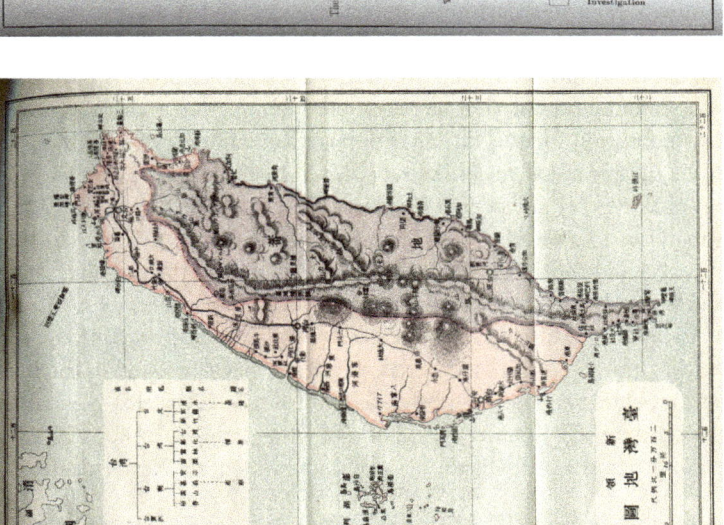

FIGURE 32. Map of Taiwan, 1895 (published in October). Akishika Kenkitsu, *Taiwan shiyō* (Tokyo: Seibidō, 1895), n.p.

194   INDIGENOUS MODERNITY

The 1905 Japanese census map (figure 33) designates the white space in its middle as the "Aboriginal Territory." This map reveals the limits of Japanese officialdom's ability to inspect, enumerate, and travel to Taiwan's interior during the camphor wars discussed in chapter 1. The census map indicates that Japanese officialdom regarded the Aborigine Territory as a limit, beyond which it could not properly conduct the basic functions of a modern state. The third map (figure 34) filled in the blank white space of the 1905 census map with culture areas. Each shaded polygon represents a *shuzoku* (race/tribe) in possession of a unique language, material culture, and corpus of myths and legends. This map was paired with a photomontage of male and female ethnic types. The polygons in figure 34 are second-order geobodies in this analysis. The pictured map was published in 1914 in a commercial publication; it was based on Inō Kanori's map in figure 2, composed between 1898 and 1900.[7]

The extension of Thongchai's geobody concept to second-order geobodies is justifiable, I think, because indigenous-territory geobodies within geobodies, like national geobodies, were strategic responses to the era's competitive imperialism. In each case, cartography was fundamentally about the mastery of space from a remote, central location at a bureaucratic apex. Whereas late nineteenth century Thai monarchs adapted an alien form of cartography to preserve autonomy in the face of an encroaching international system, the Japanese anthropologists in our story sketched their ethnic maps to extrapolate knowledge gained in limited and specific encounters to assert mastery over territories whose state of lawlessness and opacity was perceived as detrimental to the survival of the Japanese Empire.[8]

THE GLOBAL TRANSFORMATION AS THE AGE OF RACE

As self-aware non-Westerners, Japanese imperialists are said to have practiced a sort of mimesis as they internalized and reapplied race as a discursive weapon vis-à-vis other Asians, or to have refracted Western idioms in the process of becoming a full-blown colonial power. This narrative of Japanese race making as one of mimesis and/or refraction focuses our attention on the question of how race was "domesticated by the Japanese" and then redeployed in the colonies.[9] As we shall see, the mimetic framework is not without value for the study of race making in colonial Taiwan. Indeed, formally trained and westward-facing ethnologists like Inō Kanori, Torii Ryūzō, and Mori Ushinosuke had a role to play in the popularization, operationalization, and conceptualization of indigenes as members of a distinct race or races. They truly exhibited the processes of mimesis and refraction, so to speak. But their formulations were mediated, modified, and contested in the mass media by metropolitan visionaries, postcard publishers, editorialist-constables, colonized subjects themselves, and myriad others who were at best loosely affiliated with explicit programs of civilization and enlightenment or Westernization.

Moreover, the Qing precedents in aborigine administration, image production, and category construction, all of which deeply informed Japanese projects in race making, fell largely outside the history of Euro-American cultural history. In light of race's multiple and independently accreted genealogies, then, the single-origin, diffusionist model of race as subfield of European intellectual history is of limited utility for a long-term analysis of indigenous Taiwan's encounter with the global transformation.[10]

In light of these considerations, this chapter will adopt a looser construction of "race" as a category and social force. Following W. J. T. Mitchell, I regard race as a "medium," akin to a language game, rather than as a Euro-American pseudoscientific category that creates its own referent. Mitchell has argued that the medium of race provides the iconography and language for representing *any* theory, ideal, or argument that asserts the internal homogeneity and "groupness" of particular "kinds" of human beings and their distinctiveness from similarly configured groups (races). Mitchell's conceptualization recalls Thomas's definition of typification/pluralism, insofar as it minimizes the difference between "culture" and "species" as bases of invidious comparison. But it goes further. Mitchell concedes that the racial medium is often inflected with the familiar metaphor of species difference. But "race talk and race thinking" can also adopt the imagery and discourse of culture, class, status, or gender to configure difference as natural.[11] Mitchell's capacious definition is salient here because, as we shall see, photographer-anthropologists, publishers, propagandists, and merchants rarely portrayed Taiwanese racial difference in strict, Linnaean terms or even in logically consistent language or iconography. Rather, race was the thread or mediating category that conjoined a mix of ethnonyms, slurs, stereotypes, and ideals into a language of difference and hierarchy.

Mitchell, along with a number of other analysts, including Patrick Wolfe, considers modern formulations of race to be the aftereffects and not the cause of racism. In other words, racism is "what hurts." Racism is the practice of discrimination, genocide, exclusion, isolation, or segregation implemented against a race.[12] Qing-period (1700s–1895) resource wars along the frontier of Han settlement on the island of Taiwan produced a racism whose institutionalization provided the terminology and raw materials for Japanese race scientists to contend with in the Meiji period and beyond.[13] Therefore, the use of imported Western ideas involving somatological or linguistic criteria for racial classification did not produce racism in Taiwan but did provide a new language game, or medium, for framing policy options that could exacerbate or mitigate preexisting forms of racism.

To understand the genesis, meaning, and staying power of ethnically pluralist, biologically invidious, and territorially bounded indigenous formations in Taiwan, we must not only ask what men like Gotō Shinpei hoped to achieve by institutionalizing the scientifically accredited notions of hierarchy and order imbibed during his study of medicine in Germany. We must also identify and locate the dispersed interests, mechanisms, and micropolitical arrangements that allowed the medium of race to proliferate and sustain itself across vast social fields.[14] The power of anthropology and its related discourses is not to be found in connections between individual ethnologists and particular policies but rather in the rupture it introduced into discourse.

As the following sections will illustrate, even if few Japanese or Taiwanese read ethnological reports emanating from the highlands in the early twentieth century, ethnology reflected and inspired a plethora of lithographs, line drawings, paintings, ethnic maps, and photographs of indigenes. These artifacts circulated via newspapers, picture postcards, photo magazines, museum exhibitions, and exposition guides from the onset of colonial rule in 1895 right down to the end of the Pacific War in 1945. By the 1930s at the latest, it would have been impossible for tourists, colonial administrators, or politically conscious Japanese citizens to imagine a Taiwan shorn of its indigenous presence. Despite their relatively small numbers, about 2 percent of the island's population, the Indigenous Peoples produced by Japanese graphic artists, novelists, administrators, scholars, and the indigenes they interviewed, conducted trade with, photographed, and married covered half of the island's surface. The Atayal, Sediq, Truku, Bunun, Paiwan, Ami, Yami, Saisiyat, Rukai, and Tsou peoples were officially, academically, and popularly understood to be Taiwan's original inhabitants and were composed of several contiguous but distinct culture zones—in an interwar milieu that saw the conqueror's right to rule displaced by the discourse on sovereignty and authenticity.

The affirmation of indigenous autochthony and ethnic integrity was much more than the discovery of truths obscured by Sinocentric Qing discourse. As a broad-based repudiation of the notion that Taiwan's interior and eastern rift valley were inhabited by peoples "beyond the pale" (Thomas's "poorer version of the values at the center"), the creation of indigenous geobodies in Taiwan was, dialectically speaking, the negation of a negation. That is to say, the indigenous geobodies that coalesced in 1920s Taiwan did not restore Indigenous Peoples to their rightful place as original owners of the island, but rather witnessed the birth of two-way symbolic traffic between a nationalized citizenry and an excluded minority that operated, for the first time, without a mediating layer of brokers such as Kondō the Barbarian, Pan Bunkiet, or Watan Yūra. This new configuration, which I have referred to as "indigenous modernity" in chapter 3, describes an international system of nation-states riddled with pockets of quasi sovereignty. This order is sustained by the persistent and even heroic efforts of indigenes to reclaim ancestral lands and maintain corporate identities in the face of detribalization and assimilation movements. As currently configured, it also requires indigenes to perform identities in ways consistent with the aspirations, fantasies, and expectations of settler/majority populations who still control most levers of state power.

UENO SEN'ICHI AND THE PREHISTORY OF GEOBODY CONSTRUCTION IN TAIWAN

The Taiwan Government-General set up its Taipei administration in June 1895. Even before officials could safely report for duty, publications about the curious folkways of the empire's new subjects began to circulate in Japan. Especially prominent were travel accounts of hill peoples, collectively known by terms that are variations on the theme "savage," such as *banjin, seibanjin, yabanjin,* or *banzoku*.[15] Takigawa Miyotarō's *Shinryōchi Taiwantō* (Our new territory: The island of Taiwan, published in June 1895) was typical in one respect: it recycled the report of Ministry of Foreign Affairs staffer Ueno Sen'ichi, who visited Taiwan in 1881 and 1891.[16] Ueno's report, which was introduced briefly in chapter 1, is an amalgam of Ueno's firsthand observations, smatterings of cribbed material, and Ueno's translations of British Imperial Maritime Customs agent George Taylor's notes on ethnography.[17] In addition to cropping up as source material for commercial publications, Ueno's notes on Taiwan were widely disseminated within Japan's military apparatus. Thus, we can assume they had been combed over by any Japanese official, soldier, or civilian with a position of responsibility in Taiwan in the post-1895 period.

Ueno began with a discussion of Qing data and classification, continued with a digest of George Taylor's observations, and concluded with his 1891 travelogue of a visit to the environs of Quchi, home of several prominent Atayal players in the construction of indigenous modernity. To orient Japanese readers, Ueno referenced the term "eighteen tribes of Langqiao." He reminded readers that this familiar sobriquet applied only to southern Taiwanese and that there were many more than eighteen tribes, even in Hengchun. According to an 1879 Qing census of the area, wrote Ueno, there were some fifty-eight villages under the jurisdiction of Hengchun, plus another forty-six villages of the "Puyuma race" *(shuzoku),* who also lived in Hengchun district.[18]

Ueno's updates supplemented a voluminous body of Japanese records from the 1874 invasion. Much had changed in Hengchun as a result of Shen Baozhen's "open the mountains, pacify the barbarians" policies of the post-1874 period. This updated baseline data was presumably useful to Japanese constables and soldiers who fanned out across Taiwan in 1895 and 1896 to set up the rudiments of rural administration. In a less practical vein, Ueno's report also provided a somewhat confused digest of existing ethnographic information. Ueno wrote that all of Taiwan's so-called *shengfan* (raw aborigines) could be subdivided into four ethnic groups/races *(shuzoku):* the Paiwan, Zhiben (Depon), Amis, and Pingpu (Pepo). This taxonomy, inherited from Taylor, left out much of the island's indigenous population and presented some logical inconsistencies. For one, Ueno subsumed the Plains-dwelling tribes *(pingpu-zu)* under the rubric *shengfan*. In contrast, later systems considered *pingpu-zu* to be synonymous with *jukuban*, a category defined antithetically to *seiban*. Like his crude taxonomic scheme, Ueno's descriptions of origin myths followed Taylor verbatim. Taylor himself relied upon oral testimony and legends to fix ancient indigenous migration routes to Taiwan, instead of having recourse to comparative linguistic data or the maps of the global distribution of cultural traits preferred by academic ethnologists of the time. For all of its problems, this shaky overview formed the baseline for Japanese ethnologists. The "four to five different tribes of *shengfan* discovered by European writers" mentioned in Inō's 1895 manifesto refer to Taylor's classification, while Torii Ryūzō's early classificatory work also cites Taylor as a pioneer.[19]

Ueno's report described the costume, ornaments, and physical appearance of his Atayal interlocutors but did not hazard to classify indigenes into subgroups—he instead used the Chinese term *fanren* (savage). As we saw in chapter 2, Ueno's report focused instead on the cultural practices that facilitated communication between Atayal people and outsiders, to serve as a practical guide for the conduct of business. Thus, the material items it assiduously described—tobacco, glass beads, red-dyed cloth, bottled spirits—were not evidence of autochthony or cultural integrity but rather were elements of a hybrid material repertoire that had sprung up between the economically interdependent but politically independent peoples on each side of Taiwan's "savage border."

THE TAIWAN GOVERNMENT-GENERAL'S FIRST ENCOUNTER WITH INDIGENOUS PEOPLES

The newly ensconced Taiwan Government-General's first official mission to Dakekan-area Atayal peoples followed Ueno's gifting and drinking playbook, some two decades later. Mori Ushinosuke classified the Atayal members of this mission as the cismontane Dakekan tribes *(mae-Taikokan-ban)*. In the early 1900s, this group consisted of nine settlements.[20] Jiaobanshan was the largest of these.

The Japanese press and colonial bureaucracy generated at least seven written reports of the events bounded by Captain Watanabe's August 29 exploratory meeting near the Dakekan garrison and the return home of the Jiaobanshan delegation on September 12. Contemporary imagery derived from the embassy suggests that Japanese officials, writers, and publishers did not bring ethnologically informed, pluralistic categories with them to Taiwan in 1895. These would be formulated and disseminated over the course of colonial rule, on site. For example, articulate officials like Hashiguchi Bunzō and Captain Hirano Akio employed Qing terminology for "savagery" *(seiban)* and mentioned specific settlements and the names of their leaders. They did not, however, use the term *Atayal*. Nor did they attach culture zones to ethnic maps of the island. As we shall see, the first wave of Japanese-produced icons of indigeneity in Taiwan conform to Thomas's ideal-typical premodern imaginary, wherein other peoples "tend to be characterized not in any anthropologically specific terms, but as a lack or poorer form of the values of the centre."[21]

The first published Japanese illustration of an Atayal person, based on an actual face-to-face encounter, appeared in an article in the September 29, 1895, issue of the mass-circulation *Tokyo Asahi shinbun*. The article included a crude sketch of the woman known as Papau Iron, later known as Habairon. This line drawing made no attempt to capture individual features but was rather a schematic drawing of facial tattoos. According to this article, Habairon was about thirty-five years old in 1895; she is described as a woman bearing forehead and cheek tattoos, which signified her betrothal (probably an incorrect interpretation). The other female in the party of six Atayal who trekked beyond Dakekan and traveled all the way to Taipei with Hashiguchi Bunzō and Governor Tanaka (see chapter 1) was described as a nineteen-year-old woman named Washa Buta (Washiiga in subsequent sources). Washiiga lacked tattoos because she had married a Chinese man at the age of sixteen. In contrast to the "savages" *(seiban)*, Chinese did not require tattooing as part of the marriage contract, according to the report. The article also specified that female cheek tattoos consisted of four bands, indicated in the small line drawing referred to above. Despite its crudity, the newspaper drawing helped to fix the female Atayal face tattoo as one of the most easily recognizable icons of indigeneity in Taiwan.

A second, more detailed sketch portrayed two participants in the Jiaobanshan encounter—an Atayal couple who did not travel all the way to Taipei—and appeared as the back-cover illustration for the 115th issue of the *Journal of the Tokyo Anthropological Society* (see figure 35). This sketch illustrates a short narrative description of Japanese-Atayal diplomatic exchanges in September 1895. The narrative was penned by Hirano Akio, who accompanied the September 4, 1895, Hashiguchi mission to Caoling Ridge at the foot of Jiaobanshan. Like the *Tokyo Asahi* illustration, there is no attempt at ethnic or racial classification in the article. The personal names "Watan Nawi, Jiaobanshan village head, and Lemoi Maton, wife of Jiaobanshan village head" are attached, under the banner of *seiban no fuku* (savage attire). The illustration of Hirano's note, like the cruder drawing in the *Tokyo Asahi*, focuses on facial tattoos as the marker of indigenous appearance, distinguishing between male and female patterns: men wore a vertical set of bars on their foreheads, while women wore the ear-to-mouth tattoos.[22] The clothing, ornaments, coiffure, and headdress of the Jiaobanshan residents are labeled with great care. The detached coiffures and ornaments abstracted isolated cultural elements from individual historical actors to put Taiwanese *seiban* within comparative ethnography's global data set of cranial indexes, hair-strand widths, and ear shapes. At the same time, the faithfully rendered can and bottle in Lemoi Maton's backsack (see figure 11) situates the image in the shared time of frontier diplomacy, while the choice of headman Watan Nawi, who is a protagonist in the narrative account, elevates the illustration above the anonymity usually associated with "types."

These two illustrations—one mass market, the other scholarly—made gestures toward ethnographic accuracy by specifying the gender differences in tattooing

FIGURE 35. An anthropology journal sketch of Watan Nawi, 1895. *Tokyo jinruigakkai zasshi* 11, no. 115 (1895): back cover.

practices among so-called *seiban*. The next illustration, from the November 1895 issue of the general-audience magazine *Fūzoku gahō,* overlooked such niceties (see figure 36). This drawing harked back to a venerable Japanese representational practice from the 1874 expedition.

According to the *Fūzoku gahō* article's text (a faithful reproduction of excerpts from the official report filed by Hashiguchi Bunzō), the female indigenous interpreter Washiiga wears Chinese clothing and speaks an indigenous language, while the older woman, Habairon, was an unacculturated tattooed female in local garments. In the *Fūzoku gahō* illustration, however, the indigenous women lack tattoos altogether, and all of them wear a combination of Atayal capes and Chinese-style blouses.[23] In contrast to the ethnologically fastidious drawings in the anthropology bulletin described above, the men in the *Fūzoku gahō* wear facial tattoos that run from mouth to ear—a patently female pattern. More than any other detail, the tattoo mix-up confirms that the *Fūzoku gahō* artist was not working from photographs or eyewitness accounts. It is doubtful that the artist even read the text being illustrated.

Nonetheless, one element of this otherwise fanciful image did have a referent. Kabayama Sukenori, Taiwan's first governor-general, famously hosted the five Jiaobanshan emissaries and their interpreter Pu Chin in Taipei in September 1895 (see chapters 2 and 3). The inset portrait of Kabayama in figure 36 appears to be based on the commemorative photograph of the embassy.

FIGURE 36. Early mass-media illustration of the Jiaobanshan emissaries and Governor-General Kabayama. "Seiban no junfuku," *Fūzoku gahō* 103 (November 28, 1895): 17–18.

In this version of the photograph (figure 37), one Jiaobanshan emissary stares at the ground, while another is in a crouching position—not unlike the postures represented in the *Fūzoku gahō* illustration. The other Jiaobanshan emissaries adopt postures alien to the *Fūzoku gahō* drawing, however. These deviations from the photograph seem purposeful. The creative repositioning of Kabayama as a smartly attired military hero, who towers over the distorted figures of supplicant indigenes, in fact echoes 1874 wood-block prints of the Japanese expedition to Langqiao. As Robert Eskildsen has pointed out, colorful wood-block illustrations of the 1874 invasion in early Meiji-period newspapers were rife with exaggerated contrasts

影撮念紀の女男蕃生及將少田　官長政民野水 督總臺山樺
Admiral Count Kabayama, first Governor General of Formosa ; Mr. Mizuno, Chief of Civil Administration ;
Rear Admiral Tsunoda ; and man and woman aborigines, in front row.

FIGURE 37. Photograph of the Jiaobanshan emissaries and Japanese officials in Taipei, 1895. *Far left*, an unnamed foreigner, probably the Portuguese interpreter who translated from English to Taiwanese for the Hashiguchi/Tanaka mission; *4*, acting governor Tanaka Tsunatoku, who read a declaration of Japan's sovereignty to the assembled villagers near Caoling Ridge; *to Tanaka's left*, Hashiguchi Bunzō, who led the mission and became a key figure in early Japanese policy as governor of Taipei prefecture; *next*, a Jiaobanshan man named Marai (about eighteen years old); *squatting below him*, Ira Watan (about twenty-one years old), also from Jiaobanshan; *3, seated*, Civil Affairs Minister Mizuno Jun; *2, seated*, Governor-General Kabayama; *standing, between Kabayama and Mizuno*, Habairon (about thirty-five years old), from Shinajii; *seated, to Kabayama's left*, Washiiga (about nineteen years old), the Jiaobanshan woman who acted as interpreter at Caoling Ridge; *standing, behind Washiiga*, Motonaiban, an approximately forty-three-year-old Shinajii man; *to Motonaiban's right*, Pu Chin, an Atayal Chinese-language interpreter. Akiyoshi Zentarō, ed., *Nihon rekishi shashinchō kinko no kan, zohō shihan hakkō* (Tokyo: Tōkōen, 1914), 106.

that posed heroic and upright Japanese soldiers lording it over gaudily attired and obsequious Paiwanese people.[24] By 1895, however, the smartly dressed Japanese military man (figures 36 and 37), with medals and uniform, formed a contrast to both the crouching indigenes and the pike-wielding samurai of the 1870s.

From 1895 through 1900, embassy-related imagery was predominant in Japanese iconography of Taiwan's non-Han population. For example, one photograph of three Jiaobanshan emissaries (see figure 38) was converted into an etching for the *Journal of the Tokyo Anthropological Society*'s January 1896 number (see figure 39). This image illustrated a text by ethnologist Inō Kanori.

FIGURE 38. Photograph of Habairon, Motonaiban, and Washiiga, 1895. Nihon Jun'eki Taiwan Genjūmin kenkyūkai, ed., *Inō Kanori shozō Taiwan Genjūmin shashinshū* (Taipei: Jun'eki Taiwan Genjūmin hakubutsukan, 1999), 115. Photograph courtesy of the publisher: The Shung Ye Museum of Formosan Aborigines, Taipei.

FIGURE 39. Ethnographic drawing of Habairon, Motonaiban, and Washiiga that appeared in *Tokyo jinruigakkai zasshi* 11, no. 119 (1896), n.p. This drawing was titled simply "Taiwanese Savages" *(Taiwan seiban)*.

These portraits of the three emissaries Habairon, Motonaiban, and Washiiga were taken in Taipei or Dakekan walled city, to judge from the large masonry structure in the background. Whereas the *Fūzoku gahō* illustration attempted to establish a "savage territory" setting by replacing the built environment of the courtyard with a bamboo grove, Inō's commissioned etching effaced the setting of the photograph completely by whiting out everything but the sitters. This form of decontextualization was a favorite tool of visual anthropologists in the Victorian era, because it facilitated global comparisons along certain narrowly defined somatic criteria. But unlike the decontextualized picture that illustrated Hirano Akio's note (figure 35), the illustration in figure 39 does not supply labels for items of material culture. Moreover, it is puzzling (in light of subsequent fabrications) that the facial tattoos described in the *Tokyo Asahi* article—the ethnographic marker of Atayal cultural distinction in this period—have been obscured, instead of accentuated, in this etching. Inō did, however, provide readers with a sharp illustration of Atayal textile wizardry, an element that was muted in Hirano's otherwise more detailed sketch.

The photograph in figure 40 was also staged during the Jiaobanshan embassy. It became a template for several mass-circulation images, including a photograph in a middle-school geography textbook. This portrait of Habairon, Washiiga, Marai, Ira Watan, and Motonaiban, with their interpreter Pu Chin, was shot in the governor-general's reception hall in Taipei. As a comparison with figure 37 indicates, the Atayal guests sat in the governor-general's and admiral's wicker chairs for a smaller group portrait, in much less stiff poses. Ira Watan (seated) and Marai were brothers (aged twenty-one and eighteen, respectively), and Motonaiban was a forty-three-year-old widower (also seated). Washiiga and Pu Chin are standing on each side of Marai. Habairon is seated in a wicker chair. She appears to be playing a mouth harp, which also became, like facial tattoos, a marker for Atayal femininity in Japanese iconography.

As we learned in chapter 1, newspaper and magazine accounts of the Jiaobanshan embassy attached personal names to all of the emissaries pictured in figure 40, as well as the twenty-two people who greeted Hashiguchi outside Dakekan on September 8, 1895. This textbook illustration, however, is captioned *Taiwan doban*, with no other supporting information. The phrase translates to "native savages of Taiwan" and utilizes idiosyncratic characters. Japanese accounts published in Taiwan always use the character *ban*, a carryover from the Qing period, to describe indigenes. In contrast, home-island publications used a mixed and inconsistent batch of signifiers for Taiwanese, even after standardized terminology had been fixed by the government. This 1898 textbook featured only this one photograph of Taiwanese people, making the Jiaobanshan emissaries representatives of the whole island for young readers.[25]

The photograph in figure 40 reappeared in an early 1900s postcard, indicating its commercial appeal. The publishers used the more conventional term *Taiwan seiban* to label the emissaries. Like other pre-geobody-era publications, this one lumps the Atayal men and women from the Jiaobanshan embassy together with a Puyuma man and a group of Bunun or Tsou men (sitters in the other two photos), under the blanket category "savage."[26]

FIGURE 40. Photograph of Habairon, Motonaiban, Ira Watan, Marai, Pu Chin, and Washiiga, 1895. The photograph, captioned "Taiwan doban," was circulated in Satō Denzō, *Chirigaku kyōkasho: chūtō kyōiku, Nihon chizu furoku* (Tokyo: Hakubunkan, 1898), n.p. This image is reproduced from Sugiura Sosaku, *Taiwan meishō fūzoku shashinchō* (Osaka: Sugiura shōkō baiten, 1903), courtesy of the National Taiwan Library. Thanks to Joseph Allen for locating this image.

The 1897, 1898, and 1900 editions of Sanseidō's *Teikoku chirigaku kyōkasho* (Imperial geography textbook) present a radically altered version of the same photograph in a woodcut (see figure 41). Here, the artist removed Habairon's facial tattoos and mouth harp. The artist also depicted the seated Ira Watan as a standing model. The built environment, Pu Chin, Marai, Washiiga, and Motonaiban have been removed from the scene, probably to allow the reader a clearer view of the clothing and wicker chair that were thought to typify Taiwanese customs and manners *(fūzoku)* at the time. The caption, "a picture of Taiwanese" *(Taiwanjin no zu)*, obscures the indigenous or Atayal identity of the sitters. The Qing terms *seiban* (savage) and *jukuban* (acculturated savage) for indigenes do appear in the text but not in connection with this illustration. The Sanseidō text equated eastern Taiwan with the "savage territory," identifying it as home to the Mudan villagers who massacred Japanese victims back in 1874.[27] Because the tattoos on Habairon's face are not apparent in the photograph that this etching has abstracted, it is not

FIGURE 41. Textbook etching of Jiaobanshan emissaries, 1897. Kamei Tada'ichi, *Teikoku chirigaku kyōkasho* (Tokyo: Sanseidō, 1900), 152.

surprising that they were omitted. Compared to the *Fūzoku gahō* illustration in figure 36, this textbook etching is a faithful representation of the photograph on which it is based.

Yet another iteration of the Jiaobanshan embassy photograph was published concurrently, in 1900 (see figure 42). In this etching, the editors have retained Habairon's original hand and arm positions but have removed her mouth harp. The male Ira Watan now wears female cheek-to-chin tattoos, while the male Marai has been endowed with ponytails. Sheep, banana trees, and buildings on stilts have

FIGURE 42. Jiaobanshan emissaries in fanciful setting, ca. 1900. Anonymous, *Shōgaku chiri kansan* (Tokyo: Shūeidō, 1900), 29.

replaced the courtyard of Kabayama's reception area. Presumably, the point was to place the "savages" in their native habitat, symbolized here by elevated granaries, hilly topography, tropical foliage, and domesticated livestock. Although this was an educational text, it resembles the *Fūzoku gahō* illustration in its propensity for fabrication, enhancement, and misrepresentation.[28]

Two years later, an American current-events magazine called *The Independent* published a cropped version of the base photograph for these etchings (see figure 43). Its caption also erased the indigenous or non-Han identities of the sitters. Following the lead of their Japanese counterparts, they referred to Ira Watan, Marai, Motonaiban, and Pu Chin as generalized "Natives of Formosa."[29] The only other photograph in the *Independent* article is of three Atayal people (see figure 18). It suggested to American readers that typical Taiwanese were adorned with little else than striped capes or beaded vests, that women wore face tattoos, and that everyone walked barefoot (see figure 18).

The preponderance of indigenes and the paucity of Han Taiwanese in Japanese textbook portraiture—as exemplified in the five editions discussed above—was given much broader extension and a state imprimatur in the first geography textbook published, in 1903, by the Japanese Ministry of Education (see figure 44).[30] In its textbook, it adapted a photograph presumably taken on August 26, 1897 (see figure 45), when Inō Kanori visited Paalan—one of the major settlements near

FIGURE 43. Photo of Jiaobanshan emissaries in Western press, 1902. Goto Shimpei, "Formosa Under Japanese Administration," *The Independent* 54, no. 2,796 (July 3, 1902): 1,582.

Wushe, and the place where Hiyama Tetsusaburō had married into a local family two years earlier. Hiyama's father-in-law, headman Pixo Sappo, is probably the man in the photograph. According to Inō's journal, Pixo gave Inō a tour, with the help of a Sediq woman named Iwan.[31] This Iwan was probably Iwan Robao, Kondō Katsusaburō's wife.

As with the proliferation of Jiaobanshan embassy images, the people most accessible to Japanese official-scholars also became icons for an ethnic group (although their names have become lost to history). This photograph also appeared in Karl Theodor Stöpel's *Eine Reise in das Innere der Insel Formosa und die erste Besteigung des Niitakayama (Mount Morrison)*[32] and as an etching in Kamei Tadaichi's *Teikoku shin chiri* (The empire's new geography) (see figure 46).[33] A photograph of Pixo and an Atayal female with three other armed men, from the same photo shoot, was also published in the widely circulated and republished reference work by U.S. Consul James Davidson.[34]

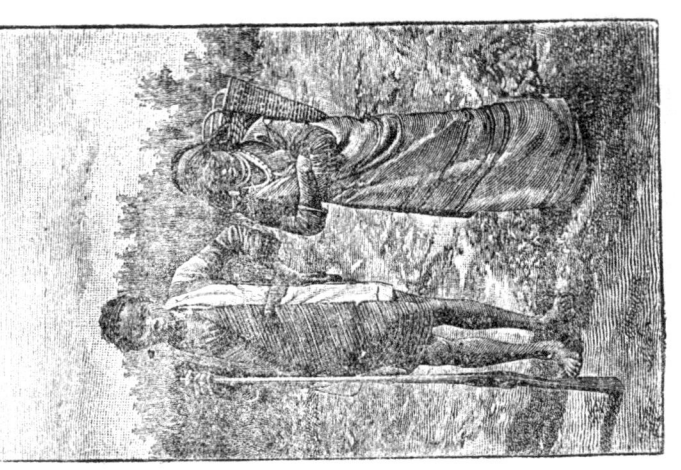

FIGURE 46. Etching of Sediq woman and Paalan headman in commercial textbook, 1908. Kamei Tadaichi, *Teikoku shin chiri* (Tokyo: Sanseidō, 1908), 138.

FIGURE 45. Photograph of Sediq woman and Paalan headman, ca. 1897. Junʼeki Taiwan Genjūmin kenkyukai, ed., *Inō Kanori shozō Taiwan Genjūmin shashinshū* (Taipei: Junʼeki Taiwan Genjūmin hakubutsukan, 1999), 142. Photograph courtesy of the publisher: The Shung Ye Museum of Formosan Aborigines, Taipei.

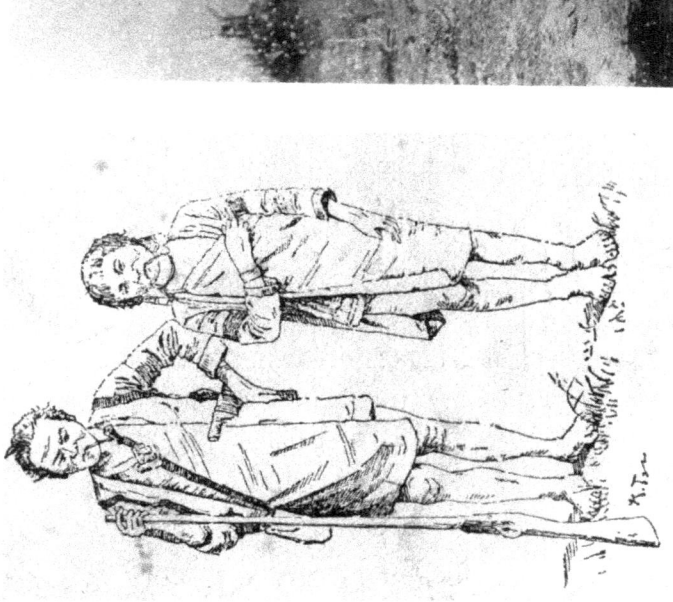

FIGURE 44. Etching of Sediq woman and Paalan headman in Ministry of Education textbook, 1904. Monbushō, ed., *Shōgaku chirisho kan ni* (Tokyo: Monbushō, 1904), 69.

The official 1903 textbook depicts a man leaning on a rifle; he wears the trademark Atayal "savage machete" *(bantō)*; he and the woman also smoke pipes. The female wears the striped Atayal cape so prominent in the other illustrations, but the stripes are muted in the illustration—only visible on the arm bands (figure 44). The photograph reveals the bolder stripes shown in the other illustrations (figure 45). This alteration can be attributed to the graphic simplification required to turn grayscale photographs into line drawings, perhaps. But there are notable fabrications here. First, the woman in the photograph is not smoking a pipe. And she is not bare-legged and barefoot, as in the drawing. Finally, as we saw in the etching of the Jiaobanshan photograph, her arms have been moved and her basket removed, presumably to accentuate the features of clothing and accoutrement that illustrators thought most salient. That exposed, well-defined, and fabricated bare feet were emphasized here suggests an imputation of savagery to the sitters—or perhaps the eroticization of the photo.[35]

The 1908 commercial textbook by Kamei (figure 46) presents readers with a more muddled etching: it is not as well defined as a line drawing, and its attempt to represent multiple shades of gray cannot be considered wholly successful. Nonetheless, it reproduces faithfully all of the elements shown in the photograph itself, with the exception of a small dog in the background.[36]

The portrait of Pixo and the Atayal female remained in print in official Japanese textbooks until the 1903 edition was replaced with the 1910 edition. On the one hand, the textbooks, official and commercial, deethnicized their Atayal subjects (ten years after Inō's ethnic labels had gained traction in official and scholarly circles) by invoking the Qing categories of *seiban* and *banjin,* respectively. On the other hand, the widely circulated textbook images highlighted ethnic markers of Atayalness such as striped clothing, pipes, machetes, and earrings. Even if commercial artists, education bureaucrats in Tokyo, and publishers did not know the difference between a Han Taiwanese, an Atayal person, or someone from Hengchun, the ethnographic lens that produced their base photographs put the identifying icons of Atayal ethnicity into play for a national audience.

Inō Kanori, who was at least indirectly involved in the production of the imagery described above, lodged an editorial complaint about the Ministry of Education textbook's illustration, but not because it was ethnographically suspect. Instead, Inō criticized the overrepresentation of indigenous peoples in textbooks. Not only was the majority population of Han Taiwanese given short shrift but also the textbook was "less than ideal" because it did not make distinctions among Hok-lo and Hakka Taiwanese. Moreover, he added, all seven indigenous ethnic groups should have been illustrated in the textbook. The 1903 Monbushō geography textbook also claimed that eastern Taiwan was largely wild and untamed, ignoring the large rift valley inhabited by cattle herders and farmers; Inō also took exception to this misrepresentation.[37]

As was the case with the Philippine Islands, where American image makers favored photographs of scantily clad Ifugao and Igorot hill peoples over suited and hoopskirted Filipino and Filipina urbanites, the visual rustification of Taiwan sketched above created the impression that Japan was colonizing an ungoverned territory. In the late nineteenth century, sovereignty was associated with "civilization" in the emergent international system. The painting of colonial acquisitions such as Borneo, Taiwan, or the Philippines as spaces of savagery, at this time, justified colonial occupation under the doctrine of terra nullius. Therefore, the predominance of Jiaobanshan embassy and Atayal imagery in early colonial-period Japanese publications does not necessarily attest to the emergence of a pluralist ethos in Japan, although in some respects it laid the groundwork for a pluralist sensibility by familiarizing large audiences with a visual vocabulary that could portray erstwhile savages as culture bearers.

THE SCIENCE OF RACE COMES TO TAIWAN

On November 3, 1895, the celebrated ethnologist and pioneer of Taiwan history Inō Kanori set out for Taiwan from Ujina Harbor aboard the *Aikoku Maru*.[38] It was around this time that Inō drafted a manifesto that linked his projects in typification, geobody construction, and race science to the sound management of Japan's new colonial possession. He wrote:

> The people of Taiwan are known by three types: Chinese *(shinajin)*, cooked barbarians *(jukuban)*, and raw barbarians *(seiban)*. As for the Chinese, of course their descendants will become obedient citizens—it should not present much difficulty to govern them. However, the raw and cooked barbarians need to be investigated from the perspectives of natural as well as conjectural science. Thereafter, an administration and an educational policy can be structured. As for "cooked" and "raw," these are general terms formerly used to reflect degrees of submission to government. If we look at it from a scientific point of view, however, there are at least four or five different tribes/races *(shuzoku)* [of aborigines], as we know from looking at the articles written by foreigners who have investigated this area. But what about the intrinsic, distinctive *(koyū)* physiologies, psychology, and local customs of the various tribes? What about their connections to the Philippine Islands and neighboring islanders? To this day, these are unsettled issues. Today, the hands of our countrymen, the clarification of these questions, will, it goes without saying, contribute to our political goals ... And we shall also obtain results in regard to our scholarly aspirations.[39]

From November 1895 to January 1896, with the help of Tashiro Antei, a high-ranking bureaucrat, botanist, and seasoned observer of Ryūkyūan customs and manners, Inō established an institutional link between the small community of Japanese anthropologists in Taiwan and Tsuboi Shogorō's Anthropological Society at Tokyo University.[40] With ambitious intellectual plans but no budget, Tashiro and Inō's society would publish its correspondence and research findings in Tsuboi's *Journal of the Tokyo Anthropological Society*. Its anthropological specimens would be stored in Inō's Taipei dormitory.[41]

The first goal of the new organization was to establish a scholarly taxonomy of names for the different non-Han tribes of Taiwan. Inō called for scientific investigations along the following lines: biological, psychological, ethnographical, linguistic, geographic, and religious.[42] In chapter 1, Kawano Shuichirō's first diplomatic mission to Yilan in November 1896 was described in some detail. One of the bicultural intermediaries, the Xitou woman named Awai, appears in Inō's first ethnological report from Taiwan. Awai acted as informant on language, village names, and local songs in the Xitou region of Yilan. Inō reproduced her testimony with his own commentary in his December 1895 digest of Tashiro's report.[43] By the time Inō published his famous 1900 synthetic ethnography, *Taiwan banjin jijō*, complete with an ethnic map of Taiwan, he had aggregated numerous interviews with bicultural interpreters such as Awai as tabular results for use by bureaucratic higher-ups who lacked direct knowledge about local populations. At this level of abstraction, Atayal interpreters like Washiiga and Awai fell out of the picture as informants, as did the "aborigine hands" Jiku Shō Min and Kondō Katsusaburō. Like Habairon, Awai's visage was turned into a crude sketch to display her facial tattoos in Inō's article, while her role as conduit of information, trade goods, and topographical intelligence was highlighted in Kawano Shuichirō's report. We can surmise that Awai's, Iwan's, and Washiiga's prolonged association with Japanese ethnologists and policemen played a role in the ethnicization of Atayal peoples.

As Vicente Rafael has observed regarding American census categories for Philippines Islands residents, the physical process of information gathering itself—rather than the reception of written digested reports—was an exercise in identity formation for both the field-level staffers who conducted surveys and the people who provided them with information.[44] Thus, it was not only anthropologists, their readers, and government officials who were buying into the new, anthropologically informed pluralist ethos. Hundreds of Taiwanese indigenes, many of them community leaders, received monetary rewards, payment in kind, or access to patronage for participating in interviews, linguistic inquiries, photo shoots, and bodily measurement exercises with Japanese survey ethnologists and census takers. They were learning, in other words, that they were Atayal, Bunun, and Paiwan peoples, instead of members of particular lineages, settlements, or ritual groups.

For Inō, the anthropologist's value-added labor was not participant observation but his global viewpoint—and ability to collate information scientifically. Referring to Lieutenant Hirano Akio's published notes,[45] Inō warned readers that amateur field reports could contribute to science only after the application of his own editorial hand. Hirano described Watan Nawi's cap as made of tanuki hide. Inō pointed out that the tanuki (a Japanese raccoon dog) did not exist in Taiwan and that other reliable eyewitnesses reported that such caps were made of deerskin. Inō insisted that such details were important for ethnologists,[46] who were set apart from men of practical affairs, such as Hirano, for their ability to construct evidence-based taxonomies, which would, in turn, provide a scientific foundation for colonial rule.

In addition to interviews with indigenes or conversations with rural policemen who themselves had daily contact with mountain dwellers, Inō relied upon Qing documents, as his January 1896 report to the *Journal of the Tokyo Anthropological Society* reveals. In this issue, Inō referenced an unnamed Chinese record to give population estimates for Dakekan. Inō also relayed a report on methods of alcohol brewing and noted that the process might be further clarified by looking at a corroborating passage in the Danshui Prefecture "Local Customs" section of the old Taiwan gazetteers.[47] In later reports, he would cite specific Qing records as evidence for a number of local practices.[48]

Timothy Tsu has argued that men like Inō represented a new force in Japanese Sinology. During the Tokugawa period, Japanese scholars read Chinese texts to understand the principles of statecraft, history, and family relations in order to become better human beings and governors. It was not uncommon for Chinese scholars to visit Japanese literary societies. They were lavishly wined and dined as they shared their expertise with provincial aficionados in Japan. Modern social-scientific approaches to data collection changed all of this. To govern Taiwan more efficiently, Japanese officials mined Chinese court records, land deeds, population registers, and treatises for evidence, not for theoretical insight or moral guidance. As Peter Pels put it in his discussion about a similar transition in colonized India, the colonial social scientists entered into a direct relationship with texts, individuals, and populations in order to correct the superstitious, backward, and parochial outlooks of local mandarins. Thus, Inō would be an energetic compiler, editor, and translator of Qing documents, but he remained committed to the idea that these documents supplied only the raw materials for scientific analysis, subject to his corrections.[49]

In the March 1896 issue of the *Journal,* Inō reproduced documentary evidence from the Qing archives to expose its *shufan/shengfan* nomenclature as anthropologically bankrupt. He documented how certain villages were classified in older Qing records as *shengfan* but reclassified as *shufan* in later gazetteers. Sometimes the two terms were used interchangeably with terms such as *yefan,* another word for "savage" with no particular ethnic referent. Inō also turned a critical eye to fellow countryman Ueno Sen'ichi, whose 1895 report for the Japanese army was summarized above. Inō chided Ueno for mistakenly using the toponym *peipoban* (plains tribe) as an ethnonym. If we recall Inō's use of the word *koyū* (particular) in his early declaration of "needs and opportunities" for Taiwan research, we can understand his objections. In the context of race studies as construed by Inō, *koyū* referred to the distinguishing characteristics of a tribe that fixed its essential nature. Terms like "unacculturated" *(shengfan)* and "plains tribe" described accidental characteristics shared by any number of tribes, villages, and confederations throughout the Qing empire.

To go beyond poking holes in other accounts, Inō had no choice but to follow the paths of Ueno, Hashiguchi, Kawano, and Hirano to gather information from and about peoples whose languages had yet to be recorded in dictionaries. One of his early informants, the woman who would become known to Japanese simply as Ai, was born around 1880 to chief *(shuchō)* Pira Omin of Kimunajii (near Dakekan). Meiji anthropologists prefaced much of their work in the language of hardship, solitary travel, danger, and exploration. Undoubtedly, such posturing reflected aspects of their experience. On the other hand—and quite sensibly, in a new colony among unknown tribes—these ethnologists, like the merchants and rural officials discussed in the previous chapters of this book, initially turned to the most willing and available informants. And these people tended to congregate around old Qing Pacification Offices and trading entrepôts, Dakekan being the most prominent.

Inō's informant Ai was seven years old when Governor Liu Mingchuan's Pacification Office was established in Dakekan in 1886. A Christian missionary named Chen Cunxin arrived circa 1890. Chen soon adopted Ai, which explains her facility in the Minnan dialect of Chinese by the time Inō showed up. As we have seen, such adoptions were common enough along the savage border, with the aim of each side to gain access to important suppliers, protectors, and patrons from across the border. Inō Kanori paid Chen and Ai a visit in January 1896. He took Ai on as a Japanese-language student while in turn interviewing her about her childhood in Kimunajii and taking rudimentary lessons in the Dakekan variant of Atayalic. This relationship continued for over a year, until Ai's tragic death on March 19, 1897, from a fever. According to Inō, Ai was making rapid progress in Japanese before she passed away. In his memorial article in the *Journal of the Tokyo Anthropological Society,* Inō characterized Ai as a shining example of Atayal people's "potential for civilization." He also acknowledged his debt to her as a native informant on language, history, and customs.[50] So, before Inō barely had time to situate himself in the new colony, he had already relied upon the services of several bicultural Atayal women, including Iwan, Awai, and Ai, to make a beginning on filling in the blank ethnological spaces on the old Qing map.

Although Inō considered himself to be a race scientist, his narrowly anthropometric investigations were peripheral to his taxonomic project. In contrast to the grim, serious, and consequential anthropometry used by United States anthropologists to lend academic legitimacy to the "one-drop rule" or to "blood-quantum" politics,[51] Inō's quantitative forays are incidental to his larger body of work or even to individual reports. For example, to determine Ai's racial status, Inō drew up a list of body parts and compared Ai's features to those of the "typical Japanese girl." Inō's method here was a far cry from Mori Ushinosuke's subsequent use of standardized forms, based on the famous British Ethnological Society Notes and Queries forms.[52] The major headings on Inō's list were even inconsistent across studies. In Ai's case, he listed skin color, bodily hair and coiffure, eye shape, and "other parts of the face" as important constituents of racial identification. For each feature, Inō used a Japanese woman as the proxy for Asian and marked "similar" or "not" (if "not," he explained how a feature was different). Under the column *bodily hair,* Inō marked "similar," but under *mouth,* he wrote that Ai's was "comparatively bigger." For all of his efforts, however, Inō believed this method of racial classification was inconclusive. For one,

Inō's sample was much too small. But even if this problem were ignored, Inō wrote, some of Ai's physical features were Asian, while others were Malayan, so there was no way to decide her racial affiliation based on his anthropometric investigations. In the end, Inō believed linguistic evidence was more definitive, because Ai's spoken *bango* (Atayal) had the flat tone (compared to the rising and falling tones of Chinese) and harsh consonants characteristic of Malay languages.[53]

Inō freely mixed cultural and somatic criteria in this case to arrive at a foregone conclusion: Ai was not Chinese or Japanese but was instead a member of the Malay race. This determination linked her ethnographically to the peoples of the Philippine Islands and the Malay Peninsula, while extracting her from the frontier political economy of Dakekan. In the years to come, Inō would labor to represent the "pure Malay" indigene graphically—an immense project to which we will return below. In a subsequent report based on a larger sample, Inō conducted anthropometric studies of the inhabitants of Wulai. Almost as if to invite the criticism of later scholars, Inō adopted different categories for measurement for his Wulai subjects than the ones he used for Ai, rendering a scientific comparison impossible. Inō had twenty-seven Wulai residents to work with, which led him to state that his statistical sample was too small to be meaningful.[54]

On the other hand, this March 1896 series of interviews, which took place in Taipei, changed the course of Japanese representational practices vis-à-vis indigenes forever and has cast a long shadow on current practices in self-representation. It was in Taipei that Inō determined that his Wulai informants were similar enough in dress, ornament, language, and comportment to his Dakekan informants to be classified as coethnics under the rubric *Atayal*.

WULAI, QUCHI, AND THE ATAYALIZATION OF THE NORTHERN TRIBES

Inō's March 1896 interviews with Wulai residents not only provided him with important clues for the classification of Taiwanese ethnic groups but also set the stage for the production of photographs by activating networks of ethnologists, military men, camphor capitalists, and headmen from the settlements along the Xindian River.

Inō Kanori's travel notes from 1897 and his 1900 ethnological report list Jiku Shō Min as his local informant for Quchi. Jiku came to Taiwan with the Imperial Guard in 1895. In 1896, under orders from first governor-general Kabayama Sukenori, Jiku made his way to Quchi to "pacify the locals."[55] Subsequently, he married into a leading Quchi family to establish a beachhead for Japanese logging concerns in conjunction with camphor entrepreneur Dogura Ryūjirō. As an adopted outsider, Jiku took the title Watan Karaho to reckon himself a true local chief *(tōmoku)*.[56] Because Inō referred to Jiku in his famous 1900 compendium as his guide to Quchi, we can surmise that Jiku himself facilitated the March 1896 exchanges between Inō Kanori and the Wulai contingent in Taipei recounted above.

A little over a year after the interviews with the twenty-seven Wulai residents in Taipei, Inō and Awano Dennojō formed an expedition crew to begin a 192-day ethnographic survey tour of Taiwan by order of the Bureau of Education. They began by recruiting two Han Taiwanese aborigine-language interpreters, named Kōan and Aki, both inhabitants of the interior for over twenty years. Both were married to indigenous women. Inō could hardly distinguish Aki from an Atayal man; he lacked a queue, wore Atayal clothing, wielded a machete, and traveled barefoot. Inō's party also hired Awai, presumably for interpreting, along with her two children, in the village of Rahao.[57] This Awai may have been the same interpreter who acted as Tashiro Antei's informant in the fall of 1895.

Jiku Shō Min organized the purchase of gifts and supplies, as well as the hiring of interpreters. When the party reached Wulai, just south of Taipei, Inō and Awano were welcomed by a young *bantei* (brave) named Watosinai, whom Inō had met previously (probably in Taipei).[58] Watan Yūra, whose name shows up in the manuscript records of Japanese rural administration as a representative of Wulai and in Inō's list of informants from the March 1896 interviews, was also present. Inō did not return to Wulai/Quchi after the May 1897 meeting, but Mori Ushinosuke, again under the aegis of Jiku Shō Min, rekindled these ethnologist-informant relationships in 1902.

Inō's island-wide survey concluded in December 1897. At this time, we should recall, etchings based on photographs of the Jiaobanshan embassy and a few actual photographs had been circulating in Taiwan and Japan as the most widely distributed illustrations of the island's peoples. On April 23, 1898, Inō Kanori made his first major intervention to controvert these ethnologically vague and, in his view, irresponsible portrayals. Shifting the ground toward a pluralist model, Inō unveiled his newly devised taxonomy of Taiwan Indigenous Peoples with a photographic montage composed of representative "types" at an exposition in Danshui.[59] On August 16, 1898, Inō's montage appeared on the cover of the first issue of *Banjō kenkyūkaishi* (Journal of the society for research on aborigine conditions).[60] The same montage was reproduced for a general readership on August 5, 1899, in *Taiwan meisho shashinchō* (A photo album of Taiwan's famous sites).[61]

Inō's montage, prefiguring the map he would publish in 1900, depicted Taiwan's ethnic groups as commensurate units, suggesting ontological parity for each. Unlike the map, however, the montage could not provide visual consistency across ethnic groups. Some of the photos are studio portraits, others were shot in situ. Some displayed noted cultural markers, others did little to distinguish their subjects from other Taiwanese. For example, the "tattooed face savage/Atayal" exemplar wears no jewelry, has no visible tattoos, and is carrying an imported weapon. This man, who hailed from Quchi, was probably familiar to Inō. In the montage, he is referred to as the "tattooed face savage" *(keimenban)*,[62] which is also glossed in furigana as *Atayal*.

The new ethnonym *Atayal* redefined the "savages" in terms of unique attributes manifested in language and material culture, neither connected to nor dependent upon their relationship to a Japanese or Qing imperial center. In other words, the ethnonym *Atayal* asserted a *presence*. But in asserting an ethnic presence, Inō also effaced the individual's identity. In contrast with the Jiaobanshan embassy sitters, whose names are easy to discover, clues regarding the identity of the man known simply as "tattooed face savage" remain fugitive.

A glass plate of Inō's "tattooed face savage" is held at the U.S. Library of Congress as part of the Bain News Service photographs,[63] along with a portrait of two well-armed "chiefs," two photographs of headhunters with fresh heads, and a picture of a skull shelf.[64] The Bain negative is captioned "typical fighting man of the head-hunters, Formosa."

The Japanese word for "savage" is also burned into the plate. The other chiefs in the Bain News Service collection are also referred to as savages, while the other three Bain negatives provide graphic evidence of *seiban* barbarity by displaying severed heads or skulls.[65] The term *Atayal* is not attached to any of these photos. Other pictures of the armed man from Inō's 1898 montage have been reproduced in the 1999 book *Kanori shozō Taiwan Genjūmin shashinshū* (Images of Taiwan indigenous peoples from the Inō Kanori archive). One shows the man seated with a rifle and a Japanese flag; the other shows him directing soldiers with weapons and again carrying a Japanese flag. The editors of this volume argue, convincingly, that he probably fought on the side of the Japanese state against Han rebels in late 1895 and 1896, as an irregular in the employ of Japanese station chiefs stationed near Quchi.[66] His image was also reproduced on cabinet cards, a popular photographic medium from the 1860s through the 1890s.[67]

In contrast to the ethnically ambiguous Atayal photographs in the 1898 montage, Inō's canonical 1900 textual description of the Atayal describes them as face-tattooed peoples, richly adorned in geometrically carved earrings and accessories that included buttons, brass, shiny metal, and colored threads.[68] To reconcile the difference between Inō's textual/cartographic representations of bounded, discrete ethnic blocks among Taiwan's non-Han population and the motley assemblage of hybrid-themed photographs in the 1898 montage, Inō commissioned a color painting for the 1900 Paris Universal Exposition.[69]

The 1900 painting adds head-feathers, necklaces, hats, and earrings to each representative "savage type" to accentuate cultural differences among them.[70] The process of fabrication is even more evident in the similarly augmented illustration for the 1907 Tokyo Industrial Exhibition, also curated by Inō.[71] In the 1900 and 1907 exposition montages, the gun has been airbrushed out of the Atayal man's hand, large bamboo earrings have been painted in, and forehead and chin tattoos have been darkened or added. In the 1898 montage, the Bain News Service photograph, and the cabinet card, the facial tattoo on the man's forehead is invisible or barely visible, and the chin tattoo is obscured by shadow. An examination under high magnification of the high-resolution negative stored in the Library of Congress reveals a very faint forehead tattoo and rules out a chest tattoo. The photos of alternative poses from the same session show no evidence of visible facial or chest tattoos. Yet the reproduction in James Davidson's 1903 book (for which Inō Kanori was the ethnological advisor) exhibits pronounced forehead, chin, and chest tattoos, the result of doctoring.⁷²

In the "ethnicized" 1900 and 1907 paintings, the female Atayal "type" shed her Chinese-style upper garment for an Atayal sleeveless vest, decorative chest embroidery, and a striped handwoven cape. The reornamented Atayal woman wears ethnologically correct earrings and necklaces, as well. Whereas the ethnicized male Atayal model was transformed with a paintbrush or pencil, his female counterpart was removed from the 1898 photomontage and replaced by a different sitter in the 1900 and 1907 composite portraits.⁷³

As curator for the 1900, 1903, 1904, and 1907 expositions, Inō Kanori was charged with educating the public about the non-Chinese population of Taiwan. In the course of preparing the visual component of his exhibits, Inō turned "savages" into Atayal and other nondescript males into Yami and Paiwan by embellishing visual documents. It would be accurate to view these fabrications, in the context of colonial census taking, mapmaking, and museum curation,⁷⁴ as exercises in top-down ethnogenesis.

MAKING PHOTOGRAPHS IN QUCHI: VISUAL CULTURE AND TOP-DOWN ETHNOGENESIS

James C. Scott's characterization of a parallel project in British Burma suggests that Inō's difficulties were not unique. As was the case with British officials, Japanese agents in upland Taiwan found even the act of naming tribes to be fraught with problems because of the hybridity they regularly encountered. Of these turn-of-the-century classificatory schemes, Scott writes that "a major reason why trait-based designations of ethnic or tribal identity fail utterly to make sense of actual affiliations is precisely that hill groups themselves, as manpower systems, absorbed whomever they could. This absorptive capacity led to great cultural diversity within hill societies."⁷⁵ These multiform, ethnically diverse "manpower-absorbing" societies were precisely the kind of formations Japanese officials encountered on the savage border circa 1900. In his study of the "Nanzhuang incident" of July 1902, Antonio C. Tavares observes that Saisiyat tribes under chieftains in the late Qing period were conglomerates of Han, non-Han, and hybrid actors, with hierarchies of power and wealth that ran counter to entrenched East Asian taxonomic spectra composed of descending markers of value from central and paramount *hua* (civilized) to peripheral and lowly *yi* (barbaric).⁷⁶ Mori's 1902 description of Watan Yūra's extended family (whom Inō met in May 1897, pictured in figures 18 and 19) illustrates how, like the Nanzhuang operators, Wulai headmen adopted outsiders to create hybrid formations, to the chagrin of ethnic cartographers like Inō:

> Wulai settlement's paramount chief Watan Yūra's eldest daughter Pazzeh and his adopted son [*yōshi*] are both about twenty years of age. This couple is the *poken*, meaning that if the line of succession is maintained, they will become chiefs . . .⁷⁷

FIGURE 47. Photograph of Mori Ushinosuke, Japanese officers, and Truku headmen, 1910. Mori is facing away from the viewer and wears the dimpled hat. Courtesy of the Rupnow Collection.

To the right of Watan Yūra is standing a plains aborigine *[peipozoku]* (cooked barbarian *[jukuban]*) male without tattoos. About twenty years ago, it is said that he entered this settlement/village and became a savage brave *[bantei]* . . . To the left are four wives of savages *[banjin]*. They are wearing Chinese-style blouses and gaiters.[78]

The networks that emerged through intermarriage, business dealings, armed conflict, and research among Japanese officials, ethnologists, merchants, and leading families from Quchi—we saw them in action during Inō's 1897 and 1898 information-gathering exercises—provided the setting for Mori Ushinosuke to make qualitatively superior photographs in the ethnographic genre. In contrast to our earliest examples of ideal-typical "head-hunting chiefs" photographed in Taipei studios (figure 21), the photographs made in Quchi during the establishment of the guardline were shot at or near the residences of the subjects (figure 19). The increased number of poses and more intricate stagecraft evident in the Quchi photographs suggest a heightened degree of familiarity between photographers and subjects.[79] Mori himself was rarely photographed. One photograph was taken circa 1914 at the end of the Truku campaigns; Mori is wearing the hat, with his back toward the viewer (see figure 47).

In one recorded instance of Mori Ushinosuke's networking prowess, on January 28, 1903, Mori brought Rimogan resident Marai Watan and his wife Yūgai Watan to Taipei to view a local theater production of *Ishiyama Gunki,* meet the staff of the *Taiwan Daily News,* and see the sights. According to the short newspaper write-up, the Rimogan couple "came down from the mountains to visit Quchi town once or twice a year, but had never been to Taipei."[80]

Since Marai's portrait was displayed at the Osaka Exposition, which opened on March 1, 1903, it is reasonable to assume that Mori photographed this couple just before or after their visit to the capital city in January. Their most widely published portrait was shot in April 1903. It was included in a number of official publications and formed the basis for at least two picture postcard designs (see figure 59). Postcards were also generated from different poses of the same couple, indicating the ideological and commercial appeal of their likenesses as rendered by Mori's camera.[81]

Instead of using painting or drawing to "Atayalize" Yūgai, Mori was able to accomplish her racialization by requesting different poses. While Yūgai's anthropometric portrait shows her Chinese-style upper garments clearly, her more commercially reproduced pose was staged to present a more "authentic" Yūgai.[82] In the latter photograph, she dons a cape of local design, which conceals her Chinese clothing. This de-Sinicized version of Yūgai's portrait showed up in various picture postcards, in a 1932 book by ethnographer Koizumi Tetsu, in a collection of government statistics, and on the sleeve for a set of Taiwan Indigenous Peoples picture postcards.[83]

During the over 150 days that it remained open, the Osaka National Industrial Exposition of 1903 drew over five million visitors.[84] The Taiwan Government-General lobbied intensively for exposition space under the energetic leadership of Gotō Shinpei. For Gotō, the Osaka Exposition presented an opportunity to educate Japanese on the home islands about the strategic importance of Taiwan, its potential economic benefits, and the cultural and culinary attractions of the island. A prevailing home-islander image of Taiwan, which Gotō hoped to dispel, was that of a savage place where demonic tribes practiced cannibalism.[85] Against this backdrop, the "tattooed face savage" photos of men with large guns glaring at cameras in studio settings were hardly appropriate. Gotō's opportunistic aversion to savagery dovetailed with Inō Kanori's preference for cultural themes in evidence in the 1900 Paris Exposition painting. Thanks to Mori's new photographs from the environs upriver from Quchi, Inō was able to accommodate both desiderata without recourse to another commissioned painting. He simply exhibited Mori's photographs.[86]

Mori shot portraits of Pazzeh Watan, daughter of the headman Watan Yūra, near Wulai in February 1903, just after his January trip to Taipei with Marai and Yūgai. Pazzeh is seated to the viewer's far left in figure 19. This group portrait shows her wearing Atayal leggings with a Chinese blouse and headdress—a common sight along the old Qing savage border. This photograph appeared in a Taiwan Government-General publication of 1911, in the general-circulation magazine *Taiyō* in 1917, and in Mori's 1915 and 1918 ethnological picture albums, as well as on Shōwa-period picture postcards.[87] It was also picked up for syndication in the United States.[88] For a different pose, Pazzeh put on bamboo earrings, locally woven fabrics, necklaces, and a diamond-shaped breast cover festooned with white buttons for her anthropometric portrait. Her bust and profile from this shot appeared in dozens of formats in Japanese and foreign publications and continues to be reproduced to this day. The differences in Pazzeh's dress and ornamentation in the two portraits from February 1903 recall Inō's alterations of the 1898 montage discussed above: features considered to be signs of autochthony and distinction were accentuated, while any other visible signs of hybridity were obscured.

THE VIEW FROM THE METROPOLE: CONSUMER DEMAND MEETS COLONIAL POLICY

Photographs, as slices of time that freeze events, cannot narrate themselves without the help of external markers, such as captioning or juxtaposition with other photographs.[89] In the case of Mori Ushinosuke's Quchi-area photographs, captions told various stories. The text for some portraits supported Mori's ethnicizing, pluralizing ethos. An early 1900s postcard of Pazzeh applied the caption "Shinkō [administrative district], Urai-sha [place name] Woman, Taiyal Tribe," sans terminology for "savage," for example.[90]

Mori's and Inō's original intentions were more often violated once they lost editorial control, because policy was moving in a different direction than representational practices favored by Japan's ethnologists.[91] In December 1902, only a couple of months before Mori took Marai's and Pazzeh's photos for the Osaka Exposition, councillor Mochiji Rokusaburō, the brains behind Gotō Shinpei's aborigine policy, issued his famous "opinion paper on the aborigine problem," which averred that "sociologically speaking, they are indeed human beings *(jinrui)*, but looked at from the viewpoint of international law, they resemble animals *(dōbutsu no gotoki mono).*"[92]

As the scorched earth campaigns were commencing, in June 1904, parliamentarian Takekoshi Yosaburō arrived in Taiwan to write a progress report.[93] In September 1905, Takekoshi published *Taiwan tōchi shi,* his encomium to Japanese rule based on his 1904 visit; he included profile pictures of Watan Yūra's daughter Pazzeh Watan, who figured prominently in Mori's Quchi photographs, as a nameless *Atayaru-zoku jo* (Atayal tribe female) next to exemplars from each officially recognized tribe. Most of these photographs were also exhibited at the 1903 Osaka Exposition. These ethnically labeled profiles and frontal shots, with blank backgrounds in the anthropometric genre, were interleaved with photos of Japanese military maneuvers and Gotō's inspection tour of camphor forests. In this context, the ethnicized portraits of Marai and Pazzeh appeared as emblems of recalcitrant Atayals, marked as an expendable race. In contrast to the photographed Jiaobanshan emissaries who arrived in Taipei in September 1895 to initiate relations between the government-general and the cismontane Dakekan tribes, the names of Watan, Marai, Pazzeh, and Yūgai were not mentioned in newspaper accounts of guardline movements in and around Quchi. And by the time their photos emerged in the flood of picture albums of Taiwan indigenes published in the 1910s, Japanese publicists and anthropologists had ceased attaching personal names to photographs of indigenes altogether.

During the era of the guardline, 1903–1915 (see chapter 1), the rhetoric on Atayal savagery was amplified and reinforced by the captions for various contemporary postcards that identify Pazzeh Watan as a *seiban,* bellicose *seiban,* or (incorrectly) as a member of the Taroko *seiban,* the most militarily resistant subgroup of Atayal peoples.⁹⁴ This view received the imprimatur of the Taiwan Government-General, which issued its second set of commemorative postcards on October 15, 1905. One featured a studio portrait of armed Atayal men captioned as "head hunters" in English and labeled "Taiwan savages" *(Taiwan banjin)* in Japanese.⁹⁵

The government-general would issue three more commemorative postcards featuring indigenes during the guardline period. Martial themes were prominent. The 1908 set, for the thirteenth anniversary of colonial rule, commemorated the Stone Gate Battle of 1874 with a colorful painting of the battlefield and a tombstone to the fallen warriors.⁹⁶ A paired card reprised an 1874 photograph of Saigō Tsugumichi surrounded by his own soldiers and several emissaries from Paiwan villages in Hengchun (figure 8).

These cards were issued two years into the administration of Governor-General Sakuma, who himself was the hero of this 1874 battle. The fourteenth-anniversary card (1909), issued on the eve of Sakuma's "five-year plan to conquer the aborigines" (see chapter 2), features the governor-general himself. Whereas his fellow veteran of the 1874 campaign Saigō sits among his Paiwan emissaries in the 1908 commemorative series, Sakuma is elevated high above the more than forty Atayal and Saisiyat men and women gathered at his residence in the photo from the 1909 series. Sakuma is placed even higher than Prince Kan'in, who was conducting a royal tour in 1908.⁹⁷

To look at the body language and positioning of Paiwan and Jiaobanshan sitters (figure 37) in their respective commemorative photographs, one might surmise that they were guests, or at least subordinate allies, at functions presided over by Saigō or Kabayama (in 1874 and 1895, respectively). But the fourteenth-anniversary photograph of Governor-General Sakuma allows for no such reading. Here, even the most highly placed indigenous person's head is even with Sakuma's feet, while most of them are huddled on the ground in positions of abjection. In fact, the 1909 postcard can be read as the wish fulfillment of the *Fūzoku gahō* artist who imagined Kabayama in a similarly commanding position over the Jiaobanshan emissaries in 1895 (figure 36).

The last of the guardline-period TGG postcards with indigenous themes was transitional. It struck a balance between a pluralist sensibility and the discourse on savagery (see figure 48). Issued in 1911, at the height of the war against Atayal peoples in and around the tramontane Dakekan tribes, it included a Mori Ushinosuke photograph of an Atayal dwelling and attached granary.⁹⁸ This scene was common in anthropological reports of the time. The card also featured a well-circulated photograph of Koalut dancers from Hengchun.⁹⁹ The photographs were innocuous

FIGURE 48. Official commemorative postcard depicting indigenous customs, 1911 ["Taiwan Aborigines Dancing" and "Taiwan Aborigine Dwelling with Granary"], ip1441, East Asia Image Collection, Lafayette College, Easton, PA, accessed May 13, 2016, http://digital.lafayette.edu/collections/eastasia/imperial-postcards/ip1441.

enough, but they were framed by a heavily embossed decorative element composed of a machete, a head-hunting backsack, a gun, some spears, and two arrows, next to a trademark Atayal wisteria-woven cap. The composition therefore connoted menace, if not danger. At the same time, it presupposed its audience's familiarity with particular cultural repertoires of the Atayal and Paiwan indigenous ethnic groups, so that viewers could read the embossed icons as symbols of indigenous bellicosity. Assuming that these mass-produced, high-quality commemorative sets were designed with great deliberation, one can conclude that the pluralistic terminology and iconography so laboriously engineered by Inō, Mori, and a cast of hundreds was gaining traction at the apex of administration in Taiwan by the 1910s, if only incrementally. The photo captions in figure 48 themselves are mute regarding ethnic designation and retailed generic words for "savage" instead.

The predominance of head-hunting and savage tropes in the government-produced postcard sets and in the state-produced and commercial punitive expedition albums reflects the power of metropolitan policy directives and consumer tastes to shape the meanings attached to widely circulated photographs of Taiwan's indigenous people. With adroit captioning and the creative deployment of design elements, Tokyo and Taipei publishers and editors yoked print culture to TGG policy and Japanese consumer tastes. At the same time, ethnologists on exposition-planning committees, editorial boards of academic journals, and lower-level corners of the colonial bureaucracy launched counterhegemonic arguments with artifacts, photographs, drawings, and texts. To be sure, advocates of a pluralist agenda such as Inō Kanori and Mori Ushinosuke were largely motivated by concerns of professional advancement in the emergent field of anthropology. They also had an eye for the survival and growth of the discipline itself. The ethnologists pursued these ambitions as they extolled Japan's modernity in the global arena of scientific publication. Whether they supported the discourse on savagery or ethnicity, the poses, set designs, captioning, and layout decisions that shaped visual culture surrounding indigenous peoples responded to dictates largely divorced from the specific locations where sitters, photographers, and stage managers came together to expose wet- or dry-plate slides to light in the presence of living beings and the environment.

To ground these images in their historically specific contexts of creation, we must return to the Atayal-dominated regions of Quchi and Jiaobanshan—each a fecund hearth of pluralist and savage-trope imagery in the early twentieth century. If indigenes themselves had anything to say about how they were being represented in Japanese photography, they exercised agency at these sites.

THE SAVAGE-BORDER MISE-EN-SCÈNE OF COLONIAL PHOTOGRAPHY IN TAIWAN

In May 1903, two months after the opening of the Osaka Exposition and the first public display of Watan Yūra's family portrait, Japanese authorities imprisoned nine Quchi men. They were used as hostages to secure the cooperation of other Quchi leaders to build a cordon sanitaire to separate camphor fields and tax-paying settlements from Atayal who were attacking camphor harvesters. This stratagem met with some success. During the years 1904 and 1905, the local knowledge, military prowess, and political agility of Quchi residents made it possible for the Taiwan Government-General to establish the toehold it needed to build its guardline across the most contested areas just south of Taipei. Thereafter, from its Quchi base, the government-general built several hundred miles of guardline across northern Taiwan.[100]

The role of Quchi auxiliaries in the advancement of the guardline is attested by two photographs produced there circa 1905. One depicts an extended family, consisting of eleven men, four women, and two children (see figure 49); the other depicts seven armed men (see figure 50), who also posed for the family portrait in figure 49. The brush-written caption to the extended family portrait places the scene at the "Guardline Control Station," meaning that it was taken in 1904 at the earliest. It was reproduced in the September 2, 1905, *Taiwan nichinichi shinpō* (Taiwan daily news). Therefore, the men, women, and children captioned as "Wulai Savages" in the newspaper were photographed about two years after Mori's famous Quchi photographs were shot in early 1903.

FIGURE 49. Men and women along the Quchi guardline, ca. 1904. Courtesy of the National Taiwan Library (Taipei). Unpublished photograph album, *Taiwan shashin* (National Taiwan Library Document 0748–71, plate 82).

The "family snapshot" (figure 49) appeared on an early 1900s postcard, in a few Japanese-language books, in several foreign publications, and in geography textbooks.[101] A comparison of the careers of the 1903 (figure 19) and 1905 Wulai (figure 49) group portraits suggests that a threshold was crossed in 1905 with the militarization of relations between the Japanese government and the Quchi-area tribes. In each group portrait, four women crouch to the viewer's left, dressed in a combination of Chinese and Atayal clothing. Standing and squatting men with pipes and diamond-shaped breast ornaments are the center of attention. Children wrapped in trademark striped Atayal capes sit in the foreground of each portrait, rounding out the cast of characters. However, the structure in the background of the 1905 photograph (figure 49) is new. This distinctive feature is a guardline control station. This military installation is not identified in the published versions of the photo, although it is indicated with a hand-brushed caption in an unpublished album housed in the former TGG library in Taipei. Therefore, editors and consumers likely viewed figure 49 as a family portrait rather than as the war photograph that it was.

In the seven Japanese-language publications that include a photo from the 1905 shoot (figures 49 and 50), only the mixed gender and age "family portrait"

FIGURE 50. Japan's Atayal allies along the Quchi guardline, ca. 1904. Courtesy of the National Taiwan Library (Taipei). Unpublished photograph album, *Taiwan shashin* (National Taiwan Library Document 0748–71, plate 102).

appears. In the 1905 and 1906 versions, the sitters are referred to as "Urai [Chinese: Wulai] tribe" people, but in the 1907, 1912, 1925, 1928, and 1933 versions, they are captioned as members of the Atayal tribe. Thus, in Japanese-language publications, the 1905 photograph of a large group in front of an unacknowledged guard station (figure 49) was captioned to ethnicize the Atayals. This framing operation was simultaneously culture-affirming and detemporalizing vis-à-vis the photograph's sitters.

In contrast, of the four English-language publications (two by Japanese publishers for foreign consumption, and two by foreigners) that picked up the 1905 shots, three adopted more explicitly martial photos of the armed men in the road (figure 50). These publications also used the term *Atayal* to describe the sitters—in 1910, 1916, and 1923. Based on this analysis, we can say that somewhere between 1906 and 1907, the term *Atayal* began to catch on with publishers, even for photographs that did not obviously illustrate the unique folkways of the sitters but instead lumped them together with the world's garden-variety savages with guns.

In sharp contrast to the shot of seven armed men blocking the road in the 1905 series, the spin-off photographs from the 1903 portrait (figure 19) eschew martial themes in favor of domestic scenes of cloth production and residential architecture. Mori took several photographs, besides the family portrait of Watan Yūra, during the same session. These scenes from daily life circulated widely as postcards and illustrations for a variety of publications.[102]

Mori Ushinosuke's Quchi-area photos, comprising subjects from Wulai and Rimogan, were reproduced in at least forty different postcard designs and in dozens of newspapers, magazines, journals, and other media in subsequent years.[103] While Mori the ethnologist may have reached dozens of anthropologists through his reports in the *Journal of the Tokyo Anthropological Society* or thousands of readers through his serialized travelogues in Taiwan newspapers, the audience for his photographs of representative Atayal culture bearers was global.

There are many reasons why the period 1903–05 was propitious for mass-circulation Atayal photographs. First, by the time Mori arrived in late 1902, a network of acquaintances connected him to several sitters and photographic sites. Therefore, as the multiple poses and variations in the Rimogan shots indicate, Mori was able to work in a better climate for photographic production than his predecessors Torii and Inō, who both operated on tight schedules among unfamiliar peoples during their forced-march surveys of the late 1890s. The state of photographic technology at the time demanded long exposure times and the participation of willing sitters to produce high-resolution, interesting, and well-composed photographs. During the period 1902–05, many Quchi people were on the government's payroll or employed by Japanese industry. Quchi residents may have charged money to be photographed, as well (a common practice a little later on), or they may have been favorably disposed toward their Japanese trade partners, employers, acquaintances, and in-laws (such as men like Jiku Shō Min).

Second, just after Mori's prints from Quchi began to arrive in Osaka for the exposition and in the Tokyo University anthropology lab for analysis, a picture postcard boom was ignited by the Russo-Japanese War. The clearest and best extant copies of the Quchi photos, the Wulai guardline photo, and even one copy of the Jiaobanshan emissary photo are in the form of collotype prints on sturdy postcard stock. In the 1903–07 period, several postcard producers availed themselves of Mori's photographs and other official sources to propagate these high-quality reproductions. Textbook publishers raided this storehouse to represent indigenous Taiwan to every grade-school student in Japan.

However, not long after these iconic individual and group portraits were shot between late 1902 and early 1903, local Quchi men overran Taiwan's first hydroelectric power station and killed fifteen workers and guards in 1905.[104] The razed power station was built on the Xindian River near Quchi village under the direction of Dogura Ryūjirō.[105] Dogura was an intimate of Jiku Shō Min and Mori Ushinosuke. He had also obtained the rights to develop hundreds of hectares of Atayal land around Quchi for camphor production in 1899. The termination of official photographic activity in Quchi coincides with these events, unsurprisingly.

The reprisals for the 1905 incident must have been harsh, though details are hard to come by. We know that within a very short time, Wulai was transformed into a hub of Japanese assimilation policies and hot-springs tourism. In December 1908, travel writer and explorer Mary T. S. Schaffer and three Canadian companions visited Wulai to get a glimpse of the world-renowned "head-hunters of Formosa." Like many a visitor after her, Schaffer wrote excitedly about the prospects of meeting a savage head taker and even purchased a postcard of a freshly taken head held by its exultant killers. But when she actually met Atayal people on the trail, she found them to be friendly and happy to pose for photographs in exchange for silver coins. Included in Schaffer's collection of magic-lantern slides was a color-tinted profile of Pazzeh Watan, the daughter of Watan Yūra (the woman in figure 19, to the viewer's far left).[106] U.S. Consul to Taiwan James Davidson also used colorized glass-lantern slide images of Mori's sitters for his public presentations.[107] In fact, all of Schaffer's and Davidson's photographs were created before 1905, when Wulai was still ethnologically available, so to speak.

The period 1903–05, then, was a window in time. Mori arrived in Wulai late enough to benefit from the networks established by Inō, Jiku, Dogura, and Watan Yūra, and from recent advances in camera technology, but early enough to ride the wave of the Russo-Japanese War postcard boom. The luck of good timing also allowed Mori to make photographs before the 1905 attacks on the power station flipped over the chessboard of frontier diplomacy along the Xindian River south of Taipei.

PUNITIVE EXPEDITION PHOTO ALBUMS

The period between the 1905 Quchi incident and the establishment of an ethnic tourism industry in Jiaobanshan in the early 1920s marks a transitional period in the politics of geobody construction in Taiwan. During this epoch, a plethora of "punitive expedition" photo albums and picture postcards of war imagery from the guardline dominated the photography of Atayal peoples.[108] Superficially, the preponderance of combat, logistics, and scenes of encampment would suggest that the pluralistic imaginary developed by Inō, Torii, and Mori was losing ground during the run-up to World War I.[109] However, second-order geobody construction in fact consolidated itself, oddly enough, in part through the circulation of war albums. While some of these guardline-focused albums eschewed the use of ethnonyms and culturally pluralist maps, others enshrined indigenous ethnic categories and normalized them by prefacing the narrative portions of their accounts with thumbnail sketches of Taiwan's ethnographic complexion. This representational strategy—which situated dynamic, eventful, and individualized photographic portraiture in a framework that presented such images to readers as illustrations of timeless ethnic traits—would continue in Taiwan to the end of colonial times.

In all such productions, which could run to over six hundred pages, the author begins the account with an atemporal, spatially organized discussion of Atayal, Saisiyat, Paiwan, Tsou, Bunun, Amis, Tsarisen/Rukai, Puyuma, and Yami social organization, material culture, ritual practices, religion, and language. These sketches are prefaced by a map that locates each second-order geobody and arrays them like nation-states on a Mercator projection. Photographs from the Mori and Inō storehouse and others in the same genre then illustrate the features of each group. The second part of such publications, beginning with war albums in the 1910s, proceeds to narrate the movement of the guardline and Japanese troops into the interior of Taiwan. Major battles are recounted, statistics of "territory mastered" are inserted. In this process, the hard-and-fast line between indigenous Taiwan and Han Taiwan was naturalized, along with the ethnic topography proposed by Inō in his 1900 *Taiwan banjin jijō* (Conditions among Taiwan's savages). This pluralizing operation worked in tandem with images and texts that paradoxically celebrated a war that portended to wipe out the cultures so lovingly portrayed between the same covers. Narita Takeshi's 1912 album, *Taiwan seiban shuzoku shashinchō* (Savage tribes of Taiwan photo album), set the tone (see figure 51).

Narita's map depicts two competing logics. Its slightly smaller inset map classifies space (Thongchai's definition of territorialization) according to its degree of submission to the colonial government. The legend associates different colors with varied military and civil conditions. The endpoint of the trajectory implied by the dynamic categories "half-submitted," "reluctantly submitted," "completely submitted," and "completely unsubmitted" is a fully "submitted" Taiwan. Narita's larger map partakes in a different temporal logic. It depicts Taiwan's indigenous ethnic groups as a system of second-order geobodies. These static categories and polygons, which were retained in dozens of official and commercial maps into the 1940s, depicted Taiwan as an eternally and essentially multiethnic geobody. The dynamic and static portraits of indigenous spaces, however, had one thing in common: the indigenous, non-Han portion of Taiwan was separated from Han Taiwan by a one-dimensional boundary line, the one depicted in figures 39 through 41.

By 1912 Narita's map could truthfully depict Quchi and Wulai as "completely submitted." However, there was an even more compliant classification, which was reserved for the Amis in the eastern rift valley, the Puyuma, and the tribes of lower Hengchun: taxable regions under normal administration. In other words, by 1912, it was possible to be classified as an indigenous tribe even if every single member of an ethnicity's second-order geobody was already a tax-paying Taiwanese subject, living in the normally administered area. Such was the case with the Amis, whose designator does not appear in 1930s statistical studies of indigenous political economy and demography. Nonetheless, the Amis' putative living space was coded as a second-order geobody and solidly colored apposite other ethnic groups on prefatory maps to these compendia.[110] Thanks to their traditions of surplus wealth production and historical familiarity with a commoditized economy, it was

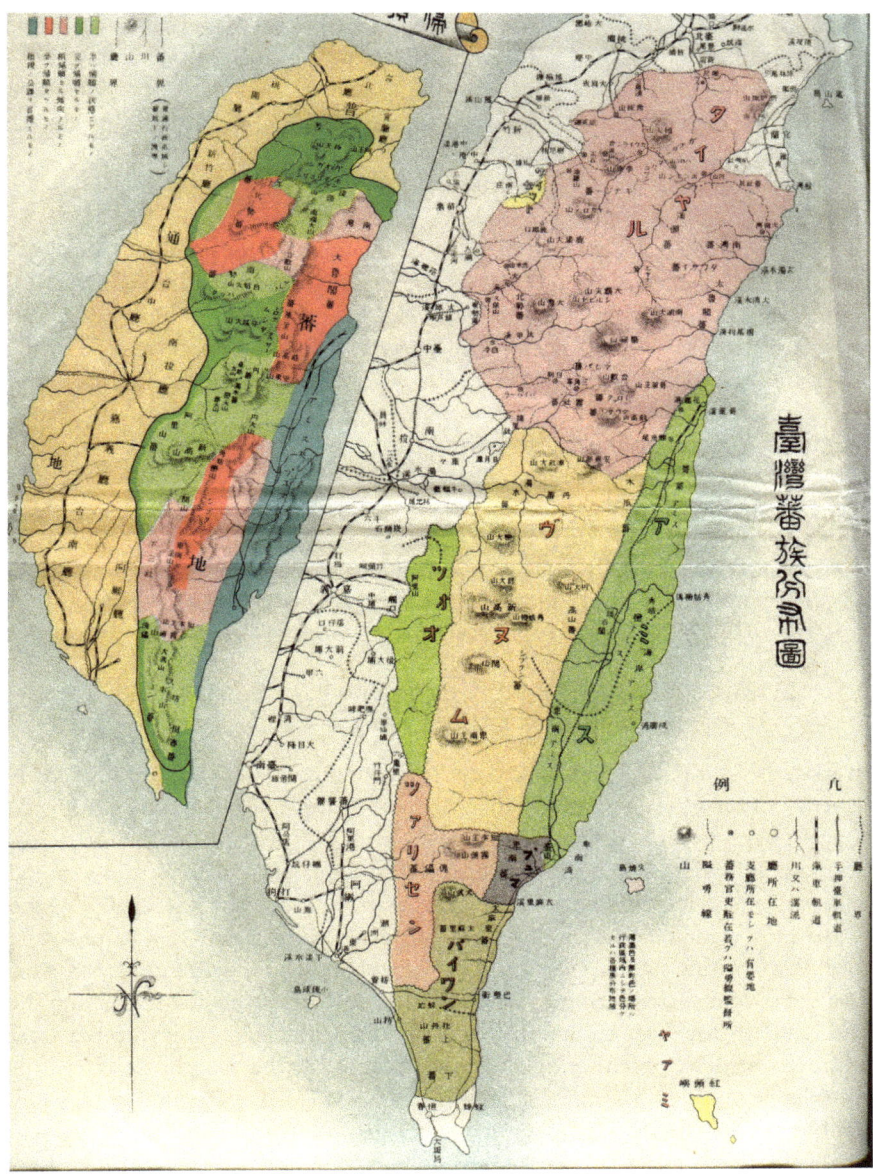

FIGURE 51. Dynamic and static maps of Taiwan's ethnic diversity, ca. 1912. Narita Takeshi, *Taiwan seiban shuzoku shashinchō* (Taipei: Narita shashin seihanjo, 1912), n.p.

possible for the Amis peoples, as well as the Tuilasok, Koalut, and Sabaree Paiwan, to move out of the "special administration" category during the first decade of the twentieth century under Japanese rule. However, the colorful polygons that marked out their separation from Han-dominated Taiwan on mass-produced, scholarly, and official ethnic maps never budged.

Over the course of Japanese rule, static ethnic maps resembling figures 2 through 4 and figure 41 were reproduced millions of times in photo albums, on picture postcards, in school textbooks, and in newspapers for public consumption in Taiwan, in Japan, and around the world. In short, while Japanese military pacification and police occupation among the Atayal, Sediq, Truku, Tsou, and Paiwan succeeded to a level unprecedented in Taiwanese history, the movement of the Qing-period savage border in concert with settler encroachment, assimilation, and state aggrandizement was finally arrested under the Japanese regime in the 1910s.

Although more punitive expeditions and forced relocation campaigns were yet to come, the notion that "special administration" in indigenous Taiwan was a temporary expedient went extinct. Administrators, scholars, and imperial subjects came to view all indigenes, no matter their outward signs of assimilation, as members of aboriginal ethnic groups that lived beyond the pale of dynamic capitalist political economy. This vision of indigeneity turned out to be a self-fulfilling prophecy.

ATTACHING PHOTOGRAPHS TO MAPS: THE CULTURAL INVESTMENT OF SECOND-ORDER GEOBODIES

In 1905, the year of the Atayal raids on the Quchi power station, the government-general cut off and surrounded Jiaobanshan, the other site of serially reproduced Atayal imagery, with fortified guard posts, clear-cut fields to aid in the detection and shooting of indigenes, and electrical wire. In 1906 Governor-General Sakuma Samata took the reins and turned up the pressure on Atayal peoples who resisted the commoditization of forest lands and subordination to a bureaucratic surplus-extracting state. Government forces embargoed recalcitrant Jiaobanshan-area tribes into surrendering their weapons by extending the guardlines into the interior. The last push culminated in a 107-day Chintōzan campaign that cost hundreds of dead on either side.[111] In local memory, the 1907 battle is considered the beginning of Japanese rule in Jiaobanshan (today's Fuxing Municipality in Taoyuan Prefecture). By 1925 the former hot spot in the camphor wars had become a show village for indigenous culture, despite its minority indigenous population. Jiaobanshan's transition from battleground to ethnic theme park, it could be argued, presents a microcosm of the island-wide processes that secured the indigenous habitations of Taiwan as second-order geobodies.

In 1908 the main trunk railway line from Jilong to Gaoxiong opened. This feat of civil engineering was the first step in the creation of a robust ethnic-tourism industry in Taiwan, though it would take years to mature. The numerous colonial railway and commercial tourist guides that followed the completion of the trunk line provide us with a window into the transformation of Jiaobanshan from ungoverned space to accessible ethnic resort town. The only Atayal person to appear in an early 1908 guide occupies the corner of a montage. The text surrounding the illustration describes the loss of Japanese life in a massacre near Beipu, the site of a major uprising in 1907. In jarring contrast to later guides, this pamphlet only mentions indigenes in connection with the establishment of rural garrisons, guardlines, and reclamation projects.[112]

In 1910 a light-gauge pushcart railway connected the walled city of Dakekan to formerly inaccessible Jiaobanshan; it was by far the most expensive and lengthy rail extension of the year's "savage territory" improvements.[113] This railway fed supplies and troops to Jiaobanshan for Japanese military actions against the tramontane Dakekan settlements known as the Gaogan tribes (an Atayal people). Endō Hiroya's *Banhi tōbatsu kinen shashinchō* (Aborigine punitive expedition commemorative photo album), dated 1911, features photographs of Jiaobanshan town occupied by Japanese soldiers and policemen. The main road is littered with military infirmaries. A few "Jiaobanshan *banjin*" are pictured standing next to policemen (see figure 52).[114]

Late 1910 marked the end of large military maneuvers against Gaogan. By 1912 Jiaobanshan was sufficiently pacified to be considered the site for a visit from the Meiji emperor himself. For the emperor's expected visit, a special reception hall, later depicted in numerous picture postcards, was erected in the main settlement area.[115] But, as a privately produced 1915 travel guide reminded its readers, even though the area was undergoing reclamation and the population was increasing, the next stop, Gaogan, was still garrisoned for defense against indigenes.[116]

Just after this 1915 guide appeared, Jiaobanshan became an obligatory stop on imperial inspection tours of Taiwan. The Imperial Household Ministry archive in Tokyo contains several lavishly illustrated albums of these tours, which included those of Prince Kan'in in 1916, Crown Prince Hirohito in 1923, and Prince Chichibu in 1925. During this liminal decade, the Japanese royals affixed commercial photographs and their own snapshots to keepsake albums. The overall impression is of Jiaobanshan as a borderland that was fast becoming an indigenous theme park.

By 1920, the light-gauge pushcart railway that connected the town of Jiaobanshan to the railway stop at Daxi (the new name for Dakekan) had become a conduit for tourists, freight, and officials. Travelers ascended the mountain pushed by two Taiwanese laborers, with rest stations and inns all along the way.[117] A 1921 travel guide emphasized the scenery and the pushcart ride. It also created the boilerplate for subsequent Jiaobanshan descriptions in the official travel guides:

> Nine *ri* and seven *cho* southeast of Daxi [Dakekan] walled city is the savage border. If you clamber your way up, you'll be able to intimately inspect conditions among the aborigines. This area is zigzagged and steep. Climbing up the mountain path by tramway is extremely slow, but descending is extremely fast, for a speedy return. At the

桃園廳角板山派出所中隊ノ廠舍枕山頭砲臺ノ遠望

角板山倉庫

FIGURE 52. Jiaobanshan as staging area for Gaogan offensives, ca. 1910. Endō Hiroya, ed., *Banhi tōbatsu kinen shashinchō* (Taipei: Endō shashinkan, 1911), n.p.

top of the mountain, things suddenly open up into orderly quadrilateral residences; this is Jiaobanshan. There is the balmy fragrance of camphor and the reception hall built from building materials from Arisan. This area is a tableland that commands a view upstream of the Dakekan ravine and is ringed by verdant linked ridgelines. . . . It is thus known not only for its steep terrain but also for its spectacular scenery.[118]

Sōyama Takeshi writes that "indigenous territory" tourism had become a mainstay by 1924, when the "injuries from indigene violence" had finally subsided and railways extended to the interior.[119] The 1924 version of the railway guide boasted that Jiaobanshan was not only a "strategic hold in aborigine administration" but also the site of two Japanese inns, a police station dispatch office, a post office, a school for aborigine children (figure 27), an aborigine trading post (figure 30), a Mitsui Corporation outpost, and a camphor company collection depot. The guide also mentioned that visitors could pick up valuable indigenous manufactures at good prices. Jiaobanshan, concluded this entry, could not be overlooked as a place to "get to know the aborigines."[120]

Jiaobanshan's reputation even extended to the rare foreign visitor. In 1925, H. L. Bagallay of the British Foreign Office described Jiaobanshan as "a 'show village' about twenty-five miles from the capital, where 'tame' savages are exhibited to official visitors and tourists . . . "[121] The 1927, 1930, and 1934 Taiwan Railway guides repeated the 1924 description above, suggesting that ethnic tourism had become routinized in Jiaobanshan by the early 1930s.[122]

The 1934 guide adds that Jiaobanshan, Wulai (see above), and Alishan, all sites for indigenous tourism, were now in "normally administered territory." However, the official 1935 Indigenous Household Register statistics indicate that all Atayal and Tsou peoples—the indigenous peoples of these three sites—resided beyond administered territory. Therefore, tourists were actually chatting with and photographing indigenes who were either visiting the tourist sites as employees or who had removed to the normally administered territory.[123] In these three popular sites, tourists could have the best of both worlds. They could enter Jiaobanshan, Wulai, or Alishan without filling out burdensome paperwork and paying extra fees required to travel beyond the line between special and normal administration and "experience savage life" without unduly upsetting their tour itineraries.[124] Ease of access and proximity to civilization were indeed the major themes in touristic imagery of Jiaobanshan in the 1930s. Photos of Japanese schools (run by police officers) filled with indigenous children and Hinomaru flags decorated magazines, atlases, and picture postcards of the 1920s and 1930s (figure 31). Much of the textual rhetoric accompanying these images extolled the conversion of a former head-hunting people into rice-growing, peace-loving subjects of the emperor.

Recall that in 1895, culturally hybrid figures—the Atayal woman Washiiga in a Chinese blouse or the Atayal man Pu Chin wearing a queue—were prominent in Japanese imagery because interpreters were the point of access to Jiaobanshan. Anthropologist Inō Kanori, in 1896, abstracted a photograph of Jiaobanshan residents taken in built environments by whiting out its background to produce more suitably anthropological types. Into the 1910s and even the 1920s, Chinese blouses like Washiiga's were prominent in photographs of Atayal women in borderland junctions such as Jiaobanshan or Wulai, as exemplified by Mori Ushinosuke's photo of a "Dakekan tribe woman" in July 1906, at the height of the camphor wars near Jiaobanshan, and by dozens of picture postcards.[125] By the 1930s, however, Chinese blouses were scarce in Japanese photography, while Japanese garments became commonplace. For ethnic-tourism operators, the question became how to balance the messages of progress and exoticism by packaging accessible villagers as avatars of a more primitive and even timeless past.

One answer was found in the skillful use of graphic arts to construct Jiaobanshan as a gateway into the Atayal geobody. This effect was achieved by manipulating particular icons of Atayal ethnicity such as facial tattoos, tobacco pipes, back-strap looms, and wicker backpacks. These icons of the unique Atayal cultural repertoire were detached from lived environments, bundled together, and marketed as portable keepsakes from an unspoiled corner of the savage territory. On a circa 1930 postcard, a woman's facial tattoos, wicker backpack, and pipe were all logoized in such a fashion (see figure 53).

The sitter for this postcard image is also the mascot for the sleeve that houses a set of eight Jiaobanshan postcards (see figure 54). Like Washiiga, Habairon, and Marai in the 1896 anthropology journal (figure 39), this woman was rendered into line art and then imaginatively placed in a new setting. But instead of the background that corresponded to blank space on the 1905 census map (figures 33 and 39), the Wakayama Prefecture–based Taishō Company placed her in front of a mountain range and Jiaobanshan's trademark suspension bridge. Tourists walked single file along this popular attraction, which connected the souvenir stands and the model school for indigenes to the mountains. The sitter in figure 53 was photographed in front of a fence and a neatly edged footpath on level ground, presumably in Jiaobanshan's model ethnic village. The graphic artist thereafter transformed her into a highlander guarding a secret passageway for the postcard sleeve titled *Bankai no hikyō* (Undiscovered savage border).

Advances in reprographic technology allowed for further abstractions and mash-ups. This sitter's tattooed face, as well as her backpack, were logoized into monochrome stamps that adorned other cards in the set, tying otherwise placid scenes that connoted settled life and domesticity to the tattooed mascot who greeted visitors to the mountainous and supposedly mysterious savage territory (figure 55). The photographs on the cards themselves depict an enclosed, flat settlement composed of Japanese-constructed dwellings and public buildings. But the last card in the set (figure 56) depicts the setting, much like the sleeve, as an extension of Taiwan's central cordillera, rather than as the island's most convenient place to sample indigenous culture in the course of a weekend tour.

FIGURE 53. Jiaobanshan woman with basket and pipe, ca. 1930. KAPPAN-ZAN TAIWAN, wa306, East Asia Image Collection, Lafayette College, Easton, PA, accessed July 26, 2017, http://digital.lafayette.edu/collections/eastasia/warner-postcards/wa0306.

FIGURE 54. Postcard sleeve, "Jiaobanshan's hidden savage border," ca. 1930 (published by Taisho of Wakayama, Japan). ["The Savage Border's Unexplored Boundary: Mt. Kappanzan's Variegated Coloration."] This image is reproduced from an Internet auction.

FIGURE 55. Couple in Jiaobanshan, ca. 1930. KAPPAN-ZAN TAIWAN, wa0288, East Asia Image Collection, Lafayette College, Easton, PA, accessed July 26, 2017, http://digital.lafayette.edu/collections/eastasia/warner-postcards/wa0288.

THE GEOBODIES WITHIN A GEOBODY   239

FIGURE 56. Mountains of Jiaobanshan, ca. 1930. KAPPAN-ZAN TAIWAN, wa0291, East Asia Image Collection, Lafayette College, Easton, PA, accessed July 26, 2017, http://digital.lafayette.edu/collections/eastasia/warner-postcards/wa0291.

Jiaobanshan worked as a show village, then, because it could provide the experience of "savage Taiwan" in such a way as to suggest that this "tame" settlement was indeed an exemplar of the rest of aborigine country. In this example, the deft use of imaginative geography, cropping, extrapolation, and logoization created a snapshot of Atayalness that was quickly apprehended and could be brought back or sent to Taipei, Gaoxiong, Tokyo, or Osaka in the form of a souvenir postcard set.

In 1935 the government-general hosted the Taiwan Hakurankai (Taiwan Expo) to celebrate its fortieth anniversary. One Taiwan Expo album held dozens of photographs that also appeared in the monthly bulletin *Riban no tomo* (Aborigine policemen's companion), published by the Keimukyoku Ribanka (Police Bureau, Aborigine Affairs Section) and in numerous postcard designs. These photographs were mostly shot by Segawa Kōkichi, an intimate of the Aborigine Affairs section chief Suzuki Hideo, and successor to Mori Ushinosuke as Japan's official portrait photographer of anthropological types.[126] In the Atayal section of the album, the Jiaobanshan photo shows the "Japanizing" of Atayal models in "various kinds of antiquated and new-style clothing." Right below it is a photo of Atayal from the Wushe settlement of Paalan, the home of Iwan Robao, Kondō the Barbarian's first wife. The Paalan men and women show no outward signs of participation in the market for imported cloth or building materials (figure 57).

FIGURE 57. Contrasting photos of Jiaobanshan and Paalan, 1935. *Top,* "New and ancient various kinds of clothing: Xinzhu-shū Kappanzan-sha"; *bottom,* "Playing the mouth-harp: two maidens: Taizhong-shū Paalan-sha," from Suzuki Hideo, ed., *Taiwan bankai tenbō* (Taipei: Riban no tomo hakkōjo, 1935), 13.

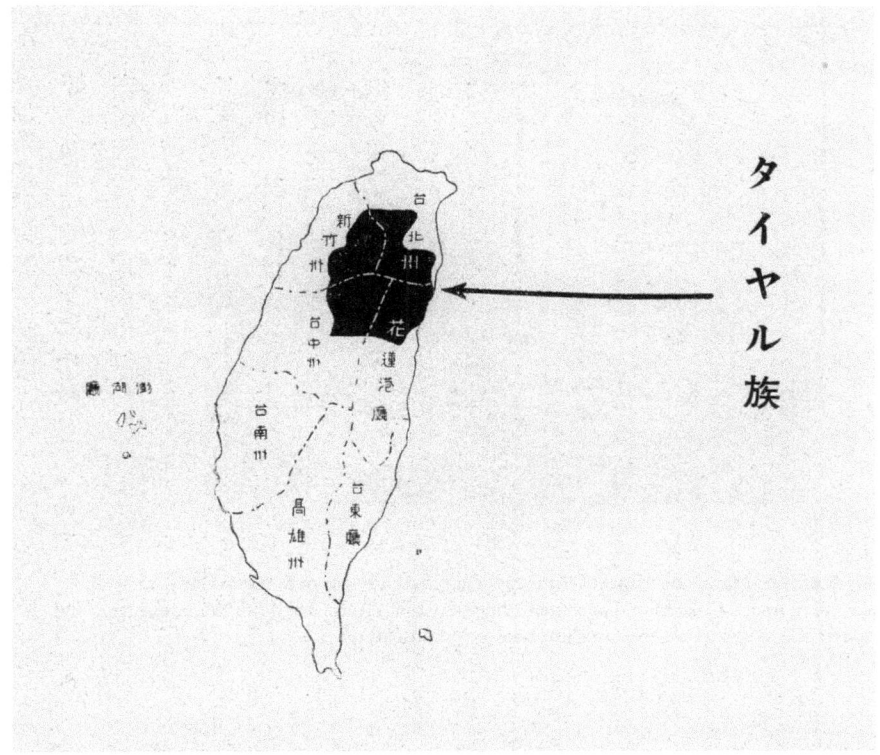

FIGURE 58. Second-order geobody of Atayal ["Taiyal tribe"]. Suzuki Hideo, ed., *Taiwan bankai tenbō* (Taipei: Riban no tomo hakkōjo, 1935), 6.

To suture these two photos together ideologically—the one displaying Japanization and the other what is being Japanized—the first page of the Atayal section of the souvenir book subsumes both images under the second-order geobody *Atayal* (figure 58). Because it was located in Atayal country and was configured horizontally within a common two-dimensional geobody, along with the visibly unassimilated inhabitants of Paalan, Jiaobanshan could represent the whole of untouched northern Taiwan, while exhibiting imperial progress toward Japanizing a wilderness that, a mere thirty years earlier, could only be represented as a borderland on the extremity of the Qing Empire. Here, in the dioramas, photographs, and ethnic maps of the 1935 exhibition, we find the fruition of the tandem operations of cartographic and racialist geobody construction. Whether strolling the fairgrounds, making a day trip to Wulai or Jiaobanshan to buy souvenirs, or perusing scholarly, commercial, or official photography of Taiwan Indigenous Peoples, Japanese people could quickly apprehend 1930s Atayal culture

FIGURE 59. Marai and Yūgai of Rimogan, ca. 1903. Customs of Savage Tribe [sic], ip1471, East Asia Image Collection, Lafayette College, Easton, PA, accessed July 26, 2017, http://digital.lafayette.edu/collections/eastasia/imperial-postcards/ip1471.

and extrapolate it across the surface of Taiwan's interior. The ensemble of artifacts, maps, performances, images, and texts associated with Jiaobanshan represented Taiwan's aborigines at once as a population frozen in time and as a race that had been rescued from the neglect of the Qing dynasty by energetic Japanese officials.

For those who could not make the trip to an exhibition or a souvenir stand, government-published textbooks—compulsory reading for nearly the whole of Japan—employed the same stratagems. When the Ministry of Education finally revised its elementary-school geography texts in 1910 and 1919, it partially heeded Inō Kanori's criticisms by including portraits of Han Taiwanese. Each edition also updated its indigenous imagery, both relying on Mori's photographs from Wulai and Rimogan. The 1910 edition displayed profile mugshot etchings of Pazzeh of Wulai and Marai of Rimogan and captioned each as generic *banjin* (savages). The 1919 edition substituted Yūgai of Rimogan for Pazzeh of Wulai to present readers with a male and a female icon from the same settlement. Mori's June 1903 photograph (see figure 59) was the source of this illustration.

A couple of months before Mori photographed the Rimogan couple, he also took a scenic photograph of Atayal dwellings near Wulai (figure 60). This composition was reproduced in several government and commercial publications throughout the colonial period. The updated 1919 textbook rendered these photographs from

FIGURE 60. Wulai dwelling and granary, ca. 1903. Source: Mori Ushinosuke, ed., *Taiwan banzoku zufu,* vol. 1 (Taipei: Rinji Taiwan kyūkan chōsakai, 1915), plate 11.

FIGURE 61. Yūgai and Marai, in textbook illustration, 1919. Monbushō, ed., *Jinjō shōgaku chirisho kan ni* (Tokyo: Monbushō, 1919), 16.

distinct Atayal settlements into emblems of the same savage territory by inserting the Rimogan portrait of Yūgai and Marai into a Wulai setting (see figure 61). For the editors of the 1903, 1910, and 1919 geography textbooks, then, all indigenous people constituted a subpopulation. The 1919 version that merged Wulai and Rimogan imagery added a physical setting to cement the view that indigenes, no matter where they were photographed, were essentially hill people.[127]

INDIGENOUS MODERNITY: A TWO-PART INVENTION

A careful student of Taiwanese history and Japanese colonial rhetoric, upon attending the 1935 Taiwan Expo, might have asked why, after forty years of colonial rule, the indigenous people of Paalan (figure 58) were still dressing in handwoven fabrics, living in drafty slate houses, and working in pursuits far removed from the booming capitalist economy of the lowlands. After all, the Japanese state had managed to mobilize resources sufficient to win the Russo-Japanese War (1904–05), dislodge the Germans from Shandong in 1915, and overrun the three northeastern provinces of China in 1931. Why had it made such a poor showing in the uplands of Taiwan after four decades of opportunity?

The answer to this question brings us back to Foucault's formulation of the "disciplinary society." A number of scholars of Japanese colonial rule in Taiwan have observed that, in the lowlands where some 97 percent of Taiwanese lived, the Japanese colonial state was able to scale back its raw displays of punitive power by 1915 or so, with the crushing of the Ta-pa-ni rebellion.[128] At the same time, the extension of the *baojia* system and the development of commercial law, public health and education, commoditization labor, and a system of safeguards for the protection of private property made great inroads into the warp and woof of daily life, in cities and in the countryside. This interlocking set of institutions and practices created a Taiwanese political economy that paid more to Tokyo in tax revenue than it cost to maintain in terms of expenditures taken from the national operating budget in Tokyo. A critical mass of lowland Han Taiwanese were, however grudgingly, bought into a disciplinary order. The incentive system that garnered this buy-in was itself expensive. To provide title deeds to land, access to commercial courts, irrigation projects, harbors, schools, hospitals, and other improvements, in such a way that they are in fact paid for by the colonized people themselves, required a "big bang" on the order of Gotō Shinpei's large spending spree of the early twentieth century. By the mid-1910s, the state—in varied degrees of alliance with Taiwanese capitalists, smallholders, professionals, policemen, officials, and *baojia* heads—had created a population that could not only produce surplus wealth but would also surrender enough of it to the government to pay for its own regulation. This form of society, wherein population increases redound to the power of the state (instead of to its detriment), is the desideratum of the disciplinary state.

Yao Jen-to has concurred, asserting that the Japanese created a disciplinary society and biopolitical regime in Taiwan based on his interpretation of the state's profligate use of statistics and its vaunted interest in "forcing Taiwanese to be healthy." Curiously, Yao overlooks the fact that the first Japanese census left the indigenous territories completely blank and that much of Taiwan still fell outside the Government-General's tax base when Japan surrendered in 1945.[129]

The lands beyond the pale of Yao's analysis were at first defined as a zone of special administration, or the indigenous territories, because they were little known to Japanese administrators and did not appear on the ready-made grid inherited from the Qing. To rectify this situation, Sakuma Samata initiated his own "big bang" in the form of coordinated military offensives that culminated in the *gokanen keikaku riban jigyō* (five-year plan to control the aborigines). As we have seen, this scorched-earth approach succeeded to the extent that rebelling subjects were mostly disarmed. The mountain territories were, in fact, made safe for land and forest surveys. Abutting forests were cleared of toll states, and the obfuscating layer of *tongshi* (bicultural interpreters) that complicated relationships between primary producers and camphor capitalists was expelled from the savage border.

This is all to say that the post-Sakuma "aborigine district" was not a product of state neglect. After 1910 especially, and into the 1930s, the state proceeded to inventory, catalog, regulate, regiment, spatially array, and even nurture indigenous populations in order to extract wealth from the highlands. While this panoptical and surveillance-like activity bore superficial marks of discipline, it excluded the most important element: the state did not produce individuals in Taiwan's indigenous territories. Rather, it produced tribes, settlements, ethnic groups, and aborigines. Collective punishment, ad hoc justice, forced relocation, fixed prices at trading posts, poorly compensated corvée labor, and nonrecognition of ownership rights in forest lands were the lot of those who lived under special administration in colonial Taiwan. In these lands beyond the pale of the Han-dominated lowlands, the state did not invest in banks, courts, high schools, train stations, and other discipline-inducing infrastructure. In the specially administered areas, Taiwanese could not secure title deeds, compete for status in a public school system, open businesses in bustling port towns, or sell agricultural produce, hunted goods, or handicrafts at market prices.

Given the bounty of natural resources to be found in the highlands and the alacrity with which indigenes learned the Japanese language and new trades, it might seem puzzling that the state did not press its apparent advantage in 1915 to bring the highlands within the profitable zone of disciplinary society. The lower Hengchun Paiwan peoples, led by Pan Bunkiet and then his son, provide a telling example. These villages were of mixed Han, *jukuban,* and Paiwan residence. They were included in the regularly administered territory of Taiwan during the period Matsuoka Tadasu has characterized as one of temporary expediency. By 1906 almost all of the lower Hengchun Paiwan settlements were recognized as being sufficiently settled to pay taxes. Therefore, their territories would no longer be closed to immigrants, and they would fall under a structure of surveillance similar to neighboring *baojia* units. Thus, along with the Amis and the Puyuma of the eastern rift valley, the lower Hengchun Paiwan were, in many respects, integrated into the empire. Nonetheless, as culture bearers and denizens of ethnically defined subgeobodies, they occupied a liminal space: they were legally, economically, and administratively considered "civilized," but they were still accounted for in population counts as members of non-Han ethnic groups—as Paiwans.[130] Moreover, they were still represented at tourist sites, in exhibitions, and in media as colorful examples of Taiwan's ethnic diversity. In a word, there was more to the permanent bifurcation of Taiwan into ethnically demarcated zones of difference than uneven capitalist development or relative levels of state neglect and oppression.

There are two major reasons for the arrested development of disciplinary society in colonial Taiwan. The first is negative. When TGG visionaries first mapped out schemes for ruling the island, Taiwan was Japan's only colony. As Japan added colonies (Karafuto and the Kwantung leased territory in 1905, Korea in 1910), the relative size and importance of Taiwan's uplands in the grand scheme of things shrank. Consequently, the cost of building a capitalist infrastructure that could produce a self-regulating disciplinary society in upland Taiwan was beyond the reach of the government-general by 1915. As we saw in chapters 1 and 2, even when the empire was relatively flush after the Sino-Japanese War, savage-border policy was run on the cheap. Although Sakuma's five-year plan to control the aborigines was announced with great fanfare and a ¥15 million budget, the funds dried up before the work was finished, and Japan declared victory in 1914 out of exhaustion.

Nonetheless, from 1915 through 1925, a series of land and population surveys was conducted throughout the highlands. These projects set the stage for not only large forest giveaways but also forced migration movements and programs to transition indigenes into intensive agriculture. As Matsuoka Tadasu has argued, up until 1915, special administration was a temporary expedient—the original plan was to economically integrate the island economy.[131] But despite the intrusions of irrigation projects, village relocation, and police government, the TGG policies kept the indigenous peoples intact as a separate population. Labor migration to the plains was discouraged; the fruits of intensive agriculture were not exported beyond the highlands but were consumed in the highlands themselves; and a majority of indigenes never paid taxes. Forced migration only occurred *within* the aborigine territory: peoples were not moved to areas under regular administration. Matsuoka documents a number of positions, including that of Governor-General Den Kenjirō, that argued for the dissolution of the indigenous territory and Taiwan's administrative integration. Nonetheless, the government-general halted in its tracks at the old savage border, partly out of bureaucratic inertia but also because the Wushe uprising showed that indigenes were in need of different treatment. Moreover, argues Matsuoka, Japanese scholar-officials in the post-Wushe era tipped the balance in favor of preservationist policies.[132]

Matsuda Kyōko's analysis of Japanese policies, practices, and representational strategies in 1930s Taiwan confirms Matsuoka's hypothesis from a different vantage. Most importantly, Matsuda demonstrates that preservationism reached beyond the small circle of intellectuals discussed above and was translated into actual policy. This brand of preservationism, Matsuda argues, forced policemen, exhibition organizers, tourism operators, and administrators to walk a fine line. On the one hand, they needed to demonstrate the efficacy of Japanization programs and policies aimed at turning supposedly rootless, violent, wandering hunters into settled and peaceful agriculturalists. On the other hand, these same social engineers recoiled in horror at the prospect of indigenes becoming dandies who might participate in the consumer culture and urban cosmopolitanism that characterized Taipei in the 1930s. The reformed yet not modern indigenous Taiwanese would always be toilers on the soil, possessed of beautiful customs. They were an ethnically separate population requiring the ministrations of a trained corps of Japanese aborigine policemen-administrators to both ease them away from the worst of their old customs and shield them from the worst excesses of modernity.

The evidence for Matsuda's general claim is abundant. For one, whereas indigenous sightseeing programs in the late 1890s through the 1910s brought small numbers of headmen and traditional leaders to urban Japan to scare them into submission by displaying Japanese military equipment and the advanced infrastructure of the home islands, tours in the 1930s involved large groups drawn from aborigine youth corps to demonstration farms within indigenous territory or to other flourishing agricultural sites in Taiwan or Japan. The goal was no longer to implant visions of Japan's overwhelming modernity and power but to educate indigenous people practically for crop production and stock breeding.[133] Here we see an echo of the representational complex exhibited in the ethnic maps and photographs from the 1935 Taiwan Expo: progress was being made among the indigenes, but they remained and would always remain a rural folk rooted to the land and engaged in useful pursuits, as members of cohesive, tradition-bound collectivities. Insofar as such a construction was a projection of Japanese conservative fantasies about the timeless virtues embodied in the imperiled and deracinated rural population of the home islands, it makes sense to view the indigenization of Taiwan's interior as a concomitant of Japanese nation building.[134]

More importantly, Taiwan-based academic, commercial, and official institutions had financial, emotional, and careerist stakes in the maintenance of the second-order geobody of the indigenous territory and its subdivision into ethnically defined language groups. Perhaps most prominent among them were the indigenous territory police and the aborigine youth corps that rose to prominence in the wake of the Wushe uprising. Both institutions were invested in the kind of modified preservationism described by Matsuda and had grown elaborate and cross-cutting organizational structures by the 1930s. The new youth leaders were fluent in Japanese, not Chinese. The lingua franca that linked them to other indigenous youth leaders separated them from Han Taiwanese, as it promoted sociability and identification with their indigenous police counterparts.

The interests of the indigenous police bureaucracy dovetailed with local boosters who lobbied for the selection of Taroko and Alishan National Parks above other sites in Taiwan. This group included primitivists like Lan Yinding and Ōzaki Hotsuma, Japanese alpinists, ethnologists at Taihoku Imperial University, musicologist Kurosawa Takatomo, and the many Japanese tourists, consumers, and collectors who were emotionally invested in the continued existence of Taiwan Indigenous Peoples as an identifiably separate and autochthonous population.[135]

To summarize, this book has considered the emergence of indigenous modernity as a two-part invention. The first part is a combination of military force sufficient to rob peoples in dynastic-state peripheries of their autonomy, coupled with an insufficiency of state resources to create disciplinary societies. In areas of Taiwan not already softened up by Chinese immigration and Qing governance, punishment remained ascendant over discipline into the 1930s. Here, it is important to consider the fact that the GMD itself, with many more resources, maintained the ethnically bifurcated form of rule in Taiwan. Its historical resilience indicates that "specially administered territory" is more than a residual category. Rather, these homelands embody positivities that gained considerable historical inertia during a moment in world-historical time marked by the ascendance of cultural pluralism.

These positivities sank roots in Taiwan coterminously with the so-called "cultural policy" in Korea, in tandem with a more diffuse, Wilsonian world order that moved sovereignty from an achieved status (civilized nations only) toward an ascribed status (all nations are ipso facto sovereign). The second part of this invention is then the construction of the second-order geobodies that formed the bulwarks of cultural pluralism in colonized Taiwan. As we have seen, the artistic, commercial, and scholarly impulses to collect, preserve, and idealize elements of indigenous cultures produced reified versions of them in museum collections, postcards, folklore anthologies, and ethnographic portraits. These preserved versions of indigenous culture have been sources of contestation, while they have also been utilized as resources for indigenous survival. The extent to which certain taxonomies, ethnonyms, or other articulations of indigenous culture are Japanese inventions is debatable. However, the shape and fundamental nature of the second-order geobody is not. It was under Japanese colonial rule that polygons such as the one illustrated in figure 58 were consolidated.

Over the course of its rule, the Taiwan Government-General zoned most of Atayal country as public land, save for a small percentage reserved for villages and their residents. This process amounted to land confiscation. Ownership of public lands was transferred to the GMD after retrocession in 1945. While the lands that were taken away from indigenes during the camphor wars and subsequent dispossession operations from 1898 through the 1930s were inhabited by myriad settlements and distinct collectivities then known as Gaogan, Dakekan, Nan'ao, or Tgdaya peoples, litigation with Taiwan's central government now aims to recover an *Atayal* homeland. In their analysis of the struggles surrounding the establishment of Maqaw National Park in north-central Taiwan, activist-scholars Yih-ren Lin, Lahuy Icyeh, and Da-Wei Kuan have argued that its proposed boundaries fall squarely within "Atayal people's traditional territory." The map they use to make this argument depicts Maqaw National Park enveloped by a much larger Atayal homeland. The space demarcated as territory to be restored to Atayal management, if not sovereignty, is not the home of a particular dialect community, ritual group, or voting district but rather is none other than the one drawn up by Japanese ethnologists, as shown in figures 2, 3, 34, 51, and 58.[136]

There are many good practical, historical, and legal reasons to consider this land as Atayal and for the central government to comanage public lands with Atayal people. There is no other effective way to configure autonomy, sovereignty, and rights in land nowadays, except territorially. The architects of the Japanese colonial project in ethnic bifurcation, who were many and not exactly in cahoots, did not predetermine how these thorny problems will be resolved. But this study suggests that they set the terms of engagement.

NOTES

INTRODUCTION

1. Wushe is in today's Ren'ai Township in Nantou Prefecture, Taiwan.
2. Taiwan sōtokufu keimukyoku, ed., *Takasagozoku chōsasho dai go hen: Bansha gaikyō, meishin* (Taipei: Taiwan sōtokufu keimukyoku, 1938), 132–33.
3. Ronald Niezen, *The Origins of Indigenism: Human Rights and the Politics of Identity* (Berkeley: University of California Press, 2003); James Clifford, *Returns: Becoming Indigenous in the Twenty-First Century* (Harvard University Press, 2013).
4. Laura R. Graham and H. Glenn Penny, "Performing Indigeneity: Emergent Identity, Self-Determination, and Sovereignty," in *Performing Indigeneity: Global Histories and Contemporary Experiences,* ed. Laura R. Graham and H. Glenn Penny (Lincoln: University of Nebraska Press, 2014), 1–5.
5. Wang Fu-chang, *Zokugun: Gendai Taiwan no esunikku imajineeshon,* trans. Matsuba Jun and Hung Yuru (Tokyo: Tōhō shoten, 2014), 86–87.
6. Anthropologist Scott Simon writes that "... today's political debates about Indigenous rights are rooted in an unfolding political dynamic that predates both the global indigenous rights movement and even the arrival of the ROC on Taiwan. What we know today as Indigenous Formosa is a co-creation of the resulting relationship between the Japanese state and diverse political constellations among many Austronesian peoples across the island." From "Making Natives: Japan and the Creation of Indigenous Formosa," in *Japanese Taiwan: Colonial Rule and Its Contested Legacy,* ed. Andrew Morris (London: Bloomsbury Press, 2015), 75.
7. "Taiwan Indigenous Peoples" is an English translation of *Taiwan Yuanzhuminzu,* the officially adopted name for indigenous peoples in Taiwan. This book will use the term *indigenes* to avoid awkward constructions and wordiness.
8. Japan's bifurcation of Taiwan fits under the category of "state-centered legal pluralism" or "strong legal pluralism," as formulated by Lauren Benton. She writes that from "the

mid-nineteenth century forward, colonial states devised formal typologies, and drew firmer boundaries, between social formations within colonial spaces that were perceived to be at different 'levels of development,' and often attributed differences to temporal lag—delimiting one zone as 'primitive' and the other 'modern.'" *Law and Colonial Cultures: Legal Regimes in World History, 1400–1900* (Cambridge: Cambridge University Press, 2002), 6.

9. The term *Austronesia* refers to a "geographic region of the language family spreading from the Western Pacific (e.g., Taiwan) to the Indian Ocean (e.g., Madagascar)." From "Editor's Note," in *Austronesian Taiwan: Linguistics, History, Ethnology, Prehistory*, ed. David Blundell (Berkeley and Taipei: Phoebe A. Hearst Museum of Anthropology and Shung Ye Museum of Formosan Aborigines, 2000), xxi.

10. The conceptual, administrative, and political vectors of continuity across the TGG and GMD periods of rule in Taiwan are complicated. Direct continuities are documented most clearly and forcefully in Matsuoka Tadasu, *Taiwan Genjūmin shakai no chihōka: Mainoriti no nijūsseiki* (Tokyo: Kenbun shuppan, 2012), 167–85. See also Nobayashi Atsushi and Miyaoka Maoko, "Araraweru senjūmin shuchō no shosō," in *Senjūmin to wa dare ka*, ed. Kubota Sachiko and Nobayashi Atsushi (Tokyo: Sekai shisōsha, 2009), 296, 306–8; 312; Chen Yuan-yang, *Taiwan Genjūmin to kokka kōen* (Fukuoka: Kyūshū daigaku shuppankai, 1999), 21–24; and Simon, "Making Natives," 82–83.

11. I am adapting James Hevia's conceptualization of re- and deterritorialization. See *English Lessons: The Pedagogy of Imperialism in Nineteenth-Century China* (Durham: Duke University Press, 2003), 20–21.

12. Michael E. Robinson, *Korea's Twentieth-Century Odyssey: A Short History* (Honolulu: University of Hawai'i Press, 2007), 47–52.

13. Takashi Fujitani, *Race for Empire: Koreans as Japanese and Japanese as Americans during World War II* (Berkeley: University of California Press, 2011), 22–25; Kyung Moon Hwang, *Rationalizing Korea: The Rise of the Modern State 1894–1945* (Berkeley: University of California Press, 2016), 9–10, 15–16.

14. Henry H. Em, "Minjok as a Modern Construct: Sin Ch'aeho's Historiography," in *Colonial Modernity in Korea*, ed. Shin Gi-Wook and Michael Robinson (Cambridge: Harvard University Asia Center, 1999), 353 (emphasis added).

15. Haruyama Meitetsu, "Shōwa seijishi ni okeru Musha hōki jiken," in *Taiwan Musha hōki jiken kenkyū to shiryō*, ed. Tai Kuo-hui (Tokyo: Shakai shisōsha, 1981), 131–36; Robinson, *Korea's Odyssey*, 49.

16. Kondō Masami, *Sōryokusen to Taiwan: Nihon shokuminchi hōkai no kenkyū* (Tokyo: Tōsui shobō, 1996), 264–66; Matsuda Kyōko, *Teikoku no shisō: Nihon "Teikoku" to Taiwan Genjūmin* (Tokyo: Yūshisha, 2014), 191–211; Sakano, *Teikoku*, 248.

17. E. Taylor Atkins, *Primitive Selves: Koreana in the Japanese Colonial Gaze, 1910–1945* (Berkeley: University of California Press, 2010); Hyung Il Pai, *Constructing "Korean" Origins: A Critical Review of Archaeology, Historiography, and Racial Myth in Korean State-Formation Theories* (Cambridge: Harvard University Asia Center, 2000); Hyung Il Pai, *Heritage Management in Korea and Japan: The Politics of Antiquity and Identity* (Seattle: University of Washington Press, 2013). For Taiwan, see Yamaji Katsuhiko, *Taiwan Taiyaru-zoku no hyaku-nen: Hyōryū suru dentō, dakō suru kindai, datsu shokuminchika e no michinori* (Tokyo: Fūkyosha, 2011), 402–5.

18. Hu Chia-yu, "Embodied Memories and Enacted Ritual Materials: Possessing the Past in Making and Remaking Saisiyat Identity in Taiwan" (PhD diss., University College London, 2006), 48.

19. Steven E. Phillips, *The Taiwanese Encounter Nationalist China, 1945–1950* (Stanford: Stanford University Press, 2003), 90–114.

20. Huang Chih Huei, "Ethnic Diversity, Two-Layered Colonization, and Complex Modern Taiwanese Attitudes toward Japan," in *Japanese Taiwan: Colonial Rule and Its Contested Legacy*, ed. Andrew Morris (London: Bloomsbury Academic, 2015), 133–53; Asano Toyomi, "Historical Perceptions of Taiwan's Japan Era," in *Toward a History Beyond Borders: Contentious Issues in Sino-Japanese Relations*, ed. Daqing Yang, Jie Liu, Hiroshi Mitani, and Andrew Gordon (Cambridge: Harvard University Asia Center, 2012), 303. An advance party for the Nationalist Party's Seventieth Army, which became the replacement authority of the defeated Japanese empire in Taiwan, landed in Jilong on October 17, 1945, while the GMD was still nominally the central government of China. In April 1949, the first planeloads of fleeing Nationalist officials arrived in Taiwan from Shanghai in the wake of Chinese Communist Party offensives. On May 19 of that year, governor of Taiwan Province Chen Ch'eng proclaimed martial law. Chou Wan-yao, *A New Illustrated History of Taiwan*, trans. Carole Plackitt and Tim Casey (Taipei: SMC Publishing, 2015): 303, 322–33.

21. Michael Rudolph, *Ritual Performances as Authenticating Practices: Cultural Representations of Taiwan's Aborigines in Times of Political Change* (New Brunswick, NJ: Transaction Publishers, 2008), 1–4, 36–38; Mitsuda Yayoi, "First Case of the New Recognition System: The Survival Strategies of the Thao," in *Taiwan Since Martial Law: Society, Culture, Politics, Economy*, ed. David Blundell (Taipei: Shung Ye Museum of Formosan Aborigines, 2012), 166–67.

22. Ku Kun-hui, "Rights to Recognition: Minorities and Indigenous Politics in Emerging Taiwan Nationalism," in Blundell, *Taiwan Since Martial Law*, 95, 98–99.

23. Rudolph, *Ritual Performances*, 55; Simon, "Making Natives," 86–87.

24. Simon, "Making Natives," 87.

25. Michael Berry, *A History of Pain: Trauma in Modern Chinese Literature and Film* (New York: Columbia University Press, 2008), 53–107.

26. Right after the Wushe uprising, highbrow general readership magazines ran feature articles on the people who had revolted against the empire. In each of these publications, the terms *banjin* (barbarian), *banzoku* (barbarian ethnic groups/tribes), and *kyōban* (bellicose barbarians) describe indigenous peoples. Authors also identified the Wushe villages as members of the larger Atayal ethnic group. Namikawa Ryō, "Taiwan no Banjin to sono minzokusei," *Kaizō* (December 1930): 42–67; Nagamatsu Asazō, "Hagyakusuru Banzoku," *Chūō kōron*, 173–86. A popular science magazine added one refinement by noting that the Wushe villages were part of the Sediq subgroup of the Atayal ethnic group. Matsumoto Akira, "Taiwan banzoku: Riban jigyō to jinruigaku," *Kagaku chishiki* 10, no. 12 (December 1930): 8–11. For representative newspaper articles, see "Musha bōdō jiken no gen'in to shinsō," *Tokyo Asahi Shinbun*, November 20, 1930, 2; "Musha no banjin hōki: keisatsu bunshitsu sono ta o shūgeki," *Taiwan nichinichi shinpō*, October 29, 1930, 1. Newspapers also used a few references to the ethnic marker Atayal amid a blizzard of pejorative terms such as *banjin* and *banzoku*.

27. Matsuda Kyōko, *Teikoku*, 189–90; Leo T. S. Ching, "Savage Construction and Civility Making: Japanese Colonialism and Taiwanese Aboriginal Representation," *Positions: East Asia Cultures Critique* 8, no. 3 (2000): 795–97, 815. Fujitani makes a related point regarding Japanese rule in Korea in *Race for Empire*, 25–26, 37–39.

28. See Uno Toshiharu, "Taiwan ni okeru 'banjin' kyōiku," *Tenbō* 4, no. 196 (April 1975): 37, for difference between *sha/she* and *shō/zhuang*; see Matsuoka, *Taiwan Genjūmin shakai no chihōka*, 41–44, for a detailed description of various Paiwan terms for units of settlement and affiliation; see the hundreds of tables in the official publication *Takasagozoku chōsasho dai san-hen: shinka* (1937), ed. Taiwan sōtokufu keimukyoku, for lists of every indigenous settlement in Taiwan categorized as a *sha/she*.

29. Inō Kanori, "Shinten chihō ni okeru Seiban no jissa (zoku)," *Tokyo jinrui gakkai zasshi* 122 (March 1896): 312–13.

30. Japanese ethnological surveys eschewed the term *Sediq* until 1915, subsuming Wushe-area residents under the label *Atayal*. For a thorough review, see Hara Eiko, "Taiyaru, Sedekku, Taroko o meguru kizoku to meishō ni kan suru undō no tenkai 1: Taroko ni okeru undō o chūshin ni," *Taiwan Genjūmin kenkyū* 7 (2003): 210. The six-volume, early 1930s compendium *Takasagozoku chōsasho* classified all Sediq peoples as Atayal, indicating that Sediq as a category remained submerged even after the rebellion. Jun'eki Genjūmin kenkyūkai, ed., *Taiwan Genjūmin kenkyū gairan: Nihon kara no shiten* (Tokyo: Fūkyōsha, 2001), 47. Popular geographies of the empire followed suit by subsuming Sediq and Truku peoples under the rubric *Taiyal*, a synonym of *Atayal*. See Nakama Terahisa, ed., *Nihon chiri fūzoku taikei dai jūgo kan* (Tokyo: Shinkōsha, 1931), 180; Yamamoto Mitsuo, ed., *Nihon chiri taikei: Taiwan hen* (Tokyo: Kaizōsha, 1930), 320–39. The latter title included mention of the Sediq as part of the Atayal group on its map but dropped the distinction in captions and descriptions of particular practices or places. General interest books on the topic included ethnic maps as a matter of course, with associated thumbnail sketches of each indigenous group, but did not adopt the term *Sediq*. For examples, see Tagami Tadayuki, *Banjin no kishū to densetsu* (Taipei: Taiwan banzoku kenkyūjo, 1935), 161, and Ōgata Tarō, *Takasagozoku* (Tokyo: Kyōseisha kōdōkyaku, 1942), 18–21. There were notable exceptions, however. For example, the TGG railway travel guides supplemented descriptions of Wushe's beautiful scenery and hot springs with detailed discussions of the 1930 uprising, while describing the rebels as Sediq members of the Atayal ethnic group. See Taiwan Sōtokufu kōtsūkyoku tetsudō-bu, ed., *Taiwan tetsudō ryokō annai* (Taipei: Taiwan Sōtokufu Kōtsūkyoku tetsudō-bu, 1935),142, Japan National Congressional Library Digital Collection, accessed 12/18/2016, http://dl.ndl.go.jp/info:ndljp/pid/1875798. In another exception, the Oriental Tour Company's Taiwan branch also separated the Sediq from the Atayal, going so far as to mark them separately on the ethnic map. Ueda Hachirō, *Takasagozoku no hanashi* (Taipei: Tōa ryokōsha Taiwan shibu, 1941), 11–13.

31. Matsuda Kyōko, *Teikoku*, 189–94.

32. Andreas Wimmer, *Ethnic Boundary Making: Institutions, Power, Networks* (Oxford: Oxford University Press, 2013), 52–55. For particulars regarding the Taiwan case, see Yamaji Katsuhiko, *Taiwan Taiyaru zoku no hyaku nen* (Tokyo: Fūkyōsha, 2011), 403–4.

33. Walter LaFeber, *The Clash: U.S.-Japanese Relations throughout History* (New York: Norton, 1998), 40–41.

34. V. I. Lenin, *Imperialism: The Highest Stage of Capitalism* (1917; repr., London and Chicago: Pluto Press, 1996), 77–78 (emphasis added).

35. Barry Buzan and George Lawson, *The Global Transformation: History, Modernity and the Making of International Relations* (Cambridge: Cambridge University Press, 2015), 2.

36. Buzan and Lawson, *Global Transformation*, 35, 63.

37. Jürgen Osterhammel, *The Transformation of the World: A Global History of the Nineteenth Century* (Princeton: Princeton University Press, 2014), xv–xx; C. A. Bayly, *The Birth of the Modern World 1780–1914* (Malden, MA: Blackwell Publishing, 2004).

38. Gabriel Popescu, *Bordering and Ordering the Twenty-first Century: Understanding Borders* (Lanham, MD: Rowman & Littlefield, 2012), 34–38.

39. Thongchai Winichakul, *Siam Mapped: A History of the Geo-Body of a Nation* (Honolulu: University of Hawai'i Press, 1994), 16–18, 52–56. (This book will use the spelling *geobody*.)

40. The Treaty of Paris was signed between Spain and the United States on December 10, 1898, to cede the Philippine Islands to the latter; it was ratified by the U.S. Senate on February 6, 1899. A large, prolonged war broke out between Philippine independence forces and the U.S. Army on February 4, 1899. On the main island of Luzon alone, the war of conquest continued well into 1902. Glenn Anthony May, *Battle for Batangas: A Philippine Province at War* (New Haven: Yale University Press, 1991), 76–77, 211–69.

41. Nicola Cooper, *France in Indochina: Colonial Encounters* (New York: Berg, 2001), 13–16; Mary Evelyn Townsend, *European Expansion Since 1871* (Chicago: J. B. Lippincott, 1941), 474, 530–31.

42. The Treaty of Shimonoseki was signed on April 17, 1895, formally ending the Sino-Japanese War and ceding Taiwan, including the Pescadores Islands, to the Japanese Empire. Wu Micha, ed., *Taiwan-shi kojiten*, trans. Yokosawa Yasuo (Tokyo: Chūgoku shoten, 2007), 137.

43. Suzuki Shogo, "Japan's Socialization into Janus-Faced European International Society, *European Journal of International Relations* 11 (2005): 137–64.

44. Jane Burbank and Frederick Cooper, *Empires in World History: Power and the Politics of Difference* (Princeton: Princeton University Press, 2011), 450.

45. Lauren Benton uses the term "quasi-sovereignty" to discuss a range of categories and legal frameworks nineteenth-century empires adopted for "enclave populations" surrounded by majority, or constitutionally governed, populations—often mountain or hill peoples. *A Search for Sovereignty: Law and Geography in European Empires, 1400–1900* (Cambridge: Cambridge University Press, 2010), 226–78. I use the term here for contemporary populations who are recognized as distinctive from national populations insofar as members of these groups have special rights, or are absolved of certain obligations, based on recognized membership in a quasi-sovereign entity.

46. W. G. Beasley, *Japanese Imperialism, 1894–1945* (Oxford: Oxford University Press, 1987), 146–47.

47. Buzan and Lawson, *Global Transformation*, 43, 171–96.

48. David Held and Anthony McGrew, David Goldblatt and Jonathan Perraton, *Global Transformations: Politics, Economics, and Culture* (Stanford: Stanford University Press, 1999), 7–27.

49. Known as Hengchun since 1875, after a series of Qing reforms sought to extend imperial rule to this former hinterland. In this book, the name Langqiao is used when referring to events that occurred before 1875, and Hengchun when referring to events after 1875.

50. Uchida Jun, *Brokers of Empire: Japanese Settler Colonialism in Korea, 1876–1945* (Cambridge: Harvard University Asia Center, 2011), 6: "The term 'brokers' also captures the intermediary position of settlers, who operated simultaneously as agents and pawns of colonial power."

51. Daniel K. Richter, "Cultural Brokers and Intercultural Politics: New York-Iroquois Relations, 1664–1701," *Journal of American History* 75, no. 1 (1988): 41: "simultaneous members of two or more interacting networks (kin groups, political factions, communities or other formal or informal coalitions), [who] provide nodes of communication . . . with respect to a community's relations with the outside world."

52. Michael W. Doyle, *Empires* (Ithaca: Cornell University Press, 1986), 25–28.

53. Lippincott, 11, 59; Sydney Giffard, *Japan Among the Powers, 1890–1990* (New Haven: Yale University Press, 1994), 33, 79.

54. Bayly, *Birth of the Modern World*, 433.

55. Eric R. Wolf, *Europe and the People without History* (Berkeley: University of California Press, 1982), 88.

56. James C. Scott, *The Art of Not Being Governed: An Anarchist History of Upland Southeast Asia* (New Haven: Yale University Press, 2009), 6.

57. Wolf refers to their structure as the "kin-ordered mode of production." Wolf, *Europe*, 88.

58. Richard White, *The Middle Ground: Indians, Empires, and Republics in the Great Lakes Region, 1650–1815* (Cambridge: Cambridge University Press, 1991).

59. John Robert Shepherd, *Statecraft and Political Economy on the Taiwan Frontier, 1600–1800* (Stanford: Stanford University Press, 1993).

60. Caglar Keyder, "Law and Legitimation in Empire," in *Lessons of Empire: Imperial Histories and American Power*, ed. Craig Calhoun, Frederick Cooper, and Kevin W. Moore (New York: Free Press, 2006), 119.

61. Adam McKeown, *Melancholy Order: Asian Migration and the Globalization of Borders* (New York: Columbia University Press, 2008), 38.

62. Peter N. Stearns, *The Industrial Revolution in World History*, 4th ed. (Boulder, CO: Westview Press, 2013), 109–20.

63. Robert Eskildsen, "Of Civilization and Savages: The Mimetic Imperialism of Japan's 1874 Expedition to Taiwan," *American Historical Review* 107, no. 2 (2002): 388–418.

64. The Mudan village incident followed a string of incidents that involved extended negotiations to recover passengers and property from distressed vessels in southern Taiwan.

65. Ian Jared Miller, "Writing Japan at Nature's Edge: The Promises and Perils of Environmental History," in *Japan at Nature's Edge: The Environmental Context of a Global Power*, ed. Ian Jared Miller, Julia Adeney Thomas, and Brett L. Walker (Honolulu: University of Hawai'i Press, 2013), 1–3; Jakobina Arch, "From Meat to Machine Oil: The Nineteenth-Century Development of Whaling in Wakayama," in *Japan at Nature's Edge*, Miller, Thomas, and Walker, 41; Peter Duus, *The Japanese Discovery of America: A Brief History with Documents* (Boston: Bedford Books, 1997), 7–11; George Feifer, *Breaking Open Japan: Commodore*

Perry, Lord Abe, and American Imperialism in 1853 (New York: Smithsonian Books and HarperCollins), 70–75.

66. John E. Herman, "The Cant of Conquest: Tusi Offices and China's Political Incorporation of the Southwest Frontier," in *Empire at the Margins: Culture, Ethnicity, and Frontier in Early Modern China*, ed. Pamela Kyle Crossley, Helen F. Siu, and Donald S. Sutton (Berkeley: University of California Press, 2006), 135–61.

67. Susan Naquin and Evelyn S. Rawski, *Chinese Society in the Eighteenth Century* (New Haven: Yale University Press, 1987), 225–27; William T. Rowe, *China's Last Empire: The Great Qing* (Cambridge: Harvard University Press, 2009), 35–39.

68. Pars Cassel, *Grounds of Judgment: Extraterritoriality and Imperial Power in Nineteenth-Century China and Japan* (Oxford: Oxford University Press, 2012).

69. Chang, Lung-chih, "From Island Frontier to Imperial Colony: Qing and Japanese Sovereignty Debates and Territorial Projects in Taiwan, 1874–1906" (PhD diss., Harvard University, 2003).

70. Rowe, *China's Last Empire*, 54.

71. Sophia Su-fei Yen, *Taiwan in China's Foreign Relations, 1836–1874* (Hamden, CT: Shoe String Press, 1965), 252–54.

72. Michel Foucault, *Discipline and Punish: The Birth of the Prison*, trans. Alan Sheridan (New York: Vintage Books, 1977), 79.

73. Foucault, *Discipline and Punish*, 82.

74. Foucault, *Discipline and Punish*, 85.

75. Foucault, *Discipline and Punish*, 85.

76. Foucault, *Discipline and Punish*, 87.

77. Hui-yu Caroline Ts'ai, *Japan's Empire-Building: An Institutional Approach to Colonial Engineering* (London and New York: Routledge, 2008), 93–94.

78. Fujitani, *Splendid Monarchy: Power and Pageantry in Modern Japan* (Berkeley: University of California, 1996), 5–11.

79. Fujitani, *Splendid*, 25.

80. Fujitani, *Splendid*.

81. Christine Kim, "Politics and Pageantry in Protectorate Korea (1905–10): The Imperial Progresses of Sunjong," *Journal of Asian Studies* 68, no. 3 (2009): 835–59.

82. Crown Prince Hirohito would visit in 1923 to much fanfare, thirty years into Japanese rule. See chapter 3.

83. E. H. Norman, *Origins of the Modern Japanese State: Selected Writings of E. H. Norman*, ed. John Dower (New York: Pantheon Books, 1975), 181, 247.

84. Kozo Yamamura, "The Meiji Land Tax Reform and Its Effects," in *Japan in Transition: From Tokugawa to Meiji*, ed. Marius B. Jansen and Gilbert Rozman (Princeton: Princeton University Press, 1986), 382.

85. Yamamura, "Meiji Land Tax Reform," 382–99.

86. Norman, *Origins*, 245–50.

87. Matthew G. Hannah, *Governmentality and the Mastery of Territory in Nineteenth-Century America* (New York: Cambridge University Press, 2000), 23, 25.

88. James I. Nakamura, *Agricultural Production and the Economic Development of Japan, 1873–1922* (1966; repr., Princeton: Princeton University Press, 2015), 7–9.

89. Ronald G. Knapp, "Settlement and Frontier Land Tenure," in *China's Island Frontier: Studies in the Historical Geography of Taiwan*, ed. Ronald Knapp (Honolulu: University of Hawai'i Press, 1980), 55–68.

90. Yao Jen-to, "The Japanese Colonial State and Its Form of Knowledge," in *Taiwan under Japanese Colonial Rule, 1895–1945: History, Culture, Memory*, ed. Liao Ping-hui and David Der-wei Wang (New York: Columbia University Press, 2006), 47, 54.

91. Yao, "Japanese Colonial State," 43.

92. Yao, "Japanese Colonial State," 48.

93. Yao, "Japanese Colonial State," 52.

94. Samuel Pao-San Ho, "Colonialism and Development: Korea, Taiwan, and Kwantung," in *The Japanese Colonial Empire, 1895–1945*, ed. Ramon H. Myers and Mark R. Peattie (Princeton: Princeton University Press, 1984), 358.

95. Ka Chih-ming, *Japanese Colonialism in Taiwan: Land Tenure, Development and Dependency, 1895–1945* (Boulder, CO: Westview Press, 1995), 55, 57.

96. Yoshitarō Takenobu, *Japan Yearbook* (Tokyo: Japan Yearbook Office, 1906), 526.

97. Beasley, *Japanese Imperialism*, 146–47.

98. Max Weber, *The Protestant Ethic and the Spirit of Capitalism*, trans. Talcott Parsons (New York: Charles Scribner's Sons, 1958), 17–18.

99. Marius Jansen, "Japanese Imperialism: Late Meiji Perspectives," in *The Japanese Colonial Empire, 1895–1945*, ed. Ramon H. Myers and Mark R. Peattie (Princeton: Princeton University Press, 1984), 65–66.

100. Takekoshi Yosaburō, *Japanese Rule in Formosa*, trans. George Braithwaite (London, New York, Bombay, and Calcutta: Longmans, Green, 1907), 138.

101. Takekoshi, *Japanese Rule*, 139.

102. Mochiji Rokusaburō, "Bansei mondai ni kansuru iken," in *Riban shikō dai ikkan*, ed. Inō Kanori (1918; Taipei: Southern Materials Center, 1995), 180–228.

103. Takekoshi, *Japanese Rule*, 230 (emphasis added).

104. Kyung Moon Hwang defines biopower as the "targeting of . . . [a] . . . population for bureaucratic outcomes regarding the people's lives, deaths, and welfare." Hwang, *Rationalizing Korea*, 9–10, 15–16.

105. Sabine Frühstück, *Colonizing Sex: Sexuality and Social Control in Modern Japan* (Berkeley: University of California Press, 2003), 17–35.

106. Achille Mbembe, "Necropolitics," trans. Libby Meintjes, *Public Culture* 15, no. 1 (2003): 25.

107. *Traces of History: Elementary Structures of Race* (London and New York: Verso, 2016), 7, 18.

108. Fujitani, *Race for Empire*, 40–66.

109. Leo T. S. Ching, "Savage Construction and Civility Making: Japanese Colonialism and Taiwanese Aboriginal Representation," *Positions: East Asia Cultures Critique* 8, no. 3 (2000): 810–15.

110. Huang Chih-huei, "The Yamatodamashi of the Takasagozoku Volunteers of Taiwan: A Reading of the Postcolonial Situation," in *Globalizing Japan: Ethnography of the Japanese Presence in Asia, Europe, and America*, ed. Harumi Befu and Sylvie Guichard-Anguis (London: Routledge, 2001), 222–50.

111. Benton, *Search for Sovereignty*, 222–78.

112. Benedict Anderson, *Imagined Communities* (London: Verso, 1983), 163–85.

113. Endō Masataka, *Kindai Nihon no shokuminchi tōchi ni okeru kokuseki to koseki* (Tokyo: Akashi shoten, 2010), 139–43.

114. Ts'ai, "Shaping Administration in Colonial Taiwan," in Liao and Wang, *Taiwan under Japanese Colonial Rule, 1895–1945,* 97–98.

115. Ka, *Japanese Colonialism*; Wang Taysheng, *Legal Reform in Taiwan under Japanese Colonial Rule, 1895–1945: The Reception of Western Law* (Seattle and London: University of Washington Press, 2000); Ming-cheng M. Lo, *Doctors within Borders: Profession, Ethnicity, and Modernity in Colonial Taiwan* (Berkeley: University of California Press, 2002); E. Patricia Tsurumi, *Japanese Colonial Education in Taiwan, 1895–1945* (Cambridge: Harvard University Press, 1977).

116. Hu Chia-yu, "Embodied Memories," 31–32.

117. Antonio C. Tavares, "The Japanese Colonial State and the Dissolution of the Late Imperial Frontier Economy in Taiwan, 1886–1909," *Journal of Asian Studies* 64, no. 2 (2005): 361–85.

118. Matsuda Yoshirō, *Taiwan Genjūmin,* 98–117, 149.

119. Rinji Taiwan kokō chōsa-bu, *Rinji Taiwan kokō chōsa kijutsu hōbun* (Taipei: Taiwan sōtokufu, 1908), 56–57.

120. Charles Hirschman, "The Making of Race in Colonial Malaya: Political Economy and Racial Ideology," *Sociological Forum* 1, no. 2 (1986): 330–61.

121. For intellectual and institutional foundations, see Pai, *Heritage Management,* 95–113; for analyses of Taiwan surveys, see Miyaoka Maoko, "Mori Ushinosuke no chosaku mokuroku oyobi jakkan no kaisetsu," *Taiwan Genjūmin kenkyū* 2 (1997), 189–99; Kasahara Masaharu, "Inō Kanori no jidai: Taiwan Genjūmin shoki kenkyū shi e no sokuen," *Taiwan Genjūmin kenkyū* 3 (1998), 54–78; Matsuda Kyōko, *Teikoku,* 82–165; Sakano, *Teikoku,* 227–39; Paul D. Barclay, "Contending Centers of Calculation in Colonial Taiwan: The Rhetorics of Vindicationism and Privation in Japan's 'Aborigine Policy,'" *Humanities Research* 14, no. 1 (2007): 67–84; Yang Nanjun, *Maboroshi no jinruigakusha: Mori Ushinosuke,* trans. and ed. Kasahara Masaharu, Miyaoka Maoko, and Miyazaki Seiko (Tokyo: Fūkyōsha, 2005); and Chen Wei-chi, *Yineng Jiaju: Taiwan lishi minzuzhi de zhankai* (Taipei: Taida chuban zhongxin, 2014).

122. The GMD picked up the nine-tribe classification in the postwar period; the classification was not amended until 2001, when the GMD was defeated by the Democratic Progressive Party, led by non-Mainlanders. Hu Chia-yu, "Embodied Memories," 45.

123. Marui Keijirō, *Buban ni kansuru ikensho, Bando Kyōiku Ikensho* (Taipei: Banmu honsho, 1914), 21–24.

124. Sōyama Takeshi, *Shokuminchi Taiwan to kindai tsūrizumu* (Tokyo: Seikyōsha, 2003).

125. Niezen, *Origins of Indigenism,* 4.

126. Prasenjit Duara, *Sovereignty and Authenticity: Manchukuo and the East Asian Modern* (Lanham: Rowman & Littlefield, 2003), 9–14, 77–78.

127. Chang Wei-chi, Ueda Akira, and Miyazaki Kiyoshi, "Nihon tōchi jidai ni okeru Taiwan no Genjūmin kankō no keisei," *Sōgō kankō kenkyū* 2 (2003): 47–55.

128. Arif Dirlik, *The Postcolonial Aura: Third World Criticism in the Age of Global Capitalism* (Boulder, CO: Westview Press, 1997), 227.

129. Hu Chia-yu, "Embodied Memories," 12. Material quoted from Marshall Sahlins, "What Is Anthropological Enlightenment? Some Lessons of the Twentieth Century," *Annual Reviews of Anthropology* 28 (1999): x.

130. See Frederick Cooper, "Modernizing Colonialism and the Limits of Empire," in *Lessons of Empire,* ed. Calhoun, Cooper, and Moore, 63–72.

131. Achille Mbembe, "Necropolitics," trans. Libby Meintjes, *Public Culture* 15, no. 1 (2003): 26.

CHAPTER 1. FROM WET DIPLOMACY TO SCORCHED EARTH

1. Ikoma Takatsune, "Musha-ban sōjō jiken chōsa fukumeisho," *Taiwan Musha hōki jiken: kenkyū to shiryō,* ed. Tai Kuo-hui (Tokyo: Shasōshi kaisha, 1981), 290–304; Igarashi Ishimatsu, *Musha jiken jikki* (Puli: Taiwan keisei shinpōsha Puli shikyoku, 1931), 6–8; Mikami Tamotsu, *Taiwan, Musha jiken no konjaku: hisan na jiken to sono uramen shi* (Chigasaki, Kanazawa: self-published, 1984), 53–55.

2. Taiwan sōtokufu, *Musha jiken no tenmatsu* in *Gendaishi shiryō 22: Taiwan (II),* ed. Yamabe Kentarō (Tokyo: Misuzu Shobō, 1971), 587; Mikami, *Taiwan,* 51–55; Mukōyama Hiroo, *Taiwan Takasagozoku no kōnichi hōki: Musha jiken* (Tokyo: Chūō keizai kenkyūjo, 1999), 43–44; Deng Xiangyang, *Kōnichi Musha jiken no rekishi,* ed. Shimomura Sakujirō, trans. Uozumi Etsuko (Osaka: Nihon Kikanshi Shuppan Sentaa, 2000), 46–47; 95–99; Chou Wan-yao, *A New Illustrated History of Taiwan,* trans. Carole Plackitt and Tim Casey (Taipei: SMC Publishing Co., 2015), 177–78.

3. Qiu Ruolong, *Wushe shijian: Taiwan yuanzhumin lixi manhua* (Taipei: Tianyuan chengshi chuban, 2001), 112–21; Wei Te-sheng, director, and John Woo, producer, *Warriors of the Rainbow: Seediq Bale* (Taipei: Central Motion Picture Corporation and ARS Film Production, 2011).

4. Robert J. Lifton, *History and Human Survival: Essays on the Young and Old, Survivors and the Dead, Peace and War, and on Contemporary Psychohistory* (New York: Random House, 1970), 101–11.

5. For details, see Zheng Anxi, *Rizhi shiqi fandi aiyong xiande tuijin yubian qian (1895–1920)* (PhD diss., National Cheng-chi University [Taipei], 2011).

6. Mahmood Mamdani, *Citizen and Subject: Contemporary Africa and the Legacy of Late Colonialism* (Princeton: Princeton University Press, 1996).

7. Leonard H. D. Gordon, *Confrontation over Taiwan: Nineteenth-Century China and the Powers* (Lanham, MD: Lexington Books, 2007), 55.

8. Sophia Su-fei Yen, *Taiwan in China's Foreign Relations, 1836–1874* (Hamden, CT: Shoe String Press, 1965), 125; Robert Gardella, "From Treaty Ports to Provincial Status, 1860–1894," in *Taiwan: A New History,* ed. Murray A. Rubinstein (Armonk, NY: M. E. Sharpe, 1999), 167. Shao-hua Liu and Shu-min Huang, "The Damming of Mudan Creek," in *Environment, Modernization and Development in East Asia: Perspectives from Environmental History,* ed. Ts'ui-jung Liu and James Beattie (London: Palgrave Macmillan, 2016), 113. A list of specific wrecks can be found in James Davidson, *The Island of Formosa Past and Present* (Yokohama: Japan Times Newspaper Company, 1903), 180–82. For another list of shipwrecks off the southern coast, see Douglas Fix, "The Changing Contours of Lived Communities on the Hengchun Peninsula,1850–1874," in *Guojia yu yuanzhumin: Ya-Tai diqu*

zuqun lishi yanjiu, ed. Hong Liwan (Taipei: Institute of Taiwan History, Academia Sinica, 2009), 278–80.

9. Chou Wan-yao, "Cong Liuqiuren chuannan shouhai dao mudanshi shijian: 'Xin' cailiao ye duoyuan quanshi de keneng," *Taiwan fengwu* 65, no. 2 (2015): 23–81.
10. Miyaguni Fumio, *Taiwan sōnan jiken* (Naha: Naha Shuppansha, 1998).
11. Ōhama Ikuko, "'Botansha jiken' saikō: Naze Paiwan-zoku wa Ryūkyūtō-min o satsugaishita no ka," *Taiwan Genjūmin kenkyū* 11 (2007): 203–23.
12. Valjeluk Mavaliu, "'Botan-sha jiken' ni tuite no shiken," trans. Miyazaki Seiko, *Taiwan Genjūmin kenkyū* 10 (2006): 38–52; "Bazuroku (Valjeluk) kara no kotoba: shinrai to kibō," trans. Ishigaki Naoki, *Taiwan Genjūmin kenkyū* 11 (2007): 224–28.
13. Gao Jiaxin, "Sinvaudjan kara mita Botan jiken ue," trans. Satoi Yōichi, *Ryūkyū Daigaku kyōiku gakubu kiyō* 72 (March 2008): 41–63; "Sinvaudjan kara mita Botan jiken shita," trans. Satoi Yōichi, *Ryūkyū Daigaku kyōiku gakubu kiyō* 73 (August 2008): 27–50.
14. Miyaguni, *Taiwan sōnan jiken,* 287; Chou, "Cong Liuqiuren," 27; Yen, *Taiwan,* 157.
15. Mavaliu, "Bazuroku," 225–26.
16. Gao, "Sinvaudjan kara mita Botan jiken ue," 47; Sugiyama Yasunori, ed., *Taiwan meisho kyūseki-shi* (Tokyo: Taiwan Government General, 1916), 251.
17. Xu Shirong, "Qingmo dao rizhi chuqi Hengchun difang de zuqun fenbu (1870–1900)," *Yuyan wenhua fenbu yu zuqun qianxi gongzuo fang* (Taipei: Taiwan Normal University, 2012), 27.
18. Mavaliu, "'Botan-sha jiken,'" 45.
19. Chou, "Cong Liuqiuren," 28–30; Sugiyama, *Taiwan meisho kyūseki-shi,* 249–52.
20. Mavaliu, "Bazuroku," 38–52.
21. Ōhama, "'Botansha jiken' saikō," 203–29.
22. Gao, "Sinvaudjan kara mita Botan jiken shita," 28.
23. Xu, "Qingmo," 38.
24. Chou, "Cong Liuqiuren," 25–26.
25. Edwin Pak-wah Leung, "The Quasi-War in East Asia: Japan's Expedition to Taiwan and the Ryūkyū Controversy," *Modern Asian Studies* 17, no. 2 (1983): 263–64.
26. James L. Hevia, *Cherishing Men from Afar: Qing Guest Ritual and the Macartney Embassy of 1793* (Durham: Duke University Press, 1995), 15–20, 116–33.
27. Mary Elizabeth Berry's discussion about the circulation of bodies in marriage, adoption, and hostage politics and about political attachments solidified by elaborate gifting practices in sixteenth-century Japan speaks eloquently to this point; see "Public Peace and Private Attachment: The Goals and Conduct of Power in Early Modern Japan," *Journal of Japanese Studies* 12, no. 2 (1986): 259–68.
28. Takeshi Hamashita, "Tribute and Treaties: Maritime Asia and Treaty Port Networks in the Era of Negotiation, 1800–1900," in *The Resurgence of East Asia: 500, 150 and 50 Year Perspectives,* ed. Giovanni Arrighi, Takeshi Hamashita, and Mark Selden (London: Routledge, 2003), 26–47. Also see Kirk W. Larsen, *Tradition, Treaties, and Trade Qing Imperialism and Chosŏn Korea, 1850–1910* (Cambridge: Harvard East Asian Monographs, 2011), 13.
29. Michael R. Auslin, *Negotiating with Imperialism: The Unequal Treaties and the Culture of Japanese Diplomacy* (Cambridge: Harvard University Press, 2006), 36–38; Gordon, *Confrontation over Taiwan,* 56–57, 73.

30. Edward J. Drea, *Japan's Imperial Army: Its Rise and Fall, 1853–1945* (Kansas City: University of Kansas Press, 2009), 36.

31. Norihito Mizuno, "An Aspect of Modern Japan's Overseas Expansionism: The Taiwanese Aboriginal Territories in the Early Meiji Japanese Perspective," *Oriental Archive* 78 (2010): 177–79.

32. W. G. Beasley, "The Foreign Threat and the Opening of the Ports," in *The Cambridge History of Japan Volume 5: The Nineteenth Century*, ed. Marius B. Jansen (Cambridge: Cambridge University Press, 1989), 267–73; Peter Booth Wiley, *Yankee in the Land of the Gods: Commodore Perry and the Opening of Japan* (New York: Penguin Books, 1990), 501–3.

33. Beasley, "Foreign Threat," 274–93.

34. Charles W. LeGendre, *Notes of Travel in Formosa*, ed. D. L. Fix and J. Shufelt (Tainan: National Museum of Taiwan History, 2012), 281, 292.

35. Davidson, *Island of Formosa*, 115–16; LeGendre, *Notes*, 251–53; Gordon, *Confrontation over Taiwan*, 56–58.

36. Fix, "Changing Contours," 235–37.

37. LeGendre, *Notes*, 254–55; Gordon, *Confrontation over Taiwan*, 59.

38. Liu Mingdeng and Wu Dating, "Taotai and General of Formosa to LeGendre, June 3, 1867," in *Foreign Adventurers and the Aborigines of Southern Taiwan, 1867–1874*, ed. Robert Eskildsen (Taipei: Institute of Taiwan History, Academia Sinica, 2005), 276–77. The section of Article Thirteen to which the Taiwan officials referred is the following, it would seem: "If the merchant vessels of the United States, while within the waters over which the Chinese Government exercises jurisdiction, be plundered by robbers or pirates, then the Chinese local authorities, civil and military, on receiving information thereof, shall arrest the said robbers or pirates, and punish them according to law." Treaty of Tianjin (Tien-tsin), 1858, University of Southern California US-China Institute, accessed January 13, 2017, http://china.usc.edu/treaty-tianjin-tien-tsin-1858.

39. Yen, *Taiwan*, 132; LeGendre, *Notes*, 257–61.

40. Xu, "Qingmo," 3–4.

41. LeGendre, *Notes*, 289.

42. Hevia, *Cherishing*, 74–118.

43. Susan Naquin and Evelyn S. Rawski, *Chinese Society in the Eighteenth Century* (New Haven: Yale University Press, 1987), 213.

44. Yen, *Taiwan*, 133.

45. LeGendre, *Notes*, 257–60.

46. Bruce Greenfield, "The Problem of the Discoverer's Authority in Lewis and Clark's History," in *Macropolitics of Nineteenth-Century Literature: Nationalism, Exoticism, Imperialism*, ed. Jonathan Arac and Harriet Ritvo (Philadelphia: University of Pennsylvania Press), 12–36.

47. Kamimura Tōru, "Parijarijao shuchō-koku' dai shuchō no zōyo kōkan keitai no tenkei to sono henkei to kussetsu tentō (zenpen): 1867-nen kara 1872-nen made no Taiwan nanbu kōshun chihō no rekishi jinruigakuteki kōsatsu," *Taiwan Genjūmin kenkyū* 18 (2014): 38–74.

48. Kamimura Tōru, "'Kōshun,'" 101–22; Xu, "Qingmo," 15–16.

49. W. A. Pickering, *Pioneering in Formosa* (London: Hurst and Blackett, 1898), 191.

50. Fix, "Changing Contours," 255.

51. LeGendre, *Notes*, 277–78.
52. LeGendre, *Notes*, 280–81.
53. LeGendre, *Notes*, 283.
54. Douglas Cassel, "Letter from Douglas Cassel to Charles LeGendre," in *Foreign Adventurers*, ed. Eskildsen, 207.
55. Pickering, *Pioneering*, 195. As Kamimura Tōru writes, the Qing host threw Toketok and his followers into "panic mode"; see Kamimura, "Parijarijao," 69–70.
56. Beasley, "Foreign Threat," 270–71; Peter Duus, *The Japanese Discovery of America: A Brief History with Documents* (Boston: Bedford Books, 1997), 92–96; LeGendre, *Notes*, 291–92.
57. LeGendre, *Notes*, 289–93, 309–24.
58. Yen, *Taiwan*, 141–42; for diplomatic correspondence on competing views between the Qing officials, see Eskildsen, ed., *Foreign Adventurers*; regarding Langqiao's Paiwan residents, see LeGendre, *Notes*, 261–77.
59. Yen, *Taiwan*, 146.
60. Edward H. House, *The Japanese Expedition to Formosa* (Tokyo: 1875), 222; Inō Kanori, *Taiwan banseishi* (Taipei: Taiwan sōtokufu minseibu shokusankyoku, 1904), 615–17.
61. Davidson, *Island of Formosa*, 169.
62. Fix, "Changing Contours," 240.
63. LeGendre, *Notes*, 309–11.
64. Shufelt and Fix, "Persons and Corporations, 1850–1875 Appearing in Notes of Travel in Formosa," in LeGendre, *Notes*, 415.
65. LeGendre, *Notes*, 311–12.
66. LeGendre, *Notes*, 310–16.
67. LeGendre, *Notes*, 316.
68. LeGendre, *Notes*, 310–14.
69. Douglas Fix, "Charles LeGendre's Travels in Formosa: A Listing of Itineraries," in Charles LeGendre, *Notes*, 442–48.
70. Marlene Mayo, "The Korean Crisis of 1873 and Early Meiji Foreign Policy," *Journal of Asian Studies* 31, no. 4 (1975): 798–801; Hamashita, "Tribute and Treaties," 46–47.
71. Namahiri Tsuneo, *Kindai Higashi Ajia-shi no naka no Ryūkyū heigō* (Tokyo: Iwanami shoten, 2014), 121–23.
72. Matsunaga Masayoshi, "Taiwan ryoyūron no keizu:1874 (Meiji 7) nen no Taiwan shuppei o chūshin ni," *Taiwan kingendai kenkyū* 1 (1978): 8; Danny Orbach, "By Not Stopping": The First Taiwan Expedition (1874) and the Roots of Japanese Military Disobedience," *Journal of Japanese Studies* 42, no. 1 (2016): 33.
73. Chen Xuan, *Meiji Nihon ni okeru Taiwanzō no keisei: Shinbun media ni yoru 1874 'Taiwan jiken' no hyōshō* (Taipei: National Taiwan University Press, 2013), 13–33; Matsunaga, "Taiwan ryoyūron no keizu," 8; Yen, *Taiwan*, 162–70.
74. Wayne C. McWilliams, "East Meets West: The Soejima Mission to China, 1873," *Monumenta Nipponica* 30, no. 3 (1975): 241–43; Yen, *Taiwan*, 180.
75. McWilliams, "East Meets West," 244; Yen, *Taiwan*, 155–56.
76. Namahiri, *Kindai Higashi Ajia-shi*, 194–95; Matsunaga, "Taiwan ryoyūron no keizu," 9; Chen Xuan, *Meiji Nihon*, 31.
77. Matsunaga, "Taiwan ryoyūron no keizu," 9; Yen, *Taiwan*, 188; Chang Lung-chih, "From Island Frontier."

78. McWilliams, "East Meets West," 265–73; Yen, *Taiwan*, 187–90; Namahiri, *Kindai Higashi Ajia-shi*, 194–95.

79. Gordon, 198–200.

80. McWilliams, "East Meets West," 274–75; Namahiri, *Kindai Higashi Ajia-shi*, 204–5.

81. Charles LeGendre, Memo No. 24 to Saigō Tsugumichi, March 31, 1874, in Japan Center for Asian Historical Records, National Archives of Japan, A03030001600, accessed on January 12, 2016, https://www.digital.archives.go.jp/das/image/M0000000000000901592.

82. Xu, "Qingmo," 20, 26; Chou, "Cong Liuqiuren," 75; Fix, "Changing Contours," 264–65; House, *Japanese Expedition*, 30–50; Cassel, "Letter," 204; LeGendre, Memo No. 24.

83. Quote from House, *Japanese Expedition*, 65–66 (emphasis added); Mizuno Jun, "Seiban shiki," in *Tairo Mizuno Jun Sensei*, ed. Tairokai (Taipei: Tairokai jimusho, 1930), 224, concurs with this version of events, as does Cassel, "Letter," 205–7.

84. Fujisaki Seinosuke, *Taiwan no Banzoku* (Tokyo: Kokushi Kankōkai, 1930), 527; House, *Japanese Expedition*, 123; Cassel, "Letter," 209–10; Taiwan sōtokufu keimukyoku, ed., *Takasagozoku chōsasho dai go-hen: Bansha gaikyō meishin* (Taipei, 1938), 307.

85. Cassel, "Letter," 212.

86. House, *Japanese Expedition*, 102.

87. Cassel, "Letter," 213.

88. Michel Foucault, *Discipline and Punish: The Birth of the Prison*, trans. Alan Sheridan (New York: Vintage Books, 1977), 3–5.

89. House, *Japanese Expedition*, 102–3; Cassel, "Letter," 215; Shidehara Hiroshi, *Nanpō bunka no kensetsu e* (Tokyo: Fuzanbō, 1938), 358–59.

90. House, *Japanese Expedition*, 133; Cassel, "Letter," 208–9.

91. Sugiyama, *Taiwan meisho kyūseki-shi*, 265.

92. Fujisaki lists the flag numbers and the names of chiefs and villages for over thirty of the flags distributed between June 19 and September 20; according to his count, the fifty-third and last flag was distributed on the latter date; see *Taiwanshi to Kabayama taishō* (Tokyo: Kokushi kankōkai, 1926), 490–93; Yamamoto Un'ichi, "Kōgun no banjin buiku ni tsuite (shita)," *Riban no tomo*, June 1, 1934, 4. For illustrations, see Paul D. Barclay, "The Relics of Modern Japan's First Foreign War in Colonial and Postcolonial Taiwan, 1874–2015," *Cross Currents: East Asian History and Culture Review E-Journal* 17 (December 2015): 131–38.

93. House, *Japanese Expedition*, 214–15; Mizuno, "Seiban shiki," 281–82; Suzuki Sakutarō, *Taiwan no banzoku kenkyū* (Taipei: Taiwanshi Shiseki Kankōkai, 1932), 506–8; Shidehara, *Nanpō bunka*, 363–64.

94. House, *Japanese Expedition*, 114–25.

95. Orbach, "By Not Stopping," 52.

96. Mizuno, "Seiban shiki," 291–95; Fujisaki, *Taiwanshi*, 494.

97. Chen Xuan, *Meiji Nihon*, 125–31; Fujisaki, *Taiwanshi*, 494.

98. Orbach, "By Not Stopping," 48.

99. Mark Ravina's intellectual biography of Saigō Takamori documents the difficulty of this conversion process for a major political figure educated under the dynastic system. *The Last Samurai: The Life and Battles of Saigō Takamori* (Hoboken, NJ: John Wiley and Sons, 2004).

100. Chen Xuan, *Meiji Nihon*, 13–21.

101. Yen, *Taiwan*, 203; Orbach, "By Not Stopping," 46.

102. Yen, *Taiwan*, 254.
103. Jürgen Osterhammel, *The Transformation of the World: A Global History of the Nineteenth Century* (Princeton: Princeton University Press, 2014), 394–95.
104. Yen, *Taiwan*, 256.
105. Byron K. Marshall, *Learning to Be Modern: Japanese Political Discourse on Education* (Boulder, CO: Westview Press, 2004), 48.
106. All quotations from Yen, *Taiwan*, 256.
107. Takekoshi Yosaburō, *Japanese Rule in Formosa*, trans. George Braithwaite (London, New York, Bombay, and Calcutta: Longmans, Green, 1907), 230.
108. Yen, *Taiwan*, 252, 261, 268; Alexis Dudden, *Japan's Colonization of Korea: Discourse and Power* (Honolulu: University of Hawai'i Press, 2005), 46–51.
109. House, *Japanese Expedition*, 190–215.
110. LeGendre, *Notes*, 295.
111. LeGendre, "Has Japan the Right to Assume Suzerainty over Aboriginal Formosa?," in *Foreign Adventurers*, 181–85; LeGendre, *Notes*, 331.
112. Yen, *Taiwan*, 257–58.
113. Hayashi Masako, "Ueno Sen'ichi: Nisshin sensō mae no Taiwan ninshiki no senkusha," *Taiwan kin-gendaishi kenkyū* 2 (1979): 30–60.
114. Ueno Sen'ichi, "Taiwantō jissen roku," *Tokyo chigaku kyōkai hōkoku* 13, no. 11 (February 1892): 21–48; Sanbō honbu, ed., *Taiwan shi* (Tokyo: Sanbō honbu, January 1895), 83–85.
115. LeGendre, *Notes*, 49–52, appended map.
116. William Hancock, "Tamsui Trade Report for the Year 1881," 32–40, archived at Douglas Fix, ed., *Formosa: 19th Century Images* (Portland, OR: Reed College), accessed on August 2, 2016, http://cdm.reed.edu/cdm4/document.php?CISOROOT = /formosa&CISOPTR = 2264&REC = 12.
117. Sanbō honbu, *Taiwan shi,* 83–85; Ueno, "Taiwantō jissen roku," 39–42.
118. In many of the details of his transit and the descriptions of his interpreter, Ueno's reports follow Hancock's so closely that they appear to be plagiarized in parts.
119. Ueno, "Taiwantō jissen roku," 42–45; Sanbō honbu, *Taiwan shi,* 90–91.
120. "Tōhō kyōkai no ensetu," *Yomiuri shinbun,* March 22, 1892, 1.
121. "Chigaku kyōkai no kōwa," *Yomiuri shinbun,* March 25, 1892, 1.
122. Ueno Sen'ichi, "Taiwantō shisatsu fukumei dai yon gō: Taiwantō seiban fūzoku," Bōei kenkyūjo toshokan, Tokyo, Japan. Document 10-Taiwan-M28-1.
123. Sanbō honbu, *Taiwan shi*.
124. See chapter 3.
125. Jiryū Yamabito, "Taiwan zakki nijū-san: Seiban kaidō (dai ikkai)," *Tokyo Asahi shinbun,* September 28, 1895, 2; "Seiban no junfuku," *Fūzoku gahō,* November 28, 1895, 18.
126. Tanaka Tsunatoku, "Dakekan seiban kaiken Taipei chiji hōkoku," in *Taiwan sōtokufu banzoku jijō kōbun ruisan genbun*, vol. 1, ed. Huang Liyun (Museum of Ethnology, Academia Sinica, Nankang, Taipei, Taiwan), n.p.
127. Hashiguchi Bunzō, "Taiwan jijō," *Tōkyō chigaku kyōkai hōkoku* 17, no. 3 (October–December 1895): 309–28.
128. Fujisaki, *Taiwan no banzoku*, 523; Mizuno, "Seiban shiki," 199–200.
129. Tanaka, "Dakekan," n.p.

130. Matsubara Iwagorō, "Seiban kōtsū shimatsu (ue)," *Kokumin shinbun*, September 28, 1895, 1; Matsubara Iwagorō, "Seiban kōtsū shimatsu (shita)," *Kokumin shinbun*, September 29, 1895, 1; Jiryū, "Taiwan zakki nijū-san," 2; Hashiguchi, "Taiwan jijō," 309–28; "Seiban no junfuku," *Fūzoku gahō*, 17–21; Davidson, *Island of Formosa*, 343.

131. Wang Peng-hui, "Faces of Ethnic Others in Press: *Daishizhai Pictorial's* Southern Chinese Empire," *Taiwan Historical Research* 19, no. 4 (2012): 114–17; Hashiguchi, "Taiwan jijō," 319–21.

132. Jiryū, "Taiwan zakki nijū-san," 2; Hashiguchi, "Taiwan jijō," 317.

133. "Taiwan shoken," *Yomiuri shinbun*, October 15, 1895, 2.

134. Hashiguchi, "Taiwan jijō," 308.

135. Inō Kanori and Awano Dennojō, *Taiwan banjin jijō* (Taipei: Taiwan sōtokufu minseibu bunshoka, 1900), 16.

136. Mori Ushinosuke, *Taiwan banzokushi dai ikkan* (Taipei: Rinji Taiwan kyūkan chōsakai, 1917; repr., Taipei: Southern Materials Center, 1996), 217–18.

137. Inō Kanori, "Juntai nichijō," in *Inō Kanori no Taiwan tōsa nikki*, ed. Kazunari Moriguchi (Taipei: Taiwan fūbutsu zasshisha, 1992), 9.

138. Inō, "Juntai," 81, 109, 124.

139. Okada Shinkō, "Arisanban chōsasho," *Taiwan kanshū kiji* 5, no. 5 (1905): 379–80.

140. Kawano's manuscript report and Shibayama's account agree on almost all particulars of this speech; however, the last line, enclosed in brackets here, is found only in Shibayama's *Taiyō* article and is not contained in the manuscript. Fujisaki summarized this outing based on his extensive official archive in *Taiwan no banzoku*, 544–45.

141. Kawano Shuichirō, "Banjin kaiken Yilan shichō hōkoku," in Huang, *Taiwan sōtokufu banzoku jijō*; Shibayama Kakuzō, "Seiban kaikenki," *Taiyō* 2, no. 4 (1896): 202–6.

142. This was probably Pixo Sappo, who was chief of Upper Paalan, the foremost of three Paalan towns (*buraku*). Inō, "Juntai," 71–72.

143. Wang Jiasheng, "Taiwan tsūshin: seibanjin no kōeki," *Yomiuri shinbun*, February 27, 1896, n.p.

144. Fujisaki, *Taiwan no banzoku*, 544.

145. Inō Kanori, ed., *Riban shikō dai ikkan* (Taipei: Taiwan sōtokufu keisatsu honsho, 1918; repr., Taipei: Southern Materials Center, 1995), 8–9.

146. Inō, *Riban shikō*, 10–11.

147. Wang Shiqing, *Qing dai Taiwan she hui jing ji* (Taipei: Lian jing chu ban, 1994), 482. Translation by Wu Haotian.

148. Inō, *Riban shikō*, 22, 125; Wang, *Qing dai*, 483.

149. "Seiban no junfuku," *Fūzoku gahō*, 18.

150. Miyanohara Tōhachi, "Seiban jijō Dakekan bukonsho no hōkoku," in *Taiwan sōtokufu banzoku jijō*, vol. 3; Miyanohara Tōhachi, "Dakekan bukonsho hōkoku," *Taiwan shinpō*, September 19, 1896, n.p. Miyanohara's forty-four-page manuscript report was reproduced in its entirety in the *Taiwan shinpō* in serial form between September 19 and October 14, 1896.

151. "Saitō bunkonsho shuji no kiso chihō shucchō," *Yomiuri shinbun*, August 20, 1897, 3.

152. *Kyū shokuminchi jinji sōran: Taiwan hen*, vol. 1 (Tokyo: Nihon tosho sentā, 1997), 78, 82–97.

153. Inō, *Riban shikō*, 14–15.

154. Ueno Shirō, "Shokuminchi tōchiki ni okeru bukonsho to Taiwan Genjūmin to no kawari ni tsuite" in *Mainoriti no koritsu to kokōsei* ed. Chūkyō Daigaku shakai kagaku kenkyūjo (Nagoya: Chūkyō Daigaku shakai kagaku kenkyūjo, 2002), 63–64.

155. Inō, *Riban shikō*, 41–42.

156. Matsuda Kyōko, "'Naichi' kankō' to iu tōchi gihō: 1897 nen no Taiwan Genjūmin no 'naichi' kankō o megutte," *Akademia* [Nanzan daigaku] (2013): 85–103; Jordan Sand, "Imperial Tokyo as a Contact Zone: The Metropolitan Tours of Taiwanese Aborigines, 1897–1941," *Asia-Pacific Journal* 12, issue 10, no. 4 (March 10, 2014), accessed February 26, 2017, http://apjjf.org/2014/12/10/Jordan-Sand/4089/article.html.

157. Inō, *Riban shikō*, 42–43.

158. Inō, *Riban shikō*, 56–57.

159. Inō, *Riban shikō*, 70–71.

160. Uchiyama Ban'yū, "Puli no tsuyu (Fukabori Taii gūnan no tenmatsu)," *Taiwan kanshū kiji* 11, no. 5 (1905): 60–66.

161. Kaku Kurata, "Chūō sanmyaku ōdan, ichi," *Taiwan nichinichi shinpō*, January 24, 1908, n.p.

162. Mori Ushinosuke, "Jūgonen no bankai, yon," *Taiwan nichinichi shinpō*, May 4, 1912, n.p.

163. Inō, *Riban shikō*, 156.

164. Takada Tomizō, ed., *Taihoku-shū ribanshi* (Taipei: Taihoku-shū keimu-bu, 1924), 304–9.

165. *Taiwan nichinichi shinpō*, December 19, 1902, n.p.

166. Gao Yongqing [Pixo Walis], *Musha hizakura no kuruizaki: gyakusatsu jiken ikinokori no shogen*, trans. Katō Minoru (Tokyo: Kyōbunkan, 1988), 13; Aui Heppaha, *Shōgen Musha jiken: Taiwan sanchijin no kōnichi hōki*, ed. Xu Jielin (Tokyo: Sōfūkan, 1985), 20; Deng, *Kōnichi Musha jiken o muguru hitobito*, 55.

167. Gao, *Musha hizakura no kuruizaki*, 13–14.

168. *Taiwan minpō*, October 9, 1903, and October 21, 1903.

169. Inō, *Riban shikō*, 455–56; *Banjin no dōyō oyobi tōbatsu no gairyaku*, in *Gendaishi shiryō 22: Taiwan (II)*, ed. Yamabe Kentarō (Tokyo: Misuzu Shobō, 1971), 509.

170. Charles Archibald Mitchell, *Camphor in Japan and in Formosa* (London: Chiswick Press, 1900), 3, 45.

171. Davidson, *Island of Formosa*, 406.

172. Takekoshi, *Japanese*, 171.

173. By 1890 world demand for the product had risen sharply because European governments were buying up supplies for the production of smokeless powder; see "Camphor," *Scientific American* 62 (April 19, 1890): 242.

174. Ka Chih-ming, *Japanese Colonialism in Taiwan: Land Tenure, Development and Dependency, 1895–1945* (Boulder, CO: Westview Press, 1995), 35.

175. Johanna Menzel Meskill, *A Chinese Pioneer Family: The Lins of Wu-feng, Taiwan, 1729–1895* (Princeton: Princeton University Press, 1979), 239–42.

176. Inō, *Riban shikō*, 28–29.

177. Iriye Takeshi, "Taiwan banchi zatsuzoku," *Fūzoku gahō* (December 10, 1896): 26–32; Meskill, *Pioneer Family*, 241–42.

178. Davidson, *Island of Formosa*, 430.

179. Kojima Reiitsu, "Nihon teikokushugi no Taiwan sanchi shihai: Musha hōki jiken," in *Taiwan Musha hōki jiken kenkyū to shiryō*, ed. Tai Kuo-hui (Tokyo: Shakai shisōsha, 1981), 63–64; Formosa Bureau of Aboriginal Affairs, *Report on the Control of the Aborigines in Formosa* (Taipei: Government of Formosa, 1911), 34–42.

180. E. Patricia Tsurumi, "Taiwan under Kodama Gentarō and Goto Shimpei," in *Papers on Japan*, ed. Albert Craig (Cambridge: Harvard East Asian Research Center, 1967), 99–101.

181. Kodama and Gotō are the "heroes" of Japanese colonization of Taiwan; they are usually given credit for ending rebellion, making the colony profitable, and reducing the military's role on the island. Comparisons to Paul Doumer's regime in French Indochina come to mind when reading of their efficiency and ruthlessness; see Edward I. Chen, "Goto Shimpei, Japan's Colonial Administrator in Taiwan: A Critical Reexamination," *American Asian Review* 13, no. 1 (1995): 29–59.

182. Ka, *Japanese Colonialism*, 51–52.

183. Mochiji's post was within the inner circle of Taiwan's central government. Only ten other civil officials (including Gotō) shared Mochiji's rank of *chokunin*. Tsurumi, "Taiwan under Kodama," 115; Ogata Taketoshi, ed., *Taiwan dainenpyō* (Taipei: self-published), 49.

184. Kaneko Fumio, "Nihon shokuminchi jinbutsu (2): Mochiji Rokusaburō no shōgai to chosaku," *Taiwan kingendaishi kenkyū* 2 (1979): 119–28.

185. Inō, *Riban shikō*, 179–228.

186. Inō, *Riban shikō*, 180–90.

187. Mochiji Rokusaburō, *Taiwan shokuminchi seisaku* (Tokyo: Fuzanbō, 1912), 380–81.

188. Julia Adeney Thomas, *Reconfiguring Modernity: Concepts of Nature in Japanese Political Ideology* (Berkeley: University of California Press, 2001), 84–110.

189. Inō, *Riban shikō*, 181.

190. Inō, *Riban shikō*, 180.

191. Ishii Shinji, "The Silent War in Formosa," *Asiatic Quarterly Review* (July 1913): 90.

192. Tōgō Minoru and Satō Shirō, *Taiwan shokuminchi hattatsu shi* (Taipei: Kōbunkan, 1916; repr., Southern Materials Center, 1996), 332; Tomoyuki Kawata, *Formosa To-day* (Osaka: Taikansha and Co., 1917), 40.

193. Inoue Toshitaka, "Taiwan sōtokufu no chikkō jigyō," in *Nihon tōchi jidai Taiwan no keizai to shakai*, ed. Matsuda Yoshirō (Tokyo: Kōyō shobō, 2012), 157–59.

194. Fujii Shizue, *Rizhi shiqi Taiwan zongdufu lifan zhengce* (Taipei: Wenyingtang chubanshe, 1997), 228.

195. Kawata, *Formosa To-day*, 13.

196. Y. Takenobu and K. Kawakami, *The Japan Year Book 1913* (Tokyo: Japan Year Book Office, n.d.), 669.

197. "Sasaki Terayama-shi," *Tokyo Asahi shinbun*, January 1934, 11.

198. Dai Nihon Teikoku gikaishi kankōkai, ed., *Dai Nihon Teikoku gikaishi*, vol. 7 (Tokyo: Dai Nihon Teikoku gikaishi kankōkai, 1928), 905, 908–9.

199. Fujii, *Rizhi shiqi*, 228.

200. Formosa Bureau of Aboriginal Affairs, *Report*, 45; Taiwan sōtokufu minseibu banmu honsho, ed., *Riban gaiyō* (Taipei: Taiwan sōtokufu minseibu, 1912), appendix 4.

201. Kojima, "Nihon teikokushugi," 62–3; see also Formosa Bureau of Aboriginal Affairs, *Report*, 16–17.

202. Taiwan sōtokufu minseibu banmu honsho, appendix 3.

203. Kojima, "Nihon teikokushugi," 62–63.
204. Government-General of Taiwan, *The Statistical Summary of Taiwan* (Tokyo: Japan Times Co., 1912), 163.
205. Kawata, *Formosa To-day*, 13.
206. Hideo Naito, *Taiwan: A Unique Colonial Record 1937–8 Edition* (Tokyo: Kokusai Nippon kyōkai, 1938), 81.
207. Caroline Hui-yu Ts'ai, "Shaping Administration in Colonial Taiwan," in *Taiwan under Japanese Colonial Rule, 1895–1945: History, Culture, Memory*, ed. Liao Ping-hui and David Der-wei Wang (New York: Columbia University Press, 2006), 108.
208. Inō, *Riban shikō*, 397.
209. Inō, *Riban shikō*, 448–49.
210. "Nantō-chō keibu-ho Itō Eitarō banjin tōbatsu ni kanshi shōyo," *Taiwan Sōtokufu Manuscript Records*, 4938-ce/7-wen, 1906–04–01.
211. Taiwan sōtokufu minseibu banmu honsho, ed., *Chiban kikō* (Taipei: Taiwan sōtokufu minseibu banmu honsho, 1911).
212. Tōgō and Satō, *Taiwan shokuminchi*, 145–46.
213. Takenobu Yoshitarō, *Japan Year Book 1914* (Tokyo: Japan Year Book Office), 702.
214. Tōgō and Satō, *Taiwan shokuminchi*, 148.
215. For a documentary/commemorative postcard of the Ninth Regiment's buglers, marchers, and the improvised arch, with troops returning to Puli in August 1914, after victory, see "[(93) The Expeditionary Force's 9th Company Entering Puli's Triumphal Arch]," tj0095, East Asia Image Collection, Lafayette College, Easton, PA, accessed July 23, 2017, http://digital.lafayette.edu/collections/eastasia/tjwar-postcards/tj0095. For a photo in the popular press of Governor-General Sakuma's triumphal return to Taipei that same year, complete with arch and parade, see "The Triumph of Governor-General Sakuma at Taihoku Station," ts0022, East Asia Image Collection, Lafayette College, Easton, PA, accessed July 23, 2017, http://digital.lafayette.edu/collections/eastasia/cpw-shashinkai/ts0022.
216. Wu Micha, ed., *Taiwan-shi kojiten,* trans. Yokosawa Yasuo (Tokyo: Chūgoku shoten, 2007), 166.
217. Drea, *Japan's Imperial Army,* 137; Mark Peattie, *Nan'yō: The Rise and Fall of the Japanese in Micronesia, 1885–1945* (Honolulu: University of Hawai'i Press, 1988), 41–42.
218. Fujii, *Rizhi shiqi*, 274.
219. Zheng, *Rizhi shiqi,* 144.
220. Tōgō and Satō, *Taiwan shokuminchi*, 145.
221. Takenobu Yoshitarō, *The Japan Year Book 1915* (Tokyo: Japan Year Book Office, n.d.), 727.
222. Takenobu Yoshitarō, *The Japan Year Book 1916* (Tokyo: Japan Year Book Office, n.d.), 708.
223. Richard White, *The Middle Ground: Indians, Empires, and Republics in the Great Lakes Region, 1650–1815* (Cambridge: Cambridge University Press, 1991).
224. Yamaji Katsuhiko, *Taiwan Taiyaru-zoku no hyaku-nen: Hyōryū suru dentō, dakō suru kindai, datsu shokuminchika e no michinori* (Tokyo: Fūkyosha, 2011), 309; Matsuoka Tadasu, *Taiwan Genjūmin shakai no chihōka: Mainoriti no nijū seiki* (Tokyo: Kenbun shuppan, 2012), 87; Matsuda Yoshirō, "Senjūmin to Nihongo kyōiku: Arisan Tsou-zoku no senzen, sengo," in *Seikatsu no naka no shokuminchi shugi,* ed. Mizuno Naoki (Kyoto: Jinbun

shoin, 2004), 153; Kondō Masami, *Sōryokusen to Taiwan: Nihon shokuminchi hōkai no kenkyū* (Tokyo: tōsui shobō, 1996), 296–97.

225. Ikoma, "Musha-ban sōjō jiken," 289.

226. Watanabe Sei, "Musha sōjō no shinsō o aku hitotsu no kagi! 'Seiban Kondō' shi no hansei o monogataru (nijū-san)," *Taiwan nichinichi shinpō*, February 5, 1931, 5; Hashimoto Hakusui, *Aa Musha jiken* (Taipei: Minamikuni shuppan kyōkai, 1930; repr., Taipei: Ch'eng Wen, 1999), 147–50; Taiwan sōtokufu, *Musha jiken no tenmatsu*, 610–11.

227. Nakagawa Kōichi et al., *Musha jiken: Taiwan Takasagozoku no hōki* (Tokyo: Sanshōdō, 1980), 59–77; Deng Xianyang, *Kōnichi Musha jiken o meguru hitobito*, ed. Shimomura Sakujirō, trans. Uozumi Etsuko (Ōsaka: Nihon kikanshi shuppan sentaa, 2001), 72–74; Hayashi Eidai, *Taiwan Hitsuwa: Musha No Hanran, Minshūgawa No Shōgen* (Tokyo: Shin hyōron, 2002), 52–55; Mukōyama, *Taiwan Takasagozoku*, 36–37; Fujisaki, *Taiwan no banzoku*, 848–49; Ikoma, 289; Mikami, *Taiwan*, 50–51.

228. Taiwan sōtokufu, *Musha jiken no tenmatsu*, 611; Hashimoto, 148–49.

229. Watanabe Sei, "Musha sōjō no shinsō o aku hitotsu no kagi! 'Seiban Kondō' shi no hansei o monogataru," *Taiwan nichinichi shinpō*, February 7, 1931, 3.

CHAPTER 2. THE *LONGUE DURÉE* AND THE SHORT CIRCUIT

1. Jürgen Osterhammel, *The Transformation of the World: A Global History of the Nineteenth Century* (Princeton: Princeton University Press, 2014), 785–90; Benedict Anderson, *Imagined Communities* (London: Verso, 1983), 43.

2. As recently as 2014, Taiwan's "national Proficiency Test of Aboriginal Languages—used to certify students seeking indigenous status in order to be eligible for government affirmative-action policies—[was] offered in a total of forty-two different language varieties." P. Kerim Friedman, "The Hegemony of the Local: Taiwanese Multiculturalism and Indigenous Identity Politics," *Boundary 2* (forthcoming, 2018). Taiwan's national government employed a team of forty-eight translators to translate President Ts'ai Ing-wen's August 1, 2016, apology to the IPT into sixteen different languages. Wu Po-wei and Jake Chung, "Apology to be Published in 18 Languages," *Taipei Times*, December 23, 2016, 4, accessed January 2, 2017, http://www.taipeitimes.com/News/taiwan/archives/2016/12/23/2003661776.

3. The Margary affair of February 21, 1875, which occurred within three months of Japan's departure from Taiwan, provides yet another example of how deadly violence, inflicted by peoples within the Qing empire but beyond its administered territories, could become an occasion for a costly foreign intervention with long-term consequences for the Qing. In this case, the death of a single British functionary at the hands of Burmese hill tribes brought the full weight of the British crown to bear on the Qing court, resulting in a round of treaty negotiations and public-apology missions. See James Hevia, *English Lessons: The Pedagogy of Imperialism in Nineteenth-Century China* (Durham: Duke University Press, 2003), 150–53.

4. Stewart Lone, *Army, Empire and Politics in Meiji Japan* (New York: Palgrave, 2000), 17.

5. Douglas R. Reynolds, "Training Young China Hands: Tōa Dōbun Shoin and Its Precursors, 1886–1945," in *The Japanese Informal Empire in China, 1895–1937*, ed. Peter Duus, Ramon H. Myers, and Mark R. Peattie (Princeton: Princeton University Press), 215–21;

Joshua A. Fogel, *Politics and Sinology: The Case of Naitō Konan (1866–1934)* (Cambridge: Harvard University Press, 1984), 12.

6. Sasa Hiroo, "Nisshin sensō to tsūyakukan," in *Nisshin sensō to Higashi Ajia sekai no henyō*, ed. Ōhata Tokushirō (Tokyo: Yumani shobō, 1997), 373–90.

7. Mori Ushinosuke, "Taiwan banzoku ni tuite," in *Taiwan banzokushi dai ikkan* (Taipei: Rinji Taiwan kyūkan chōsakai, 1917; repr., Taipei: Southern Materials Center, 1996), 2.

8. Sasa, "Nisshin sensō to tsūyakukan," 373–90.

9. Ōe Shinobu, "Shokuminchi sensō to sōtokufu no seiritsu," in *Iwanami kōza: Kindai Nihon to shokuminchi, Teikoku tōji no kōkoku*, vol. 2 (Tokyo: Iwanami Shoten, 1992), 3–10.

10. Furuno Naoya, *Taiwangun shireibu: 1895–1945* (Tokyo: Kokusho kankōkai, 1991), 58–77.

11. "Kenpeitai-zuki tsūyakukan no saiyō," *Yomiuri shinbun*, September 9, 1895, 2.

12. Taiwan sōtokufu keimukyoku, ed., *Taiwan sōtokufu keisatsu enkakushi* (Taipei: Taiwan sōtokufu keimukyoku, 1938; repr., Tokyo: Rokuin shobō, 1986), 5: 912. Hereafter abbreviated *TSK*.

13. He Dongquan, "Taiwan nansei roku: shoken zakki," *Yomiuri shinbun*, September 1, 1895, 1.

14. Figures compiled and analyzed from pages of *Kyūshokuminchi jinji sōran: Taiwan hen*, vol. 1 (Tokyo: Nihon tosho sentā, 1997), hereafter abbreviated *KJS*.

15. *TSK* 5: 914–15.

16. *TSK* 5: 916.

17. Lone, *Army*, 52.

18. "Dogo senkō iin," *Taiwan kyōkai kaihō* 9 (1899): 61.

19. *TSK* 5: 916–18.

20. For the best illustration of the budgeting shell game that disguised diminished per capita spending on education under the banner of "increased participation," see Kitamura Kae, *Nihon shokuminchika no Taiwan Genjūmin kyōiku shi* (Sapporo: Hokkaidō Daigaku shuppankai, 2008), 238–40. One of many Japanese postmortem investigations into the causes of the Wushe uprising also noted the neglect of aborigine administration in the 1920s as a problem. See Ikoma Takatsune, ed., "Musha-ban sōjō jiken chōsa fukumeisho," in Tai Kuo-hui, ed., *Taiwan Musha hōki jiken: kenkyū to shiryō* (Tokyo: Shasōshi kaisha, 1981), 318.

21. Kondō Masami, *Sōryokusen to Taiwan: Nihon shokuminchi hōkai no kenkyū* (Tokyo: tōsui shobō, 1996), 263.

22. Yamaji Katsuhiko, *Taiwan Taiyaru-zoku no hyaku-nen: Hyōryū suru dentō, dakō suru kindai, datsu shokuminchika e no michinori* (Tokyo: Fūkyosha, 2011), 307–11; Matsuoka Tadasu, *Taiwan Genjūmin shakai no chihōka: Mainoriti no nijūsseiki* (Tokyo: Kenbun shuppan, 2012), 86–88.

23. Kondō, *Sōryokusen*, 294–99; Matsuda Kyōko, *Teikoku no shisō: Nihon "Teikoku" to Taiwan Genjūmin* (Tokyo: Yūshisha, 2014), 189–90; Matsuda Yoshirō, "Senjūmin to Nihongo kyōiku: Arisan Tsou-zoku no senzen, sengo," in *Seikatsu no naka no shokuminchi shugi*, ed. Mizuno Naoki (Kyoto: Jinbun shoin, 2004), 153.

24. Matsuda, "Senjūmin," 158–59.

25. Robert Swinhoe, "Notes on the Ethnology of Formosa," in *Natives of Formosa: British Reports of the Taiwan Indigenous People, 1650–1950*, ed. Henrietta Harrison (Taipei: Shung Ye Museum of Formosan Aborigines, 2001), 66.

26. Douglas Fix, "The Changing Contours of Lived Communities on the Hengchun Peninsula,1850–1874," in *Guojia yu yuanzhumin: Ya-Tai diqu zuqun lishi yanjiu,* ed. Hong Liwan (Taipei: Institute of Taiwan History, Academia Sinica, 2009), 271.

27. Xu Shirong, "Qingmo dao rizhi chuqi Hengchun difang de zuqun fenbu (1870–1900)," *Yuyan wenhua fenbu yu zuqun qianxi gongzuo fang* (Taipei: Taiwan Normal University, 2012), 20–24.

28. W. A. Pickering, *Pioneering in Formosa* (London: Hurst and Blackett, 1898), 143.

29. Joseph Beal Steere, *Formosa and Its Inhabitants,* ed. Paul Jen-kuei Li (Taipei: Institute of History [Preparatory Office], Academia Sinica, 2002), 314.

30. Paul D. Barclay, "Cultural Brokerage and Interethnic Marriage in Colonial Taiwan: Japanese Subalterns and Their Aborigine Wives, 1895–1930," *Journal of Asian Studies* 64, no. 2 (May 2005): 323–60.

31. Chang, Lung-chih, "From Island Frontier to Imperial Colony: Qing and Japanese Sovereignty Debates and Territorial Projects in Taiwan, 1874–1906" (PhD diss., Harvard University, 2003), 105–7.

32. Kurosaki Michio, "Seibanchi Marai-sha tanken (shūzen)," *Tokyo Asahi shinbun,* March 4, 1896, 3; Jiang Guizhen, *Zaixian chuangtong de shijian, Wulai Taiyazu de wenhua tuxiang* (Taipei: National Museum of History, 2010), 58.

33. Kirsten L. Ziomek, "The Possibility of Liminal Colonial Subjecthood: Yayutz Bleyh and the Search for Subaltern Histories in the Japanese Empire," *Critical Asian Studies* 47, no. 1 (2015): 123–50.

34. Chang, "Island Frontier," 95–101.

35. Fujisaki Seinosuke, *Taiwan no banzoku* (Tokyo: Kokushi Kankōkai, 1930), 455.

36. Inō Kanori, *Taiwan banseishi* (Taipei: Taiwan sōtokufu minseibu shokusankyoku, 1904), 551–54.

37. Hashiguchi Bunzō, "Taiwan jijō," *Tokyo chigaku kyōkai hōkoku* 17, no. 3 (1895): 311–17.

38. Jiryū Yamabito, "Taiwan zakki nijū-san: Seiban kaidō (dai ikkai)," *Tokyo Asahi shinbun,* September 28, 1895, 2; "Seiban no junfuku," *Fūzoku gahō* 103 (November 28, 1895), 17–18.

39. Hashiguchi, "Taiwan jijō," 313–18; Hashiguchi Bunzō, "Dakekan chihō seiban kaiken no tame shutchō jihōkoku," in *Taiwan sōtokufu banzoku jijō kōbun ruisan genbun,* vol. 1, ed. Huang Liyun (Museum of Ethnology, Academia Sinica, Nankang, Taipei, Taiwan), n.p.; Tanaka Tsunatoku, "Dakekan seiban kaiken Taipei chiji hōkoku," in *Taiwan sōtokufu banzoku jijō kōbun ruisan genbun,* vol. 1; Inō Kanori, "Taiwan tsūshin dai sankai," *Tokyo jinruigakkai zasshi* 119 (1896): 179–84; Inō Kanori, ed., *Riban shikō dai ikkan* (Taipei: Taiwan sōtokufu keisatsu honsho, 1918; repr., Taipei: Southern Materials Center, 1995), 4; Jiryū Yamabito, "Taiwan zakki nijū-yon: Seiban kaidō (dai nikai)," *Tokyo Asahi shinbun,* September 29, 1895, 2.

40. Hashiguchi, "Taiwan jijō," 317–18.

41. Mori, "Taiwan banzoku ni tuite," features extended discussions of cross-cultural misapprehension surrounding terms like *surrender* and *alliance* between Japanese and Atayalic speakers.

42. Kawano Shuichirō, "Banjin kaiken Yilan shichō hōkoku," in *Taiwan sōtokufu banzoku jijō kōbun ruisan genbun,* vol. 1; Shibayama Kakuzō, "Seiban kaikenki," *Taiyō* 2, no. 4

(1896): 203–5; Takada Tomizō, ed., *Taihoku-shū ribanshi,* vol. 1 (Taipei: Taihoku-shū keimubu, 1924), 1; Fujisaki, *Taiwan no Banzoku,* 544–45.

43. Inō Kanori, "Taiwan tsūshin dai ikkai," *Tokyo jinrui gakkai zasshi* 117 (1895): 97–98.

44. Kawano Shūichirō, "Banjin kaiken," n.p.; Shibayama, "Seiban kaikenki," 202–6; Takada, *Taihoku-shū ribanshi,*1.

45. Nakajima Takemuro, "Seibanchi tankenki jō," *Taiyō* 2, no. 21 (1896): 247–48.

46. Saitō Kenji, "Taiwan no shōnō seizō (setsuzen gō)," *Taiwan kyōkai kaihō* 4 (1899): 15–16.

47. Iriye Takeshi, "Taiwan banzoku zue," *Fūzoku gahō* 129 (December 1, 1896): 17.

48. Mori, *Taiwan banzoku shi,* 176–77.

49. Laura Lee Junker, *Raiding, Trading, and Feasting: The Political Economy of Philippine Chiefdoms* (Honolulu: University of Hawai'i Press, 1999); Matsuoka Tadasu, "Gendai Taiwan Genjūmin shakairon *chūtàn*: 'Tōmoku' o tegakari to shite," *Taiwan Genjūmin Kenkyū* 8 (2004): 83–84.

50. Margery Wolf, *Women and the Family in Rural Taiwan* (Stanford: Stanford University Press, 1972), 171–90.

51. Saitō Otosaku, "Morrison kikō (zoku)," *Taiyō* 3, no. 14 (July 5, 1897): 180.

52. "Taiwan minji shibu: tsūyakukan no Taiwan tsūshin," *Yomiuri shinbun,* September 30, 1895, 5.

53. Iriye Takeshi and Hashimoto Shigeru, "Taiwan banchi zatsuzoku," *Fūzoku gahō* 130 (1896): 29–30; Chiwas is identified in Mori Ushinosuke, "Sūsū no kishiki ban monogatari," *Taiwan nichinichi shinpō,* June 21, 1925, 3; Pixo Sappo is identified in Mori Ushinosuke, "Bankai no konjaku (jū-ni)," *Taiwan nichinichi shinpō,* July 18, 1915, and Inō Kanori, "Juntai nichijō," in *Inō Kanori no Taiwan tōsa nikki,* ed. Kazunari Moriguchi (Taipei: Taiwan fūbutsu zasshisha, 1992), 73.

54. Araki Masayasu, ed., *Shinbun ga kataru meijishi,* vol. 2 (Tokyo: Hara shobō, 1979), 79. Meiji Japan's most revered student of northern aborigine languages and culture, Mori Ushinosuke, recalled Hiyama's marriage to a Wushe *banpu* as the first official Japanese action to assert itself among the Atayal of Nantou Prefecture (*Taiwan nichinichi shinpō,* May 4, 1912).

55. "Hiyama Tetsusaburō-shi no donchi," *Yomiuri shinbun,* May 19,1895, 3.

56. "Hiyama Tetsusaburō-shi no gōtō kyōsa kengi," *Yomiuri shinbun,* June 1, 1897, 3; "Hiyama Tetsusaburō kōin ni tsuite," *Yomiuri shinbun,* June 11, 1897, 3.

57. Suimoto Sei'ichi, *Taiwan hitsuwa* (Taipei: Nihon oyobi shokumin sha, 1928), 259.

58. Torii Ryūzō, "Taiwan chūō sanmyaku no ōdan: shōzen," *Taiyō* 7, 9 (1901): 131; Uchiyama Ban'yū, "Puli no tsuyu (Fukahori Taii gūnan no tenmatsu)," *Taiwan kanshū kiji* 11, no. 5 (1905): 66; Inoguchi Yasuyoshi, ed., *Riban shikō dai nikan* (Taipei: Taiwan sōtokufu keimukyoku, 1921; repr., Taipei: Southern Materials Center, 1995), 232.

59. Suimoto, *Taiwan hitsuwa,* 259–61. This account has many chronological inconsistencies; it sounds like an oral history based on Kondō's memory; it was published two years before the Wushe Rebellion. It is therefore not completely reliable.

60. Yamamoto Ryōichi, "Kaitakusha Kondō Katsusaburō to sono shūi: Miyatake Shōtarō-shi no genkō o moto ni," *Gendai Taiwan kenkyū* 19 (2000): 107–8.

61. Japanese sources use the word *dohi* (brigand, bandit) to describe rebels against the state, since they refused to impute any but the basest motives to the rebels' acts of sabotage, robbery, and resistance to Japanese occupation.

62. Takekoshi, *Japanese Rule*, 93–94.
63. Inō, *Riban shikō*, 22.
64. *Taiwan nichinichi shinpō*, December 21, 1930.
65. Inō Kanori identified him as Tsitsok, father of Iwan. Inō was introduced to Iwan, who led him to Tsitsok, by an interpreter (probably Kondō) whom Inō met near Puli; the interpreter's name is left blank in Inō's diary. Inō, "Juntai," 71.
66. *Taiwan nichinichi shinpō*, December 21, 1930; Ide Kiwata, *Taiwan chisekishi* (Taipei: Taiwan nichinichi shinpōsha, 1937), 278.
67. *Taiwan nichinichi shinpō*, December 21, 1930; Fujisaki, *Taiwan no banzoku*, 606.
68. *Taiwan nichinichi shinpō*, December 25, 1930; Yamabe Kentarō, ed., *Gendaishi shiryō 22: Taiwan (II)* (Tokyo: Misuzu Shobō, 1971), 509; Toyonaga Tōhei, "Aa, Fukahori Tai'i," *Riban no tomo* (January 1, 1936): 2–3.
69. *Taiwan nichinichi shinpō*, December 25, 1930.
70. *Taiwan nichinichi shinpō*, January 13–14, 1931; Fujisaki, *Taiwan no banzoku*, 614–16.
71. Higashiyama Kyoko, "Taiwan ryōyūki ni okeru tai-Genjūmin seisaku: Fukahori Yasuichirō tankentai to Nagano Yoshitora ikensho kara no ikkō satsu," *Shakai kagaku kenkyū* 32, no. 2 (2012): 283–86.
72. "Puli-sha shishō-chō hokuban junshi heiko Fukahori Tai'i ichigyō sōnan ibutsu hakken hōkoku," *Taiwan sōtokufu kōbun ruisan*, 4627-ce, 2-wen, 1900–05–01.
73. "Hokuban daishū-chō no shukushi," *Taiwan kyōkai kaihō* 1 (1898): 102; "Hokuban koō kettō no zu," *Taiwan kyōkai kaihō* 6 (1899): 76–77.
74. Inō, "Juntai," 7.
75. Xia Shengli, et al., *Hyakunen Cangsang: Dogura Ryūjirō to Taihoku Kameyama suiryoku hatsudenjo*, trans. and ed. Dogura Masao and Dogura Nobuko (Sakurai-shi: Dogura Masao, 2006).
76. "Seiban no raisha," *Taiwan nichinichi shinpō*, January 30, 1903.
77. "Jiku Shō Min yori seiban," *Taiwan sōtokufu kōbun ruisan*, 4534-ce, 2-wen, 1897–07–01.
78. Torii Ryūzō, "Taiwan chūō sanmyaku no ōdan," *Taiyō* 7, no. 9 (August 5, 1901): 131–32; Inō, "Juntai," 70–71.
79. Torii Ryūzō, "Keimenban joshi no tōkei," 555–56; "Horisha hōmen nite chōsaseshi jinruigakuteki jikō," 525–29; "Taiwan Horisha [Musha] ban [tōbu yūgeimenban] no shinwa," in *Torii Ryūzō zenshū* 11 (Tokyo: Asahi shinbun, 1976), 557–58.
80. Inō, *Riban shikō*, 148–49.
81. *KJS* 1: 22–23.
82. *KJS* 1: 78, 82–97.
83. "Saitō bunkonsho shuji no kiso chihō shucchō," *Yomiuri shinbun*, August 20, 1897, 3.
84. Inō, *Riban shikō*, 105.
85. Inō, *Riban shikō*, 45.
86. Mio Yūko, "'Bango hensan hōshin' kara mita Nihon tōchi shoki ni okeru Taiwan Genjūmingo chōsa," *Nihon Taiwan gakkaihō* 11 (2009): 157–69.
87. Inō, *Riban shikō*, 96–97; *TSK* 5: 915.
88. Kitamura, *Nihon shokuminchika*, 176–77.
89. Inō, *Riban shikō*, 504–55; *TSK* 5: 923–24.

90. At the time of this writing, there are sixteen officially recognized indigenous groups in Taiwan. P. Kerim Friedman has termed the proliferation of localism the "hegemony of the local" and refers to these subgeobodies as "fractal." His larger argument is that redefinition of "locality" in Taiwan along ethnic lines within the population of non-Mainlanders has diffused anti-GMD nationalism by atomizing locality to the point where it becomes harmless in terms of national-scale political mobilization. Friedman asserts that such "fractal recursivity" has its origin in the Japanese colonial period. Friedman, "The Hegemony of the Local."

91. Inō, *Riban shikō*, 707–9.
92. Inō, *Riban shikō*, 455–56.
93. Inō, *Riban shikō*, 457.
94. Zheng Anxi, *Rizhi shiqi fandi aiyong xiande tuijin yubian qian (1895–1920)* (PhD diss., National Cheng-chi University [Taipei], 2011).
95. "Nantō-chō keibu-ho Itō Eitarō banjin tōbatsu ni kanshi shōyo," *Taiwan sōtokufu kōbun ruisan*, 4938-ce/7-wen, 1906–04–01.
96. For a description of the guardline, its staffing, and its movements, see chapter 2.
97. Inō, *Riban shikō*, 533–34.
98. Watanabe Sei, "Musha sōjō no shinsō o aku hitotsu no kagi! 'Seiban Kondō' shi no hansei o monogataru (nijū-ichi)," *Taiwan nichinichi shinpō*, February 2, 1931, 5.
99. Watanabe Sei, "Musha sōjō no shinsō o aku hitotsu no kagi! 'Seiban Kondō' shi no hansei o monogataru (nijū-ni)," *Taiwan nichinichi shinpō*, February 3, 1931, 5.
100. Watanabe Sei, "Musha sōjō no shinsō o aku hitotsu no kagi! 'Seiban Kondō' shi no hansei o monogataru (nijū-san)," *Taiwan nichinichi shinpō*, February 5, 1931, 5.
101. Inō, *Riban shikō*, 638–39; Deng Xianyang, *Kōnichi Musha jiken o meguru hitobito*, ed. Shimomura Sakujirō, trans. Uozumi Etsuko (Ōsaka: Nihon kikanshi shuppan sentaa, 2001), 20.
102. Aui Heppaha, *Shōgen Musha jiken: Taiwan sanchijin no kōnichi hōki*, ed. Xu Jielin (Tokyo: Sōfūkan, 1985), 179–80.
103. Watanabe Sei, "Musha sōjō no shinsō o aku hitotsu no kagi! 'Seiban Kondō' shi no hansei o monogataru (nijū-kyū)," *Taiwan nichinichi shinpō*, February 15, 1931, 5; "Kanyū genya kashiwatasu kyoka (Kondō Katsusaburō)," *Taiwan sōtokufu kōbun ruisan*, 6821-ce/6-wen.
104. Igarashi Ishimatsu, *Musha jiken jikki* (Puli: Taiwan keisei shinpōsha Hori shikyoku, 1931), 118–21.
105. Yamabe, *Gendaishi shiryō*, 694.
106. Watanabe Sei, "Musha sōjō no shinsō o aku hitotsu no kagi! 'Seiban Kondō' shi no hansei o monogataru (nijū-hachi)," *Taiwan nichinichi shinpō*, February 10, 1931, 5.
107. Paul D. Barclay, "'They Have for the Coast Dwellers a Traditional Hatred': Governing Igorots in Northern Luzon and Central Taiwan, 1895–1915," in *The American Colonial State in the Philippines: Global Perspectives*, ed. Julian Go and Anne Foster (Durham, NC: Duke University Press, 2003), 232.
108. Hayashi Eidai, *Taiwan hitsuwa: Musha no hanran, minshūgawa no shōgen* (Tokyo: Shinhyōron, 2002), 43–45, 103.
109. Yanagimoto Michihiko, *Taiwan Musha ni ikiru* (Tokyo: Gendai shokan, 1996), 39; Hayashi, *Taiwan hitsuwa*, 56–57.
110. Yanagimoto, *Taiwan Musha*, 43–47; Hayashi, *Taiwan hitsuwa*, 57–58.

111. Mikami Tamotsu, *Taiwan Musha jiken no konjaku: hisan na jiken to sono uramen shi* (Chigasaki, Kanazawa: self-published, 1984), 110–11.

112. Hayashi, *Taiwan hitsuwa*, 84.

113. Taiwan sōtokufu, "Musha jikenshi," in *Taiwan Musha hōki jiken: kenkyū to shiryō*, ed. Tai Kuo-hui (Tokyo: Shasōshi kaisha, 1981), 374.

114. Mikami, *Taiwan Musha jiken*, 108.

115. Hayashi, *Taiwan hitsuwa*, 64.

116. Taiwan sōtokufu, "Musha jikenshi," 375; Mikami, *Taiwan Musha jiken*, 109–10; Yamabe, *Gendaishi shiryō*, 614–15.

117. Chiang Yu-lan, "Japanese Policies Toward the Formosan Aborigines: The Wu-she Incident of 1930" (MA thesis, University of Oklahoma, 1974), 30.

118. Hayashi, *Taiwan hitsuwa*, 51.

119. E. Patricia Tsurumi, *Japanese Colonial Education in Taiwan, 1895–1945* (Cambridge: Harvard University Press, 1977), 16.

120. Edward H. House, *The Japanese Expedition to Formosa* (Tokyo, 1875), 64; "Letter from Douglas Cassel to Charles LeGendre," in *Foreign Adventurers and the Aborigines of Southern Taiwan, 1867–1874*, ed. Robert Eskildsen (Taipei: Institute of Taiwan History, Academia Sinica, 2005), 206.

121. Zhuang Yongming, *Taiwan fang qing song 5: Taiwan yuan zhu min* (Hong Kong: Yuan-Liou Publishing Co., 2001), 83–90; Abe Akiyoshi, *Taiwan chimei kenkyū* (Taipei: Bango kenkyūkai, 1937), 283–84; Matsuda Yoshirō, *Taiwan Genjūmin no Nihongo kyōiku* (Kōyō shobō, 2004), 8.

122. Miyaguni Fumio, *Taiwan sōnan jiken* (Naha: Naha Shuppansha, 1998), 311.

123. Inō Kanori, "Ryōtaigo no riban (shōzen)," *Tōyō jihō* (February 1912): 42–43; Suzuki Sakutarō, *Taiwan no banzoku kenkyū* (Taipei: Taiwan shiseki kankōkai, 1932; repr., Taipei: Southern Materials Center, 1988), 512.

124. Rokkoki Shōgorō, "Taitōshō kannai shisatsu fukumeisho," *Zhongguo fangzhi congshu: Taiwandiqu*, no. 311 (Taipei: Chengwen, 1984), n.p.; Inō Kanori, "Langqiao no Daibanmoku Pan Bunketsu," *Taiwan kyōkai kaihō* 88 (1906): 21–22; Sagara Nagatsuna, "Taitō fukin banjin kijun kōshun shutchōjo hōkoku," in *Taiwan sōtokufu banzoku jijō kōbun ruisan genbun*, vol. 1, ed. Huang Liyun (Museum of Ethnology, Academia Sinica, Nankang, Taipei, Taiwan), n.p.

125. Takekoshi Yosaburō, *Japanese Rule in Formosa*, trans. George Braithwaite (London, New York, Bombay, and Calcutta: Longmans, Green, 1907), 93.

126. Sagara, "Taitō fukin," n.p.

127. Matsuda Yoshirō, *Taiwan Genjūmin*, 42.

128. Sagara, "Taitō fukin," n.p.; Inō, *Riban shikō*, 157.

129. "Taiwanjin jokun," *Tokyo Asahi shinbun*, December 18, 1897, 2.

130. Inō, *Riban shikō*, 157–58; Inō, "Langqiao no Daibanmoku," 21–22.

131. Suzuki, *Taiwan no banzoku kenkyū*, 512–13.

132. Kitamura, *Nihon shokuminchika*, 69–72.

133. Byron K. Marshall, *Learning to Be Modern: Japanese Political Discourse on Education* (Boulder, CO: Westview Press, 1994), 47–49; Leonard H. D. Gordon, *Confrontation over Taiwan: Nineteenth-Century China and the Powers* (Lanham, MD: Lexington Books, 2007), 68.

134. Kitamura, *Nihon shokuminchika*, 68.
135. Xu, "Qing modao."
136. Inō, "Juntai," 118–19.
137. Inō Kanori and Awano Dennojō, *Taiwan banjin jijō* (Taipei: Taiwan sōtokufu minseibu bunshoka, 1900), 222.
138. Jun'eki Taiwan Genjūmin kenkyūkai, ed., *Inō Kanori shozō Taiwan Genjūmin shashinshū* (Taipei: Jun'eki Taiwan Genjūmin hakubutsukan, 1999), 183–84.
139. Inō, *Riban shikō*, 326–32.
140. Xu, "Qing modao," 15.
141. Taiwan sōtokufu keimukyoku, ed., *Takasagozoku chōsasho*, vol. 3 (Taipei: Taiwan sōtokufu keimukyoku, 1937), 11.
142. Shao-hua Liu and Shu-min Huang, "The Damming of Mudan Creek," in *Environment, Modernization and Development in East Asia: Perspectives from Environmental History*, ed. Ts'ui-jung Liu and James Beattie (London: Palgrave Macmillan, 2016), 120–21.
143. Matsuda Yoshirō, *Taiwan Genjūmin*, 11.
144. Tsurumi, *Japanese Colonial Education*, 18.
145. Department of Educational Affairs of the Government-General of Formosa, Japan, ed., *A Review of Educational Work in Formosa 1916*, in Hattori Hitsuji, ed., *Nihon shokuminchi kyōiku seisaku shiryō shūsei (Taiwan-hen) dai ikkan* (Tokyo: Ryūkei shosha, 2007), 38.
146. Kitamura, *Nihon shokuminchika*, 70; Matsuda Yoshirō, *Taiwan Genjūmin*, 47–49.
147. Department of Educational Affairs, *Review of Educational Work*, 39.
148. In 1905, the Tuilasok institute was incorporated into the nearby Mantsui Common School; Kuskus, on the other hand, opened an Aborigine Common School that same month. Kitamura, *Nihon shokuminchika*, 70.
149. Taiwan sōtokufu kanbō bunsho-ka, *The Progress of Taiwan (Formosa) for Ten Years, 1895–1904* (Taipei: Taiwan sōtokufu kanbō bunsho-ka, 1906), 43.
150. Kitamura, *Nihon shokuminchika*, 277, 291.
151. Eika Tai, "The Assimilationist Policy and the Aborigines in Taiwan Under Japanese Rule," *Current Politics and Economics of Asia* 6, no. 4 (1999): 277.
152. Tai, "Assimilationist Policy," 279–80.
153. Kitamura, *Nihon shokuminchika*, 112–14; Kondō, *Sōryokusen*, 292.
154. Inō, *Riban shikō*, 849–50.
155. Ōe Shinobu, "Shokuminchi sensō to sōtokufu no seiritsu," in *Iwanami kōza: Kindai Nihon to shokuminchi, Teikoku tōji no kōkoku*, vol. 2 (Tokyo: Iwanami Shoten, 1992), 3–10.
156. This text is reproduced in the original Japanese in Matsuda Yoshirō, *Taiwan Genjūmin*, 53 (translation by author).
157. Sakano Tōru, *Teikoku Nihon to jinruigakusha, 1884–1952* (Tokyo: Keishobo, 2005).
158. Tsurumi, *Japanese Colonial Education*, 20–21.
159. Inō, *Taiwan bansei-shi*, 52; Xu, "Qing modao," 36.
160. Matsuda Yoshirō, *Taiwan Genjūmin*, 53–54.
161. Kitamura, *Nihon shokuminchika*, 114.
162. Hayashi, *Taiwan hitsuwa*, 64.
163. Matsuda Yoshirō, *Taiwan Genjūmin*, 55.

164. *Banjin dokuhon maki san* (Taipei: Taiwan sōtokufu, 1916), 45–47; *Banjin dokuhon maki yon* (Taipei: Taiwan sōtokufu, 1917), 20, 34. All four volumes are reprinted in Li Rongzhi and Chen Shuying, ed., *Banjin dokuhon* (Fukushima: Kurume Daigaku, 2001).
165. Tai, "Assimilationist Policy," 285.
166. Kitamura, *Nihon shokuminchika*, 238–43.
167. Uno Toshiharu, "Taiwan ni okeru 'banjin' no kyōiku," in *Taiwan Musha hōki jiken kenkyū to shiryō*, ed. Tai Kuo-hui (Tokyo: Shakai shisōsha, 1981), 44–45.
168. Chou Wan-yao, trans. Carole Plackitt and Tim Casey, *A New Illustrated History of Taiwan* (Taipei: SMC Publishing Co., 2015), 185–86; Deng Xiangyang, *Kōnichi Musha jiken no rekishi,* trans. Shimomura Sakujirō and Uozumi Etsuko (Osaka: Nihon kikanshi shuppan sentaa, 2000), 69–71.
169. Matsuda Yoshirō, "Senjūmin," 160.
170. Matsuda Yoshirō, "Taiwan senjūmin," 160; Kitamura, *Nihon shokuminchika*, 250–52.
171. Kondō, *Sōryokusen,* 291–93.
172. Schools under regular administration were paid for out of local tax moneys and student fees. Kitamura, *Nihon shokuminchika,* 238; Tsurumi, *Japanese Colonial Education,* 240–41.
173. Kondō, *Sōryokusen,* 295.
174. Kitamura, *Nihon shokuminchika,* 174–78.
175. The composition and functions of the youth corps are described in Aoki Setsuzō, *Haruka naru toki Taiwan: Senjūmin shakai ni ikita aru Nihonjin keisatsukan no kiroku* (Osaka: Kansai tosho shuppan, 2001), 128–34; Matsuda Yoshirō, *Taiwan Genjūmin no shakai teki kyōiku jigyō* (Tokyo: Kōyōsho, 2011), 91–120; Kondō, *Sōryokusen,* 294–305; Matsuoka, *Taiwan Genjūmin,* 82–85.
176. Kondō, *Sōryokusen,* 262–300; Matsuda Kyōko, *Teikoku,* 190–92.
177. Leo T. S. Ching, "Savage Construction and Civility Making: Japanese Colonialism and Taiwanese Aboriginal Representation," *Positions: East Asia Cultures Critique* 8, no. 3 (2000): 810–15.
178. U.S. Consul Gerald Warner and his wife, Rella, toured the main sites on the indigenous ethnic-tourism route in 1939, just after Sayon's death. Several of Warner's snapshots at inns and on trails suggest that Sayon was not exceptional as a female burden-carrier for hire. See http://digital.lafayette.edu/collections/eastasia/warner-negs-taiwan/gr0277.
179. Tai, "Assimilationist Policy," 273.
180. Tai, "Assimilationist Policy," 281.
181. Fujino Yohei, "Nihon tōchika Taiwan ni okeru tainichi kanjō: Kanzoku to Genjūmin no hikaku kara," *Minzoku bunka kenkyū* 5 (2004): 52–54; Wu Micha, ed., *Taiwan-shi kojiten,* trans. Yokosawa Yasuo (Tokyo: Chūgoku shoten, 2007), 164.
182. Wu Micha referred to this event as the watershed that divided Han resistance into an earlier period of armed uprisings and a later period of nonviolent sociopolitical movements, *Taiwan-shi,* 173.
183. Paul R. Katz, *When Valleys Turned Blood Red: The Ta-pa-ni Incident in Colonial Taiwan* (Honolulu: University of Hawai'i Press, 2005).
184. Paul R. Katz, "Governmentality and Its Consequences in Colonial Taiwan," *Journal of Asian Studies* 64, no. 2 (2005): 389.

185. Ts'ai, "Shaping Administration in Colonial Taiwan," in *Taiwan under Japanese Colonial Rule, 1895–1945: History, Culture, Memory*, ed. Liao Ping-hui and David Der-wei Wang (New York: Columbia University Press, 2006), 97–98.

186. Ming-cheng M. Lo, *Doctors within Borders: Profession, Ethnicity, and Modernity in Colonial Taiwan* (Berkeley: University of California Press, 2002), 37.

187. Wang Taysheng, *Legal Reform in Taiwan under Japanese Colonial Rule, 1895–1945: The Reception of Western Law* (Seattle and London: University of Washington Press, 2000).

CHAPTER 3. TANGLED UP IN RED

1. James Davidson, *The Island of Formosa Past and Present* (Yokohama: Japan Times Newspaper Company, 1903), 173–74.

2. James L. Hevia, *English Lessons: The Pedagogy of Imperialism in Nineteenth-Century China* (Durham, NC, 2003), 31–48; Robert Gardella, "From Treaty Ports to Provincial Status, 1860–1894," in *Taiwan: A New History*, ed. Murray A. Rubinstein (Armonk, NY: M. E. Sharpe, 1999), 167.

3. Yŏnghŏ Chŏe, "Yanagi Muneyoshi and the Kwanghwa Gate in Seoul, Korea," in *Sources of Japanese Tradition*, 2nd ed., vol. 2, abridged pt. 2, ed. Wm. Theodore de Bary, Carol Gluck, and Arthur E. Tiedemann, ed. (New York: Columbia University Press, 2006), 144–47; Yuko Kikuchi, "Refracted Colonial Modernity: Vernacularism in the Development of Modern Taiwanese Crafts," in *Refracted Modernity: Visual Culture and Identity in Colonial Taiwan*, Yuko Kikuchi, ed. (Honolulu: University of Hawai'i Press, 2007), 222–29.

4. C. W. LeGendre, *Reports on Amoy and the Island of Formosa* (Washington, DC: Government Printing Office, 1871), 33.

5. Thomas Francis Hughes, "Visit to Tok-e-Tok, Chief of the Eighteen Tribes, Southern Formosa," in *Aborigines of South Taiwan in the 1880s*, ed. Glen Dudbridge (Taipei: Shung Ye Museum of Formosan Aborigines and Institute of Taiwan History, Academia Sinica), 32.

6. Charles W. LeGendre, *Notes of Travel in Formosa*, ed. D. L. Fix and J. Shufelt (Tainan: National Museum of Taiwan History, 2012), 267–69.

7. Douglas Fix, "The Changing Contours of Lived Communities on the Hengchun Peninsula,1850–1874," *Guojia yu yuanzhumin: Ya-Tai diqu zuqun lishi yanjiu*, ed. Hong Liwan (Taipei: Institute of Taiwan History, Academia Sinica, 2009), 246–47.

8. Edward H. House, *The Japanese Expedition to Formosa* (Tokyo, 1875), 143.

9. House, *Japanese Expedition*, 143.

10. House, *Japanese Expedition*, 141.

11. "Letter from Douglas Cassel to Charles LeGendre," in *Foreign Adventurers and the Aborigines of Southern Taiwan, 1867–1874*, ed. Robert Eskildsen (Taipei: Institute of Taiwan History, Academia Sinica, 2005), 205, 209.

12. Tania Murray Li, "Indigeneity, Capitalism, and the Management of Dispossession," *Current Anthropology* 51, no. 3 (June 2010): 385–414, draws on several examples from colonized Southeast Asia to demonstrate how outsiders' estimations of indigenous economic innocence, incompetence, or corporatism became reified in the form of separate legal regimes that shielded them from market forces.

13. Kamimura Tōru, "Parijarijao shuchō-koku' dai shuchō no zōyo kōkan keitai no tenkei to sono henkei to kussetsu tentō (zenpen): 1867-nen kara 1872-nen made no Taiwan

nanbu kōshun chihō no rekishi jinruigakuteki kōsatsu," *Taiwan Genjūmin kenkyū* 18 (2014): 38–74.

14. Antonio C. Tavares, "The Japanese Colonial State and the Dissolution of the Late Imperial Frontier Economy in Taiwan, 1886–1909," *Journal of Asian Studies* 64, no. 2 (2005): 361–85.

15. Kondō Masami, "Taiwan sōtokufu no riban taisei to Musha Jiken," *Iwanami kōza: Kindai Nihon to shokuminchi, Teikoku tōji no kōkoku*, vol. 2 (Tokyo: Iwanami Shoten, 1992), 43–44; Melissa L. Meyer, "'We Can Not Get a Living as We Used To': Dispossession and the White Earth Anishinaabeg, 1889–1920," *American Historical Review* 96, no. 2 (1991): 384.

16. Scott Simon, "Making Natives: Japan and the Creation of Indigenous Formosa," in *Japanese Taiwan: Colonial Rule and Its Contested Legacy*, ed. Andrew D. Morris (London: Bloomsbury Press, 2015), 75–92.

17. Hu Chia-yu, "Taiwanese Aboriginal Art and Artifacts: Entangled Images of Colonization and Modernization," in *Refracted Modernity: Visual Culture and Identity in Colonial Taiwan*, ed. Kikuchi, 201.

18. Yamaji Katsuhiko, *Taiwan Taiyaru-zoku no hyaku-nen: Hyōryū suru dentō, dakō suru kindai, datsu shokuminchika e no michinori* (Tokyo: Fūkyosha, 2011), 402–5; Hu, "Taiwanese," 201–2; Kikuchi, "Refracted Colonial Modernity," 218–22; Tierney, *Tropics of Savagery: The Culture of Japanese Empire in Comparative Frame* (Berkeley: University of California Press, 2010), 64–65.

19. Wakabayashi Masahiro, "A Perspective on Studies of Taiwanese Political History: Reconsidering the Postwar Japanese Historiography of Japanese Colonial Rule in Taiwan," in Liao Ping-hui and David Der-wei Wang, eds., *Taiwan under Japanese Colonial Rule, 1895–1945* (New York: Columbia University Press, 2006), 19–36.

20. Nicholas Thomas, *Entangled Objects: Exchange, Material Culture, and Colonialism in the Pacific* (Cambridge: Harvard University Press, 1991).

21. John L. Comaroff and Jean Comaroff, *Ethnicity, Inc.* (Chicago: University of Chicago Press, 2009).

22. Kamimura Tōru, "'Kōshun shitaban' shuchōsei no seikaku: mae—Nihon ryōyūki Taiwan nanbu sanchi no kosumorojii no henbyō," *Nanpō bunka* 24 (1997): 101–22.

23. Henrietta Harrison, "Clothing and Power on the Periphery of Empire: The Costumes of the Indigenous People of Taiwan," *Positions* 11, no. 2 (2003): 337.

24. Mami Yoshimura, "Weaving and Identity of the Atayal in Wulai, Taiwan" (master's thesis, University of Waterloo, 2007), 166–67; Tamoto Haruna, "'Genjūmin kōgei' no hyōshō to seisaku o meguru ikkōsatsu: Taiwan Genjūmin no orimono fukkō o jirei ni," *Shigaku (Mita shi gakkai)* 81, no. 3 (2012): 97, 104; Yamaji, *Taiwan Taiyaru-zoku no hyaku-nen*, 402–5.

25. Hu, "Taiwanese," 207–11.

26. P. Kerim Friedman, "The Hegemony of the Local: Taiwanese Multiculturalism and Indigenous Identity Politics," *boundary 2* (forthcoming); Haidy Geismar, *Treasured Possessions: Indigenous Interventions into Cultural and Intellectual Property* (Durham and London: Duke University Press), 2013; Tomoto, "Genjūmin kōgei," 92; Hu, "Taiwanese," 210–11.

27. Hu Chia-yu, "Embodied Memories and Enacted Ritual Materials: Possessing the Past in Making and Remaking Saisiyat Identity in Taiwan," (PhD diss., University College London, 2006), 233–238.

28. Laurence G. Thompson, "The Earliest Chinese Eyewitness Accounts of the Formosan Aborigines," *Monumenta Serica* 23 (1964): 177–78.
29. Leonard Blussé, Natalie Everts, and Evelien French, eds., *The Formosan Encounter: Notes on Formosa's Aboriginal Society: A Selection of Documents from Dutch Archival Sources* (Taipei: Shung Ye Museum of Formosan Aborigines, 1999), 1.
30. Blussé, Everts, and French, *Formosan Encounter,* 29 (emphasis added).
31. Wayne C. McWilliams, "East Meets East: The Soejima Mission to China, 1873," *Monumentica Nipponica* 30, no. 3 (1975): 237–75; Mizuno Jun, "Seiban Shiki," in *Tairo Mizuno Jun Sensei,* ed. Tairokai (Nagoya: Tairokai, 1930), 188.
32. Mizuno, "Seibanki," 188–93.
33. George Taylor, "A Ramble through Formosa," in *Aborigines of South Taiwan in the 1880s: Papers by George Taylor,* ed. Glen Dudbridge (Taipei: Shung Ye Museum of Formosan Aborigines and Institute of Taiwan History, Academia Sinica, 1999), 122–23.
34. Ueno Sen'ichi, "Taiwan shima jissen roku," *Tokyo chigaku kyōkai hōkoku* 13, no. 11 (1892): 21–48; Sanbō Honbu, ed., *Taiwan shi* (Hiroshima: Sanbō honbu, 1895).
35. *Tokyo Asahi shinbun,* September 28, 1895; *Fūzoku gahō,* November 28, 1895.
36. Hashiguchi Bunzō, "Dakekan chihō seiban kaiken no tame shucchō jihōkoku," *Taiwan sōtokufu banzoku jijō kōbun ruisan genbun,* vol. 1, ed. Huang Liyun (Taipei: Museum of Ethnology, Academia Sinica); Hashiguchi Bunzō, "Taiwan jijō," *Tokyo chigaku kyōkai hōkoku* 17, no. 3 (1895): 313–18.
37. Hashiguchi, "Taiwan jijō," 313–14.
38. Hashiguchi Bunzō, "Banmin ni shinamono keiyo no gi hōkoku," in *Taiwan sōtokufu banzoku jijō kōbun ruisan genbun,* vol. 1, ed. Huang Liyun (Taipei: Museum of Ethnology, Academia Sinica).
39. Inō Kanori, ed., *Riban shikō dai ikkan* (Taipei: Taiwan sōtokufu keisatsu honsho, 1918; repr., Taipei: Southern Materials Center, 1995), 14–15.
40. "Taiwan tsūshin," *Yomiuri shinbun,* September 30, 1895.
41. *Taiwan sangyō ryakushi* (Tokyo: Nōshōmu daijin kanbō bunsho-ka, 1895), 40–41, 52–53.
42. *Taiwan sōtokufu minseikyoku shokusanbu hōbun dai ikken dai ni satsu* (Tokyo: Taiwan sōtokufu minseikyoku shokusanbu, 1896), 15.
43. Taihoku-shū, ed., *Taihoku-shū ribanshi* (Taipei: Taihoku-shū keimubu, 1924), 141.
44. Taihoku-shū, *Taihoku-shū ribanshi,* 172.
45. Iriye Takeshi and Hashimoto Shigeru, "Taiwan banchi zatsuzoku," *Fūzoku gahō* 130 (1896): 29–30.
46. "Hokuban no sensō," *Taiwan nichinichi shinpō,* May 10, 1898, 5.
47. Paul D. Barclay, "Bansan kōekijo ni okeru 'banchi' no shōgyōka to chitsujoka," *Taiwan Genjūmin kenkyū* 9 (2005): 93–96.
48. Inō, *Riban shikō,* 102.
49. Taihoku-shū, *Taihoku-shū ribanshi,* 304–10.
50. Tavares, "Japanese Colonial State," 361–85.
51. Inō, *Riban shikō,* 163.
52. Taihoku-shū, *Taihoku-shū ribanshi,* 248.
53. Tavares, "Japanese Colonial State," 361–85.
54. Kondō, "Taiwan," 38.

55. Inō, *Riban shikō*, 408–10.
56. Inō, *Riban shikō*, 457, 465.
57. Inō, *Riban shikō*, 723–25.
58. Inoguchi Yasuyoshi, ed., *Riban shikō dai nikan* (Taipei: Taiwan Sōtokufu Keimukyoku, 1921), 63; Uesugi Mitsuhiko, "'Takasagozoku' e no jusan seisaku: kōeki seisaku o chūshin to shite," *Takachihō ronsō* 26, no. 4 (1992): 59.
59. Taiwan sōtokufu, ed., *Riban gaiyō* (Taihoku: Taiwan sōtokufu minseibu banmu honsho, 1912), 55–56.
60. Marui Keijirō, *Buban ni kansuru ikensho, Bando Kyōiku Ikensho* (Taipei: Banmu honsho, 1914), 71.
61. Inoguchi, 531.
62. Mori Ushinosuke, "Taiwan shinrin to banjin no kankei ni tsuite," *Taiwan jihō* 89 (1917): 9–19.
63. Masuya Sei, "Banjin no keizai kannen to kanshū," *Riban no tomo*, October 1, 1935, 8–9.
64. From 1998 through 2015, I visited roughly fifteen museums or theme parks that feature biographical information about these men, or feature the artifacts they collected or photographs they produced, in Pingdong, Tainan, Fuxing, Nantou, Hengchun, Wulai, and several sites in Taipei.
65. Inō Kanori, "Taiwan tsūshin dai rokkai," *Tokyo jinruigakkai zasshi* 11, no. 121 (1896): 274–76.
66. Inō, "Taiwan tsūshin dai rokkai," 301–13.
67. Hu, "Taiwanese," 200–211.
68. Jiang Guizhen, *Zaixian chuangtong de shijian, Wulai Taiyazu de wenhua tuxiang* (Taipei: National Museum of History, 2010), 96–106.
69. Li Tsu-ning et al., *The Story of Collection in a Century: National Taiwan Museum Centennial Edition*, trans. Christopher Findler and Ruby Li (Taipei: National Taiwan Museum, 2009), 49–53.
70. Monbushō, ed., *Jinjō shōgaku chiri ken ni: jidō yō* (Tokyo: Monbushō, 1910), 21; Tanaka Hirokichi, *Shin kyōkasho kiga no kaisetu oyobi toriatsukai hō: shūshin chiri rekishi no bu* (Tokyo: Kōbundō, 1911), 102.
71. Satō Haruo, "Wushe," in *Nihon tōchiki Taiwan bunka: Nihonjin sakka hinshū, bekkan (Naichi sakka)*, ed. Kawahara Iwao (Tokyo: Rokuin shobō, 1998), 29.
72. "Chinki na bussan ni gokyō mo fukashi," *Tokyo Asahi shinbun*, April 18, 1923, 2.
73. "Chichibunomiya denka no Taiwan Onari," *Taiwan jihō* (July 1925): 12; "Kappanzan bansha ni onari no Asakanomiya denka," *Taiwan jihō* (December 1927): frontispiece.
74. Ozaki Hotsuma, "Jūyō bijutsu no hozon to Taiwan no Banzokuhin," *Riban no tomo*, April 1, 1933, 2.
75. E. Taylor Atkins, *Primitive Selves: Koreana in the Japanese Colonial Gaze, 1910–1945* (Berkeley: University of California Press, 2010), 124.
76. "Banjin banchi ni kansuru jimu oyobi jōkyō," *Taiwan zongdu fu gongwen leizuan shuwei hua dang'an*, July 1, 1900, 4625-5-3.
77. Harrison Forman, "Diary: Japan, Taiwan, Korea [1938]," Harrison Forman Papers, box 1, folder 7, item 6. Special Collections and University Archives, University of Oregon Libraries.

78. Harrison Forman, letter to the editor, *Natural History* 47, no. 4 (1941): 182–83.

79. Michael Rudolph, *Ritual Performances as Authenticating Practices: Cultural Representations of Taiwan's Aborigines in Times of Political Change* (New Brunswick, NJ: Transaction Publishers, 2008), 7.

80. Scott Simon, *Sadyaq Balae!: L'Autochthonie Formosan dans tous ses états* (Quebec City: Les Presses de L'Université Laval, 2012), 89–90; Rudolph, *Ritual Performances*, 107–08, 117.

81. Rudolph, *Ritual Performances*, 6–7, 106; Simon, *Sadyaq Balae!*, 82–84; Ku Kun-hui, "Rights to Recognition: Minorities and Indigenous Politics in Emerging Taiwan Nationalism," in *Taiwan Since Martial Law: Society, Culture, Politics, Economy*, ed. David Blundell (Taipei: Shung Ye Museum of Formosan Aborigines, 2012), 93.

82. Rudolph, *Ritual Performances*, 114–27; Simon, *Sadyaq Balae!*, 14–16, 228–33; Mitsuda Yayoi, "First Case of the New Recognition System: The Survival Strategies of the Thao," in *Taiwan Since Martial Law: Society, Culture, Politics, Economy*, 169–70.

83. Hu, "Embodied Memories," 248.

84. Shahid Amin, *Event, Metaphor, Memory: Chauri Chaura, 1922–1992* (Berkeley: University of California Press, 1995); Gyan Prakash, *Mumbai Fables* (Princeton: Princeton University Press, 2010).

85. Simon, *Sadyaq Balae!*, 28–33; "Gov't officially recognizes two more aboriginal tribes," *China Post*, June 27, 2014, accessed January 8, 2015, http://www.chinapost.com.tw/taiwan/national/national-news/2014/06/27/411066/Govt-officially.htm.

86. Rudolph, *Ritual Performances*, 107–15; Mitsuda, "First Case," 170.

87. Arif Dirlik, *The Postcolonial Aura: Third World Criticism in the Age of Global Capitalism* (Boulder, CO: Westview Press, 1997), 227.

88. James Clifford, "Identity in Mashpee," in *The Predicament of Culture: Twentieth-Century Ethnography, Literature, and Art*, ed. James Clifford (Cambridge: Harvard University Press, 1988), 277–348.

89. Hsiau A-chin, *Contemporary Taiwanese Cultural Nationalism* (London: Routledge, 2000), 162–64; Rudolph, *Ritual Performances*, 55–59; Ku, "Rights to Recognition," 104, 122.

90. Simon, *Sadyaq Balae!*, 220–25.

91. Rudolph, *Ritual Performances*, 60–62.

92. Hu, "Embodied Memories," 10.

CHAPTER 4. THE GEOBODIES WITHIN A GEOBODY

1. Achille Mbembe, "Necropolitics," trans. Libby Meintjes, *Public Culture* 15, no. 1 (2003): 26.

2. Nicholas Thomas, *Colonialism's Culture: Anthropology, Travel, and Government* (Princeton: Princeton University Press, 1994), 71–72.

3. Inō Kanori, "Shinajin no Taiwan doban ni kansuru jinshu teki kansatsu," *Taiwan kanshū kiji* 5, no. 8 (August 1905): 52.

4. Inō, "Shinajin no Taiwan," 54.

5. Thomas, *Colonialism's Culture*, 71–72.

6. The dotted dividing line on the map (published in 1895) in figure 32 bifurcates Taiwan into the *banchi* (savage lands) and the unmarked rest of Taiwan; Akishika Kenkitsu, *Taiwan*

shiyō (Tokyo: Seibidō, 1895), n.p. Charles LeGendre's 1870 map has a similar bifurcating line; it is annotated with the characters for "savage border lands" *(doban chikai),* dividing the island between zones occupied by "Aborigines" and "the portion of the island occupied by Chinese"; LeGendre, *Notes,* 385. Both maps allocate more than half of Taiwan's territory to the non-Chinese, or aborigines.

7. Takeuchi Sadayoshi, *Taiwan* (Taipei: Taiwan nichinichi shinpō, 1914), 620.

8. Sakano Tōru, *Teikoku Nihon to jinruigakusha, 1884–1952* (Tokyo: Keishobo, 2005), 230; Paul D. Barclay, "An Historian Among the Anthropologists: The Inō Kanori Revival and the Legacy of Japanese Colonial Ethnography in Taiwan," *Japanese Studies* 21, no. 2 (September 2001): 117–36.

9. Peter Duus, *The Abacus and the Sword: The Japanese Penetration of Korea, 1895–1910* (Berkeley and Los Angeles: University of California Press, 1995), 424–34; and Robert Eskildsen, "Of Civilization and Savages: The Mimetic Imperialism of Japan's 1874 Expedition to Taiwan," *American Historical Review* 107, no. 2 (2002): 388–418.

10. Patrick Wolfe has recently reenergized the notion that *racism,* as opposed to *racialization,* is a particularly European construct and is ultimately bound up with white imperialism and shifting configurations of white supremacy. See *Traces of History: Elementary Structures of Race* (London and New York: Verso, 2016), 7, 18.

11. W. J. T. Mitchell, *Seeing Through Race* (Cambridge: Harvard University Press, 2012), 34–35.

12. Mitchell, *Seeing Through Race,* 17; Wolfe, *Traces of History,* 101.

13. Ke Zhiming, *Fantou jia: Qing dai Taiwan zuqun zhengzhi yu shufan diquan* (Taipei: Zhongyang yanjiuyuan shehuixue yanjiusuo, 2001); Emma Jinhua Teng, *Taiwan's Imagined Geography: Chinese Colonial Travel Writing and Pictures, 1683–1895* (Cambridge: Harvard University Press, 2004).

14. Michel Foucault, "Two Lectures," in *Culture/Power/History: A Reader in Contemporary Social Theory,* ed. Nicholas B. Dirks, Geoff Eley, and Sherry B. Ortner (Princeton: Princeton University Press, 1994), 213.

15. These terms have extremely pejorative connotations and have been replaced in official and popular discourse with the general term *Yuanzhumin/Genjūmin.*

16. Takigawa Miyotarō, ed., *Shinryōchi Taiwantō* (Tokyo: Kokondō, June 12, 1895), 160–202.

17. Ueno Sen'ichi, "Taiwantō jissen roku," *Tokyo chigaku kyōkai hōkoku* 13, no. 11 (February 1892): 21–48; Sanbō honbu, ed., *Taiwan shi* (Tokyo: January 1895).

18. Sanbō honbu, *Taiwan shi,* 71.

19. Inō Kanori, "Yo no sekishi o nobete sendatsu no kunshi ni uttau," in *Inō Kanori no Taiwan tōsa nikki,* ed. Moriguchi Kazunari (Taipei: Taiwan fūbutsu zasshisha, 1992). Compare Sanbō honbu, *Taiwan shi,* 72–79, and George Taylor, "Formosa: Characteristic Traits of the Island and Its Aboriginal Inhabitants," in *Aborigines of South Taiwan in the 1880s: Papers by George Taylor,* ed. Glen Dudbridge (Taipei: Shung Ye Museum of Formosan Aborigines and Institute of Taiwan History, Academia Sinica, 1999), 154–59. Torii Ryūzō himself, in a short retrospective on this classificatory project, identified Taylor's work as the first widely accepted taxonomy of the island's aborigines; see "Jinruigaku kenkyū, Taiwan no Genjūmin (ichi) joron," in *Torii Ryūzō zenshū,* vol. 5 (Tokyo: Asahi shinbunsha, 1976), 9.

20. Mori Ushinosuke, *Taiwan banzokushi dai ikkan* (Taipei: Rinji Taiwan kyūkan chōsakai, 1917; repr., Taipei: Nanten Shokyoku, 1996), 49–52. According to Mori's accounting, there were 69 households and 389 inhabitants of Jiaobanshan-sha, ca. 1915.

21. Thomas, *Colonialism's Culture*, 71.

22. Hirano Akio, "Taiwan seiban kisatsu no gaikyō," *Taiwan jinruigakkai zasshi* 115 (1895): 6–8.

23. "Seiban no junfuku," *Fūzoku gahō*, November 28, 1895, 17–21.

24. Eskildsen, "Civilization and Savages," 388–418.

25. Satō Denzō, *Chirigaku kyōkasho: chūtō kyōiku, Nihon chizu furoku* (Tokyo: Hakubunkan, 1898), n.p.

26. Taipics.com, "Aboriginal Daily Life—Set 6," accessed January 27, 2017, http://www.taipics.com/abo_daily_life6.php.

27. Kamei Tadaichi, *Teikoku chirigaku kyōkasho* (Tokyo: Sanseidō, 1900), 152.

28. *Shōgaku chiri kansan* (Tokyo: Shūeidō, 1900), 29.

29. Gotō Shinpei, "Formosa Under Japanese Administration," *The Independent* 54, no. 2,796 (July 3, 1902): 1,582.

30. Monbushō, ed., *Shōgaku chirisho kan ni* (Tokyo: Monbushō, 1903), 69.

31. Inō Kanori, "Juntai nichijō," in *Inō Kanori no Taiwan tōsa nikki,* ed. Moriguchi Kazunari (Taipei: Taiwan fūbutsu zasshisha, 1992), 70–73.

32. Karl Theodor Stöpel, *Eine Reise in das Innere der Insel Formosa und die erste Besteigung des Niitakayama (Mount Morrison)* (Buenos Aires: Companñía sud-americana de billetes de banco, 1905), 42.

33. Kamei Tadaichi, *Teikoku shin chiri* (Tokyo: Sanseidō, 1908), 138.

34. James Davidson, *The Island of Formosa Past and Present* (Yokohama: Japan Times Newspaper Company, 1903), 568; Jun'eki Taiwan Genjūmin kenkyūkai, ed., *Inō Kanori shozō Taiwan Genjūmin shashinshū* (Taipei: Jun'eki Taiwan Genjūmin hakubutsukan, 1999), 141.

35. See Lee Ju-ling, "Constructing an Imaginary of Taiwanese Aborigines through Postcards (1895–1945)," in *Translation, History and Arts: New Horizons in Asian Interdisciplinary Humanities Research,* ed. Meng Ji and Ukai Atsuko (London: Cambridge Scholars, 2013), 111–35.

36. Kamei, *Teikoku shin chiri*, 138.

37. Bai In [Inō Kanori], "Kokutei chiri kyōkasho chū Taiwan no bu no sakusen," *Taiwan kanshū kiji* 4, no. 9 (1904): 816–17.

38. Tōno Municipal Museum, ed., *Inō Kanori: kyōdo to Taiwan kenkyū no shōgai* (Tōno, Iwate-ken: Tōno shiritsu hakubutsukan, 1995), 68.

39. Inō, "Yo no sekishi."

40. At the time, Inō was an employee of the Records Office at a salary of twenty yen per month.

41. Moriguchi, *Inō Kanori*, 357; Inō Kanori, "Taiwan tsūshin dai nikai," *Tokyo jinruigakkai zasshi* 118 (1896):149–51.

42. Inō, "Taiwan tsūshin dai nikai," 149–54.

43. Inō Kanori, "Taiwan tsūshin dai ikkai," *Tokyo jinrui gakkai zasshi* 117 (1895): 97.

44. Vicente L. Rafael, "White Love: Surveillance and Nationalist Resistance in the U.S. Colonization of the Philippines," in *Cultures of United States Imperialism,* ed. Amy Kaplan and Donald E. Pease (Durham, NC: Duke University Press, 1993), 185–218.

45. Hirano, "Taiwan seiban," 6–8.
46. Inō, "Taiwan tsūshin dai nikai," 153.
47. Inō, "Taiwan tsūshin dai nikai," 152.
48. Inō Kanori, ed., *Taiwan shi,* vol. 1 (1902), 8–14, contains an extensive bibliography of Chinese-language materials on Taiwan known to Japanese officials. In 1904, Inō's translation and compilation of Qing records pertinent to the non-Han areas of Taiwan was published; it continues to be a primary source for historians. Inō Kanori, ed., *Taiwan banseishi* (Taipei: Taiwan sōtokufu minseibu shokusankyoku, 1904).
49. Timothy Y. Tsu, "Japanese Colonialism and the Investigation of Taiwanese 'Old Customs,'" in *Anthropology and Colonialism in Asia and Oceania,* ed. Jan van Bremen and Akitoshi Shimizu (Richmond, Surrey: Curzon Press, 1999), 197–218; Peter Pels, "From Texts to Bodies: Brian Houghton Hodgson and the Emergence of Ethnology in India," in *Anthropology and Colonialism in Asia and Oceania,* ed. Jan van Bremen and Akitoshi Shimizu (Richmond, Surrey: Curzon Press, 1999), 65–92.
50. Inō Kanori, "Seibanfu Ai o itamu," *Tokyo jinruigakkai zasshi* 12, no. 138 (1897): 499–500.
51. Melissa L. Meyer, "'We Can Not Get a Living as We Used To': Dispossession and the White Earth Anishinaabeg, 1889–1920," *American Historical Review* 96, no. 2 (1991): 387.
52. Mori Ushinosuke, *Chūō sanmyaku ōdan tanken hōbun,* 1914, MS 0762/14 (vol. 1), Taipei: National Taiwan Library, Taipei. This manuscript copy of Mori's journal from the Sakuma-campaign years contains several standardized Notes and Queries forms for recording face, eye, nose and teeth shapes, and other physiological traits of individuals. These forms are filled in, without names.
53. Inō Kanori, "Taiwan tsūshin dai yonkai," *Taiwan jinruigakkai zasshi* 11, no. 120 (1896): 224–30.
54. Inō Kanori, "Taiwan tsūshin dai rokkai," *Taiwan jinrui gakkai zasshi* 11, no. 121 (1896): 274.
55. "Jiku-shi no banjin buiku to Koore bansha no kijun," *Tokyo Asahi shinbun,* November 22, 1897, 6.
56. "Hokuban daishū-chō no shukushi," *Taiwan kyōkai kaihō* 1 (1898): 102; Harada Zenshichi [原田善七], "Hokuban ko'o kettō no zu," *Taiwan kyōkai kaihō* 6 (1899): 76–77.
57. Inō, "Juntai," 8, 13.
58. Inō, "Juntai," 9.
59. Hu Chia-yu, "Taiwanese Aboriginal Art and Artifacts: Entangled Images of Colonization and Modernization," in *Refracted Modernity: Visual Culture and Identity in Colonial Taiwan,* ed. Yuko Kikuchi (Honolulu: University of Hawai'i Press, 2007), 198; Hu Jiayu and Yilan Cui, eds., *Taida renlei xuexi yi neng cangpin yanjiu* (Taipei: Guoli Taiwan daxue chuban zhongxin, 1998), 263.
60. *Banjō kenyūkaishi* 1 (August 16, 1898): front matter. Thanks to Hu Chia-yu for sending me an intact copy of this issue.
61. Ishikawa Gen'ichirō, ed., *Taiwan meisho shashinchō* (Taipei: Taiwan shōhōsha, 1899), n.p.
62. Torii Ryūzō used the terms *Yūgeiban* and *Yūgeimenban* to designate Atayal peoples, while Inō Kanori used the term *Atayal.*

63. "Typical head hunter, Formosa," George Grantham Bain Collection, Library of Congress Prints and Photographs Division, Washington, DC, Prints and Photographs Online Catalog, accessed April 3, 2013, http://www.loc.gov/pictures/item/ggb2004002272/.

64. The two grisly Bain News Service photos were used to illustrate the short piece, suggesting that they had been made available to American publishers before that time. "Electricity Used to Capture Head Hunters," *Popular Mechanics*, May 1909, 444, Google Books, accessed on January 9, 2015, https://books.google.co.jp/books?id = mt8DAAAAMBAJ&lpg = PA444&ots = k1snqUUX5J.

65. "Head Hunting Natives and Japanese Police in Group around a Head," "Head Hunters Seated With Their Head, Formosa," and "Skull Shelf of Head Hunter, Formosa," George Grantham Bain Collection, Library of Congress Prints and Photographs Division, Washington, DC, Prints and Photographs Online Catalog, accessed July 23, 2017, http://www.loc.gov/pictures/collection/ggbain/.

66. Nihon Jun'eki Taiwan Genjūmin kenkyūkai, *Inō Kanori*, 108–11.

67. A high-resolution scan of this cabinet card and its reverse side was posted on eBay by the seller eby071 on December 14, 2010.

68. Inō Kanori and Awano Dennosuke, *Taiwan banjin jijō* (Taipei: Taiwan sōtokufu minseibu bunshoka, 1900), 15, stipulates that some Atayal wore ornaments, while others did not. The popularized versions of Inō's sketch that appeared in Davidson, *Island of Formosa*, 565, and Takekoshi Yosaburō, *Japanese Rule in Formosa*, trans. George Braithwaite (London, New York, Bombay, and Calcutta: Longmans, Green, 1907), 221, are less subtle, like the placards at the exhibitions and the captions for postcards.

69. Hu Jiayu and Yilan Cui, *Taida renlei xuexi*, facing 263.

70. Hu Chia-yu, "Taiwanese," 198–99.

71. Ishizaka Tonan, *Photographs of Formosa: Collected in Commemoration of the Tokyo Industrial Exhibition in 1907*, 13, in Sōtokufu archives, National Taiwan Library, Taipei. This drawing was reproduced in an early travel guide, before tourists could actually visit indigenous settlements; see untitled railway guide, ed. Taiwan sōtokufu tetsudō bu (Tokyo: Eriguchi shōkai, 1908), 57, in Sōtokufu archives, National Taiwan Library, Taipei.

72. Davidson, *Island of Formosa*, 563.

73. Ishikawa, *Taiwan meisho*.

74. Benedict Anderson, *Imagined Communities* (London: Verso, 1983), 163–85.

75. James C. Scott, *The Art of Not Being Governed: An Anarchist History of Upland Southeast Asia* (New Haven: Yale University Press, 2009).

76. Antonio C. Tavares, "The Japanese Colonial State and the Dissolution of the Late Imperial Frontier Economy in Taiwan, 1886–1909," *Journal of Asian Studies* 64, no. 2 (2005): 361–85.

77. "Mori Ushinosuke to Tsuboi Shōgorō, September 2, 1902," *Tokyo jinruigakkai zasshi* 199, October 20, 1902, 39.

78. "Taiwan banjin fūzoku shashin zusetu," *Tokyo jinruigakkai zasshi* 213 (December 20, 1903): 109.

79. Paul D. Barclay, "Playing the Race Card in Japanese Governed Taiwan, or: Anthropometric Photographs as 'Shape-Shifting Jokers'" in *The Affect of Difference: Representations of Race in East Asian Empire*, ed. Christopher Hanscom and Dennis Washburn (Honolulu: University of Hawai'i Press, 2016), 38–80.

80. "Seiban no raisha," *Taiwan nichinichi shinpō,* January 30, 1903; "Taiwan banjin fūzoku," *Tokyo jinruigakkai zasshi,* 108.

81. Taiwan Government Bureau of Aborigine Affairs, ed., *Report on the Control of the Aborigines in Formosa* (Taipei: Taiwan Government General, 1911), facing 3; Ishii Shinji, *The Island of Formosa and Its Primitive Inhabitants* (London: China Society, 1916), plate VIII; Fujisaki Seinosuke, *Taiwan no banzoku* (Tokyo: Kokushi Kankōkai, 1930), 248; "Taroko Tribe Husband and Wife," ip1225, East Asia Image Collection, Lafayette College, Easton, PA, accessed March 30, 2013, http://digital.lafayette.edu/collections/eastasia/imperial-postcards/ip1225.

82. "Aborigines [sic] Woman, Formosa (33)," ip1020, East Asia Image Collection, Lafayette College, Easton, PA, accessed March 30, 2013, http://digital.lafayette.edu/collections/eastasia/imperial-postcards/ip1020.

83. See the postcard reproduced in Narita Takeshi, *Taiwan seiban shuzoku shashinchō* (Taipei: Narita shashin seihanjo, 1912), 31; Koizumi Tetsu, *Bankyō fūzokuki* (Tokyo kensetsusha, 1932), plate 13; "All about the Aborigine Territories postcard collection," lw0522, East Asia Image Collection, Lafayette College, Easton, PA, accessed March 30, 2013, http://digital.lafayette.edu/collections/eastasia/lewis-postcards/lw0522; Richard Goldschmidt, *Neu-Japan; Reisebilder aus Formosa, den Ryukyuinseln, Bonininseln, Korea and dem südmandschurischen Pachtgebiet* (Berlin: J. Springer, 1927), 65.

84. Matsuda Kyōko, *Teikoku no shisen: hakurankai to ibunka hyōshō* (Tokyo: Yoshikawa kōbunkan, 2003),15–19.

85. Kuni Takeyuki, *Hakurankai no jidai* (Tokyo: Iwata shoin, 2005), 176.

86. Barclay, "Senzen no media ni shiyō sareta Mori Ushinosuke no Taiwan Genjūmin 'Kusshaku-ban' shashin: hakurankai, shinbun, kyōkasho, ehagaki, zasshi de no shiyō rei no kentō," *Taiwan Genjūmin kenkyū* 19 (2015): 53.

87. Taiwan Government Bureau of Aborigine Affairs, ed., *Report,* facing 3; *Taiyō* 23, no. 7 (June 15, 1917); Mori Ushinosuke, ed., *Taiwan banzoku zufu,* vol. 1 (Taipei: Rinji Taiwan kyūkan chōsakai, 1915), plate 23; "two Quchi savages of Taiyaru tribe, Farmosa [sic]," lw0002, East Asia Image Collection, Lafayette College, Easton, PA, accessed July 28, 2013, http://digital.lafayette.edu/collections/eastasia/lewis-postcards/lw0002.

88. "Hunting Head Hunters with Live Electric Wires," *Detroit Free Press,* April 4, 1909.

89. Elizabeth Edwards, introduction to *Anthropology and Photography: 1860–1920,* ed. Elizabeth Edwards (New Haven: Yale University Press, 1992), 11.

90. [Shinkō, Urai-sha Woman, Taiyal Tribe], ip1448, East Asia Image Collection, Lafayette College, Easton, PA, accessed July 23, 2017, http://digital.lafayette.edu/collections/eastasia/imperial-postcards/ip1448.

91. "Wiping Out the Formosans: Japan's War of Subjugation on Their Newly Taken Island," *Washington Post,* June 30, 1907, E14.

92. Inō Kanori, ed., *Riban shikō dai ikkan* (Taipei: Taiwan sōtokufu keisatsu honsho, 1918; repr., Taipei: Southern Materials Center, 1995), 182.

93. Takekoshi, *Japanese Rule in Formosa,* 230.

94. See figure 3 and "THE BARBARIC WOMAN OF FORMOSA," lw0384, East Asia Image Collection, Lafayette College, Easton, PA, accessed March 30, 2013, http://digital.lafayette.edu/collections/eastasia/lewis-postcards/lw0384; "Woman of Savage," lw0391, East Asia Image Collection, Lafayette College, Easton, PA, accessed March 30, 2013,

http://digital.lafayette.edu/collections/eastasia/lewis-postcards/lw0391. For details regarding the dozens of publications that included Pazzeh's portrait, see Barclay, "Senzen," 47–75.

95. "Head hunters in Formosa," lw0264, East Asia Image Collection, Lafayette College, Easton, PA, accessed March 30, 2013, http://digital.lafayette.edu/collections/eastasia/lewis-postcards/lw0264.

96. See Paul D. Barclay, "The Relics of Modern Japan's First Foreign War in Colonial and Postcolonial Taiwan, 1874–2015," *Cross Currents: East Asian History and Culture Review*, no. 17 (December 2015): frame 3, accessed July 23, 2017, https://cross-currents.berkeley.edu/e-journal/issue-17/barclay.

97. [Under Prince Kan'in at the Taiwan Governor-General's Residence], ip0192, East Asia Image Collection, Lafayette College, Easton, PA, accessed May 13, 2016, http://digital.lafayette.edu/collections/eastasia/imperial-postcards/ip0192.

98. Mori, *Banzoku*, vol. 1, plate 15.

99. This village on the South Cape was the combatant tribe during the 1867 *Rover* incident (see chapter 1); the men in the picture are wearing Qing hairstyles; Koalut was moved to normal administration in 1904.

100. Inō, *Riban shikō*, 349; Fujii Shizue, *Riju shiqi Taiwan zongdufu de lifan zhengce* (Taipei: Guoli Taiwan shifan daxue lishi yanjiusuo, 1989), 190–91.

101. For example, *Saishin Nihon chiri kyōkasho* (Tokyo: Sanseidō, 1925), 95; *Joshi kyōiku: saishin nihonchiri* (Tokyo: Sanseidō, 1928), 96; *Saishin Nihon chiri kyōkasho* (Tokyo: Sanseidō, 1933), 131.

102. Barclay, "Senzen," 54.

103. Three photos of Watan Yūra's extended family, at least five different poses for portraits of Marai Watan, three poses for Yūgai Watan, two poses for Pazzeh Watan, and a panoramic shot of an Atayal house and granary set in the mountains were the subjects of these photos. See Barclay, "Senzen."

104. Inō, *Riban shikō*, 375–76.

105. Xia Shengli, et al., *Hyakunen Cangsang: Dogura Ryūjirō to Taihoku Kameyama suiryoku hatsudenjo*, trans. and ed. Dogura Masao and Dogura Nobuko (Sakurai-shi: Dogura Masao, 2006).

106. Michele Lang, *An Adventurous Woman Abroad: The Selected Lantern Slides of Mary T. S. Schaffer* (Vancouver: Rocky Mountain Books, 2011), 258–63.

107. The colorized bust and profile of Marai, as well as several anthropometric shots included in Takekoshi Yosaburō's 1905 book, are preserved in the James Wheeler Davidson Collection at the University of Calgary, accessed March 4, 2017, http://contentdm.ucalgary.ca/cdm/search/collection/jwd/.

108. For a detailed analysis of an exemplary album from this period, see Okada Shigehiro, "Takamatsu-miya kashi no 'Banhi tōbatsu kinen shashin-chō' ni tuite," *Gakushuin Daigaku shiryōkan kiyō* 14 (March 2007): 77–154.

109. The term "encampment" is taken from Joseph Allen's essay on Meiji-period photographic albums of Taiwan, "Colonial Itineraries: Japanese Photography in Taiwan," in *Japanese Taiwan: Colonial Rule and Its Contested Legacy*, ed. Andrew D. Morris (London: Bloomsbury Press, 2015), 25–48.

110. Taiwan sōtokufu keimukyoku, ed., *Takasagozoku chōsasho dai san-hen: shinka* (Taipei: Taiwan sōtokufu keimukyoku, 1937).

111. Taiwan sōtokufu minseibu banmu honsho, ed., *Riban gaiyō* (Taipei: Taiwan sōtokufu minseibu banmu honsho, 1912), 92–96.

112. Untitled railway guide, ed. Taiwan sōtokufu tetsudōbu (Tokyo: Eiguchi shōkai, 1908), 57–58, in Sōtokufu archives, National Taiwan Library, Taipei.

113. Yamabe Kentarō, ed., *Taiwan (II),* vol. 22, *Gendaishi shiryō* (Tokyo: Misuzu shobō, 1971), 416.

114. Endō Hiroya, *Banhi tōbatsu kinen shashinchō* (Taipei: Endō shashinkan, 1911), in Sōtokufu archives, National Taiwan Library, Taipei.

115. Ide Kiwata, *Taiwan chisekishi* (Taipei: Taiwan nichinichi shinpōsha, 1937), 707.

116. Hashimoto Hakusui, ed., *Taiwan ryokō annai* (Taipei: Fujisaki Tomisō, 1915), 78.

117. A. B. Kirjassoff, "Formosa the Beautiful," *National Geographic Magazine* 37, no. 3 (1920): 246–92.

118. Taiwan sōtokufu tetsudōbu, ed., *Tetsudō ryokō annai* (Taipei: Taiwan sōtokufu tetsudōbu, 1921), 32.

119. Sōyama Takeshi, *Shokuminchi Taiwan to kindai tsūrizumu* (Tokyo: Seikyōsha, 2003), 243–46.

120. Taiwan sōtokufu tetsudōbu, ed., *Tetsudō ryokō annai* (Taipei: Taiwan sōtokufu tetsudōbu, 1924), 69.

121. H. L. Bagallay, "The Savage Territory of Formosa" [May 1925], in *Taiwan: Political and Economic Reports 1861–1960, vol. 7: 1924–1941,* ed. Robert L. Jarman (Slough: Archive Editions, 1997), 24.

122. Taiwan sōtokufu kōtsūkyoku tetsudōbu, ed., *Taiwan tetsudō ryokō annai* (Taipei: Taiwan sōtokufu tetsudōbu, 1927), 88; Taiwan sōtokufu kōtsūkyoku tetsudōbu, ed., *Taiwan tetsudō ryokō annai* (Taipei: Taiwan sōtokufu tetsudōbu, 1930), 97; Taiwan sōtokufu kōtsūkyoku tetsudōbu, ed., *Taiwan tetsudō ryokō annai* (Taipei: Taiwan sōtokufu tetsudōbu, 1934), 67.

123. Abe Akiyoshi, *Taiwan chimei kenkyū* (Taipei: Sugita shoten, 1937), 8–9.

124. Taiwan sōtokufu kōtsūkyoku tetsudōbu, ed., *Taiwan tetsudō ryokō annai* (1934), 9.

125. Mori, *Taiwan banzoku zufu,* vol. 1, plate 33; a common postcard displaying Atayal women in Chinese, Japanese, and Atayal clothing, ca. 1920, "Chest-nuts by female savages of Ataiya' trive [sic] (5)," lw0189, East Asia Image Collection, accessed August 12, 2016, Lafayette College, Easton, PA, http://digital.lafayette.edu/collections/eastasia/lewis-postcards/lw0189.

126. Paul D. Barclay, "Peddling Postcards and Selling Empire: Image-Making in Taiwan under Japanese Colonial Rule," *Japanese Studies* 30, no. 1 (May 2010): 81–110.

127. Barclay, "Senzen," 58–59.

128. Ming-cheng M. Lo, *Doctors within Borders: Profession, Ethnicity, and Modernity in Colonial Taiwan* (Berkeley: University of California Press, 2002); Ka Chih-ming, *Japanese Colonialism in Taiwan: Land Tenure, Development, and Dependency, 1895–1945* (Boulder, CO: Westview Press, 1995); Wang Taysheng, *Legal Reform in Taiwan under Japanese Colonial Rule, 1895–1945: The Reception of Western Law* (Seattle and London: University of Washington Press, 2000).

129. Yao Jen-to, "Governing the Colonised: Governmentality in the Japanese Colonisation of Taiwan, 1895–1945" (PhD diss., University of Essex, 2002).

130. Inō, *Riban shikō,* 326–33, 474–76.

131. Matsuoka Tadasu, *Taiwan Genjūmin shakai no chihōka: Mainoriti no nijū seiki* (Tokyo: Kenbun shuppan, 2012), 39–40.

132. Matsuoka, *Taiwan Genjūmin*, 101–17.

133. Matsuda Kyōko, *Teikoku no shisō: Nihon "Teikoku" to Taiwan Genjūmin* (Tokyo: Yūshisha, 2014), 190–92.

134. Hashimoto Mitsuru, "Yanagita Kunio's 'Japan,'" in Stephen Vlastos, ed., *Mirror of Modernity: Invented Traditions of Modern Japan* (Berkeley: University of California Press, 1998), 133–43; Marilyn Ivy, *Discourses of the Vanishing: Modernity, Phantasm, Japan* (Chicago: University of Chicago Press, 1995), 68–73.

135. Matsuda Kyōko, *Teikoku*, 190–92.

136. Yih-ren Lin, Lahuy Icyeh, and Da-Wei Kuan, "Indigenous Language-Informed Participatory Policy in Taiwan: A Socio-Political Perspective," in *Documenting and Revitalizing Austronesian Languages,* ed. Victoria Rau and Margaret Florey (Honolulu: University of Hawai'i Press, 2007), 138.

GLOSSARY

Terms used in text	Characters or kana
aiyū	隘勇
Alishan	阿里山
Amis	阿美
Atayal	泰雅
Awai	亞歪
banba	蕃婆
bandō kyōikujo	蕃童教育所
bango	蕃語
banjin	蕃人
banjin banchi mondai	蕃人蕃地問題
banjo	蕃女
Bankai no hikyō	蕃界の秘境
banpu	蕃婦
banzoku	蕃族
baojia	保甲
Baoli	保力
Bayao Bay	八瑤湾
Beipu	北埔
bentuhua	本土化
bunka seiji	文化政治

293

Bunun	布農
Chen Ansheng	陳安生
Chen Xilai	陳溪瀨
Chiankoey	雙溪
Dakekan	大料崁
dogo	土語
domoku	土目
Dongpushe	東埔社
Du Tingdong	杜庭動
Ernai	爾乃
fan	番
fanren	番人
Fengshan	鳳山
Fukahori Yasuichirō	深堀安一郎
fukenju	撫墾局
fukutsūyaku	副通訳
Fūzoku gahō	風俗画報
Gantaban	干卓萬
genjin	原人
gishu	技手
gokanen keikaku riban jigyō	五か年計画理蕃事業
Gotō Shinpei	後藤新平
guihuashengfan	帰化生蕃
Hakka	客家
hannin	判人
Hashiguchi Bunzō	橋口文蔵
Hengchun	恒春
Hewen (Hha-hoi)	合脗
hitsudan	筆談
Hiyama Tetsusaburō	檜山鉄三郎
hontōjin	本島人
Huang Qiying	黄祈英
Huozhang	夥長
Igarashi Ishimatsu	五十嵐石松
Inō Kanori	伊能嘉矩
inshu no reigi	飲酒の礼儀

Ishii Shinji	石井眞二
Itō Shūkichi	伊藤修吉
Iwan Robao	伊娃莉・羅拔俄
Jiaobanshan	角板山
Jiayi	嘉義
Jiku Shō Min	竺紹珉
jimu shokutaku	事務嘱託
Joseon	朝鮮
jukuban	熟蕃
junho	巡補
junsaho	巡査補
Kagoshima	鹿児島
Kaku Kurata	賀来倉田
Kawano Shuichirō	河野主一郎
kegai	化外
keimenban	黥面蕃
kekkon o yaku	結婚を約
kijun	帰順
Koalut	亀好児
koin	傭員
Kondō Gisaburō	近藤儀三郎
Kondō Katsusaburō	近藤勝三郎
Kondō Yoshio	近藤義雄
koshu	戸主
koyū	固有
Kuomintang / Guomindang	国民党
Kuskus	高士佛
Lan Yinding	藍蔭鼎
Langqiao	瑯{王+喬}
Li A'long	李阿龍
lifan tongzhi	理番同知
Linyipu	林圯埔
Liu Mingchuan	劉銘傳
mae-Taikokan-ban	前大科崁蕃
Mao Jian	毛奸
Marai	馬来

Mehebu	馬赫坡
Mei-hai	梅海
mekake	妾
metoru	娶る
Miyakojima	宮古島
Mochiji Rokusaburō	持地六三郎
Mona Ludao	菓那・魯道
Mori Ushinosuke	森丑之助
Mosu	墨宿
Mudan	牡丹
mukōyoshi	婿養子
Murakami Yoshio	村上義雄
Myōzai	名西
Nagakura Yoshitsugu	長倉吉次
naien no otto	内縁の夫
Nakamura Yūsuke	中村雄助
Nan'ao	南澳
Neng'gao	能高郡
Order of the Sacred Treasure, Sixth Rank	叙勲六等, 授瑞寶章
Ortai	鄂爾泰
Ōtsu Rinpei	大津麟平
Paiwan	排湾
Paalan	芭蘭
Pan Bunkiet	潘文杰
Pan Laolong	藩老龍
Papau Iron	パパウ・イロン
Pixo Doleh	貝克・道雷
Poliac	保力
Pu Chin	蒲靖
Puli	埔里
Pushige	璞石閣
Puyuma	卑南
Quchi	屈尺
Riban no tomo	理蕃の友
Rukai	魯凱
Sabaree	射麻里

Sagara Nagatsuna	相良長綱
Saisiyat	賽夏
Sakuma Samata	佐久間左馬太
sancengzhi zuqun fenbu jiagou	三层制族群分布架构
Sandiaoshe	三貂社
Sanjiaoyong	三角湧
Saprek	射不力
Sasaki Yasugorō	佐々木安五郎
Satō Haruo	佐藤春夫
Satomi Yoshimasa	里見義正
Sazuka Aisuke	佐塚愛祐
Sediq	賽德克
seiban kyōhi	生蕃饗費
seibanjin	生蕃人
seinendan	青年団
seiryokusha	勢力者
Seiyūkai	政友会
sha	社
Shang Tai	尚泰
sheding	社丁
shegun	社棍
shengfan	生番
sheshang	社商
Shimaigahara	姉妹ヶ原
Shina kanwa	支那官話
Shō (dynasty)	尚
Shōjiro Kunitei	彰城邦貞
Shoucheng Dashan	守城大山
Shuangxikou	双渓口
shūchō	酋長
shujiho	主事補
shuryō	首領
shutchōjo	出張所
shuzoku	種族
Suzuki Hideo	鈴木秀夫
Taidong	台東

tairiku rōnin	大陸浪人
Taiwan bankai tenbō	台湾蕃界展望
Taiwan banzoku zufu	台湾蕃族図譜
Taiwan doban	台湾土蛮
Taiwan dogo	台湾土語
Taiwan gahō	台湾画報
Taiwan jihō	台湾時報
Taiwan Yuanzhuminzu	台灣原住民族
Takasagozoku	高砂族
Takekoshi Yosaburō	竹越与三郎
Tanaka Tsunatoku	田中綱常
Taroko	太魯閣
Tata	達達
Tgdaya	德固達雅
Thao	邵
Toda	都達/道澤
tōmoku	頭目
tongshi	通事
Torii Ryūzō	鳥居龍蔵
Truku	德路固
Tsou	鄒
tsūben	通辯
tsūyakukan	通訳官
tsūyakusei	通訳生
Tuilasok	猪朥束
Urashō	浦庄
Wanda	萬大
Wangsha	網紗
Watan Yūro	瓦丹有洛
wu-pin	五品
Wu Sha	呉沙
Wushe	霧社
Xalut	白狗
Xincheng	新城
Xinzhu	新竹
Xitou	溪頭

Xiyanlaowa	四煙老瓦
Yami	雅美
Yang Youwang	楊友旺
Yawai Taimu	亜娃伊・泰目
Yilan	宜蘭
Yūkōmaru	有功丸
Zhang Shichang	張世昌
Zhang Xinzhang	張新丈
Zhang Yichun	張義春
Zheng Yan'ning	鄭延寧

INDEX

aborigine administration (*riban*), 4, 90–92, 119–120, 271n20
aborigine common schools (*banjin kōgakkō*), 148–150, 153
aborigine territory, 2, 32–33, 58*map*, 80*map*, 102, 193*map*, 194
aborigine youth schools (*bandō kyōikujo*), 149, 152
aiyū-sen. See guardline
Akamatsu Noriyoshi, 68–69
Aki (the interpreter), 122–123, 124*fig.*, 217
Akinaga Nagakichi, 139
alcoholic beverages, 44, 74, 81, 85–87, 97, 165, 174
Alliance of Taiwan Aborigines, 5
Alok (Paiwan warrior), 69
Amis (ethnic group), 7*map*, 8*map*, 59; as attendees of aborigine common schools, 149; as dancers, 167; as minority in Langqiao, 59; in Ueno Sen'ichi's ethnic classification, 197; language, 144; under "normal administration," 144, 230–232, 246
annex schools (*bunkyōba*), 142–148
anthropologists: as preservationists, 163, 171, 182–183; 188–189, 248; as taxonomists, 6, 35, 198; as theorists of indigenism, 38; cultural pluralism and, 184, 191–192, 213, 225; ethnogenesis and, 194–195, 213; photography and, 216–222; wet diplomacy and, 86
anthropology: authenticity and, 120; cultural pluralism and, 35–36, 167, 182, 191, 196; in colonial Taiwan, 212; race science and, 35, 215
Arao Kiyoshi, 115
Atayal (ethnic group), 7*map*, 8*map*; alcohol consumption and, 44, 45*fig.*, 85–86; as combatants, 28–32, 39, 46, 48*fig.*, 49*fig.*, 70, 90, 94, 102, 109, 136–137, 178; as "innocent aborigines," 173–175; colonial education and, 149–155; cultural renaissance, 188–189; ethnogenesis of, 6, 9, 167, 183, 198–228, 236–244; interpreters and, 79, 85, 122–128; land rights, 249; language, 140; textiles, 40, 161–162, 167, 169–171, 174, 182–187; trade, 79; tourism and, 184, 233–236; wet diplomacy and, 82–85, 87, 91, 125–128
Atkins, E. Taylor, 252n17
Aui Heppa, 96
Aui Nukan, 137
authenticity, 3, 36–37, 188, 196
Awai, 124–126, 213–217

bandō kyōikujo. See aborigine youth schools
banjin kōgakkō. See aborigine common schools
banpu (female indigene), 123–128, 133, 136
baojia, 31, 119, 146, 157, 244
Bassau Bōran, 131
Bayly, C.A., 11, 15–17, 36
Beasley, W.G., 26–27
Beinan, 9*fig.*, 143
Beipu incident, 156–157, 233

302   INDEX

Bell, Admiral H. H., 56–57
benmusho (District Administrative Office), 85, 134
Benton, Lauren, 12, 13, 251, 252n8, 255n45
biculturalism, 60, 121–122, 133
bifurcated sovereignty, 3, 13, 17–18, 119, 149, 192, 248, 283n6
big bang (of government outlays), 13, 29, 32, 102, 244–245
biopolitics/biopower, 29–32, 258n104
Bukonsho. See Pacification Office
Bunkiet, Jagarushi Guri (Pan Wenjie), 70, 142, 144, 145*fig*., 146–148, 245
Bunun, 7*map*, 8*map*, 9*fig*., 94, 96–97, 102, 11, 167
Burbank, Jane, 12–13
Bureau of Aboriginal Affairs (*banmu honsho*), 103, 139
Buzan, Barry, 11, 13

camphor: industry, 87, 94, 98, 124, 132, 162, 174, 178–179; monopoly, 32, 98–101, 118, 188, 178; wars, 28, 32, 70, 95, 98–106, 175, 225–228
Cassel, Douglas, 61, 68–70, 75, 125, 164
Cassel, Pars, 20
casualties, 98–100, 103, 105–106, 110, 176
census: categories, 135, 150, 213; ethnogenesis and, 213; of Taiwan, 25, 33, 47, 48, 51, 193*fig*.,196, 197
Checheng, 53*map*, 59, 60, 142
Ching, Leo, 30
Chiwas Ludao, 119, 137, 138
Chou Wan-yao, xvii, 50, 75
citizens (*kokumin*), 21, 23, 33, 78, 92, 149, 152, 157
competitive imperialism, 2, 17, 27, 38, 96, 194
Cooper, Frederick, 12–13
cultural rule: in Korea, 3–4, 9, 37; in Taiwan, 6, 9
cultural survival, 2, 37, 248, 253n21

Dakekan (Atayal subgroup), 9*fig*., 71, 198; as combatants, 178–179, 223, 233; as culture-bearers, 183, 216, 236; at parleys, 83, 125; dialect, 125, 215
Dakekan (place), 7*map*, 58*map*, 80*map*; administrative seat, 83–84, 89–91, 122–125, 204–205, 214, 233; junction town, 82, 84*fig*., 89–91, 125, 172–174, 198, 204–205, 214, 233
Deng Tianbao, 52, 55
Deng Xiangyang, 5, 96, 154
dialects, 90, 117, 133, 138
Dirlik, Arif, 37
discipline: regime of, 13, 21–33, 99, 118–119, 156–157, 244–248
Duara, Prasenjit, 36

dynastic state, 11–21, 31, 38–39, 75–77, 114, 192, 264n99

economic competence, 3, 6, 147, 167, 180–181, 279n12
education, 77, 120, 146–157
Eighteen-Tribe Confederation (of Langqiao), 59–65, 163, 169, 197
Em, Henry, 4
embargoes, 59, 95–96, 135, 169, 176–181
entangled objects, 168–178
Eskildsen, Robert, 77, 201
ethnic enclave, 31, 119
ethnic classification, 135, 147, 183, 195–199, 213–217, 230, 259n122, 284n19
ethnogenesis, 219–222
ethnography. See anthropology
ethnologists. See anthropologists
ethnology. See anthropology

Fangliao, 58*map*, 62, 75
favoritism, 46, 113, 140
feasts, 52, 64–74, 79, 83, 86, 146, 176; aborigine administration (*riban*) and, 89–91, 96, 111–112, 178
Fenggang, 53, 53*map*, 60, 62, 75
five-year plan to manage the Aborigines (*gokanen keikaku riban jigyō*), 29, 49*fig*., 104–110, 138–139, 179, 245–246
flogging, 3, 156–157
Foucault, Michel, 21–23, 28–29
Friedman, P. Kerim, 275n90
Frühstück, Sabine, 29
Fujii Shizue, 104
Fujisaki Seinosuke, 75, 112
Fujitani, Takashi, 23, 29–30, 77, 254n27
Fukahori Yasuichirō, 95–96, 130–131
Fukushima Kunari, 68
Fukushima Yasumasa, 116

Gao Jiaxin (Lianes Punanang), 50, 52
Gaoshifo. See Kuskus
geobody, 18–19, 33, 65, 162, 194. See also second-order geobody
gifts, 39–40, 162–163, 261n27; aborigine administration (*riban*) and, 82–96, 175–179; frontier diplomacy and, 46, 60, 64, 70–71, 81–82, 123, 173–174, 217; in redistributive political systems, 65, 128; in ritual exchange, 61, 165–166; Yoshimura beating incident and, 43
Gantaban, 9*fig*., 96–97, 97*fig*., 112–113

global transformation, 11–17, 36–38, 191–195
Gotō Shinpei, 25–26, 29, 99, 111, 178–179, 221
governmentality, 23–29, 32–33, 38, 99
guardline (*aiyū-sen*), 39, 46–47, 47*fig.*, 97–106, 108*fig.*, 109*fig.*, 111–113, 135–139, 223–233, 226*fig.*, 227*fig.*, 233
gunboat diplomacy, 56, 88
Gungu. *See* Hōgō
Guomindang (Nationalist Party), 3,5, 187, 248–249, 252*n*10, 253*n*20, 252*n*122

Habairon (Papau Iron), 199–200, 202*fig.*, 203*fig.*, 204, 204*fig.*, 205–206, 206*fig.*, 207, 213
Hakka (*Kejia*), 52, 56–62, 85, 121, 134, 178
Hamashita, Takeshi, 54–55, 166
Hanaoka Ichirō (Dakis Nobing), 153–154
Hanaoka Jirō (Dakis Nawi), 153–154
Hancock, William, 79
Hannah, Matthew, 21–27
Haruyama Meitetsu, 167–168
Hashiguchi Bunzō, 82–88, 125–126, 174, 199–200, 202*fig.*, 205
headmen. *See* tōmoku
Hengchun: lower, (Paiwan subgroup), 9*fig.*, 59, 71, 74*fig.*, 142, 146–148, 151, 164, 181, 223, 230, 245–246; Peninsula, 39, 72, 121, 143, 197, 223; upper, (Paiwan subgroup), 147, 181; walled city, 53*map* 122, 142, 148
Hevia, James, 252*n*11
high velocity capitalism, 18–22, 33, 103, 166
Hirschman, Charles, 33
Hiyama Tetsusaburō, 88–89, 93, 129–130, 176, 209, 273*n*54
Hōgō (Gungu), 9*fig.*, 97*fig.*, 135, 137, 153–154
Hok-lo, 52, 60, 134, 211
horizontal integration, 21, 39, 48, 75, 77–78, 119, 146
House, Edward, 68–71, 163–166
Hu Chia-yu, 37, 167, 187, 189
Huang Chih-huei, 30
Hyung Il Pai, 252*n*17

identity: aborigine territory police and, 156; Atayal, 167, 206–213, 218; censuses and, 33–34, 213; Korean, 4,6; modern indigenous, 2, 37, 188, 219; Saisiyat, 37, 89; Taiwan Indigenous Peoples, 6, 9, 154, 187, 189; Taiwanese, 187
imperial subjectification (*kōminka*), 30–31, 119–120, 154
indigenism, 2, 13, 36–40
indigenous youth corps. *See* seinendan
Inō Kanori: as colonial collector, 183, 189; as critic, 191, 211; as ethnologist, 85–86, 131, 133, 146, 182, 202, 212, 215–216; ethnic classification and, 10*fig.*, 35, 135; ethnogenesis and, 188, 219–221; ethnonym "Atayal" and, 6, 217
interiority, 6, 112
intermarriage, 39, 46, 121–122, 127, 146–147
intermediaries, 12, 20, 79, 88, 95, 111–113, 121–122, 128, 165
international law, 17, 28, 77–78, 192, 222
international system, 2, 11–15, 23, 33, 77, 194–196
interpreter. *See* tongshi
Ira Watan, 202*fig.*, 203*fig.*, 204*fig.*, 205–208, 206*fig.*, 209*fig.*
Iriye Takeshi, 98, 127–128
Isa (of Sabaree), 59, 64–74, 88, 164–166
Ishizuka Eizō, 4
isshi dōjin (impartiality, non-discrimination), 46, 113
Iwan Robao, 96, 124, 130, 133–137, 209

Jiaobanshan (Atayal subgroup), 9*fig.*, 198
Jiaobanshan (place), 7*map*, 9*fig.*, 80*map*; as battlefield, 48*fig.*, 109, 232, 234*fig.*; emissaries, 84–88, 125, 174, 182, 198–202, 202*fig.*, 205–212; school, 152, 153*fig.*, tourism and, 184, 229, 232–242; trading post, 177*fig.*
Jiku Shō Min, 131–133, 216–217, 228–229
Jilong Harbor, 103
Johnson, James, 63–64, 68–69, 72*fig.*

Ka Chih-ming, 29
Kabayama Sukenori, 83, 85, 90, 200–201, 202*fig.*, 223
Kagoshima. *See* Satsuma
kaishan fufan (open the mountains, pacify the barbarians), 122, 142–144, 197
Kamimura Tōru, 165, 263*n*55
Kasahara Masaharu, 259*n*121
Katz, Paul, 156–157
Kawano Shuichirō, 87–88, 126
kensho. *See* stipend
Kido Takayoshi, 76–77
Kitamura Kae, 141, 146, 152, 154
Koalut, 9*fig.*, 53*map*, 56–61, 142, 147–148, 151, 223, 232
Kōan (the interpreter), 123, 124*fig.*, 217
Kodama Gentarō, 96, 99, 102, 118, 268*n*181
kokugo denshūjo (Japanese language institutes), 141–142
kokumin. *See* citizens
kōminka. *See* imperial subjectification

304 INDEX

Kondō Gisaburō, 112–113, 137*fig.*, 138
Kondō Katsusaburō, 96, 129–133, 130*fig.*, 135–138
Korean Government-General, 3–4
koseki (Japanese household registration), 138, 140
kula ring, 165
Kuskus, 9*fig.*, 50, 52, 53*map*, 59, 70–71, 147, 277*n*148

LaFeber, Walter, 18
land tax reforms: in Japan, 24–25, 29; in Taiwan, 25–27
Langqiao: Peninsula, 14, 21, 51*map*, 53*map*, 55–63, 67–72, 75–79, 90, 121, 165, 256*n*49; village of, 53*map*, 61
Lawson, George, 11–13
legal centralism, 17–19, 33, 38
LeGendre, Charles, 56–69, 71, 79, 88, 149, 163–166, 192
Lemoi Maton, 84*fig.*, 199
Lenin, V.I., 11, 17–18, 21
Leung, Edwin Pak-wah, 54, 75
Li Hongzhang, 67, 76
Lianes Punanang. *See* Gao Jiaxin
liquor. *See* alcoholic beverages
Liu Deshao (Liu Tek-chok), 142–144
Liu Mingchuan, 20, 122–124, 215
Liu Mingdeng, 57–64
Lo, Ming-cheng M., 158
Ludao Bai, 112, 137

Mackenzie, Lieutenant Captain, 56–61
Malay (race), 33–36, 150–152, 216
Malepa, 7*map*, 112, 139–140, 179
Mamdani, Mahmood, 47, 111
Marai (eight-village settlement), 79
Marai (of Jiaobanshan), 202*fig.*, 205–208, 206*fig.*, 209*fig.*
Marai (paramount chieftain near Wulai), 122
Marai Watan (of Rimogan), 220–222, 242*fig.*, 243*fig.*, 244
March 1 Movement, 3–4
Masitoban, 7*map*, 9*fig.*, 136, 140
Matsuda Kyōko, 247
Matsuda Yoshirō, 154
Matsuoka Tadasu, 32, 151, 245–246
Mbembe, Achille, 29
Mehebu, 1, 6, 7*map*, 9*fig.*, 43, 137
Meiji Emperor, 23–24, 65, 104
Meiji Restoration, 54, 65–68, 114
meritorious service awards: for compliant indigenes, 177; for Qing-period *tongshi* (interpreters), 64, 142; for *tōmoku* (headmen), 111; on the guardline, 106, 117, 136
Mia. *See* Miya.
middle ground, 18, 32, 111
Ministry of Education (Monbusho): as textbook publisher, 150, 211
Minseitō (Popular Government Party), 4
Mio Yūko, 134
Mitchell, W.J.T., 195
Mitsuda Yayoi, 187
Miya, 60–64, 68–69, 121
Miyanohara Tōhachi, 89–91
Mizuno Jun: as Kabayama Sukenori's translator, 72, 72*fig.*, 83; as Taiwan Government-General civil administrator, 129, 166, 202*fig.*; mission to Dakekan (1873), 172–173
Mizuno, Norihito, 55
Mochiji Rokusaburō, 28, 102, 192, 222
Mona Ludao, 1, 6, 9, 43, 47, 112
Mongolian (race), 33
Mori Ushinosuke: as Chinese-language translator, 116, 182; as critic, 180–182; as curator, 182, 184; as ethnic taxonomist, 35–36, 135, 198; as ethnographer, 86, 128–129, 182, 215, 225; as photographer, 182–183, 220–223, 228–230, 236, 239, 242–243
Motonaiban, 202*fig.*, 203*fig.*, 204, 204*fig.*, 205–206, 206*fig.*, 208
Mudan (Paiwan subgroup), 9*fig.*, 63, 72, 135, 147–148
Mudan (place), 9*fig.*, 51*map*, 53*map*, 58*map*
Mudan village incident, 19–21, 50–75
Murakami Yoshio, 178

Nagano Yoshitora, 93–94, 176
Nakamura Yūsuke, 143, 143*fig.*
Nan'ao (Atayal subgroup), 7*map*, 9*fig.*, 83, 87, 175
National Taiwan Museum, 161, 182
nationalism: as analog to *isshi dōjin*, 46; as nineteenth century phenomenon, 2, 38; geobodies and, 192–194; Korean, 4, 9; postcolonial, 5, 188; Satsuma domain, 76; Taiwanese, 5
Native Americans, 16, 30, 78, 111, 215
Native Authority, 47–48; 111–113; 155
native peoples: as *dojin* (Taiwanese), 117, 171, 208; as objects of discipline, 29; empires and, 16; in Qing dynasty, 20, 76, 191–192; vs. settlers, 16–17; Wilsonianism and, 36
necropolitics, 29
Niezen, Ronald, 2, 36, 38

normal administration, 110, 147–151, 156–157, 230, 235, 289n99
Northern Tribes, 9fig.

Obin Nukan, 137
Okada Shinkō, 87
Ōkubo Toshimichi, 21, 23, 68, 76–78
Ōkuma Shigenobu, 67–68
open the mountains, pacify the barbarians. *See kaishan fufan*
Osaka Exposition (1903), 221–222
Oshikawa Noriyoshi, 90–93
Osterhammel, Jürgen, 11–13, 77
Ōtsu Rinpei, 106, 136–138, 141
Ōyama Tsunayoshi, 66

Paalan, 7map, 9fig., 88, 96–97, 97fig., 113, 135–137, 176, 208, 210fig., 239–244, 244fig.
Pacification Office: *Bukonsho* (Japanese period), 90–95, 92fig., 103, 129–134; *Fukenju* (Qing-period), 87, 89, 215
Paiwan (ethnic group), 8map, 9fig.; as culture-bearers, 162, 169, 185, 224; as noble savages, 164, 167; as tribute-takers, 59–63; as wreckers, 62–63; during *kaishan fufan* (open the mountains, pacify the barbarians), 146–147; in Mudan village incident, 20, 50, 52, 68–72, 72fig., 75, 202; Rover incident and, 56; social structure during Qing period, 56, 59, 165–166; Qing views of, 76; *tōmoku* (headmen), 111; under Japanese colonial rule, 142–149, 181, 232, 245–246; U.S. Consul LeGendre's views of, 78. *See also* Eighteen-Tribe Confederation (of Langqiao)
Pan Wenjie. *See* Bunkiet, Jagarushi Guri
panopticism, 22, 31
Parijarijao, 165
Paris Universal Exposition (1900), 183, 218, 221
Pazzeh Watan, 124fig., 219, 221–223, 229, 242, 289n94, 289n103
Perry, Commodore Matthew, 55, 114
photography, 161, 182, 225–229, 236, 241
Pickering, William, 59–61, 121
Pixo Doleh, 139–140
Pixo Sappo, 129, 209–211, 266n122, 273n53
Pixo Walis (Gao Yongqing), 96
pluralism: cultural, 36, 191–195, 212–213, 217–229, 248; legal, 17–22, 251–252n8
Poliac (Baoli), 52–53, 53map, 59, 61, 72, 121, 142
police: aborigine territory 32, 43–44, 47,119, 133, 138–139, 151–152, 156, 179, 232, 246–248; as feature of modern sovereignty, 21, 31;

as teachers, 149–152; attacks on, 1, 112, 158; camphor production and, 28; Foucault and, 23; in colonial Korea, 3; in guardline (aiyū-sen) movements, 66, 99–110, 233; military (kenpeitai), 117, 125; Pacification Office and, 90, 93; political marriages and, 136, 139–141; trading posts and, 180
police stations: as language schools, 120, 153, 155; Jiaobanshan, 235; Kasumigaseki (Taiwan), 136; Wushe, 1, 112
primitivism, 40, 163, 169
Pu Chin, 85, 124–126, 200, 202fig., 205–208, 206fig., 235
public power, 22–23, 78, 82, 93, 103, 112, 155
Puli, 7map, 58map, 88; as administrative center, 97, 97fig., 139; as contact zone, 88–89, 96, 130–131; elementary school (*shōgakkō*), 153–154; Fukahori mission and, 95; Pacification Office, 91–93, 129–131; Qing-period guardline and, 98
punishment: regime of, 21–23; 26–32, 118, 248
punitive expeditions (*tōbatsu*): Qing-period, 20, 28; Japanese-period, 30–31, 96, 99, 103–105, 131, 169, 224, 229–233. *See also* guardline.
Puyuma (ethnic group), 8map, 9fig., 59, 122, 135, 142–144, 143fig., 144fig., 165–166, 197, 205, 230, 246

Qiu Ruolong, 5
quantification (calculation/rationality), 27, 76, 179
quasi-sovereignty, 13, 196–197, 255n45
Quchi (Atayal subgroup), 9fig., 79, 122–123, 216–222, 225–228, 226fig., 227fig., 230
Quchi (place), 7map, 79–81, 80map, 122–123, 131, 132fig., 149, 150fig., 197, 216, 228

race: administrative bifurcation and, 34fig., 150–152; biopolitics and, 30; ethnic classification and, 35, 191–192; expendable, 223; in settler colonialism, 29–30; mimetic colonialism and, 194–195; second-order geobodies and, 194; social Darwinism and, 102; W.J.T. Mitchell's definition of, 195–196; science of, 212–216. *See also* racism.
racism: against indigenes, 37; as logical and temporal antecdent of "race," 195; as Western invention, 284n10; "polite" vs. "vulgar," 29–30; scientific, 35
Raga, 9fig., 133
Rainbow and Dragonfly exhibit, 161–162, 182
renaissance: indigenous cultural, 5–9, 13, 40, 168, 187–188, 190

306   INDEX

Ri Aguai, 32, 98, 178
Richter, Daniel, 256n51
Rimogan, 7map, 9fig., 79, 80map, 132, 183, 221, 228, 242–244
Rover incident, 56–57, 62
Rowe, William T., 20
Rudolph, Michael, 187
Rukai (ethnic group), 8map, 120–121, 135, 169
Ryūkyūans: massacre of fifty-four, 19, 48–55, 62–68, 75, 172

Sabaree, 9fig., 53map, 146–148, 151, 163, 232
Sagara Nagatsuna, 142–144, 148
Saigō Tsugumichi, 19, 55, 67–76, 72fig., 142, 146, 223
Saisiyat, 7map, 8map, 32, 37, 135, 169, 189, 219
Saitō Makoto, 3–4
Saitō Otosaku, 91, 128, 176–177
Sakano Tōru, 151
Sakuma Samata, 29–30, 72, 103–106, 136, 223, 245
Salamao incident, 112–113, 138
salt: as inducement, 89, 174, 176; as trade item, 172, 177, 180; as weapon, 93, 172, 178–180; embargoes of, 93–96; Taiwan Government-General monopoly, 99
Sasaki Yasugorō, 104
Satsuma, 51map, 56, 65–67, 76
Sayon, 156, 278n178
Sazuka Aisuke, 140–141
Scott, James C., 219
second-order geobody: defined, 31–33; aborigine territory as, 36, 135, 156, 247; as product of colonial visual culture, 232–241; indigenous ethnic groups and, 40, 194, 229–230, 248. *See also* geobody
Sediq, 5–9, 7map, 8map, 9fig., 43, 49, 88, 93, 96, 138, 140–141, 154, 253n26
Seediq Bale (film), 5, 43
Segawa Kōkichi, 239
seinendan (youth corps), 9, 31, 119, 155, 247–248, 278n175
seiryokusha (men of influence), 111–112, 119, 155
Seiyūkai (Friends of the Constitution), 4
self-determination, 36
senkusha (pioneers), 115, 119
settlers: as "brokers of empire," 256n50; as ideal type in world history, 15–17; Han, in Qing-period Taiwan, 59, 79–82, 123, 165
sha/she (administrative units), 6, 9fig., 147, 152, 254n28
shatei (local men), 127–128
Shen Baozhen, 20, 72

Shepherd, John R., 16
Shimaigaseki (Bukai) incident, 96–97
Shimoyama Hajime, 139–141
Shimoyama Jihei, 139–141
shipwrecks, 18–19, 48–50, 54–56, 60–67, 75, 260n8
Shiron (of Quchi), 123
Siaoliao, 53map, 56, 59–60, 63–65, 68
sightseeing tours (for indigenes), 94, 152, 247
Simon, Scott, 167, 187, 251n6
Sino-Japanese War, 116, 129
social Darwinism, 17, 102–104
Soejima Taneomi, 66–67, 172
sovereignty: along the "savage border," 94–95, 202fig.; as achieved status, 212, 248; bifurcated, 13, 17–18, 119; denial of, 15; dynastic-state, 12, 17–18, 38–39, 55; global transformation and, 11; high-velocity capitalism and, 22; horizontal integration and, 22; indigenous conceptions of, 6, 9, 136, 249; international system and, 11, 15, 18, 21, 33; Meiji period Japan and, 19, 23, 55; nationalist conceptions of, 9, 11–12, 16–17, 33, 77, 192; post-World War I conceptions of, 37, 196, 248; public power and, 78; Taiwan Government-General and, 14, 48, 82, 94. *See also* quasi-sovereignty
statistics. *See* quantification
stipends (*kensho*), 118, 134, 155
Stone Gate Battle, 53map, 69–71, 223
surrenders: to Saigō Tsugumichi (1874), 73fig.; to Taiwan Government-General, 32, 46, 48fig., 104, 112, 135–136, 144, 179, 232, 272n41
Suzuki Hideo, 239
Swinhoe, Robert, 120–121

Tadao Mona, 43–44, 49
Tai, Eika, 149
tairiku rōnin (continental adventurer), 104, 115
Taiwan hakurankai (Taiwan Expo, 1935), 239, 244, 247
Taiwan Indigenous Peoples (*Taiwan Yuanzhuminzu*): 169, 188, 248, 251n7
Takekoshi Yosaburō, 28, 77, 222
Tanaka Tsunatoku, 82–84, 125–126, 202fig.
Ta-pa-ni incident, 156–157, 244
Tappas Kuras, 131
Tata Rara, 142–144, 143fig., 144fig.
Tavares, Antonio C., 166, 178, 219
tax base: criteria for inclusion, 6, 47, 230; expansion of, 17, 21, 63, 110; incomplete extension of, 225, 245; Qing, 20

tax revenue: Japanese government, 244; Taiwan Government-General, 101*table*
taxation: for schools in Taiwan, 278*n*172; on land, 24, 26; on Qing frontier, 76; reform of, 24–25
Taylor, George, 173, 197–198, 284*n*19
textiles. *See* Atayal:textiles
Tgdaya (Wushe Sediq), 9*fig.*, 88–89, 95–96, 112–113, 129–131, 135–138, 140, 179
Thomas, Nicholas, 168, 191
Toda, 7*map*, 9*fig.*; as Sediq settlement, 131, 180; as Tgdaya enemies, 96, 112–113, 137–138, 176; guardline and, 136–138, 179
Toketok, 56, 59–68, 71, 142, 162–165, 263*n*55
Tokugawa shogunate, 18–22, 24, 55–56, 65, 214
tōmoku (headmen), 59, 81, 111–113, 119, 154–155, 165, 216
tongshi (interpreters/translators), 121–129, 162, 166, 245
Torii Ryūzō, 35–36, 133, 194, 198, 284*n*19, 182, 228, 286*n*62
tourism, 3, 36–37, 156, 184–190, 229–236, 278*n*178
trading posts, 79, 87, 96, 139–140, 176–184, 245
translation, 69–70, 114, 163
translators. *See tongshi*
Treaty of Peace and Amity (US-Japan 1854), 55
Treaty of Shimonoseki (1895), 28, 255*n*42
Treaty of Tianjin (1858), 57, 98, 120, 162, 262*n*38
treaty-port: era, 98, 122, 127, 165–166, 172, 192; powers, 22; system, 54, 57, 61–65, 78, 88, 103
tributary system, 48, 54, 62, 65–67, 122
Truku (ethnic group), 9*fig.*, 110, 137*fig.*, 220*fig.*, 254*n*30
Truku (Sediq subgroup, prewar), 7*map*, 9*fig.*, 112–113, 131, 136–137, 176
Ts'ai, Caroline Hui-yu, 23, 106, 157
Tsou (ethnic group), 8*map*, 86–87, 121, 181, 205, 235
Tuilasok, 9*fig.*, 53*map*, 59, 61–65, 68, 70–74, 142–148, 145*fig.*, 151, 232, 277*n*148

Uchida, Jun, 14, 256*n*50
Ueno Sen'ichi, 78–82, 166, 173–175, 197, 214

Valjeluk Mavaliu, 50, 52

Washiiga, 125, 199–206, 202*fig.*, 203*fig.*, 204*fig.*, 206*fig.*, 213, 235–236
Watan Nawi, 199, 200*fig.*, 213
Watan Yū. *See* Watan Yūra
Watan Yūra, 86, 122–124, 174, 183, 196, 217–225
Watanabe (garrison commander), 82, 84*fig.*, 125, 174, 198
Watosinai, 86, 217
Weber, Max, 27–28
whalers, 19, 55
White, Richard, 16, 111
Wilsonianism, 36–37, 151, 248
Winichakul, Thongchai, 12, 18
Wolf, Eric, 16, 36
Wolfe, Patrick, 29, 195, 284*n*10
World War I. *See* Wilsonianism
wreckers, 19, 67, 114
Wu Micha, 278*n*182
Wulai, 7*map*, 9*fig.*, 58*map*, 80*map*. *See also* Quchi (place)
Wushe (Sediq subgroup). *See* Tgdaya
Wushe (place), 1, 7*map*, 53*map*, 58*map*; 112, 135–140, 153–154, 176, 180, 209, 239
Wushe Rebellion, 1, 43; causes of, 39, 49, 113, 119, 129, 140–141, 153–154; in popular culture, 5, 43–44; impact on aborigine administration (*riban*), 30, 119, 155, 246–247; ramifications in Japan, 4

Xilai'an incident. *See* Ta-pa-ni incident
Xitou (Atayal subgroup), 7*map*, 9*fig.*, 87–88, 126, 175, 213

Yamagata Aritomo, 29, 104
Yamaji Katsuhiko, 167
Yanaihara Sakimitsu, 66–67
Yang Youwang, 52, 121
Yao Jen-to, 21, 25–26, 245
Yawai Taimu, 119, 140
Yayutz Beriya, 124
Yilan, 7*map*, 58*map*, 80*map*, 83, 87–88, 122–126, 135, 175–178, 213
Ying Gui, 57, 62
Yoshimura Katsumi, 43–44, 49, 113
Yūgai Watan, 220–222, 242*fig.*, 289*n*103

Zongli Yamen, 21, 23, 76

www.ingramcontent.com/pod-product-compliance
Ingram Content Group UK Ltd.
Pitfield, Milton Keynes, MK11 3LW, UK
UKHW021000260226
468435UK00004B/80